american ethnologist

The Journal of the American Ethnological Society

ISSN 0094-0496

VOLUME 9   NUMBER 4   NOVEMBER 1982

NORMAN E. WHITTEN, JR., *EDITOR*

Special Issue Editors

Janet W. D. Dougherty   Emiko Ohnuki-Tierney

James W. Fernandez   Norman E. Whitten, Jr.

Theresa L. Sears, *Editorial Associate*
Thomas N. Krizay, *Production Editor*

special issue: SYMBOLISM AND COGNITION II

contents

635 Whitten and Ohnuki-Tierney / **when paradigms collide: introduction to *symbolism and cognition II***
644 Herzfeld / **the etymology of excuses: aspects of rhetorical performance in Greece**
664 Galt / **the evil eye as synthetic image and its meanings on the Island of Pantelleria, Italy**
682 Boddy / **womb as oasis: the symbolic context of Pharaonic circumcision in rural Northern Sudan**
699 Edwards / **something borrowed: wedding cakes as symbols in modern Japan**
712 Roberts / **"comets importing change of Times and States": ephemerae and process among the Tabwa of Zaire**
730 Sallnow / **a trinity of Christs: cultic processes in Andean Catholicism**
750 Stoller / **signs in the social order: riding a Songhay bush taxi**
763 Dougherty and Keller / **taskonomy: a practical approach to knowledge structures**
775 Quinn / **"commitment" in American marriage: a cultural analysis**
799 Goodwin / **"instigating": storytelling as social process**
820 Dougherty and Fernandez / **afterword**

The code at the bottom of the first page of an article indicates the copyright owner's consent that copies of the article may be made for personal or internal use or for the personal or internal use of specific clients, *provided* that the copier pay the stated per-copy fee through the Copyright Clearance Center, Inc., P.O. Box 765, Schenectady, NY 12301, for copying beyond that permitted by Sections 107 or 108 of the U.S. Copyright Law. To request permission for other kinds of copying, such as copying for general distribution, for advertising or promotional purposes, for creating new collective works, or for resale, write the publisher.

Copyright © 1982 by the American Ethnological Society. All rights reserved.

Published quarterly (February, May, August and November) by the American Ethnological Society, 1703 New Hampshire Ave., N.W., Washington, DC, 20009. Printed in the U.S.A. Second class postage paid at Washington, DC, and additional mailing offices.

You are cordially invited
to join us during Mardi Gras
for

TEXT, STORY, and PLAY

the 105th Annual Meeting
of the
AMERICAN ETHNOLOGICAL SOCIETY

11-14 February 1983
Prince Murat Hotel
Baton Rouge, Louisiana

in conjunction with the
Southern Anthropological Society
and the
Association for the Anthropological Study of Play

Edward M. Bruner
AES President and Meeting Convenor
University of Illinois, Urbana-Champaign

Miles Richardson
AES Program Chairman
Louisiana State University

when paradigms collide: introduction to *symbolism and cognition II*

NORMAN E. WHITTEN, JR.
University of Illinois, Urbana

EMIKO OHNUKI-TIERNEY
University of Wisconsin, Madison

In August 1982 the *American Ethnologist* published a special issue on *Symbolism and Cognition* (vol. 8, no. 3), culminating, we thought, a process of scholarly development that began with an idea introduced during the first editorial board meeting in 1979 under Whitten's editorship. More recently, we published a complement to that issue, *Economic and Ecological Processes in Society and Culture* (vol. 9, no. 2), that opened with a discussion of the etymology of both economy and ecology from the Greek root *oikos* (Gudeman and Whitten, AE 9:223, 1982). This discussion of the fundamental duality lying at the heart of systems of human management led to an arrangement of papers that began with neo-Marxian-inspired analyses, then proceeded from micro-analyses based on a theory of optimal foraging as constituted by cost/benefit metaphors, on through an econometric critique of the "perfect market" model, to end the issue on a decidedly human note:

> The struggle to construct a world so that we may be is a continual one, and one from which, for the human creature, there is no escape. . . . we are constantly at the job of building cultures; shaping, molding, fitting together materials produced not only by experience of social interaction but also from materials produced by nature. Transformed by the magic of symbols, these objects shape our lives even as we shape them; and in this manner, caged but free, driven but heroic, we are (Richardson, AE 9:434, 1982).

By seeking a balanced presentation between the structure of thought and ideas (cognition and symbolism), on the one side, and the organization of wealth and resource utilization, on what many anthropologists now take to be "the other side," we continued to raise the same fundamental questions.

As we developed the volume on economy and ecology, comments on the first symbolism and cognition issue flowed with sufficient frequency and intensity to convince us that the task of setting forth salient exemplars of the ideational realm in society and culture was still partially at hand. Rather than sprinkle the papers coming to us in various issues of volumes 9 and 10, we decided to do a "follow-up" special edition to make available an expanded body of work for richer comparison and more precise judgment. In reviewing the communication, and in the process of critical peer review of the many papers sent to our office for possible publication since the issuance of *AE* 8(3), it became increasingly clear that the range of approaches and perspectives represents a provocative stage of development of anthropological thought, one reflecting not only disciplinary growth but also a renewed sense of mutual interest among many scholars in the humanities, social sciences, and scientific philosophy. Because of this, we asked Janet Dougherty and James Fernandez, who introduced 8(3), to prepare an Afterword.

The cross-subdisciplinary (symbolic-cognitive) endeavor seems to come mainly from those primarily interested in the nature of symbols and in the nature of mind. Many scholars, of course, justifiably question whether the term "symbol"—something that stands for or represents another thing—is really appropriate in any technical sense, in that its very polysemy ranges from precise mathematical sign to elusive trope. Be that as it may, increasing attention is being turned to the ramifying consequences of human symbolization in social and cultural domains, to the expansion of domains themselves, and to the creative transcendence of domain boundaries.

Many of our colleagues have broken through the barriers presented by a stage of polarization between those emphasizing system or structure, on the one side, and those focusing on the individual, as actor, and interpersonal communication among individuals, as a social process, on the other. During the period of paradigmatic polarization discussed in *AE* 8(3), the replication of existing models, or their refutations, seemed to be a primary goal of scholarly communication. We would now appear to be at a point best described as a reasonably comfortable existence (characterized by reciprocal provocations) of multiple models, while new syntheses and fresh intellectual directions continue to emerge.

symbolon

Reflection on the bases that propel some symbolists and cognitivists to see "convergence" turns our attention to the Greek root *symbolon* and its significance to human identity, to human positioning within society, and to the cultural importance of identity and position of the self vis-à-vis others (specific and general) in the flow of human lifeways. Quite obviously, *symbolon,* from whence "symbol" derives, is also the base upon which studies of human cognition are constructed. *Symbolon* means "contract, token, insignia, and a means of identification" *(Encyclopedia Britannica* 17:900, 1976).

> Parties to a contract, allies, guests, and their host could identify each other with the help of parts of the *symbolon.* In its original meaning the symbol represented and communicated a coherent greater whole by means of a part. The part, as a sort of certificate, guaranteed the presence of the whole and, as a concise meaningful formula, indicated the larger context. The symbol is based, therefore, on the principle of complementation. The symbol object, the picture, the sign, the word, and the gesture require the association of certain conscious ideas in order to fully express what is meant by them. To this *it has an esoteric and at the same time exoteric, or a veiling and a revealing, function.* The discovery of its meaning presupposes a certain amount of active cooperation. As a rule, it is based on convention of a group that agrees upon its meaning. Symbols, however, may also be individual and subjectively constructed (*Encyclopedia Britannica* 17:900, 1976; emphasis added).

A sharp epistemological bifurcation with regard to the "discovery of meaning" has permeated social and behavioral science methodology over the past several decades. The rift, or divide, is framed in global perspective by the "science versus humanities" polarity (e.g., introductions to *AE* 8(3) and 9(2)) and in disciplinary perspective by many (sometimes crosscutting) polarities, a salient one of which remains that of the specific methodological rigor of cognitivist *analysis* versus the interpretive symbolist *synthesis* in anthropological discourse. The dichotomy, of course, is unfortunate, and probably spurious, since *symbolon* presumably provides the semantic root structure for each branch of Western ethnographic and ethnological endeavor.

The essence of the symbol, without a doubt, is its *constitutive* nature. This simply means, according to *Webster's New World Dictionary* (2nd college edition), "having power to establish, appoint, or enact ... making a thing what it is; basic ... forming a part (of). ..." In the world of human beings, having the power to form or establish—to constitute— means to veil and to unveil, to reveal and to mystify. As mystical religions grow and their revelations develop, they often purport to be based on acknowledged, rational procedures of "science" (e.g., scientific creationism); and as scientific "truths" unfold through rigorous methodologies, they become mystified by magical rhetoric based on theory-constitutive metaphors (e.g., the law of supply and demand). The symbol is dynamic and constitution of its meaning takes place at many levels; hence, the nature of human thought is to not only comprehend revealed meaning—often polysemic, polarized, condensed, evocative, emotionally charged—but to cloak the revelation, as it were, in the veil or mantle of the allusive, obscure, or mystical.

Herein lies the ramifying bifurcation of our *symbolon* tap root. By precisely stating the parameters of meaning, cognitive anthropology documents with precision born of innovative method the boundaries between meanings using the well-known criteria of contrast, hierarchy, and classification. Cognition studies emphasize that meaning must be contained and the semantic space doing that job cannot be violated lest an anomaly develop, in which case "disambiguation" is a necessary analytical goal. By contrast with the modern cognitivists, symbolists not only collect exegeses that expand meanings into and across semantic space (some of them relishing the nature of anomaly itself), but they themselves expand on inevitable elaborations of meanings, thereby muddling models or "blurring genres," as Clifford Geertz so aptly puts it. By judiciously exploring the ramifications of exegesis, on the one hand, and using thought processes inherent in the nature of the *symbolon* root itself (including metaphor, metonymy, synecdoche, or irony), on the other, the symbolist demonstrates how human groups and individuals, as public and private actors, consciously transcend meaningful boundaries and, by so doing, construct and constitute novel formations out of the ordered debris of shared cognitive categories and meanings.

Clash of paradigms, or *paradigms in collision,* is perhaps an appropriately provocative way to depict the "convergence" discussed in *AE* 8(3) between cognitive and symbolic concerns. The collision that gave birth to dialogues and dialectics is epistemological in historical development but has become manifest and salient through the differentiation of research aims and methodologies.

The authors of this introduction have made their own attempts at cognitive/symbolic resolution without arguing for a "convergence." Ohnuki-Tierney (*AE* 8:451–467, 1981), in her analysis of the catfish in Japan, argues that contrastive methodologies leading to sophisticated understanding of seemingly diverse symbolic meanings (fish as species; as evocative, allusive symbol; as icon) must be approached at complementary levels, phases, or stages which, in turn, must be related to one another through appropriate understanding of the mechanisms of mental transformation. The goal, then, becomes one of understanding the *transformations from one level to another,* rather than trying to "merge" the methods or perspectives at the same level. Whitten (*AA* 80:836–859, 1978; *Cultural Transformations and Ethnicity in Modern Ecuador,* 1981) provides another dimension of cognate thought when he seeks to understand the allusive ecological *imagery* of Upper Amazonian peoples evoked during times of social upheaval. Such imagery involving domain merger (a signal of impending catastrophe presaged by the unleashing of power) depends on analysis of intradomain lexical order, as set forth, for example, by the cognitivist work of O. Brent Berlin and his colleagues. Whitten's work and that of Berlin develop from contrasing methodologies, but they complement one another at different levels. Ohnuki-Tierney's model provides a conceptual framework for appropriate cognitive-symbolic transformation from intradomain lexical order, through symbolic elaboration, to an understanding of the ordering of chaos.

Although often characterized as regarding "ideology" as a systematic obfuscation, or mask, of social realities born of economic processes, certain branches of neo-Marxism also provide a mode of thought relevant to the sorts of transformations we have discussed. For example, Dolgin, Kemnitzer, and Schneider introduce their collection of essays in *Symbolic Anthropology* (1977) by drawing careful attention to the concept of *praxis*—which refers to the meaning of and the intention implied by a thought or an act. Thought and action together operate as a unified construct subject to interpretations not only in the mind of the anthropologist, influenced by his methods and disciplinary traditions, but also in the minds of natives vis-à-vis significant others, including the anthropologist. Innovative non-Marxists such as Clifford Geertz, Victor Turner, Keith Basso, Bruce Kapferer, Roger Keesing, and Gerardo Reichel-Dolmatoff also stress this process of continuing, reciprocal interpretation *in* culture and *of* culture.

Marxists, however, go on to "ground" the analysis of every situation in industrial society in an ultimate, analytical cognizance of the "dominating" growth of capitalism, or of the nation-state, depending on emphasis and perspective. As Dolgin et al. (1977:37) put it, "Every action situation is the site or negotiation for, or struggle against, domination." A similar argument, with documentation from folklore of money-commodity transformation, is given by Michael Taussig in *The Devil and Commodity Fetishism in South America* (1980). Such forays by Marxian-inspired thought into the nature of cognition and symbolism through the elusive notion of *praxis* are premised on the idea that at certain levels of public discourse, ideology is an interpretable exegesis. Moreover, interpretation of bundles of meaning that reveal and obfuscate the nature of human consciousness must be made by reference to the growing omniscence of the expansionist state.

Such neo-Marxian analyses that seek to "read" ideology as a critical text diverge from the structuralism of Claude Lévi-Strauss (who also acknowledges a debt to Marx). In this divergence, the duality implied by the *symbolon* root again emerges. Lévi-Strauss, from the 1940s through the 1970s, at least, seems to proceed by inferring (rather than inducing) high-level metaphors analogous to cognitive (lexical) categories for natural species and social relations, noting their correspondence structure and underlying logic. He then turns to inconsistencies between the correspondences to "explain" ideological structure as a "mask," "cloak," or other form of obfuscation that forever propels culture and its bearers toward self-mystification. For the analyst, but not for the native, structural analysis peels away the obfuscations of ideology to offer homologies between natural and social phenomena. Such analysis takes us not to a deeper understanding of symbols that are constitutive of *a* culture, but rather to the mechanisms of Culture and Mind themselves. Revelatory and obfuscatory dimensions of culture are seen processually as complementary facets of symbolism. Such structuralist procedure eventually reveals the nature of mind mythologized by culture.

Dissatisfaction with this process perhaps led Dan Sperber to eschew the entire concept of "meaning" in restoring structuralism as a viable means by which to understand symbolism and mental processing. It may also have led Maurice Godelier to develop "structural Marxism" by moving "infrastructure" into the domain of social organization or even "religion," and perhaps influenced Marshall Sahlins to reintroduce "history" (rather than diachrony) to the understanding of metaphorical structure. In one way or another, each of these scholars, including Lévi-Strauss, is concerned in a tantamount way with the *mechanisms of transformation*—the reorganization of form—*from one level to another,* and from one domain to another, both in the construction of theory and in the understanding of the flow of symbols in culture. It is such a focus on transformation that potentially unites the diverse works included in this special issue.

from excuses to instigation

Given this discussion, it is fitting that we open with a symbolic treatment of rhetorical performance in Greece, especially since Michael Herzfeld turns his attention to the "etymology of excuses." Could anything be more salient for the study of symbolism and cognition than a system in which every revelation of causal blame is cloaked in its multilayered rhetoric emphasizing "It's not my fault" as soon as it appears? In an equally fitting manner, the issue ends with a detailed, painstaking social-linguistic analysis of the process of "instigating," moving us to the very micro-processes that motivate symbol flow in emotionally charged settings across and through the barriers of neat structure and intradomain elegance. Here, Marjorie Goodwin demonstrates, in a Black American setting, just what "gossip-dispute activity" *does* to actors in specified settings, to the structure itself, and to motivational forces in what must be the *praxis* of social life where act and thought are unified in the constitutive process.

To explore the contributions to symbolism and cognition, let us now follow some themes as they are embodied in, or suggested by, the ten papers that ensue. Herzfeld's piece takes us directly to the Marxian-inspired view of domination as a pivotal feature of continuity of rhetorical form within a system of transformation. His own perspective is not a Marxian one but rather a view sketched by Max Weber, a major critic of Marx. Weber argued that Marx's focus on classes as primary relations of production in an industrializing world missed the critical feature of bureaucratic perseverance from preindustrial through industrial development as an instrument of domination. Although Weber was a late-19th-century German nationalist, a descendant of German idealism, a contemporary of Freud, and a proponent of action-oriented symbolic analysis within every social formation, his contributions have recently been cast—incorrectly, or inappropriately—as rigidly identified with a system of inflexible "ideal types." Herzfeld returns to some of the preoccupations of German sociology of the early 20th century to demonstrate the ways by which bureaucracy in Greece is linked to fatalism in active ideology construction.

Moreover, Herzfeld productively sets forth the way by which oppositional processing of complex symbolic materials through recognized Greek rhetorical stratagems resolves the paradox of Greek selfhood: fatalism-linked-to-bureaucracy "is a stereotype held *by* the Greeks about others and *about* the Greeks by unsympathetic observers." By dealing with a key symbol—fate—as it corresponds at different levels and in different contexts to a social institution—bureaucracy—the author is able to take us from interpersonal to international relations and back again, demonstrating the viability of advanced, macrosymbolic analysis of one of the key social features of a contemporary world. He demonstrates that the concept "fatalism," while descriptively and analytically inadequate as a term defining a key, or dominant, symbol in Greek thought, nonetheless emerges as a significant element in the rhetoric of Greek discourse itself. Greeks regard fatalism as an explanation of *other* nations' failures, just as they attribute their own setbacks to the machinations of external agencies:

> The rhetoric of blame attribution . . . furnishes a strategic means of defining national, cultural, ideological, and social boundaries. Acceptance of an excuse expresses and articulates the common experience of speaker and addressee. It also entails recognition that speaker and addressee share a common code.

In the next article, Anthony Galt turns to an analysis of the "evil eye," taking issue, in part, with an analysis offered by Herzfeld in *AE* 8(3). Galt's article is exemplary of a major interest in symbolic anthropology today—reconciling universals with cultural particulars. On one end of the spectrum is the renewed insistence of a culture, as championed by Geertzian emphasis on "thick description" of a particular lifeway and a search for its ramifying (as opposed to "deeper and deeper") meanings. The thick and broad strategy of analysis, also carried out by other contributors to this issue, reacts against a Lévi-Straussian approach to Culture or Mind—the universal symbolic structures that lie in the unconscious of peoples of various cultural backgrounds. Rodney Needham, who positions himself near the middle of the Geertz–Lévi-Strauss spectrum, has endeavored to synthesize the two by proposing a conceptual tool called *synthetic image,* a symbolic counterpart to Jungian psychoanalytic archetype, to neo-Marxian dominant symbol, or to anthropology's familiar key symbol.

Galt, following Needham, anchors synthetic imagery in the system of social inequality in a small Italian community where to be powerfully envied is to be marked as upwardly mobile in a three-tier system. The system is composed of elites, a middle group, and dispersed marginals in terms of economic wherewithall and in terms of the corresponding system of ranked grades of social honor. By understanding domain shifts from an individual's malign glance to an important individual's malign glance, on through the "glance" of the community at large or, better still, society as a whole, Galt demonstrates that there is a confluence of symbolization wherein the particular (the Italian community) and the general (conceptualized society as a system of interclass mobility marked by gradations of social honor) flow together in a system of synthetic imagery. While apparently directed by neither Marxian nor Weberian social thought, Galt brings his work into the sphere of analysis to which Marxists manifest their greatest focus of attention: "Being envied is promoted in the hegemony of modern capitalism as a positive value that aids in the constant expansion of markets so necessary for the system's persistence."

By bringing the imagery of bureaucratic omnipresence and the expansion of capitalism to bear on enduring rhetorical strategy and persistent blame attribution, contemporary anthropology lends its hand to the clarification of complex issues predominant in the understanding of Western symbolism over the past several centuries. Perceptive examples of Western symbolism itself are presented by Roland Barthes (*Mythologies*, 1957), who undertakes a symbolic analysis of French culture, and by Sahlins (*Culture and Practical Reason*, 1976), who offers a symbolic treatment of Western social science theories.

As capitalism (or any other doctrine of economic expansion borne by nation-states) as a system of signs and rhetoric for the transformation of values expands, systems caught up in its structure of dominance persist. The theme of persistence binds the next group of articles by Janice Boddy, Walter Edwards, Allen Roberts, and M. J. Sallnow. The enduring power of a key symbol—fertility—is dramatically brought to light as Boddy demonstrates its ramifying webs of significance beginning with the threatened and controversial custom of female circumcision in Northern Sudan, in the very face of governmental and Orthodox Islamic attempts to eradicate this form of "gender mutilation." Although influenced by new techniques, and even some forms of subterfuge, "Pharaonic circumcision . . . [remains] deeply embedded in [Sudanic] culture. It is a salient expression of interiority, an idiom that informs much of village daily life."

By sharpest contrast with the persistence of an idiom embedded in an "esoteric" custom, Walters takes the Western reader to an imported, commercial, "exoteric" item in Japan—the wedding cake—to demonstrate how such a "new element" in contemporary Japanese culture nonetheless is incorporated into custom as a metaphor for social reproduction. In the process of developing his point, one that is not to be found in conscious exegesis of the modern Japanese, the author blends semiotics, Lévi-Straussian-inspired structuralism, and the cognitivist-derived concept of "cultural grammar."

In the same vein, but with a strong diachronic perspective, Roberts focuses on the Tabwa of Zaire and their persistent ideas about the symbolism of transition or transformation—or unpredictability and the importation of inequality—as they build correspondences between their observations of an anomaly in the celestial vault and their observations of worldly technology. Through time they see the comet as importing wealth and corresponding Christian ideology to Europeans, as sorcery and dependency increase within their own society. Analogies such as pistol:comet::technogen:external domination suggest themselves. Roberts skillfully blends Victor Turner's extensive work on processes of liminality with Ohnuki-Tierney's transformational phases from the natural through iconic in a framework of the pending unleashing of power. By so doing, he approaches the analytical horizons also explored in various ways by James L. Peacock (*Consciousness and Change,* 1975), Paul Rabinow (*Symbolic Domination: Cultural Form and Historical Change in Morocco,* 1975), James Boon (*Anthropological Romance of Bali, 1597–1972,* 1977), Eva Hunt (*The Transformation of the Hummingbird,* 1977), Geertz (*Negara: The Theatre State in Nineteenth-Century Bali,* 1980), Abner Cohen (*The Politics of Culture,* 1981), and Sahlins (*Historical Metaphors and Mythical Realities,* 1981). This is done by skillfully merging native exegesis with anthropological interpretation set in history with an eye to worldwide encompassments attendant on the expansion of high-energy technology.

In many ways, the article by Sallnow draws together the themes of persistence manifest in the prior articles and links them directly to the etymology suggested earlier, wherein "parties to a contract, allies, guests, and their host could identify each other with the help of parts of the *symbolon.*" In the Central Andes, the author argues, shrines are constitutive of social, physical, and ethnic space. Developing an argument inspired by Lévi-Strauss and pioneered by Edmund Leach in British structuralism, Sallnow "reveals" the concentric dualism wherein three images of Christ correspond in their mutual polysemy to various oppositional paradigms: center/periphery; political/ritual; order/rebellion; dominance/challenge. Throughout Central Andean history, the structure of dominance has generated systems of rebellion as the order of disguise became revealed in processual rhetoric. Syncretism built upon syncretism and the concept of "belonging," in a universal sense, generated compartmentalizations represented by the trilogy of shrines. These, in turn, came to emphasize various oppositions embedded in the concept of Christ.

With Paul Stoller we return to the theme on which our special issue in *Economic and Ecological Processes* ended—the hermeneutics of reflexivity wherein Paul Ricoeur's ("The Model of the Text" in *Interpretive Social Science,* Rabinow and Sullivan, eds., 1979) problematic of "being in the world" is of central concern. Once again, the structure of domination is present, if subtly recognized. As the paper proceeds, we see the anthropologist striving to enter the system of Songhay signs that enclose the order of negotiations within the bush-taxi vehicle. But—and herewith the structure—the author finds a limit to negotiations within the hermeneutic since "the rights and duties of many of the roles remain by and large fixed—controlled, as they are, by external forces." This central correspondence of external control, which comes to the vehicle's riders via a complex reading of the system of signs, fixes ultimately on the power wielded by "the absent owner." Again, even within the constitutive set that allows the sensitive observer to relate sign upon sign, we confront that which Marxian-inspired methodology tells us to seek—the conjunction of act and thought vis-à-vis the structure of domination.

As Stoller argues, in line with the foregoing articles, that the ramification of correspondences of signification across social contexts provides the analyst with breadth of perspective, Janet Dougherty and Charles Keller carry us to the brink of paradigm collision. In this brief piece the authors find *task specificity* to be a central key to cognition, seemingly contradicting the viewpoint that it is by reference to the ramifying relations of significance that one may perceive the nature of context specificity itself. It is as though the Songhay bush taxi, in stopping for repairs at a local blacksmith shop, threw the entire world of the analyst following the spiral of meanings outward into a new, inner dimension. Both analysts begin with the actor-inducing-meaning, but where the symbolist (Stoller, in this case) casts ever outward to find his enclosed "situation" within the bush taxi (until he comes upon the system of external control), the cognitivists (here Dougherty and Keller) "situate" their conceptual order in the specific task at the blacksmith's hand. Whether these outward/inward perspectives come to reflect the macro-/micro- division in economic analysis discussed in our previous special issue, or whether they can be resolved by transformation rules or processes of intellectual "convergence," remains to be seen. Just as Gudeman and Whitten did in discussing the *oikos* root in *AE* 9(2), we introduce this point to provoke the reader, to drive home the inherent semantic ambiguity of the *symbolon* root, and not to detract from the generative value in what, to us, remains the divergent perspectives represented here.

More divergence seems apparent as we move "deeper" into the cognitive dimensions of this special issue. Where Dougherty and Keller offer "an anti-Whorfian argument that is very different from the universalist conclusions previously derived from ethnoscientific work . . . ," Naomi Quinn, in the article that follows, gives us an "unabashedly Whorfian claim," in that a "scenario word" ("commitment") is treated in terms of the polysemy of three syntactic patterns, "promise," "dedication," and "attachment," to develop a sense of pan-contextual semiotics of marriage in at least one segment of American society. She eventually tells us that the word "commitment" itself is a *complex story* about American marriage, containing, as it does, bundles of concepts that adhere by syntax, metaphor, formulaic language, and a "sense of utterance." These, in turn, overlap to produce a web of recognizable, and communicable, significances that is clearly culture bound, but not context bound.

In our closing essay, Marjorie Goodwin focuses on a segment of Black America—on young girls in a working-class neighborhood of west Philadelphia—to demonstrate through face-to-face talk just how a constituted act is transformed into "actionable offense," a process that the girls themselves call *instigating*. Just as Quinn demonstrates the tremendous power of *condensation* in the symbol—where one word tells a story about American marriage to those capable of "debundling" its many revealing and obfuscating meanings—Goodwin shows how complex *elaboration* occurs in face-to-face talk scenarios: "I am concerned . . . with the problem of how the description of the past is constructed in the first place such that it is a recognizable cultural object appropriate to the ongoing social project of the moment." To focus talk on the "social project," Goodwin turns to Turner's notion of the "social drama." This drama is a processual structure that is initiated by a "breach" (here an insult in the he-said-she-said frame), moves toward "crisis" (where the past statement is revealing of a person's defect), on through "restitution" or "resolution" (where cloaking or mystifying occurs), to "reentry," to other forms of talk, until "instigation" again occurs. By tying "talk" to "face-to-face interaction" to "social drama," Goodwin bypasses sterile claims that "everything is a story" and introduces the constitutive nature of past, future, and fantasy in a liminal present, thereby linking persistence and change in culture to micro-analysis of the interactions of discrete individuals.

In reflecting on these excellent papers, one cannot escape the point that the methodological rigor of the ethnoscientists of a past era, which stressed intradomain positioning of lexemes and their hierarchical ordering, led us to intradomain precision at the expense of interdomain ramification. Each of the three final papers contributes to breaking, in one manner or another, from the statics of lexeme organization, substituting task-orientation process, bundling tropes by condensation, and social drama in face-to-face talk as more dynamic analytical modes. Yet, each of these modes remains intradomain, by contrast with the first seven papers.

What unites the ten disparate papers is a sustained effort to "read" one form or another of native exegesis as a critical text on salient issues and hidden agendas. This unity returns us to the bases for separation and divergence of cognitive anthropology and symbolic anthropology. Cognitivists in the United States started with a decisively scientific tone by emphasizing classification as the mode of human thought that specializes in separation of meanings so as to heighten criteria of contrast and discrimination as primary analytic tools. These techniques also wed the analyst to native consultants and demonstrated the rational precision embedded in the seemingly exotic. Some symbolists on both sides of the Atlantic also based their analyses on "classification," but they did so at another level of human thought wherein meanings are bundled together through complex symbolic processes, including metonym and metaphor. The emphasis in the latter series of symbolic developments is on synthesis and in the integrating capacity of human mind as expressed in spoken, written, or enacted tropes. Here, too, analyst thought became conjoined with that of native exegete, but in a very different way.

The dual foci on classification could not, by any epistemological set of premises, lead to "convergence." Yet, many anthropologists did forge on to combine methodological rigor of the ethnosemanticists with the synthetic imagery of the tropic analysts. The result would seem to be the development of fresh polarities crosscutting the symbolic-cognitive one. We can illustrate one such "crosscut" by opposing the structuralism of Lévi-Strauss with the action-oriented symbolism of Turner. A Lévi-Straussian *bricoleur* begins his search for the constitutive format of culture with major structural principles, or themes, in a people's lifeways. These find expressive and meaningful outlet in a number of symbols. Such correspondences, then, become the focus for analytical synthesis. Our Turnerian or Geertzian analyst, on the other side, begins with the very polysemy (or multivocality) of symbols themselves, the meanings of which must be ferreted out at various levels, in each context of occurrence. The appeal of tropic analysis—the study of figures of speech, whether directly recorded or bundled into a key word—as discussed by Colby, Fernandez, and Kronenfeld in *AE* 8(3), by contributors to J. David Sapir and J. Christopher Crocker's *The Social Use of Metaphor* (1977), and by Keith Basso's *Portraits of the Whiteman* (1979), offers insights into broad, or deep, structural correspondences, while at the same time retaining the strategic value of symbol deployment in specific contexts. The analysis of tropes satisfies anthropology's productive yearning toward the general and its rigorous acknowledgment of context specificity.

Another dichotomy develops, richly illustrated in our previous special issue on *Economic and Ecological Processes,* by contrasting transactional approaches, as pioneered, for example, by Fredrik Barth, with hermeneutics that comes strongly to our discipline through the writings of Geertz and Turner. Both hermeneutic and transactional perspectives, in turn, are compatible with the European sociology of Émile Durkheim and Max Weber, in definite contrast with the influence of Karl Marx. We are clearly historical heirs to mixed legacies of odd pairings and equally odd polarities, none of which overlay nicely. We close, then, by inviting readers to rethink cherished polarities and favorite "bundlings," and to reflect critically on the provocations that should thereby emerge.

Acknowledgments and Editor's Note. We wish to thank William Belzner, Theresa Sears, and especially Janet Dougherty for valuable comments on various drafts of this Introduction. Naomi Quinn suggested the "when paradigms collide" title. Responsibility for interpretations and provocations remain ours. References cited are omitted due to space constraints. The Introduction and Afterword were prepared by their respective authors at the same time under pressures of a rigid publication schedule; consequent overlap or contradiction may thereby result. The American Ethnological Society and the *American Ethnologist* gratefully acknowledge the support of the Wenner-Gren Foundation for Anthropological Research (Grant #4233).

the etymology of excuses: aspects of rhetorical performance in Greece

MICHAEL HERZFELD—*Indiana University*

idioms of blame

Folk responses to bureaucratic and political intransigence are often stereotypically dismissed as "fatalistic." The label suggests a problematic relationship between the cosmology of chance and the ways by which people conceptualize the much more mundane caprices of little minds and big governments. What it does not do, however, is explore the relationship itself. This paper begins that exploration.

Fatalism, as ordinarily conceived, is a passive resignation to the future dictates of chance. From the standpoint of technological rationalism, therefore, it represents the worst kind of inefficiency. As such, it also belongs to that broad spectrum of supposedly maladaptive and inflexible values that are ranged against the benefits of technological progress (e.g., Banfield 1958; Diaz 1966). In such a view, the symbolic universe constitutes a rigid barrier to the practical.

That perspective, however, fundamentally misconceives the symbolic side of the opposition: the fact that values are expressed in an apparently unchanging *form* (e.g., moral terminology) should not be taken to imply that their *content* is equally static (see also Meeker 1979:30). Cultural continuity does not necessarily imply cultural sclerosis, and it certainly does not mean that indigenous populations cannot conceptualize innovation; on the contrary, it may indicate the assimilation of intrusive ideas and experiences to a preexistent understanding of events (e.g., Ardener 1970; Ossio 1977). The practical common sense of so-called modern or technologically oriented societies is itself part of a culturally peculiar symbolic universe (Crick 1976:142–148). There is thus no reason to suppose that an intrusive

---

Excuses often take strikingly similar rhetorical forms in widely divergent kinds of situation. These forms, according to J. L. Austin, may work by evoking ideas about impersonal agencies such as fate through etymological allusion; their conventionality makes them socially acceptable as well as highly adaptable. Using the example of modern Greece, this essay explores some implications of Austin's insight for the study of blame attribution in particular cultures by examining parallels in rhetorical treatment of fate, the national bureaucracy, and the international superpowers as agents of disaster. Particular emphasis is placed on the retrospective character of blame attribution in all three domains and on the consequent inadequacy of "fatalism" as a descriptive and analytical construct.
[etymology, semiotics, symbolism, rhetoric, excuses, cultural construction of events, Greece]

Copyright © 1982 by the American Ethnological Society
0094-0496/82/040644-20$2.50/1

organizational form will be accorded the same significance that it had in its previous cultural context.

Bureaucratic systems illustrate this issue well. They are taken by their inventors to be rational, efficient, goal-directed organizations. These attributes, however, are not eternal verities about some kind of cultural universal; they are culturally specific interpretations of a complex artifact. Most intrusive bureaucratic systems confront indigenous populations with an operational ethic that then gets interpreted, often in quite novel ways.

Unfortunately, most of what has been written about bureaucratic systems sidesteps this question of how people apparently confront them with a ready-made set of responses. Sociological studies, for example, tend to focus predominantly on the workings of bureaucratic institutions as such (e.g., Blau 1963; Gouldner 1954; Mouzelis 1975; Weber 1958 [1946]). Handelman's (1976) sensitive treatment of Israeli official-client relations, by contrast, approaches the ideological and moral framework primarily for its relevance to those bureaucratic encounters themselves and does not suggest extensive parallels between bureaucratic and other kinds of encounter. Yet the existence of such a framework is a remarkable phenomenon in its own right. Unless we assume that it sprang into existence out of nowhere, it forces us to consider how existing cultural frames of reference might affect the perception of novel forms of social experience.

Taking Greece as my example, I suggest that the idiom in which people conceptualize responsibility and blame—bureaucratic and otherwise—may be both *indigenous* (in the sense that it precedes the importation of formal bureaucratic protocols and structures chronologically) and *plastic* (in that it provides a recognition for types of experience that actors may not have experienced before). Some vaguely perceived connection with traditional ideas may have prompted the characterization of political and bureaucratic attitudes as "fatalistic" (e.g., Kasperson 1966:61-62; cf. also Legg 1969:35). But this kind of label hardly constitutes an explanation. It is, rather, a stereotype derived from the very ethnocentrism that generated the "traditional-symbolic/modern-practical" dichotomy in the first place.

the shape of excuses

The kinds of utterance dealt with here depart from the usual sense of fatalism in one important respect: they are all attributions of blame for events that have already occurred. They are excuses for past failures, rather than for present or future inaction. They are also highly patterned, in that they show a certain consistency of vocabulary, imagery, and sequencing. Whether people believe them or not, they are evidently willing to countenance such excuses, provided only that the excuses exhibit certain appropriate, stereotypical characteristics. To focus on the *credibility* of the excuses thus seems a red herring; their *acceptability*, which is far more easily demonstrated, still demands an explanation. Indeed, acceptability is a precondition for credibility: "Even prophets have to be socially *accepted* in order to be right; if not, they are wrong" (Eco 1976:256).

Acceptability is also a precondition for a successful performative utterance (Austin 1975 [1962]). In each performance, existing social relations may be recast within a prevailing idiom according to the performers' skills (cf. Bauman 1977:43-45). J. L. Austin's (1971 [1956-57]) eloquent "Plea for Excuses" seeks cultural explanations for the acceptability and conventionality of ways of excusing various kinds of failure and misdeed. It does so in part by appealing to historical speculations about the idioms in which people excuse themselves.

Austin argues that the manner in which people present their excuses for personal failure has to fit a set of conventions in order for the excuses to succeed. This is a question of performative appropriateness rather than of some abstract measure of right or wrong; after all, as he points out elsewhere (Austin 1975:37), it is no good to announce a dueling challenge to pistols at dawn to someone who is not interested in the honor code associated with formal duels. Similarly, an excuse must *look* good. People are more likely to accept it if it is well presented—as, of course, every trial lawyer knows.

Moreover, Austin argues, the efficacy of an excuse depends to a considerable extent on its ability to draw on a substratum of ideas about causation, even though these ideas may belong to long forgotten or radically transformed systems of thought. Some trace of their earlier meaning lingers, implicitly, in the present form of the excuse, and the immediate familiarity of the idiom confers a kind of respectability that only the cleverest of novel excuses could hope to match. Thus, to cite "accident" is to draw on the implications of the Latin *accidit,* with its suggestion of an impersonal fate falling from on high as the efficient cause of disaster. People do not necessarily articulate these connections between a current idiom of self-justification and some past concept of causation. Austin's (1971:99–100) description of the links as "trailing clouds of etymology" is thus suitably indefinite; his account of excuses lends itself to understanding why they are accepted without obliging us to judge the ultimately irreducible issue of their truthfulness.

The etymological connections in question are thus a form of indirect allusion. They are not links between referential meanings as such. Rather, they subsist between preexisting cosmological *explanations* of events and current *idioms for describing* similar events. I would add that the chronological implications of this argument are largely immaterial; there is no reason why, for example, a person should not claim something "was an accident" while *simultaneously* attributing other actions to "fate" or some similar cosmological force.

Greek excuses draw on a rich fund of conventional motifs and thus furnish a valuable ethnographic corpus with which to explore the usefulness of Austin's suggestive essay. Ethnographically, the existence of so many common conventions may make it easier to see why and how Greeks have been thought fatalistic, even when their responses to disaster do not explicitly include mention of such concepts as fate and destiny. Through analysis of the ways in which Greeks talk about fate itself, we can see that fatalism is not an appropriate label; there is also no reason to assume that it will work any better for attitudes toward bureaucracy or politics. The fact that it has been used for all three sets of attitudes, however, is suggestive, since it implies that some level of conceptual homogeneity lies behind the stereotype.

The label of fatalism is crucial to this discussion in another way: it is a part of the same rhetoric of which it has been so inadequately used; it is a stereotype held *by* the Greeks about others and *about* the Greeks by unsympathetic observers. Greeks usually reject the stereotype as applicable to themselves. There is some uncertainty about this, however, and Greek social critics certainly do recognize the tendency to blame impersonal forces for disaster as an endemic problem. Such ambivalence reflects a central problematic of Greek cultural identity: Are Greeks *Evropei* (Europeans)? Stereotypically, Europeans are neither fatalistic nor inefficient. Thus, the question of fatalism can usefully be viewed as an aspect of the rhetoric of national identity and as integral part of the internal Greek debate about the past and present role of Greece in the evolution of European culture.[1]

specific ethnographic context

Greece may be thought insufficiently homogeneous to be treated as a single ethnographic entity. The country exhibits a considerable range of variation in social institutions, moral ideologies, language, and political orientations (Dimen and Friedl 1976; Herzfeld 1980a; Browning 1969:119-134; Legg 1969:324-327). Equally, however, Greeks themselves generally recognize a supraregional or national level of cultural identity. National media necessarily operate within this broad cultural context; newspaper articles, which have furnished a generous proportion of the data discussed below, thus resemble other forms of popular literature in being pitched to a cultural common denominator (cf. also Howe 1981: 279). Extracts from large-circulation newspapers presumably represent a construction of events couched in a familiar, shared code.[2] It should be remembered that all such discussions are conducted *in Greek*—that is, in a language that protects them from foreign criticism.[3] Although Greek newspapers are public *within* Greece, their language lends them a certain privacy with regard to the "Europeans" by whose alleged cultural standards Greek journalists often claim to judge Greek society.

For the purposes of this discussion, I have drawn primarily on three independent national dailies sympathetic to the Panhellenic Socialist Movement of Andreas Papandreou. Of these, *Eleftherotipia* ("Free Press") probably has the most radical reputation; *To Vima* ("The Platform") has usually adopted a more conventional, restrained tone; and *Ta Nea* ("The News") usually comes somewhere in between the other two in terms of both political stance and rhetorical flamboyance. All three are strongly critical of the American military presence in Greece, Anglo-American policies in Cyprus, and Great Power manipulation generally; all three have made a point of carrying feature articles on matters of cultural and historical interest; and all three, though in varying degrees, pride themselves on their investigative reporting of government activities under the conservative New Democracy party (1974-81). A fourth paper, *Akropolis,* is essentially pro-New Democracy, although it does carry reports on administrative mismanagement from time to time.

For the material on personal interaction, and on the ideology of fate and character, I have drawn on published ethnographic materials. In moving from local-level interaction to newspaper reportage, we also move to a very different kind of discourse. Journalistic writing is not very friendly, on the whole, to petty excuses. Denuded of such gestural support as the helpless shoulder shrug, for example, excuses can be made to look quite absurd in print, where they are placed in an entirely different context. Journalistic writing is nevertheless not devoid of excuses, and these may indeed take conventional forms. Newspapers are also a good place for the social critic to begin taking those forms apart.

By and large, journalists' discussions of bureaucratic behavior are of the accusatory kind. When they shift to questions of international politics, by contrast, much depends on the ideological sympathies and motives of the writers. Whether they excuse or accuse, however, all the journalists whose writing is discussed below operate within a common rhetorical idiom. To accuse the government of complaisance in Great Power machinations, for example, is a way of saying that one's ideological opponents are of poor moral caliber; to defend Greece as a country on the grounds of Great Power intervention is to excuse one's own people's collective failure.

blame and self-justification

Journalistic writing in Greece reproduces on a grander scale the agonistic conventions of everyday discourse. In ordinary speech, people attribute the failure of others to character flaws. One's own failures, conversely, are the result of bad luck, and it is one's successes that are attributed to character. An important character trait in these rhetorical ploys is that of how hard a person works. To many Greek villagers (see du Boulay 1974:52; Herzfeld 1981:564), the attitude that outsiders would call fatalism is really just indolence. Despite its name, it is thus a *character* attribution. The few who say they are resigned to the whims of chance are thought to be making excuses for their inaction. The morally good life is above all one of unceasing struggle—whether against nature or against other people (Friedl 1962: 75)—even when the cause seems hopeless.[4] At the very moment that an individual seeks to justify past failure on the grounds of ill fortune, measures should already be underway to set matters right. These ideas, moreover, seem to be widely distributed throughout Greece.[5]

The components of the overall pattern that are essential to the present analysis may be summarized: (1) the social character of blame and self-justification; (2) the close involvement of concepts of destiny with ideas about the inheritance of both *characterological properties* and *material property*; and (3) the pervasive image of fate as "writing" its decision.

Some brief discussion of these aspects is necessary before we proceed to bureaucratic and political embodiments of similar concepts.

the social dimension   Although character is invoked as the explanation of successes and fate for Ego's failures, there are occasions when self-accusation is appropriate. Such outbursts of candor are not necessarily expressive of a guilty conscience, but represent collective self-criticism within the reference group; this perhaps explains why outside observers get to hear such outbursts relatively rarely.

Self-criticism implies at least an implicit admission of collective responsibility. When voiced to outsiders, it may seem a betrayal of social boundaries. Thus, at the beginning of the 1974 Cyprus crisis, a Pefkiot remarked to me that it was all the fault of "our own donkeys [*ghaidhouria*]"—a venomous insult usually reserved for outsiders to the reference group.[6] To understand this apparent solecism, it must be understood that my informant was (1) extremely unpopular with his fellow villagers; (2) unusual among them in his willingness to associate with foreigners (such as myself); and (3) known as someone who systematically violated village canons of appropriate behavior. He can thus be seen as reversing those canons in accordance with his own outsiderlike status within the community. Another reason for seeming to take the blame is that it allows one to present oneself as the person in charge. Thus, for example, when a Pefkiot is worsted in some competitive encounter, he is likely to say that it was *his* fault for *allowing* his rival to compete with him in the first place; he thereby tries to claim a degree of personal autonomy that the actual course of events otherwise belies. In the reverse phenomenon, a Pefkiot may grant others that degree of control in order to blame them for the outcome. In Glendi, cardplayers sometimes complain that others, by making so much noise, "don't allow" them to win at cards. The latter is a significant usage in the present context; as we shall see, national humiliation over the Turkish invasion of Cyprus in 1974 is conventionally ascribed to American refusals to "allow" the Greeks to retaliate.

More generally, however, the public or social nature of blame distribution requires that one explicitly attribute personal difficulties that have become common knowledge to the wickedness of others. Indeed, the act of retaliation can itself be construed as a symbolic statement about the locus of blame. A Glendiot unsuccessfully attempted to persuade a close friend to give a daughter in marriage to the first man's dishonored son. This ploy ended in a public rejection by the second man of the entire relationship between the two households. His response can be read as an unambiguous attempt to pin the blame for the entire situation on his erstwhile friend, and his own comments on the situation support that interpretation.

The relation between the attribution of bad character to others and the need to take personal initiative against it oneself is nicely (if somewhat hypothetically) illustrated by

Pefkiot responses to allegations of Turkish atrocities in Cyprus in 1974. Their anger was vented in the form of a frequently reiterated call for the extermination of every Turkish woman and child. Not only were they able to endorse this programmatic crusade with an unorthodox interpretation of New Testament theology,[7] but they were also thereby able to ignore the official Greek policy of forbearance toward the unarmed Turkish-Cypriot civilian population. Their justification was expressed at two levels: first, that of indignation at the unprovoked slaughter of *Greek* women and children by the Turks;[8] second, that of the need for the total extirpation of the Turkish people so as to prevent any future recurrence. Thus, in the face of disaster, the attitude is clearly not one of fatalism in the conventional sense, but instead a call to action in the immediate future. That the disaster in question has *already occurred* is another matter entirely; this can be blamed on external agencies, whether fate, the United States, or NATO.

fate, character, and inheritance   Personal and group character is said to be inherited and thus predictable. Published ethnographies, however, make it clear that this "prediction" is in practice a thinly disguised form of retrospection; gossip treats shameful deeds as confirming a reputation that may not in fact have been clearly articulated up to that point (e.g., de Boulay 1974:183) and can take a form that corresponds to the "I always did say" formula of some English speakers.

In determining the distribution of inheritable property, by contrast, the retrospective character of villagers' recognition of fate's intervention is entirely obvious, since there is no way of knowing how the distribution will work out *before* lots are cast. The appeal to fate through the casting of lots concerns different types of property in different parts of Greece, and it seems likely that in each case the aim is to avoid family conflict over the items of material property most likely to provoke it (Herzfeld 1980b).

Interestingly, at least in Pefko, the "lot" is conceptually opposed to the "gift." Property distributed by lot is automatically transmitted to the succeeding generation, so that gifts (*dhora*) have come to represent a perversion of the normative practice (i.e., transference of a parent's land to someone other than his/her offspring). Property is thus distributed through the decision of fate, which is conceptualized as an act of "writing"; and the decision of a parent to "write" property on anyone other than a son or daughter is an act of defiance against the writ of fate.

the image of writing   Writing is the supreme act of definition. Rather than asking for a person's name, one is likely to inquire (especially in formal contexts), *pos ghrafese?* ("How are you written?").[9] The irrevocability of fate's decisions is symbolized by the image of a written decree (see Politis 1874:218–219). In the hands of humans, the phrase "writing the property" is used to indicate a legally documented act of transfer that conflicts with the writ of fate revealed in the custom of dividing property by lot and may not be in accordance with local property transmission norms (cf. also Gavrielides 1976:268); this encapsulates the notion that an appeal to (codified) law involves arrogating to oneself the prerogative of destiny and is expressed as "writing the property upon" the beneficiary. More generally, when someone has to explain a failure, it is described as "written" (i.e., predestined). A Glendiot who was losing badly at cards explained, "It wasn't written that I should win." Note that he did not stop playing at this point; instead, he was setting the scene for the likely outcome, but at the same time he may also have been trying to manipulate fate's own malice—fate is expected to do the opposite of whatever one thinks it will.[10] Even in confronting fate itself, then, he is not being fatalistic, in the usual sense of that term; he goes on trying to influence the course of events as long as he can.

In what follows, we shall meet some of these themes repeatedly. In particular, the image of writing pervades all the accounts of bureaucratic behavior, and it is also a feature of allegations about Great Power plans to subvert Greek political interests. It is further developed in the image of the paternalistic bureaucrat who "shares out" (*mirazi*) favors and of Great Power designs to "share out" (*mirazi*) dominion over the entire world. In addition, both bribery and betrayal are denoted by terms etymologically cognate with *dhoro* (gift)—that is, with the category of property transfer that most subverts the correct order. Etymological links of this sort enable people to recognize certain standard images like these as familiar rhetorical devices and therefore as socially and aesthetically acceptable ones.

the letter and the spirit: civic attitudes

There are several symbolic correspondences between the respective attitudes to fate and bureaucracy. Above all, bureaucracy resembles fate in that it is seen generically as an immovable force. This view seems to be rooted in direct experience: it is thought that the only people with sufficient power to alter the system are those whose vested interests are best served by its perpetuation (see *To Vima*, 7/7/76, p. 2). While the prevalence of patronage doubtless explains much of this sentiment (see Campbell 1964:260-261; Argyriades 1968), the persistent experience of bureaucrats' everyday unwillingness to take any initiative has undoubtedly reinforced that impression.

This inflexibility most characteristically takes the form of a punctilious insistence on accurate documentation in accordance with the exact provisions of the law. A widow remarried and reported to the local police station to have her identity card altered accordingly. She took with her a copy of her marriage certificate.

> The relevant Inspector told me that instead of the marriage certificate, I should have brought a certification issued by the Borough. I brought the Borough document; the relevant official did not approve it, because the profession of my husband was written down as "Pensioned Dentist" and it should have said "Dentist on pension." I took him that too. . . . Three months have gone by, and I have still not been given a new identity card (*To Vima*, 7/7/76, p. 2).

Without such a card, one has no official existence as a Greek citizen; in common speech the same term (*taftotita*) is used for both "identity card" and "identity."

Associated with the insistence on correct documentation is the concept of *efthinofovia* (fear of responsibility), the unwillingness to take the initiative in any even slightly anomalous situation. *Efthinofovia* is seen by social critics as endemic (e.g., *Akropolis*, 4/16/76, p. 2; *To Vima*, 8/4/76, p. 2; Tamiolakis 1976:90-91; Dimou 1976:45) and is cited as the reason for many of the delays and inefficiencies of the bureaucracy. In one incident, a 20-minute power outage disabled all the electrical equipment of an Athens hospital. There was a generator in the main hall, bought at considerable cost for just such an eventuality.

> The generator, however, was left to rot, as the bureaucratic procedures for determining who was responsible for its functioning had not been resolved. Truly, if "someone had died of disgust" [i.e., during the power outage], who would have been responsible? (*To Vima*, 8/5/76, p. 2).

Perhaps the extreme of *efthinofovia* arises in conjunction with the verification of personal identity. This is especially well illustrated by the procedures that a male Greek studying abroad has to undergo in order to have his military service deferred:

> He must take a Borough certificate of identity verification to the Military Board. The Borough, in order to give him the certificate requires him to go to the Civil Court or to a notary public and get a sworn affidavit to the effect that the person studying abroad is the same as the one who was born in such-and-such a place and is registered in the roster of male inhabitants of such-and-such a Borough (*Akropolis*, 11/10/77, p. 2).

The journalist who raised this issue commented that the need for such a complex procedure was dubious at best, on the grounds that "in that case it would be a straightforward case of false identity, which is indeed severely punishable by law. And we do not believe that there exist families that would expose their children to such a danger." Clearly, however, the existing legal arrangement encourages dependence upon written forms; indeed, the civil servants' national organization has consistently rejected the view that it is possible for government employees to do anything other than apply the letter of the law with unwavering strictness, since they are themselves liable to sanctions from above in an unbroken stream of "buck-passing" that only ends with a fatelike "unknown manager" (*To Vima*, 7/7/76, p. 2).

As an impersonal and malignant power, the bureaucracy itself may be explicitly blamed for individual misfortunes. This happened, for example, when villagers, desperate to gain control of afforested land long before the tedious bureaucratic procedure had ground to its appointed end, set fire to the forest and then held the bureaucracy responsible for what they had done (Resvanis 1977:7). Similarly, du Boulay (1974:269-270) reports a tendency to blame intracommunal hostilities on the arbitrary application of land-tenure legislation by a local court.

A set of written instructions (*endoli*) allows no flexibility and provides a formulaic excuse in the face of the most reasonable complaints. Thus, the owner of a country house near Athens discovered that his telephone service had been cut off. When he complained, he was told that his bill had not been paid.

> So he thought that nothing could be more natural than to put an end to the whole adventure by showing his paid invoice.... But this—supposedly—official document, the receipt with official stamp and signature attesting payment, was of no interest to the telephone company employee, who simply declared, "This is the *endoli* I received"—that is, to charge the hapless subscriber over again.

The latter was thus obliged to pay his bill twice, as well as a fine and a reconnection fee (*To Vima*, 8/5/76, p. 2). Other complaints are met with the equally conventional response, "That's what the directive [*engiklios*] says." Here, too, we encounter a bitter comment on the apparent priority of written orders over standard practice: "... and it's well known that public service offices function with directives which they regard as above the law" (T. Paraskevopoulos, letter in *To Vima*, 8/21/76, p. 5).

What these extracts from journalistic commentary make very clear is that such incidents are commonplace and formulaic. The appeal to a directive, though often recognized as *efthinofovia*, is conventionally acceptable, since it conforms to previously encoded experience. Many of the problems in question do not arise from the administrative apparatus as such, but from the literal application of the principle that, as it were, the last directive to be received always takes precedence. Note that appeals to fate work in a very similar way: since the edict of fate cannot be known until after the event, each new development requires a further appraisal or interpretation of what the edict actually "wrote."

For many Greek commentators, the problem is one of bureaucratic mentality. Whether the attitudes in question are confined to bureaucrats is itself dubious; a doctrinally far from orthodox folk interpretation of the sign of the cross illustrates the radical distrust of altruistic initiative (see Figure 1).[11]

Moreover, the similarities between attitudes toward fate and bureaucracy respectively suggest something far more fundamental to Greek cultural recognition than is likely to have appeared with the relatively recent importation of an essentially foreign bureaucratic system. It is true, however, that the educated Greeks had a long and intimate involvement with Ottoman administrative practice (see Dakin 1973:16-21), and some commentators (e.g., Bakoyannis 1977) see the present pattern of bureaucrat-client interaction as "nothing

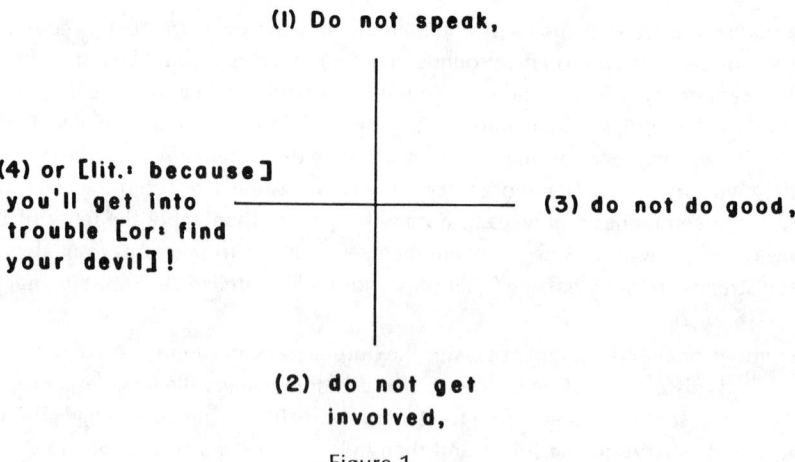

Figure 1.

but a continuation of the landlord-serf relationship of Turkish times." Such statements require careful evaluation. While a senior official may behave with calculated rudeness to illiterate country folk (e.g., Campbell 1964:227-228, 241-242), the junior clerk often turns out to be a cowed and unctuous underling in the presence of administrative superiors. The description of the bureaucratic system as a continuation of Turkish practices and attitudes is a popular and not altogether unconvincing device in Greek political rhetoric, one which goes back to the earliest years of Greek statehood (Dakin 1973; Katsoulis 1975:216; Kiriakidou-Nestoros 1975:238). Employees claim that they too are victims of the bureaucratic system (e.g., *To Vima*, 8/4/76, p. 2). What can they do? History, the Turks, even the hot climate (Paleologos 1976), are all blamed for the endemic evasion of bureaucratic responsibility, a feature that is nevertheless accounted as a national failing. Clearly, the Greeks do not lack the capacity for collective self-criticism, but it is softened for them by the convention of attributing ultimate responsibility to some impersonal, external agency, even while the problem itself is energetically (if perhaps inconclusively) tackled. This provides a rhetoric that satisfies the ever-present concern with potential criticism from abroad.

Despite the bitter complaints about bureaucracy in general, the attitude of *efthinofovia* and the appeal to written directives appear to be a conventionally appropriate idiom of self-defense by bureaucrats. This does not mean, of course, that all statements of this sort will be accepted, any more than will every attempt to explain a personal failure as the work of fate. But the recognition of the directive motif as a recurrent characteristic suggests, at the very least, an expectation on the part of the bureaucrats themselves that it will sometimes prove persuasive. This is very different from what are seen as *violations* of the same code by officials and wealthy clients whose trade in bribes offends the sensibilities of others in a less fortunate position (e.g., *To Vima*, 8/18/76, p. 2). Bribery, in Greek, is denoted by a term (*dhorodhokia*) that can be rendered literally as "gift-giving." This translation is misleadingly innocent-sounding, however, since its connotations in Greek are almost entirely negative and smack of the underhand dealings of the unscrupulous and powerful. Although the term probably originated in the neoclassical *katharevousa* language, its component lexemes are sufficiently close to their ordinary-language equivalents for there to be no ambiguity. Here, again, the "gift" represents a diversion of benefits from their rightful destinations (see especially *To Vima*, 8/18/76, p. 2), as in the "gift" that violates a traditional rule for the transmission of property and arrogates the power of an impersonal and remote power to a few individuals.

betrayal from within

Given the extremely high value Greeks attach to hospitality (e.g, Friedl 1962:106), this negative evaluation of "gift-giving" may seem surprising. This, however, is a question of context. Just as excessive generosity may be socially as disruptive as a total failure to engage in normative reciprocity, so too "gift-giving" can become a symbol of other kinds of deviancy. On Crete, for example, the covillager who directs a sheep-thief from elsewhere to one's flocks and assists in their disposal is known as the *dhotis,* "one who gives or betrays." More generally, the standard Greek term for betrayal, *prodhosia,* is yet another etymological cognate. Once again, there is the sense of the immoral disposal of something held in trust and the enrichment of one partner to the detriment of others.

In the aftermath of the Turkish invasion of Cyprus in 1974, both NATO in general and the United States in particular were accused by many Greeks of *prodhosia* (but see critiques in Vatikiotis 1977; Grigoriadis 1981).[12] This usage is instructive in that the English translation is clearly inadequate. English does not use "betrayal" for the actions of the larger social group of which the speaker is a member; it applies only to the actions of an at least nominally equal partner or member. One can only be betrayed from within. In the Greek use of *prodhosia* for the actions of the NATO allies, there is in fact an explicit sense of the father (the United States) who makes an unfair distribution of his property between two quarrelsome sons—his image is part of the rhetoric of both the right wing, where it is meant to imply that NATO is a "family affair" (e.g., *Ta Nea,* 4/4/77, p. 16), and the liberal and left-wing groups, for which the theme of paternalism is not necessarily a positive one (cf., e.g., *To Vima,* 4/4/77, p. 2), especially as "The British gave both to Turkey in Cyprus; the Americans gave both to Turkey in the Aegean conflict over oil" (*To Vima,* 8/15/76, p. 1). It is perhaps significant in this regard that most of the active opposition to patronage and influence peddling, especially in its exploitation of kinship and spiritual kinship, has come from the socialist PA.SO.K. party and its supporters (e.g., *Eleftherotipia,* series of articles during September 1976).

The concept of *prodhosia* provides an "explanation of misfortune" (Evans-Pritchard 1937), but this must be seen in terms of a larger symbolic context: How does one explain such national misfortunes when the received wisdom also has it that "one Greek is worth ten Turks"? External agency must be invoked, and the long historical experience of constant Western failures to come to the aid of beleaguered Greek Christians may have furnished a model.[13] Above and beyond the perfidy of squabbling allies, moreover, Greek popular imagery attributed the Fall of Constantinople (1453) to the "will of God" (*thelima Theu*). The vicious internal feuds of the last years of Byzantium, by contrast, were internal to Orthodox Christianity and perhaps for this reason did not provide a palatable explanation for Greek singers.

Appealing to the will of God fits the retrospective pattern of attributions to fate. Indeed, so strong was the presumption of divinely ordained disaster and so exceptional the successful repulse of the invaders that when Malta successfully withstood a Turkish siege in 1565, the "will of God" was assumed to have occasioned a disaster that in fact never occurred (Passow 1860:365, #485d)! *After* the sack of Constantinople, by contrast, traditions immediately began to form that predicted the regaining of the City of Constantine for Christianity (see especially Politis 1904:21–22, 656–674). These optimistic traditions were later emblematically adopted by Greek irredentists for their own secular purposes, with a success that further demonstrates how far the Greeks' orientation to future events is from being fatalistic (Herzfeld 1982:129–138).

As we turn again to events in the recent past, it is clear that divine intervention as such is no longer a widely accepted explanation for disaster. Instead, the impersonal force called *Ameriki* is said to "want" (*theli*) Turkish victory; the assumption that the Great Powers can do as they wish is so prevalent that one Glendiot even claimed that the Americans had lost the war in Vietnam "because they wanted to"! Again, this is a widespread idiom: Glendiots who find they are losing at cards will exclaim, "It [a card] doesn't want [*theli*] me!" While part of the aim may be to inspire overconfidence in the opposing player, such expressions also seem to appear when the game has become manifestly irretrievable. In this context, note that the sequence of cards (*i sindhesi tu khartiu*) is perceived as dependent on how the cards are dealt; the term for "dealing" (*mirazi*) is also used: (1) for the activity of fate in general (*i mira mirazi*, [fate divides]; the pun shows etymological awareness); (2) for the division by lots, especially by a father; (3) for the distribution of political favors; and (4) for the division of the world arranged by the Great Powers at Yalta. Public awareness of Yalta is fostered by some newspapers, as, for example, when fears of a "new Yalta" were expressed in an article (*To Vima*, 8/15/76) that also accused the United States of setting Greece and Turkey at each other's throats in order to gain influence as mediators in the ensuing conflict.

Conflict, indeed, is seen as "in the program" (*proskhedhiasmenos, proghrammatismenos*) in both ordinary speech and journalism (e.g., *To Vima*, 8/24/76, p. 5). The image has long figured in political rhetoric, having been used in the 19th century to explain setbacks in the gradual enlargement of the Greek territorial boundaries (e.g., Vivilakis 1866). The image here is that instrument of destiny, the pen. Internally, especially during periods of repression, it carries the sinister implications of *fakellosi* ("having one's political life recorded in a dossier"); as one Glendiot remarked, there is a "huge pencil" (*moliva*) that records every false step and thus restricts the ambitions of all but the politically well connected. Externally, the same image is attached to Great Power treaties that condemn the small nations to effective servitude. The superpowers, it is said, "do not allow us" (*dhe mas afinun*) to fight the Turks and beat them as we would otherwise easily do. Sometimes, the agent is not specified; "they" do not allow the Greeks or their leaders to act in the nation's best interests. This rhetoric is as popular with the extreme right wing as it is with the opposition parties; for example, a projunta functionary who somehow managed to remain in the civil service after the collapse of the colonels' regime claimed that Ioannidis, the junta leader responsible for the Cyprus fiasco of 1974, had not been "allowed" to carry out his task to its appointed conclusion; the same official claimed that Karamanlis, the first postjunta prime minister, had been a traitor (*prodhotis*) (*To Vima*, 8/14/76, p. 1). By far the commonest use of this rhetoric nevertheless remains the complaint that the NATO powers have subordinated Greek interests to their own; or, in the words of a proverb often cited in this connection, "The big fish eats the little one."

friendship, politics, and identity

In short, the Greeks' experiences of internal administration and international politics have often been extremely discouraging. The effects of foreign interference and domination in both arenas are well documented (e.g., Couloumbis, Petropulos, and Psomiades 1976; Couloumbis and Iatrides 1980; Freeman 1975). In the present discussion I have been less concerned with the historical causes of these problems than with the ways in which Greeks try to make some sense of them. By encoding their accounts of specific events in an imagery derived from the rhetoric of personal interaction, they represent seemingly uncontrollable forces in a more accessible way.

The emphasis here is on the rhetorical, rather than on the personal in any literal sense. Greeks conventionally represent political conflicts in terms of personal relationships between political leaders. Two qualifications need to be made, however. First, it is no longer an invariable feature of newspaper commentary that "friendship" can be invoked as a serious principle of international relations (e.g., *To Vima*, 8/15/76, p. 10; Vatikiotis 1977). The bitterness often expressed by villagers at the perfidy of the Greek allies of World War II is no longer always the persuasive argument it once was; during my most recent visit (1981) to Glendi, at least one young man explicitly *denied* the possibility that "friendship" had any role to play in international politics. Second, even within the conceptual framework of older generations, it is clear that the personal character of political forces is of a highly stylized kind; it is cast in the image of an implacable being with a pen, with opaque but ultimately destructive designs upon the speaker's side. Friendship is formulaic: under the guise of representing events in personal terms, it actually recasts them stereotypically.

In addition, while friendship is a highly prized virtue in rural Greece, it does not impose the stable obligations that are associated with kinship, affinal, and spiritual ties. In some communities, of which Pefko is an example, *filia* is even explicitly pointed out as an inferior kind of relationship.[14] Thus, the attribution of "friendship" to political allies is in fact a metaphor for the *instability* of that relationship, which may, in addition, be essentially one of asymmetrical patronage (cf. Loizos 1975:89–92). The dependency relationship is even more explicitly spelled out, of course, in the representation of America as a "parent."

The ambivalence of the friendship between Greece and the Western powers reproduces in the political domain the ambiguity that Greeks express about their cultural relationship with the West. Torn between conflicting ideologies, one of which stresses the European status of their classical heritage, while the other looks to the more recent periods of Byzantine and Turkish domination as the main source of cultural models, the Greeks have long experienced a degree of uncertainty that is reflected in the double sense of *Evropi* (Europe) as both inclusive and exclusive of the Greeks themselves (Herzfeld 1982:10–11, 53–60). The semantic ambiguity of *Evropi* thus expresses a pervasive unease about the status and identity of modern Greek culture.

The desire to be included in *Evropi* generates a certain defensiveness about cultural traits thought to derive from the Turkish experience. One such trait is the evasion of personal responsibility in bureaucratic interaction (cf. Argyriades 1968:342). Some foreign commentators have concluded that Greeks suffer from a basic incapacity for self-awareness (e.g., Holden 1972). This view, however, apparently reflects the commentators' insensitivity to their own status as outsiders. Among themselves, Greeks are often quite severely critical of what they see as national failings, and their coinage of a term for the evasion of responsibility (*efthinofovia*) implies a fairly general recognition of that particular problem.

Many critics of the bureaucracy point out that it combines fear of personal accountability with an institutionalized exploitation of the underdog and that these two features prevent it from conforming to the European ideal (e.g., Bakoyannis 1977; Filippidis 1977; cf. also *To Vima*, 1/25/77, p. 8). These critics are clearly responding to external criteria of excellence.[15] Both the desire to be European and the contempt for what is seen as the oriental fatalism of the Turks are aspects of an orientalist thesis that itself largely derives from Western European cultural ideologies (cf. Said 1978:102). The conservative New Democracy party had as its 1981 election slogan "We belong to the West"—a claim that was hotly contested by the political left. Similarly, right-wing social critics decry what they see as un-European attitudes blocking their political integration with the European Economic Community; their opponents criticize the domination of political and administrative life by a pro-Western elite. *Both* groups, in short, argue their respective positions in terms of a symbolic opposition between Europe and the Orient. The long predominance of political conservatism, inspired by the concept of Greece as the quintessence of European culture and assiduously fostered by the Western powers, has probably been primarily responsible for locking the debate into this particular symbolic format.

Attitudes toward personal and collective responsibility cannot be understood independently of the Eurocentric cultural yardstick. The accusation that the Turks are fatalistic reproduces on an Aegean-wide scale the local-level charge of laziness brought against particular individuals (see, e.g., Herzfeld 1981:565): it says that the Turks, although neighbors, are unworthy of serious consideration and are to blame for their own woes. It also says that they are not European. By contrast, when the Greeks turn to self-characterization, they take pains to deny that they are fatalists, since this would be tantamount to excluding themselves from the conceptual unity of Europe. Admitting to fatalism would thus involve accepting from foreigners the very taint that the Greeks themselves stereotypically confer on the Turks. The charge of fatalism expresses a moral differentiation; it serves as a negotiable means of justifying social boundaries in terms of what are presented as fixed truths about selves and others.

Thus, Greeks usually deny charges of fatalism when these are leveled by foreigners. In this they conform to a more general pattern of presenting a stereotypically European face to the outside world. Internally, however, a good deal of doubt remains. Even when the charge of fatalism as such is absent, Greeks worry about the implications of endemic *efthinofovia* for the national self-image and well-being, and—in an ironic echo of the very rhetoric we are discussing—attribute it stereotypically to "four centuries of Turkish rule" (Argyriades 1968:342; but cf. Kiriakidou-Nestoros 1975:235).

This cultural ambivalence cannot today be treated separately from the somewhat similar attitude toward political relationships with the West. Just as Western Europe was long seen as the repository of the values first generated by classical Greece, so the NATO alliance is represented by its Greek supporters as a necessary counter to the "Slavic dogma" of communism; these are long-standing rhetorical terms in Balkan history. For most Greeks, in the ordinary course of events, both the European virtues and the steadfast friendship of the West are at best rather vague and problematic concepts, fraught with the doubt born of actual experience. Among themselves, Greeks often *oppose* their culture to that of *Evropi;* I have already mentioned the comparably double-edged nature of the friendship metaphor for international alliances.

Given these mixed feelings, it is hardly surprising that Greeks should represent both bureaucratic and international setbacks in the agonistic idiom of personal interaction. This does not mean that they literally attribute every such setback to personal malice; on the contrary, just as the imagery of fate depersonalizes one's individual accountability for failure, so the rhetoric of European identity and political friendship provides a flexible idiom for impugning the character of others while blaming one's own failures on crushingly superior and implacable forces. In these terms, the charge of fatalism is best seen as a device for creating cultural otherness, which it does by creating discrete oppositions out of a cultural and social continuum.[16]

Fate is something to be struggled against until there is no hope left. Possibly this is true of all societies; it is at least certain that the old stereotype of the fatalistic peasant has already lost a good deal of ground in anthropological thinking, where its uncritical use could only be evidence of a persistent strain of Eurocentrism. In fact, many authors have already shown how misleading it can be as a descriptive tool (see Ingersoll 1966; Joseph 1974; Srinivas 1976). It is no more apposite in those areas of social life where the concept of fate itself is iconographically replaced—as, in the Greek materials given here, when its role is taken over by the faceless bureaucracy or the impersonal superpowers. In these cases, too, the charge of fatalism fails to capture the retrospective and strategic character of the speaker's evasion of blame. Greek villagers may indeed say that it does not matter for whom they vote, as the Americans will intervene anyway. Not only does this declaration not prevent them from campaigning for anti-American candidates, but it may also be a part of the electoral strategy itself, much like the cardplayer's ploy to lull his opponent into a false sense of security. It is also good insurance for the future: if and when events eventually seem to have justified it, it falls neatly into place as part of the retrospective etiology of political life.

conclusions

Much of what has been called fatalism in Greek culture turns out to consist of a set of rhetorical strategies. The key question thus shifts from how belief in fate influences action, to how declarations about fate constitute a form of action—the performative action of excuses. Instead of literal statements of belief in fate, it addresses performances that invoke the idea of fate through oblique allusion. How, then, is such indirection a source of efficacy in the performance of excuses?

The first thing to realize in answering this question is that fate is not necessarily the object of religious activity as such. Villagers do not specify the attributes of fate as consistently as they do those of deity or the saints. In Pefko, for example, there are no visual icons of fate, verbal accounts are minimally descriptive, the relationship between fate and the pluralized "fates" is unclear, and the role of God in directing the activities of fate seems to deprive fate of an autonomous identity. Questions about "the fates" may elicit an identification of them with "angels." Asking whether people believe in fate is therefore of dubious relevance. Religion is the domain of belief; the fates, although historically cosmological, have been elbowed aside by Christian ideology.

They have not, however, lost their evocative or allusory significance in the process. While Greek villagers may take pride in their rejection of paganism as such, the pre-Christian etymology of their rhetoric of fate remains a source of implicit validation. In such a context, the ethnographer's questions about belief in fate are impertinent both socially and methodologically.

Excuses that appeal to fate are thus not necessarily believed. They are nevertheless often accepted, and their acceptability seems to draw on a generous fund of discourse conventions. Even these, however, are not sufficient to guarantee acceptance, since an explanation that works in front of one audience may flop disastrously in front of another. The composition of the audience, too, must be appropriate to the excuse offered. A hostile addressee will discount the speaker's appeal to fate; this is a form of dissociation from the speaker's interpretation of experience.

In the same way, when individuals blame some mishap on the bureaucracy; there is always an implied appeal to shared experience. If those addressed accept that appeal, they will always be able to recall similar occasions when they themselves were victimized by some unsympathetic official; if they do not want to accept that appeal, they will in effect suggest that *they* would not have made such a mess of things. Whether they share in the speaker's experience or differentiate it from their own is thus not usually a question of plausibility alone. Most Greeks *can* draw on a fund of negative experiences of the bureaucracy; they do not always choose to do so. In the same way, ideological considerations will affect the extent to which individuals are willing to accede to criticisms of superpower intervention in Greek politics.

The rhetoric of blame attribution thus furnishes a strategic means of defining national, cultural, ideological, and social boundaries. Acceptance of an excuse expresses and articulates the common experience of speaker and addressee. It also entails recognition that speaker and addressee share a common code.

This complex recognition of cultural commonality is triggered, at least in part, by the implicit etymological links between ways of representing the various domains of social experience. The forms of blame evasion are unmistakably Greek, and an individual must adopt those forms in order to encode a personal experience so that it will be understood sympathetically by others. They, in turn, recognize the experience as belonging to a known *type* of situation. Recognition, in this sense, occurs when an event "comes to be viewed by an addressee as the expression of a given content" (Eco 1976:221), and it is immaterial that this content may—as here—be a vaguely formulated situation type. The lack of specificity is highly significant. Greeks do not usually explicate the etymological link. They do not, for instance, represent their responses to political crisis as resembling traditional ideas about fate (but cf. Dimou 1976:46); perhaps this is because any such parallelism might imply that they were fatalists. The situation type, and the explanation for it, are articulated through a set of images such as writing, sharing, and gift giving. These images may be partly conveyed by words, but they are not *articulated in* words or collected together under a simple categorical label. For this reason the rhetorical code cannot simply be reduced to a verbal folk taxonomy.

In general, since no purely linguistic description of the code will suffice, I also hesitate to describe the code as possessing a symbolic syntax (cf. Crick 1976:73, 77). "Symbolic syntax" is a linguistic metaphor and the component images do not exhibit the combinatorial complexity of linguistic syntax. Such linguistic metaphors may be misleading and they are certainly also unnecessarily restrictive.

Austin's (1971) view of etymology, by contrast, has semiotic rather than purely linguistic implications. Ardener (1971:222–227) has already stressed the etymological character of much of the informant exegesis on which anthropologists build their analyses of predominantly nonverbal symbolic systems. By combining these two insights, we see that verbal idioms may be sustained in use by their ability to invoke inchoate images; the "trailing clouds of etymology" that make an excuse conventionally acceptable do so by investing it with a virtually iconographic flavor. The implacable pen hardly loses its force, for example, as it passes from the writing hand of fate to those of bureaucracy and the superpowers; on the contrary, bitter experience confirms its aptness. Austin himself was mainly interested in the etymological suggestiveness of words, and we have seen how certain verbal etymologies strengthen the fatelike appearance of the more mundane bureaucratic and political powers. Nevertheless, that resemblance does not entirely depend on purely verbal links; the writing and gift-giving *images* might well have sufficed even if all the *verbal* etymologies had vanished.

Austin's framework can be expanded to incorporate nonverbal elements of the discourse itself. An expressive shrug of the shoulders, or a journalist's exclamation mark, may serve indexically to remind the audience of the fatelike implacability of bureaucracy. These elements are part of the code and possess at least a crudely etymological suggestiveness in linking people's reactions to quite different areas of social and political experience.

Nonverbal elements also demonstrate still further the priority of the implicit over the verbally explicit in the rhetoric of excuses. Like verbal etymologies, they operate at a subdued level; spelling out the cosmological allusions would simply deflate the rhetoric and possibly provoke all the usual defensiveness about fatalism.[17] The apparent vagueness of these etymological allusions, a counterpart to the "fuzzy concepts" of recent linguistics and logic (cf. Eco 1976:82), may have deterred anthropologists from making use of the "Plea for Excuses" when it originally appeared in 1956-57.[18] At that time, too, the term "etymology" smacked of unfashionable, diachronic concerns. Today, however, these objections have lost much of their force. The present explosive increase in the anthropological study of rhetoric should prove highly conducive to a more general exploration of the central issue discussed here: that of how etymology lends acceptability to particular interpretations of events.

notes

Acknowledgments. For their provocative commentary at various stages in the development of this paper, I wish to record my gratitude to J. K. Campbell, Van Coufoudakis, Jane K. Cowan, Loring M. Danforth, S. K. Frangos, Cornelia Mayer Herzfeld, Martha B. Kendall, Leonidas Sotiropoulos, Spyros Stavrakas, and Lilo Stern; I would also like to thank the editor and anonymous reviewers of the *American Ethnologist* for their helpful observations in the final stages.

[1] The core of the debate is the question of how much emphasis should be given to the classical elements in the modern Greek heritage; this aspect of Greek identity was a preoccupation of Greek thinkers long before independence and statehood (Henderson 1970) and was the focus of an ideological struggle that revealed itself most clearly in the development of an indigenous scholarly tradition in ethnology (Herzfeld 1982). It proved especially divisive in the still partially unresolved "language question" (*ghlossiko zitima*), or diglossic problem, the socioeconomic and ideological dimensions of which have been discussed with great clarity by Sotiropoulos (1977). See also Augustinos (1977) and Clogg (1976).

[2] In rural communities, men usually read national newspapers with great avidity; women less so, as newspapers are principally read in the coffeehouses, which they do not frequent. On the historical development of the Greek press, see Dimakis (1977). McNeill (1978:242-244) stresses the heavy influence of imported television programs. It should not be thought, however, that villagers necessarily *believe* media reports; much depends on their ideological position, and in any case people's political convictions are extremely opaque (cf. Loizos 1975:301).

[3] The general attitude is that Greek is too difficult for foreigners to learn properly. This reproduces a parallel view that local dialects cannot be learned by outsiders; du Boulay (1974:48) recounts a story illustrative of this kind of linguistic localism that I have also heard about the national language. In both cases, language is viewed as a defense against inquisitive outsiders.

[4] In Crete, I was told (1981) that suicide was wrong even for a person in immense pain; one should struggle up to the appointed end of one's life.

[5] My own field data from two strongly differentiated communities in Rhodes (Pefko) and Crete (Glendi) appear to corroborate the folklorists' accounts in several matters of detail (see especially Politis 1874:207-236; Lawson 1910:120-130; see also Blum and Blum 1970:100, 313). "Pefko" and "Glendi" are pseudonyms; for further details, see Herzfeld (1980a, 1980b, 1981).

[6] The point of this insult seems to be that the donkey is unpredictable, and this, in conjunction with viciousness, is thought to be an attribute of outsiders, rather than of those one knows well through everyday interaction; see also Herzfeld (1980a:346).

[7] The reference, taken entirely out of context, is to Jesus' response to the disciple who cut off the ear of the high priest's servant, one of those who came to take Jesus before Pilate: "Then said Jesus unto him put up again, the sword into his place: *for all they that take the sword shall perish by the sword*" (Matt. 27:52). This injunction thus inveighed against the very code of vengeful behavior my informants sought to justify by it; its particular sense of the inevitability of Jesus' death comes far closer to the stereotypical notion of "fatalism" than any comparable village usage.

[8] "How is she/it at fault for *you*?"—where "you" refers to the Turk.

[9] See below on the homonymy of personal identity with the document that attests it.

[10] Glendiots, when asked how they are, usually reply, "Let's say 'well' " (*as ta leme(ne) kala*). This is apparently an apotropaic formula; too positive a reply might attract the evil eye (*thiarmos*) or some other active embodiment of envy. In both Pefko and Glendi, there is a general reluctance to admit to good fortune, either present or prospective, for this reason; pessimistic predictions, conversely, are thought to improve one's chances. Glendiots also play on the delicate balance between the ironic, the strategic, and the apotropaic when they assure their cardplaying opponents that the latter will win.

[11] Recorded in Pefko in 1974, but apparently derived from the informant's conversations in Rhodes Town. This folk exegesis shows that Jesus is perceived as the ultimate victim of too keen a desire to "get involved" and in particular to tangle with government on behalf of some good cause.

[12] A popular post-1974 slogan is NATO-SIA [=C.I.A.], PRODHOSIA. Note that this device absolves not only the nation as a collectivity, but also individuals whose acts might otherwise portray the nation in an unfavorable act abroad. Thus, when a Greek arsonist was convicted of setting fire to a Moslem (i.e., "Turkish") school, the prosecutor [sic] claimed that "the Great Powers were at least the moral culprits in the crime of the accused" (*To Vima*, 8/24/76). More right-wing journalists, apparently identifying their perspective with the generally pro-Western stance of the New Democracy party, discount some of the more extreme accounts of Anglo-American involvement in the 1974 crisis.

[13] Historically, consciousness of "the West" (*i dhisi*) has shifted its exact referents. The bitter experience of 1204, when the Crusaders sacked Byzantium, left scars that were hardly appeased by the indifference of the Christian powers to the later collapse of the Byzantine Empire and the advance of Ottoman power. Indeed, there is evidence that on several occasions, notably in Crete in 1645, the local population welcomed the Turks as saviors from the oppressive rule of the Christian powers (Venice in the case of Crete).

[14] In Pefko, this is in part because nonkin are ideally also non-Pefkiots; the community is normatively endogamous.

[15] See Langrod (1965:40), Munkman (1958), and McNeill (1978:226–228) for illustrations of these technocratic criteria applied to Greece by foreigners.

[16] I use the notion of "continuum" in Drummond's (1981:657, n. 4; cf. 1980) sense of "intersystem": "a conceptualized system of identity/difference/relations that ties 'We' to 'Other,' as a fundamental attribute of culture."

[17] To Greek commentators, however, such parallelisms may also seem too *obvious* to be worth discussing. In either case, we see here the process that Douglas (1975:3–8) has called "backgrounding."

[18] A major difficulty seems to be that such indeterminacy is not, and cannot be, catered for by formalized techniques for data collection in the field; on this, see Karp and Kendall (1982).

references cited

Ardener, Edwin
   1970   Witchcraft, Economics and the Continuity of Belief. *In* Witchcraft Confessions and Accusations. Mary Douglas, ed. pp. 141–160. ASA Monographs, 9. London: Tavistock.
   1971   Social Anthropology and the Historicity of Historical Linguistics. *In* Social Anthropology and Language. Edwin Ardener, ed. pp. 209–241. ASA Monographs, 10. London: Tavistock.
Argyriades, D.
   1968   The Ecology of Greek Administration: Some Factors Affecting the Development of the Greek Civil Service. *In* Contributions to Mediterranean Sociology. J. G. Peristiany, ed. pp. 339–349. The Hague: Mouton.
Augustinos, Gerasimos
   1977   Consciousness and History: Nationalist Critics of Greek Society, 1897–1914. Boulder, CO: East European Quarterly.
Austin, J. L.
   1971 [1956–57]   A Plea for Excuses. *In* Philosophy and Linguistics. Colin Lyas, ed. pp. 79–101. London: Macmillan.
   1975 [1962]   How To Do Things with Words. J. O. Urmson and Marina Sbisá, eds. Cambridge: Harvard University Press.
Bakoyannis, P.
   1977   Opisthodhromisi s' olus tus tomis. To Vima, 3/15/77, p. 5.
Banfield, Edward C.
   1958   The Moral Basis of a Backward Society. New York: Free Press.
Bauman, Richard
   1977   Verbal Art as Performance. Rowley, MA: Newbury House.
Blau, Peter M.
   1963   The Dynamics of Bureaucracy: A Study of Interpersonal Relationships in Two Government Agencies. Chicago: University of Chicago Press.
Blum, Richard, and Eva Blum
   1970   The Dangerous Hour: The Lore of Crisis and Mystery in Rural Greece. London: Chatto & Windus.
Browning, Robert
   1969   Medieval and Modern Greek. London: Hutchinson.

Campbell, J. K.
　1964　Honour, Family, and Patronage: A Study of Institutions and Moral Values in a Greek Mountain Community. Oxford: Clarendon.
Clogg, Richard, ed.
　1976　The Movement for Greek Independence, 1770-1812: A Collection of Documents. New York: Barnes & Noble.
Couloumbis, Theodore A., and John O. Iatrides, eds.
　1980　Greek American Relations: A Critical Review. New York: Pella.
Couloumbis, T. A., J. A. Petropulos, and H. J. Psomiades, eds.
　1976　Foreign Interference in Greek Politics. New York: Pella.
Crick, Malcom
　1976　Explorations in Language and Meaning: Towards a Semantic Anthropology. New York: John Wiley.
Dakin, Douglas
　1973　The Greek Struggle for Independence, 1821-1833. London: Batsford.
Diaz, May N.
　1966　Tonalá: Conservatism, Responsibility, and Authority in a Mexican Town. Berkeley: University of California Press.
Dimakis, John
　1977　The Greek Press. In Greece in Transition: Essays in the History of Modern Greece, 1821-1974. John T. A. Koumoulides, ed. pp. 209-235. London: Zeno.
Dimen, Muriel, and Ernestine Friedl, eds.
　1976　Regional Variation in Modern Greece and Cyprus: Toward a Perspective on the Ethnography of Greece. New York: New York Academy of Sciences. (Annals of the New York Academy of Sciences 268:1-465.)
Dimou, Nikos
　1976　I dhistikhia tu na ise ellinas. Athens: Ikaros.
Douglas, Mary
　1975　Implicit Meanings: Essays in Anthropology. London: Routledge & Kegan Paul.
Drummond, Lee
　1980　The Cultural Continuum: A Theory of Intersystems. Man(NS)15:352-374.
　1981　The Serpent's Children: Semiotics of Cultural Genesis in Arawak and Trobriand Myth. American Ethnologist 8:633-660.
du Boulay, Juliet
　1974　Portrait of a Greek Mountain Village. Oxford: Clarendon.
Eco, Umberto
　1976　A Theory of Semiotics. Bloomington: Indiana University Press.
Evans-Pritchard, E. E.
　1937　Witchcraft, Oracles and Magic among the Azande. Oxford: Clarendon.
Filippidis, Khristos
　1977　Dhimosia Ipiresia. Akropolis, 3/6/77, p. 2.
Freeman, John, gen. ed.
　1975　Ksenokratia: To Apokaliptiko ton Ksenon Epemvaseon stin Elladha (1944-75). Athens: Papiros.
Friedl, Ernestine
　1962　Vasilika: A Village in Modern Greece. New York: Holt, Rinehart, and Winston.
Gavrielides, Nicolas
　1976　The Cultural Ecology of Olive Growing in the Fourni Valley. In Regional Variation in Modern Greece and Cyprus: Toward a Perspective on the Ethnography of Greece. M. Dimen and E. Friedl, eds. pp. 265-274. New York: New York Academy of Sciences. (Annals of the New York Academy of Sciences 268:1-465.)
Gouldner, Alvin W.
　1954　Patterns of Industrial Bureaucracy. Glencoe, IL: Free Press.
Grigoriadis, Solon
　1981　Mia Traghodhia khoris "Katharsi." Epikera 23 (677):17-23.
Handelman, Don
　1976　Bureaucratic Transactions: The Development of Official-Client Relationships in Israel. In Transaction and Meaning: Directions in the Anthropology of Exchange and Symbolic Behavior. Bruce Kapferer, ed. pp. 223-275. Philadelphia: Institute for the Study of Human Issues.
Henderson, G. P.
　1970　The Revival of Greek Thought, 1620-1830. Albany: State University of New York Press.
Herzfeld, Michael
　1980a　Honour and Shame: Problems in the Comparative Analysis of Moral Systems. Man (NS) 15:339-351.
　1980b　Social Tension and Inheritance by Lot in Three Greek Villages. Anthropological Quarterly 53:91-100.

    1981   Meaning and Morality: A Semiotic Approach to Evil Eye Accusations in a Greek Village. American Ethnologist 8:560-574.
    1982   Ours Once More: Folklore, Ideology, and the Making of Modern Greece. Austin: University of Texas Press.
Holden, David
    1972   Greece Without Columns: The Making of the Modern Greeks. London: Faber & Faber.
Howe, James
    1981   Fox Hunting as Ritual. American Ethnologist 8:278-300.
Ingersoll, James, ed.
    1966   Fatalism in Asia: Old Myths and New Realities. Anthropological Quarterly 39:143-253.
Joseph, Roger
    1974   The Idiom of Fatalism in North African Society. Manifest 2:52-60.
Karp, Ivan, and Martha B. Kendall
    1982   Reflexivity in Field Work. *In* Explaining Human Behavior: Consciousness, Human Action and Social Structure. H. Secord, ed. pp. 249-273. Beverly Hills: Sage.
Kasperson, Roger E.
    1966   The Dodecanese: Diversity and Unity in Island Politics. Research Paper No. 108. Department of Geography, University of Chicago.
Katsoulis, George D.
    1975   To Katestimeno sti Neoelliniki Istoria. Athens: Nea Sinora.
Kiriakidou-Nestoros, Alki
    1975   Laoghrafika Meletimata. Athens: Olkos.
Langrod, Georges
    1965   Réorganisation de la fonction publique en Grèce. Paris: Organisation de Coopération et Développement Économiques.
Lawson, John Cuthbert
    1910   Modern Greek Folklore and Ancient Greek Religion: A Study in Survivals. Cambridge: Cambridge University Press.
Legg, Keith R.
    1969   Politics in Modern Greece. Stanford: Stanford University Press.
Loizos, Peter
    1975   The Greek Gift: Politics in a Cypriot Village. Oxford: Blackwell.
McNeill, William H.
    1978   The Metamorphosis of Greece since World War II. Chicago: University of Chicago Press.
Meeker, Michael E.
    1979   Literature and Violence in North Arabia. Cambridge: Cambridge University Press.
Mouzelis, Nicos P.
    1975   Organisation and Bureaucracy: An Analysis of Modern Theories. London: Routledge & Kegan Paul.
Munkman, C. A.
    1958   American Aid to Greece: A Report of the First Ten Years. New York: Praeger.
Ossio, Juan M.
    1977   Myth and History: The Seventeenth-Century Chronicle of Guaman Poma de Ayala. *In* Text and Context: The Social Anthropology of Tradition. Ravindra K. Jain, ed. pp. 51-93. Philadelphia: Institute for the Study of Human Issues.
Paleologos, Il.
    1976   To klima ghrafi istoria. To Vima, 7/14/76, p. 1.
Passow, Arnold
    1860   Carmina popularia Graeciae recentioris. Leipzig: Teubner.
Politis, N. G.
    1874   Neoelliniki Mitholoyia. Part 2. Athens: N. B. Nakis & Karl Wilberg.
    1904   Paradhosis. Athens: Marasli
Resvanis, Kostas
    1977   Ke... i Ghrafiokratia kei ta Dhasi! Ta Nea, 4/6/77, pp. 7, 10.
Said, Edward
    1978   Orientalism. New York: Random House.
Sotiropoulos, Dimitri
    1977   Diglossia and the National Language Question in Modern Greece. Linguistics 197:5-31.
Srinivas, M. N.
    1976   The Remembered Village. Berkeley: University of California Press.
Tamiolakis, Mikhail
    1976   Maties sti Zoi ton Ghrafion. Thessaloniki: private publication.
Vatikiotis, P. G. [= P. J.]
    1977   Aftapates, dhilimmata ke mithi tis ellinikis eksoterikis politikis. To Vima, 1/28/77.
Vivilakis, E.
    1866   O proyeghrammenos Kris i o fatriasmos tis Kendrikis Epitropis (The Cretan Predestined by Writ...). Athens: Tipoghrafion Radhamanthios.

Weber, Max
   1958 [1946]   Bureaucracy. *In* From Max Weber: Essays in Sociology. H. H. Gerth and C. Wright Mills, eds. pp. 196-244. New York: Oxford University Press.

Submitted 30 October 1981
Revised version received 2 April 1982
Accepted 7 April 1982
Final revisions received 22 April 1982

the evil eye as synthetic image and its meanings on the Island of Pantelleria, Italy

ANTHONY H. GALT—*University of Wisconsin, Green Bay*

Little has been written about the evil eye in contemporary anthropology. A recent volume (Maloney 1976) contains a number of case studies of the phenomenon and several attempts at widely inclusive and ambitious theoretical explanations of it as a circum-Mediterranean symbolic complex (Roberts 1976; Garrison and Arensberg 1976). Subsequent to those writings, Herzfeld's (1981) article appeared in a special issue of this journal. Herzfeld, following Crick (1976:109-127), sees evil eye as a category for analysis that is best "dissolved" in favor of particularistic analysis of values and semantic systems. For reasons to be presented, the explanations in the Maloney volume cannot be accepted as conclusive, and Herzfeld's desire to abolish the evil eye as a useful category must be seen as overrash.

The perspective taken here, stated simply, is that the evil eye symbolic system has a wide distribution through the circum-Mediterranean area precisely because it is an evocative image with characteristics that allow, and even invite, the attachment of meaning at various levels, both social and individual. The notion of evil eye, I argue, has diffused and persisted because it is culturally, situationally, and individually useful; in fact, its usefulness comes not exclusively from any of the specific functions attributed to it in various cases but rather from its *flexibility of significance*. The evil eye is a member of a class Needham (1978:23-50) calls "synthetic images," and my task is to show how this synthetic image is expressed and utilized in the culture of the Island of Pantelleria, Sicily. While such images probably cannot be ascribed universal meanings, functions, or causal explanations, they do serve as symbolic frames, or boxes, which can be filled flexibly with local and even individual meanings.

Garrison and Arensberg's overgeneralized assertion that the evil eye is a reflection of patron-client systems in circum-Mediterranean societies, and Herzfeld's particularistic argument that the evil eye is not a useful unit for local cultural analysis, are found to be inadequate. Needham's synthetic image concept is offered as a fresh view of evil eye; it mediates the cross-cultural and historical existence of the belief, on the one hand, and fills the need for careful analysis in given locales, on the other. The evil eye synthetic image as it is constituted on the Island of Pantelleria, Italy, is explored as an example of such a perspective of a persistent symbolic complex. [Italy, evil eye, symbolism, envy, synthetic image, magic]

Copyright © 1982 by the American Ethnological Society
0094-0496/82/040664-18$2.30/1

previous general interpretations

Recent anthropological attempts to provide a general theory of evil eye are found in the Maloney volume noted above. The first (Roberts 1976) is a statistical, cross-cultural approach that provides correlates for the phenomenon's presence in contemporary and past societies; the second is an ambitious argument made by Garrison and Arensberg (1976) that the evil eye system occurs and is a symbolic projection in societies characterized by patron-client relationships.

Roberts (1976:227) admits that his cross-cultural treatment of evil eye is methodologically crude. His analysis probably shows that the evil eye belief system is not a universal thing as some previous, and now antiquated, works have claimed (see, e.g., Elsworthy 1970 [1958]:ix ff; Westermarck 1926, I:477–478), but is clustered in the circum-Mediterranean and Near Eastern cultures—among what Garrison and Arensberg (1976:290), following the latter's longstanding classification, call the "peoples of the book."[1] Naturally, evil eye beliefs of these Old World peoples have diffused into the New World with migrants. Otherwise, cases of evil eye seem sporadic. Many of them among Pacific, Amerindian, South of Sahara African, and East and Southeast Asian peoples are uncertain and possibly products of Old World diffusion. Thus, Galton's problem looms large for Roberts's study because cases in his sample cluster in a single, highly interconnected part of the world, making claims of causal association between sociocultural and economic factors and the evil eye immediately suspect and inconclusive if only because of diffusion. This is particularly the case, as evil eye has long associations with the three great religions of the area—Christianity, Islam, and Judaism—which, at least at the folk level, provide symbolic contexts for its diffusion (Moss and Cappannari 1976:5–8).[2]

High correlations with cultural complexity, dairying and milking, cereal agriculture, bride price or bride wealth, social stratification, and so on, are thus not at all surprising because these are traits that can be taken as typical of the "peoples of the book." Roberts's cross-cultural study, while interesting, does little more than possibly associate evil eye with a geographic and culturally contiguous area. Any further investigation of the phenomenon cross-culturally must look at variance in the belief system within that area and hypothesize concomitant variance in other variables while controlling for internal diffusion. This is almost impossible given problems of data control and the widespread movements of peoples and ideas so historically characteristic of the zone.

The detailed discussion provided by Garrison and Arensberg is intriguing and must be considered at length. It rests on Arensberg's assumption that a "cultural form" such as the evil eye can be "explained as an emergent from an underlying regularity of social action best represented as a minimal-sequence model of interpersonal behavior" (Garrison and Arensberg 1976:288). This assumption—and of course it is just that, for there are other competing kinds of explanations for cultural forms—leads Garrison and Arensberg (1976:288, emphasis added) to look about in the circum-Mediterranean culture area for "*the* social process or institution putatively symbolised in the evil eye." Their approach immediately excludes the possibility that there could be more than one institution symbolized by the complex, either in a given locale or over the entire range of cultures involved. That there is only one social process or institution symbolized by the evil eye among such a wide range of peoples does not follow necessarily from the previous assumption that symbolic complexes are "emergent" from underlying social structures.

By this assumption, Garrison and Arensberg propose a relationship between the evil eye and patronage. This is based on the idea of the evil eye containing "a minimal sequence of interpersonal action: a gaze or suspected gaze, gazee's raising of protection, and thereby the deflection of gazer (or his power) from seizure, expropriation, or destruction" (Garrison and Arensberg 1976:293). This is seen as emergent from the invocation of the power of a patron by a client in situations involving actual or possible seizure or destruction by such figures as "tax collectors," "Janiseries," "raiders," or "corrupt officials" (1976:293). Thus, the minimal social-structural unit defined for patronage is a patron appealed to by a client in the face of impending threat from a rapacious third party. The deflection of the evil eye through the use of symbols invoking higher powers is deemed congruent with protecting oneself from seizure or destruction through patronage. Patronage of this kind is found, the authors argue, in "a system of plural, stratified, societies organized in unstable states with redistributive economies" (1976:303). Such systems, they further note, are typical of the circum-Mediterranean area, particularly of the Near East, where evil eye symbolism is assumed to have originated.

Garrison and Arensberg assert that variations in evil eye beliefs are concomitant with variations in the nature of patronage in the area of its distribution. Thus they differentiate "gazer prophylaxis" (where the person expressing admiration of something spits, or otherwise symbolically detaches himself from a desire to cast the evil eye) and "gazee prophylaxis" (where the potential victim seeks protection from a gazer). The former is claimed to be characteristic of northern Europe, where social relations are seen as more "dyadic" (i.e., not involving the use of patrons against potential enemies), while the latter is ascribed to the circum-Mediterranean region where Garrison and Arensberg (1976: 305-315) see the evil eye as most developed. This distinction is empirically questionable. The common southern European device of avoiding making compliments is surely a form of gazer prophylaxis; the literature for the area reports verbal formulae to be uttered when a compliment is made (see, e.g., descriptions for Greece in Herzfeld 1981:572, note 8; Westermarck 1926:417-419). Gazee prophylaxis can be documented in northern Europe (examples from South Wales are reported in Morris, Collett, Marsh, and O'Shaughnessy 1979:143-144).

The Garrison and Arensberg article may be correct in its interpretation, but the argument is made with a rather selective use of evidence and in such a way that validation is impossible. For instance, they assume that the harm caused by the evil eye is of the nature of seizure, expropriation, or destruction. Even among the case studies in the Maloney volume, however, these words by no means always accurately describe the harm caused. Appel (1976:17) states that evil eye victims on the Murgia dei Trulli in southern Italy suffer headaches, sleepiness, exhaustion, depression, hypochondria, and spirit possession, illnesses linked to the sense of being "acted upon by powerful and unknown forces," but with the exception of "spirit possession" (which would seem a separate category from *malocchio* pure and simple), are not necessarily clearly characterizable as seizure or confiscation. A similar list is supplied for a pseudonymous Aegean island called "Nisi" by Dionisopoulos-Mass (1976:45), although added to it are sudden death of children and animals, withering of vines, and the splitting of an olive press. Teitelbaum (1976:64-65) reports that only living things are hurt by the evil eye and that the Tunisian Arabic usage for describing the affliction includes the notion of being "taken by the evil eye." There is a kind of seizure implied, but the recipient of it is unclear or highly abstract. A child whose death is caused by evil eye does not become the property of, or a benefit to, the gazer, even though, emically, evil eye may be thought to operate through envy. It stretches the case too much to make the gazer in the evil eye complex correspond with a person in a social-structural role or status (such as tax collectors, raiders, or Janiseries), who would seize and make into property people, produce, or objects.[3] The occupants of such roles benefit from seizure; projectors of the evil eye are rarely thought to do so.

Spooner (1976:78), writing of the evil eye in Islamic areas, notes a large variation in specific beliefs, and states that the affliction may cause "any misfortune" from the most trivial to sudden death, though a *gradual* wasting sickness is thought of as its most characteristic effect. Seizure or confiscation for the benefit of a gazer does not seem to be clear for the Middle East either.

Only in Ethiopia do seizure and confiscation find a clear symbolic model in evil eye lore. Here the gazers are the *buda* people of different ethnic origin from the Mänze Amhara. The *buda* are thought capable of changing themselves into were-hyenas at night and attacking through the evil eye under such guise. According to Reminick (1976:88-91), the *buda,* in so doing, "eat" others to better their lot among the Amhara. The resemblances to general sub-Saharan witchcraft beliefs are unmistakable, as Reminick (1976:99) notes, and thus this particular marginal case of evil eye in which seizure by the gazer is clearly defined cannot be used to generalize to the whole area of its occurrence.

Further, Garrison and Arensberg seize upon the notion of raising a protective amulet as a symbolic invocation of the protection of powerful patrons vis-à-vis threatened seizure, confiscation, or destruction. In support of this position they note that evil eye prophylactic amulets and rituals often have specific references to sources of power at higher levels of authority. Crosses, images of saints, or verses from the Koran are commonly used. Garrison and Arensberg (1976:308) further assert that all anti-evil-eye symbols "are, or at least were once, symbols of placement and rank." Beyond conjecturing that some of them have reference to items once associated with luxury trade—indigo (as in blue beads), gold, or iron—this assumption is not well supported. They ignore the strong sexual, particularly phallic, connotations of such well-known anti-evil-eye charms as the horn, the horned hand (and hornlike objects such as red chilies, crab claws, sharks' teeth, and boars' tusks), the "fig" gesture (Morris et al. 1979:145-160), keys, and plowshares (de Martino 1966:Figure 5). They also fail to deal with the common North African open-hand symbolism and the consequent use of the number 5 as evil eye prophylactic measures (Westermarck 1926:445-453).

In trying to invoke with the evil eye the image of an individual making it known to a potential seizer, confiscator, or destroyer of property, such as a tax collector or a barbary pirate, that he has the protection of a powerful patron, Garrison and Arensberg (1976:294) write that "the sign of protection raised says, in effect, 'Beware, I am protected, and I or my powers, my patron, saint . . . God, will get you if you harm me.'" This assertion overstretches the ethnography of the phenomenon by reading into it the idea of supernatural retaliation toward the gazer, an idea which is, in fact, very rare in the evil eye belief system, as Garrison and Arensberg (1976:316) themselves point out.

Finally, if the symbols of evil eye beliefs evoke the social fact of patronage, then the evocation is fragmentary and redundant with other symbol systems. The patron-client relationship, as a number of authors have pointed out, is one of continuing, unbalanced exchange (see Boissevain 1966; Foster 1963; Galt 1974; Paine 1971; Wolf 1966). Garrison and Arensberg suggest that evil eye prophylactic magic has reference to high power and rank, but if that reference is present in the use of a blue bead, or a red strip of cloth, or a boar's tusk, it is surely distant and vestigial at best and any evocation of a relationship of exchange with an entity of higher power or rank is certainly lost in the abstraction. Furthermore, one wonders why two symbolic systems emergent from patron-client relationships are necessary: as others have pointed out (e.g., Kenny 1960), that relationship is clearly figured in the expression of personal relationship with saints. Garrison and Arensberg (1976:295-296) themselves note that in popular Judaism, Islam, and Christianity, God is reached through patronlike intermediaries but they do not explain why the social institution of patronage must be twice invoked at the symbolic level.

In fact, little is said in the article about why the evil eye symbolic system is *the* "emergent" expression of patronage over so vast an area as opposed to other symbolic systems, or vice versa, or why it is patronage and not some other relationship that is symbolized by the evil eye. In other words, other than noting a geographical congruence between the two notions, no necessary and convincing causal or explanatory link is made between them beyond the assertion that one mirrors the other. Perhaps their image of a threatened individual invoking patronal aid vis-à-vis a threatening outsider can serve as a "just-so" story for the origins of the evil eye somewhere in the remote past in its area of distribution; but as a minimal behavioral sequence that continues to generate evil eye notions everywhere in that area, it has inadequate fit with the ethnographic facts. The evolution of a trait and its subsequent functions are best not confused, as Diener, Nonini, and Robkin (1980) point out. It would be intriguing to know the origin of evil eye symbolism, but, even if by some marvelous archaeological discovery we could see with such clarity into the past, that origin might have little to do with understanding present configurations of culture that include evil eye.

the evil eye as a dissolving category

At the opposite pole from Garrison and Arensberg's generalizations is the recent particularistic analysis of Herzfeld (1981). This author would see such categories as evil eye abolished as "ethnographic facts" in favor of painstaking semiotic analyses within particular cultural systems. Herzfeld's analysis of evil eye accusations in a Greek village is an excellent piece of what Geertz (1973) calls "thick description." In this approach to the evil eye category, Herzfeld follows Crick (1976:109–127), who would "dissolve" witchcraft as a unit for analysis, in a "reagent" labeled "moral space," because of its overgenerality as a category and its Western culture-bound nature. He opts, instead, for particularistic symbolic analysis. Herzfeld's (1981:571) conclusion is that only "if it can be shown that the evil eye fits into comparable systems wherever it has been reported" will "cross-cultural generalization," or the "search for a unified theory," prove other than a "misdirected enterprise." His call for careful symbolic analysis is certainly well taken, but we are left with a kind of Boasian charge to wait until all the data are gathered before making any sort of generalization at all.

I think it would be rash to view the evil eye concept in that way. First of all, if Roberts is correct, it has a regional locus. Second, there is a coherence and clustering to the set of features that compose it. Third, the name "evil eye," or a close variant thereof, translated into the languages of the cultures in which it occurs, labels the phenomenon consistently and preserves with it a simple image that has very direct evocative qualities, something the label "witchcraft" does not do. Herzfeld and Crick seem to regard single peoples and cultures—even villages—as the most appropriate units for analysis of this sort of phenomenon, but that is difficult to sustain for an area such as the circum-Mediterranean, where the evil eye is observed to have sufficiently consistent qualities to make it an "ethnographic fact" across cultural and even historical boundaries. A Greek and a Sicilian sailor do not share exactly the same ranges of meaning about the evil eye, but each grasps familar things about the other's concept and there are ample grounds for a lively comparison of notes. In the Mediterranean area we are dealing with peoples who have a long history of movement and contact and therefore of such conversations, or at least awareness of each other's belief systems. We are dealing not with an etic concept invented by anthropologists but rather with an image of great historical depth, wide diffusion, and a quality of persistence.

the evil eye as synthetic image

A middle ground between the overgeneralization of Garrison and Arensberg and the particularism of Herzfeld and of Crick can be explored using the "synthetic image" concept of Needham (1978). It is a concept that certainly allows for the valuable particularistic analyses advocated by Herzfeld, but at the same time it keeps present the important notion that each of those analyses concerns a variant of a wider phenomenon.

For Needham (1978:41) a synthetic image is a cluster of "disparate phenomena" grouped together under a regularly occurring, empirically observable label.[4] The disparate phenomena are what he calls "primary factors," by which he means evocative and widely found "vehicles for significance," which "do not convey explicit universal meanings" (1978:11). Such primary factors are elements of experience that have the qualities of simplicity and immediacy and that capture the imagination. As examples of primary factors, Needham lists such things as temperature contrasts, the opposition of right and left, color (particularly red, white, and black), numbers (sacred, odd, and even), and percussive sound. He defines these primary factors as heterogeneous in that the discovery of some of them cannot lead to the deduction of others.

Synthetic images persist through time and space because they are evocative, because they provide for and stimulate the play of human cultural imagination and invention. As a simile, one could say that they are like the chords to a widely known song upon which jazz musicians improvise new but related melodies. Through time and across regions, cultures have received (and in some cases invented) synthetic images and integrated them through modification, through selective emphasis of elements, and through addition of elements. I think it is useful to call this kind of integration in a given time and a given locale the *construction* of a synthetic image.

One of the important and salient characteristics of such synthetic images is their very evocative quality—their ability to capture the imagination of individuals or even to preoccupy a culture. Needham (1978:4) notes as illustrative the way the astrophysical concept of the black hole has done just that in modern Euro-American society. One might also mention the interest the modern world has (mostly through film) in the character of Dracula (man-wolf-vampire-bat-red-black-white-death-undeath-blood-sucking-kissing), mostly concocted by a minor late-19th-century British novelist, Bram Stoker, on a folkloristic basis.

The "primary factors," or building blocks, of which the evil eye synthetic image is composed are not absolutely constant from place to place, but there seems to be a minimal set that hangs together widely across cultural boundaries in the circum-Mediterranean area. Perhaps most fundamental is the act of gazing itself. Eye contact and eye images are attached some significance everywhere and are probably deeply embedded not only in the human ethogram, but also throughout the animal kingdom as well, as Argyle and Cook (1976:1-25) note. A second primary factor is the notion of magical harm, an idea that is basic in almost all belief systems and combines with other primary factors to form other synthetic images such as the witch or the image of automatic harm as a consequence of violating a rule—taboo.

Third among the dimensions of this synthetic image is the idea of envy as the trigger firing the mechanism of evil eye. In their search for a single etic minimal interaction sequence, Garrison and Arensberg (1976:326) have dismissed envy as emic and therefore as "an underlying linear cause" of the belief system. In this they are perhaps right, but the primary factor of envy cannot be excluded from the synthetic image, which, I submit, is best understood as a roving emic phenomenon. Envy, as Foster (1972) and Schoeck (1969) have pointed out, is a powerful human feeling that certainly stimulates imagination, particularly in societies with inequality in the distribution of resources. Every study in the Maloney anthology mentions envy as part of the symbolic complex. In fact, it may be more elegant to define evil eye as a regional case of a more pervasive synthetic image that links envy to involuntary magical harm through various possible mechanisms. For example, there is a Japanese belief reported by Embree (1939:257) in which a "fox spirit" is projected upon victims by envious fellow villagers. However, something explicitly labeled in many languages as "evil eye" and clearly involving envy exists and can be taken as a unit for analysis.

A fourth primary component in the synthetic image is, of course, the prophylactic measure used to divert, repel, or otherwise ward off or protect from the evil eye. This is a richly elaborated component that contains a number of primary factors itself. Common emic explanations of prophylactic power have to do with the attention-getting qualities of amulets. Thus, intensely colored objects are commonly adopted and displayed so as to divert attention from the object or creature on which they are displayed. Obscene gestures such as the "fig," and symbols of undeniable phallic reference such as the *mano cornuto,* the horn, and keys, are widespread as protective devices and are often explained emically as being startling enough to distract malignant gaze from its target. In particular, the horn has an ancient history as a primary factor that first shows itself in the upraised hand of the upper paleolithic Venus of Laussel in the Dordogne and continues to crop up in the ancient world, especially at Çatal Hüyük in Turkey, where it is a key ritual theme. Other prophylactic measures, as Garrison and Arensberg stress, emphasize whatever sources of supernatural (or more rarely, political) power might be available in the belief system of a given society. Still other prophylactic imagery concerns turning the eye's power back on itself or otherwise injuring it through homeopathic magic. Westermarck (1926:445) reports the use of mirrors as amulets and the phrase in Arabic "five in your eye," accompanied by a gesture, as a prophylactic measure in Morocco (1926:446). Of course, protection from evil eye is often accomplished by direct means such as covering things (e.g., goods or women) that might be coveted. These practices follow logically from the image of gaze as primary. Thus, prophylaxis seems to have three major common emic subcomponents: (1) diversion of gaze, (2) appeal to stronger powers, and (3) injury or blockage of the offending eye.

The final primary element is the notion of diagnosis and cure of symptoms brought on by evil eye. Here there is rather wide variation. Many of the cures make appeals to supernatural sanction in promoting the gazee's well-being. Some cures make use of the gazer or the gazer's clothing (Spooner 1976:81). Divining the identity of the gazer generally has the purpose of gaining his or her cooperation rather than being a preliminary to punishment or retaliation. In sum, the circum-Mediterranean synthetic image of evil eye contains at the most abstract level the notions of a gazer causing harm, usually through envy, to a gazee; ideas about preventing that harm; and ways to cure it once it has happened. This is a simple and evocative image that provides material for improvisation of local cultural detail and selective emphasis of components in such a way as to integrate with social structures, economic settings, and other belief systems.

The Greek villagers that Herzfeld describes, for instance, have inserted the evil eye image into a broader system of meanings pertaining to the moral boundaries of their village; they seem most concerned with the condition of the gazer as an antisocial and morally flawed individual "who is nevertheless a member of the best of all communities, one's own" (Herzfeld 1981:570). As I show below, the residents of the Island of Pantelleria have given more emphasis to the components having to do with envy of the gazee, cure, and prophylaxis. In these cases, and in most others reported from the region, and despite emphasis on particular elements, the synthetic image as defined above persists (see Herzfeld's first three cases, although we are told nothing about protection and cure, which are surely present in some form) and conceivably remains subject to further imaginative possibilities and reuse as other conditions change. It is useful, then, to maintain the evil eye category as a synthetic image because the discovery of its particular construction in a given time and place may thrust the investigator toward asking important social-structural questions.

the evil eye synthetic image on Pantelleria

The Island of Pantelleria, an Italian island with about 8000 inhabitants, emerges from the sea roughly halfway between the western tip of Sicily and the Tunisian coast. Its inhabitants are primarily small-proprietor grape growers who, by southern Italian standards, led a fairly prosperous existence in the late 1960s and early 1970s when the data that follow were gathered. Most information about the evil eye was obtained in the village of Khamma, an agricultural settlement of about 2000 people in the northeastern quadrant of the island. Inquiries were also made with several informants in the village of Scauri.[5]

It is safe to assume that the evil eye synthetic image has been part of the culture of the island since remote antiquity, at least since the time when, under the name Hiranim, it was a Punic colony (Verger 1966) and thus heir to lore from the ancient Near East, the reputed origin, according to the weight of opinion, of the evil eye. All subsequent ethnic groups that occupied the island are well known to have included evil eye in some way within their belief systems (Romans, Byzantines, Arabs, Jews, Italians, and Spaniards, to name the more important ones—see Moss and Cappannari 1976). Diffusion of the image to the island therefore happened very early and reoccurred as populations of differing ethnicity migrated to its shores, bringing with them variants of elements of circum-Mediterranean culture. Since very little that is descriptive of island social life or even folklore exists before my work, it is impossible to reconstruct the processes of change and assimilation that must have occurred with respect to the evil eye synthetic image; reluctantly, we must be content with a synchronic description and analysis. Currently, the belief system continues in a way that is pervasive but that could not be called obvious to the outsider as a major cultural theme. It is neither a "traditional belief" that is "dying out" nor a constant concern, and there is a casualness about its discussion.

On Pantelleria the evil eye is called *u malocciu,* or more simply *l'occiu* (the eye). It is transmitted through the act of either verbal or mental admiration and this, in turn, implies envy. One who is struck by the evil eye is said to be *pigghiatu ad occiu* (taken by means of the eye), and this usage seems to underscore the generally sudden character of the affliction.[6] For instance, an informant recounted that one day he was walking to his fields in a new pair of work snoes when a man of his acquaintance approached and said, jokingly, "You must sleep in those shoes for fear someone will steal them!" Suddenly the informant felt intensely ill and could go no further. He returned home and was cured of evil eye by his wife Za Fidela (see below for further discussion of this curer).

Pantescan informants emphasize that the ability to cast harm through envy is a power that is unpredictable and that passes around among everyone since no one is free of envy. No label for the consistent gazer could be collected despite efforts in that direction. The south Italian word *jettatore* (Appel 1976:24–25), which in some other parts of southern Italy refers to the consistent knowing or unwitting gazer, elicited no recognition from Pantescan informants. Za Fidela, who can be considered an expert on the subject in the village of Khamma, stated that "we each have a time to give the evil eye." The Pantescans have made a cultural choice against elaborating the component of gazer in the synthetic image and have devoted little folk imagination, at least in their current construction, to questions of boundaries across which the *occiu* is thought to operate, or to the fit of gazers into "moral space." Casters of the evil eye are unwitting and inconsistent and therefore thought of by the islanders as morally neutral. The Pantescan construction of the synthetic image differs, therefore, from that described by Herzfeld for the Rhodian village he studied, in which, as noted, primary emphasis seems to be placed on boundaries and the use of accusation of gazer status in defining antisocial individuals in the social setting.

Although no consistent gazers were identified by informants, if the perpetrator of the evil eye in a given instance can be readily identified, that person may be employed in the cure. There is no stigma attached to being so utilized. An instance involved my wife, Janice, while we were enjoying a protracted stay in the village of Scauri on the southern side of the island. One morning she went with our hostess to a neighboring household to buy some milk. When they arrived and were taken to the cow, my wife, thinking herself polite in a North American way, praised it as looking healthy. Two mornings later the cow's owner came and asked that the *signora americana* come and "touch the cow," as it had not given milk since the morning before. She was led to the animal and asked to touch its side while repeating a spell lifter, the gist of which was that she had put the evil eye on the cow and now took it off. The process of cure when the gazer is identifiable and at one's disposal can be rather simple and casual and attaches no particular stigma to that person.[7]

Not all Pantescans queried admitted belief in evil eye, but such belief did not necessarily vary inversely with educational attainment or experience in the outside world. Several accounts were collected from individuals who had spent long periods either at the university or as migrant factory workers. For instance, Leonardo (a pseudonym), a young man who had earned a university degree in science, was driving one morning in Khamma and slowed down to greet a friend when, for no perceivable reason, his car stopped running. After looking under the hood to check for obvious causes, finding none, and wondering why the car had stopped at precisely that moment, he walked a short distance to a local curer's house. She came to the car and performed the oil and water oracle over it. On the basis of the oracle she decided that both the car and Leonardo's hands had been afflicted and through her efforts cured both so that he could proceed. (Note that machines as well as living beings can be targets of the evil eye on Pantelleria.) This helped convince him of the reality of the *occiu*, although his fetching of the curer suggests openness to belief in the first place. Another man, who had spent several years in Germany and who was a skilled worker on the island, recounted that he had fallen ill suddenly after a woman had told him how plump and healthy he looked. Evil eye was diagnosed and cured. Typically, more experienced and educated people prefaced their professions of belief with statements to the effect that once they had been skeptical but that through a personal experience with the evil eye they had become convinced.

The most common oracle/cure for evil eye is the oil and water procedure. This cure is reported in one form or another elsewhere in the literature from southern Italy, but it is seldom described in much detail (Appel 1976; de Martino 1966:13-14; Gallini 1973:133). On Pantelleria it can be used as an oracle to diagnose evil eye by anyone, but it only has the power to cure in the practice of a woman like Za Fidela of Khamma.[8] She is a practitioner who specializes in the cure of evil eye and of another magical affliction called *scantu*—"fright."[9] Za Fidela's services, like those of other Pantescan curing women, are given free of charge because she feels that she must not ask money for something that is a *dunu di Diu* (gift of God), acquired through birth at 8:00 A.M. on the day of the Immaculate Virgin. Charging for services is also believed to endanger curing power. Such a morning birth on a holy day may bring about the ability to cure, as may having a close relative who is a curing woman—Za Fidela's grandmother had the ability. In her 70s when interviewed, she first became aware of her powers at the age of 10 or 11.

Za Fidela's practice is carried out in the kitchen of her house. For the oil and water oracle the equipment consists of a standard pasta bowl and an antiquated *cannila*—ceramic oil lamp—which has a dished base used to hold salt out of which rises a stalk with a shallow cup on top to hold oil. The patient sits in a chair while Za Fidela fills the pasta bowl with freshly drawn rainwater from the cistern outside and adds a pinch of salt from the base of the *cannila*. She then holds the bowl in front of the client's chest and touches it with her finger, at intervals of several centimeters, about 50 times, saying *oraziuni* (orations) under her breath. When questioned as to the nature of the *oraziuni* she replied that they were *Pater Nosters* and *Ave Marias*. Another informant volunteered that such utterances could consist of rapid recitations of the days of the Holy Week culminating in Easter Sunday. Clearly what is important is that the client understand that they are words deriving their power from holy sources. This phase is concluded when she makes the sign of the cross over the bowl, touching its rim at the end point of each sweep of her hand. Next, using her finger, she places three drops of oil from the cup of the *cannila* onto the surface of the water. At this point the oil may either remain in discrete droplets or "mix" with the water by spreading out over its surface. If the latter occurs it is immediately apparent to the patient and to Za Fidela that the former has been *pigghiatu ad occiu* because the power of the affliction has caused oil and water to mix—a phenomenon that informants understand as impossible normally and therefore only likely in the presence of unusual conditions.[10]

Whatever the initial reading, the bowl is now passed near the patient's head, trunk, arms, and legs, from the front; the same is repeated from the back. Changes in configuration of the oil indicate more specific diagnoses. For instance, a negative initial reading that becomes positive when the plate is passed near the client's back indicates that he or she was *pigghiatu* from behind. If the oil suddenly forms many tiny droplets after having "mixed" with the water the subject has been envied by a number of people at once, as in the case of a group of men standing on the corner commenting on someone. If the oil leaves a film on the surface of the water that reflects iridescent colors, the patient has maladies that should be treated by a doctor. If during the first run of the oracle there is a positive reaction, it is repeated with new water and salt two more times or until the oil droplets remain floating on the surface of the water without "mixing" with it. When the oil no longer "mixes" the patient is cured and the contents of the bowl are thrown out the door. If by the third trial the droplets still refuse to remain discrete the indication is that the patient was gazed upon on a Friday and will have to return on successive Fridays to repeat the cure until a negative outcome appears, or the third Friday's positive trials are completed. Beyond that Za Fidela's powers diminish and it may be necessary to seek out a more powerful cure in Sicily or elsewhere in Italy—an expensive proposition because city cures cost about 50,000 lire (about $80) in 1969, not to mention the expenses of travel and lodging. There is a sense among Pantescans that just as more cosmopolitan centers have more highly trained doctors and better medical facilities, the cities produce more efficacious, but more expensive, evil eye curers.

The emphasis on diagnosis and even on divining vague details about the act of transmission of the evil eye underscore an important characteristic of the synthetic image on Pantelleria that meshes with the aforementioned lack of interest or concern about the specific identity of gazers. The potential evil eye victim seeks an explanation and cure for symptoms or malfunctions, generally of a sudden or intense nature such as painful headaches. Most often it is not a distinctly remembered episode of envy or admiration that brings about a visit to a curer such as Za Fidela. Her reading of the oil in the water may prompt a recollection about some instance in which the *occiu* might have been cast, but it does not pin down details or lay the blame at anyone's feet. Most of her clientele, then, consists of people who simply feel bad, rather than individuals with specific narratives to relate, such as those reported above. In fact, Za Fidela said that many of her patients are children with various symptoms, brought to her by their mothers.

The measures taken to prevent affiliction by evil eye are similar to those taken elsewhere in the circum-Mediterranean area (see Moss and Cappannari 1976) in that amulets of various kinds, such as the ubiquitous *mano cornuto* (horned hand) and the simpler *corno* (horn), are worn on the person, attached to animal trappings, or hung in automobiles. Thought to have particular local efficaciousness are amulets made of the movable half of the claw of the *migrosciu,* the spinous spider crab *(Maja squinado H.).* One informant ("Giuseppe Shotgun," discussed below) carried a red chili pepper in his pocket which served as on-the-spot seasoning for pasta as well as for an amulet. Gold horns are given to babies at baptism by godparents and worn around their necks under their clothing. Babies and children are also protected with *abitini* pinned inside their clothing, which on Pantelleria consist of small bags of red cloth (sometimes heart-shaped) that look like pin cushions and contain a *figurinu* (saint card), a small gold horn, or a crab claw, and a bit of red cloth or a piece of iron.

The elaboration of the synthetic image of the evil eye on Pantelleria gives special emphasis to the components having to do with cure and prophylaxis and, I will show, to the place of the gazee in several arenas of village society having to do with stratification and consequently with envy. One must keep in mind, however, that what was observable about the evil eye on Pantelleria in the late 1960s and early 1970s is but a "snapshot" taken from what must be a long process of structuring and restructuring of a symbolic set that has existed on the island since at least classical times. As I have shown elsewhere (Galt 1980), the stratificational aspects of Pantescan social structure have changed considerably over the last 200 years and it can be expected that some covariance in the local construction of the synthetic image of the evil eye should have taken place as well. Ardener (1970) gives an excellent demonstration of this sort of point for Bakweri witchcraft. Unfortunately, data are not available to present such a demonstration.

interpretation of evil eye on Pantelleria

A useful framework for probing the meanings of the evil eye image on Pantelleria is provided by Rappaport's (1971:25) definition of rituals as "conventional acts of display through which one or more participants transmit information concerning their physiological, psychological, or sociological states either to themselves or to one or more of their participants." His discussion leads one to ask questions about the nature of messages that are communicated through publicly observable activity connected with belief systems and about the possible material, psychological, and social causes and consequences of those activities. In essence, what are people who participate in the belief system of evil eye communicating by doing so? Similarly, as Crick (1976:121) notes, "Meaning is part of a game whose conventions have some purpose." What "game" is being played on Pantelleria through the evil eye synthetic image?

While the particular construction of evil eye on the island has at least one material consequence, the social-structural and individual consequences of activities associated with it seem more immediate.[11] The most readily observable events having to do with evil eye consist of the rituals of cure and the display of amulets. Associated with such events may be conversations about them. Going to the curer is an observable social act. Little movement in the settlements of Pantelleria escapes the attention of others (elderly women invisible behind the cane blinds that cover doors are often watching) and the identities of curing women are well known. Thus, a woman leading a child to Za Fidela's door would be a sign to watching neighbors that a cure is being sought. One who visits a curer is likely to have had some amount of conversation about it with family or friends before the visit (or perhaps along the way) or, in fact, may be making it at their suggestion. At the very least there is social interaction with the curer herself. Naturally, contacting the gazer and involving him or her in a curing ritual is a social interaction likely to cause comment.

The messages conveyed by these observable social phenomena connected with evil eye operate, of course, at several levels. At the manifest level, a person who displays an amulet is conveying the message that he or she fears and seeks protection from the evil eye—from envy. A person seeking a cure communicates to others his or her suspicion of having been *pigghiatu ad occiu*. A person who is diagnosed by a curer as an evil eye target has that suspicion confirmed in the eyes of those who participate in the belief system through her divinely sanctioned power. And last, a person who cannot be cured by the local practitioner, or whose cure takes more than one session, conveys that he or she has been very strongly afflicted.

At a latent level, however, there is a simultaneous set of related messages. In order to be envied a person must somehow be enviable. Thus, to display an amulet says to the observer, "I might be envied for some quality I have." To seek a diagnosis or cure from a woman like Za Fidela says, "I think I have been envied." To obtain a positive diagnosis and cure from a curing woman says, "Oil and water have mixed to show that I have been envied, and divinely sanctioned powers have been used to cure me." To fail to obtain a cure from a local practitioner such that further help must be sought away from the island states that, "I have been powerfully envied indeed!" I suggest that in the social structure of the island at the mid-20th century these messages are important to some individuals.

Elsewhere (Galt 1980) I have portrayed the social stratificational system of Pantelleria as composed of three broad groups—a socially distanced group, separated because its members fell short of the mark mostly in terms of honor and reputation; a large and inclusive middle group that contains most island families and is relatively egalitarian; and a small group that claims elite status in the system, but to which such rank is not automatically accorded by the middle group except when it is expedient to do so, as, for instance, in the context of a patron-client relationship. This social structure has at its base a relatively broad and uniform distribution of the island's productive wealth—land—among small-proprietor households.[12] I suggest that such a setting provides several significant arenas in which statuses are easily called into question and which therefore become arenas in which the conventions of the Pantescan construction of the evil eye synthetic image come to have heightened significance. These arenas are (1) the lower margin of the central group in which families and individuals attempt to keep from falling into the lower group (which is labeled *poveri disgraziati* [poor dishonored people]); and (2) the upper margin of the central group in which families and individuals attempt to claim elite status in the structure and find their peers unwilling to concede rank to them. I do not suggest that these arenas exhaust the possibilities for use of the synthetic image of the evil eye in present-day Pantelleria. It is likely, for instance, that evil eye imagery finds a fit in purely individual psychological contexts, as Parsons (1969) shows in discussing the case of an Italo-American woman with paranoid delusions; but as a cultural phenomenon in the island's villages it is important that its most likely social-structural concomitants, in this case of a stratificational kind, be identified. I suggest, then, that it is in the arenas defined above that some people are most likely to claim symbolically that they are envied by others as an unconscious strategy in the "game" of stratification.

The examination of several cases helps to illuminate this generalization. "Giuseppe Shotgun" (a pseudonym for his nickname—he likes to hunt) showed unusually great and open concern with the evil eye. He was in the habit of carrying in his pocket a red chili pepper or other amulet that he would display on occasion as having great power. He would extract the object from his pants pocket, hold it cupped in his hands as if it had great potency, and flash only brief glimpses of it to his audience as if, left in the open too long, it would leap from his hands. Giuseppe Shotgun was also very careful to publicly deny the quality of things he produced, such as wine, sometimes claiming that he had none at all. Further, he was quite concerned not to stare directly into the lens of a camera while he was being photographed, possibly for fear of *malocciu*. Giuseppe thus showed public concern with being a potential evil eye victim through demonstrations that he was protected and by carefully avoiding envy by openly denigrating potential targets for it, such as the fruits of his labor. His behavior, which was exaggerated in its openness, becomes more understandable through examination of his place as a household head in the social structure of Khamma.

Giuseppe Shotgun did not quite measure up to the image of household head solidly within the inclusive middle-group system of honor and rank. Although his moral reputation in Khamma was not severely questioned—even though he drank a little too much by local standards—he teetered on the lower border of the large central category of people because he lacked the household self-sufficiency considered ideal. He had rather less than the average amount of land even for a *bracciante agricolo* (agricultural worker) and made his living through sharecropping a few bits and pieces of land and by working for others. His daughter's marriage was a topic of gossip because her husband beat her brutally (a shameful and unusual situation on the island) and seemed to have mental problems. This embarrassed Giuseppe because the sort of marriage a child makes reflects on the reputation of his parents. Further, he had once inherited a local tavern, which had previously been a thriving business and a center of mens' activities, but had proven himself incapable of running it. A saving grace for Giuseppe was a warm manner and a fondness for children, coupled with skill at hunting and fishing that earned him a place in the male society of the village *piazza* and barbershop and a reputation as a good neighbor. But he was sometimes the object of derision in public, some of it to his face, as when another man suggested to the frequenters of the barbershop that Giuseppe save money by shaving at home on Saturdays. This wounded him deeply because the barbershop is a public arena for men and the weekend shave in Khamma is a ritual celebrating male sociability. The comment suggested that he did not belong to the middle group by virtue of poverty and was a deeply unkind cut for which he sought the sympathy of others for weeks after. In Giuseppe Shotgun we see a socially marginal man who showed preoccupation with being envied and thus conveyed the claim that he was indeed a worthy individual deserving admiration. The claim of enviability is seen as a strategy to shore up a damageable reputation and possibly Giuseppe Shotgun's self-concept.

Another case concerns a young woman I shall call Anna, who was the victim of a most pernicious case of evil eye, the symptoms of which consisted of intense headaches. Her affliction had not succumbed to local cure, and she had purchased a powder in Rome (where she had successfully taken civil service examinations) that she carried on her person and that helped. Anna was the daughter of a man who had risen from the occupation of agricultural worker holding a marginal amount of land to a position where he commanded a secure and fairly substantial income (by local standards) deriving from government employment. This family was accused by its neighbors of flaunting wealth and of seeking higher rank than it deserved. Anna and her mother were considered *muntati* ("stuck up") by their contemporaries. In the early 1970s the family moved into a newly constructed house that contained all of the amenities including plumbing, a tiled bathroom, and a kitchen equipped with the latest appliances. Further, the family had married its other daughter to the owner of an appliance store in the port of Pantelleria—the urban settlement.

The arena for envy in this case has to do with several related components. First, we see a case of conspicuous consumption. Pantelleria is fully part of the "consumer society" of modern Italy. Messages about consumption reach the island in a number of ways, and those means of communication have expanded and increased in the years since World War II with the introduction of television and radio, the greater diffusion of print media, and more recently the living example of summer tourists, some of whom have been affluent popular entertainers and large industrialists from the north who have built villas. During my years of fieldwork there, the island was even a sample area for a northern Italian market research firm. In conversation Pantescans often recognize their propensities toward consumption and keeping up with their neighbors in the accumulation of kitchen appliances, television sets, telephones, and automobiles. Many of these things were becoming de rigueur in dowries as the 1960s closed. "Who has bought what?" is a common topic of conversation, as is the arrival of large packages from mail-order companies, which are displayed stacked in full view at the village post office. Clearly, the evil eye does not operate as a leveling mechanism in the sense that fear of envy keeps people from the acquisition of things or from their conspicuous display. Dowry goods, for instance, are openly displayed in an arrangement before the wedding for the admiration of friends, neighbors, and relatives.

Pantelleria, I suggest, participates in the modern world of consumption in that many of its inhabitants have accepted the idea that the envy of others for what one has is a desirable thing. The fear of envy, possibly a universal feeling before the advent of mass consumption in modern industrial society, seems to have fallen before the forces of marketing and advertising that consistently promote the desirability of being envied by one's peers. One can argue, in fact, that being envied is promoted in the hegemony of modern capitalism as a positive value that aids in the constant expansion of markets so necessary for the system's persistence.[13] Although that expansion is surely promoted by other motives alongside conspicuous consumption, the latter is undeniably a force and has in the course of the 20th century, on Pantelleria as elsewhere, shifted from the exclusive domain of the wealthy to become a far more widespread phenomenon that touches all in some way. Part of Anna's concern with the evil eye, then, had sprung from the need to demonstrate that she and her family in its good fortune and prosperity were powerfully envied.

The strategic usefulness of evil eye symbolism in this kind of situation is not exhausted in the explanation above, however. The claim of powerful envy on the part of the community can be used to turn its criticism back on itself. The socially climbing family absolves itself from its neighbors' accusations of being *muntata*—of being morally at fault—by claiming the criticism is merely invidious (a sentiment that at the manifest level is recognized as negative, although understandable, in the gazer) and demonstrates this through a particularly intense case of evil eye. In the case of Anna and her family, the criticism was particularly intense and their claim to higher rank locally was doubtful because of their relatively humble origins. These interpretations help to account for the cases of evil eye collected from relatively educated and sophisticated individuals, all of whom fit into the arena of the upper margin of the central stratificational group.

These usages of the evil eye synthetic image on Pantelleria help, I suggest, to explain the vagueness of the components having to do with the gazer's identity. The gazer could be anyone in the Pantescan construction, not merely a social deviate or an outsider, and therefore by extension of logic is everyone—the community at large. There is little to be gained in this "game" in being envied by marginal or antisocial individuals; rather, if I am correct, it is important to be envied by people with full community standing, or better, by society in general.

conclusion

I have argued that although a universal theoretical explanation of the evil eye, such as that attempted by Garrison and Arensberg, is likely to be fruitless, it would be a hasty decision to discard the notion of evil eye as a useless abstraction, as Herzfeld seems to suggest we do. Rather, by understanding it as a synthetic image with a core of regionally shared components, it can be used as a key to open understanding of significant structures and themes in circum-Mediterranean society. Herzfeld has successfully used it to understand the boundaries of "moral space" in the village he studied, and I have used it to illuminate junctures in the stratificational system of the village of Khamma on Pantelleria. The key to its use in a given situation is to discover which of its components receive emphasis and to attempt an explanation of the particular construction of the image. Ultimately, it may be shown to have a limited number of logical possibilities for adaptation and readaptation in local settings, and the variance in those possibilities may be explicable. We are as yet far from that point, and I offer my account of the construction of the evil eye synthetic image on Pantelleria as a possibility that seems to have escaped ethnographic attention.

notes

Acknowledgments. The data presented herein were gathered on two field trips to Pantelleria, the first from September 1968 through January 1970 and funded through an NIH predoctoral grant and fellowship, and the second during the summer of 1974 and funded through an NSF grant to the University of Wisconsin-Green Bay matched by the Rockefeller Foundation. The funding agencies noted above have my gratitude. Special gratitude is owed to George Saunders of Lawrence University who read and commented on an early draft of this article. The reviewers who read the first version submitted to the *American Ethnologist,* although their identities are unknown to me, wrote extremely useful and lengthy comments and deserve my thanks.

[1] Unfortunately, the distribution suggested by Roberts must be taken as inconclusive. Raters scaled societies from 1 through 8 according to whether evil eye was present or not. Very few societies were rated 1 (definitely not present) or 8 (definitely present). Thus, there is doubt either way for most of the societies included in the sample. No minimal definition of what criteria raters were to use to indicate evil eye belief is supplied in the article. The ability to harm through glance is sometimes found in descriptions of mythological characters and is not considered characteristic of normal humans. Also, harm may spring from envy but through mechanisms other than glance (see text below and Embree 1939:257). Roberts associates evil eye with envy but does not specify whether raters keyed on "harm through glance" or "harm through envy" or both, in their perusal of the literature. Thus the occurrence data he reports leave many questions open.

[2] It is interesting to note that this has been reported among Islamic Chinese (Maloney 1976:xi).

[3] Those who subscribe to the notion of the "image of limited good" (Foster 1965) might argue that an individual's loss through evil eye would automatically benefit others, such as the gazer. It seems to me that there are three logical possibilities that follow from "limited good" assumptions: (1) the gazee's loss would benefit the gazer; (2) the gazee's loss would benefit society at large and benefit to the gazer would thus be diluted to an extent depending on the size of the social group; (3) the gazee's loss would benefit a third party and thus not the gazer. In a society with a "limited good" world view, harm through evil eye would not necessarily logically benefit the gazer. I emphasize the point that, emically, gazers are not thought to benefit from possessing the evil eye and thus cannot be compared directly to the statuses Garrison and Arensberg mention as actors in social interactions on which they claim the evil eye belief system is modeled.

[4] Needham's concept needs some contextualization to place its utility in relief against some other terms for powerful symbols. First of all, while denying adherence to Jungian psychology as a whole, Needham (1978:45–46) acknowledges the similarity of his concept to that thinker's *archetype* concept. Synthetic image has much broader derivation from world ethnographic sources and more explicit cross-cultural applicability.

Several other terms for powerful symbols have, of course, been coined. Sapir's (1958:564–568) "condensation symbol" is in some ways a similar concept, although as Sapir defined it such a symbol need not have the persistence and pervasiveness in time and space that Needham makes explicit for his concept, and, of course, was heavily colored by the psychoanalytic approach in that it allowed for "the ready release of emotional tension in conscious or unconscious forms" (Sapir 1958:565). Needham's concept is not psychoanalytically charged. Also, synthetic images could well be given constructions in some situations that create emotional tensions as well as release them. C. Wright Mills's (1961:36–37) "master symbol" idea is more limiting in that it concerns those symbols used as tools for power and control exclusively. Synthetic images might become "master symbols" in particular times and places, but do not necessarily have to do with political power.

Closer to Needham's concept, at least as I have employed it in this article, is Ardener's (1970:159) notion of "template" discussed, to my knowledge, only in a footnote to his excellent essay on Bakwari witchcraft and economic change. Ardener invokes Lévi-Strauss's (1962) image of the *bricoleur* to talk about the imaginative combination and recombination of elements from a "template" carried through time in a culture—in this case having to do with zombies and economics. However, this concept, certainly applicable here to evil eye, does not seem to have been further and more explicitly developed and is not construed as having relevance across cultural boundaries. Needham's more fully developed ideas of "primary factors" and "synthetic images" as stimuli for human imagination thus seem to be the right ones to employ for this analysis.

[5] In both field sessions, residence was taken up in Khamma and visits were made elsewhere on the island to collect data. All place names and the names of individuals are actual except where indicated.

[6] Note that this is the exact usage reported by Teitelbaum (1976) in Arabic for nearby Tunisia.

[7] In this situation the cow was also visited by a veterinarian who said that it had eaten some plants which would have caused the loss of milk. Subsequent to both actions, the cow began to produce again, verifying both diagnoses of its ailment and deciding for neither. The example demonstrates that on Pantelleria evil eye is but one possible cause of misfortune and that a person ought to consult "great tradition" medical people as well as rely upon local magical remedies. Even though the cow was subject to behavior on the part of a human admirer that would logically lead to affliction by the evil eye, the owner sought veterinary help because, since there are no consistent gazers, not every act of envy or admiration leads to affliction.

[8] *Za* is an honorific title applied to all women of advanced years; *Zu* is the corresponding masculine form.

[9] "Fright" or *scantu* (pronounced /škántu/) is another magical illness. The symptom is a general "out-of-sorts" feeling and the cause is a sudden frightening event that makes one's body proportions appear slightly wrong. The theory is that a person's height when standing with feet together ought to equal his armspan. The practitioner measures the height with a piece of thread and then uses it to compare height with armspan. If the thread is too short the test is positive. The thread is then doubled over and over into a little bundle and the resulting loops are cut to yield many short pieces. The patient sits down and the curer places three threads on each of his or her joints while reciting prayers. Then the threads are removed and rolled into a ball. The victim is told to burn them the next day after saying some prayers. He or she is also told to drink *centelvo,* which is an infusion of rue *(Ruta chaliepensis)* in alcohol or of horehound *(Marrubbium vulgare)* in wine.

[10] Note that both Gallini (1973:133) for Sardinia and Appel (1976:18) for the Murgia dei Trulli in Apulia report that the oracle works in the opposite way. For the people they interviewed evil eye affliction is present if the oil remains in discrete droplets. Gallini reports that the droplets are called *occhi* (eyes) and are thus signs of the evil eye.

[11] A factor that may be seen as a material consequence of the construction of the evil eye synthetic image on the island (as in other places), and thus may partially explain it, is the custom of bestowing protective amulets made of precious metals on infants at baptism by godparents. In 1969 a child's parents could expect to see him receive about $50 worth of gold in the form of medals, amulets, chains, and earrings. Later in life people acquire more amulets. Even the locally efficacious spider crab claw is often seen in a silver mounting. Precious metal amulets provide a means of savings and even investment that has the property of cash redeemability without particularly weakening evil eye protection, for such amulets can always be substituted by less valuable measures such as gestures or even plastic horns.

[12] These statements are documented statistically and in comparison with other southern Italian locales (Galt 1980). Both the present stratificational profile and the processes leading to it are described. Here suffice it to say that roughly 70 percent of the households in the village of Khamma, the reference group referred to in this article, are those of self-sufficient small proprietors. The rest are either agricultural workers who own a little land or merchants and artisans who also typically own some land.

[13] For instance, there is a spray-on cleaning product marketed in the United States by the Johnson Wax Corporation called "Envy." The implication is, I suppose, that those who use it will be the envy of their neighbors for the shiny surfaces it will produce. The phrases "Be the first on your block to own...," or "Be the envy of your neighbors....," are now advertising clichés.

references cited

Appel, Willa
    1976   The Myth of the Jettatura. *In* The Evil Eye. C. Maloney, ed. pp. 16–27. New York: Columbia University Press.

Ardener, Edwin
   1970   Witchcraft, Economics and the Continuity of Belief. *In* Witchcraft Confessions and Accusations. Mary Douglas, ed. pp. 141-160. ASA Monograph 9. London: Tavistock.
Argyle, Michael, and Mark Cook
   1976   Gaze and Mutual Gaze. Cambridge: Cambridge University Press.
Boissevain, Jeremy
   1966   Patronage in Sicily. Man (NS)1:18-33.
Crick, Malcolm
   1976   Explorations in Language and Meaning: Towards a Semantic Anthropology. New York: John Wiley.
de Martino, Ernesto
   1966   Sud e Magia (South and Magic). Milan: Feltirnelli.
Diener, Paul, Donald Nonini, and Eugene Robkin
   1980   Ecology and Evolution in Cultural Anthropology. Man (NS) 15:1-31.
Dionisopoulos-Mass, Regina
   1976   The Evil Eye and Bewitchment in a Peasant Village. *In* The Evil Eye. C. Maloney, ed. pp. 42-62. New York: Columbia University Press.
Elsworthy, Frederick
   1970[1958]   The Evil Eye. London: Collier-Macmillan Limited.
Embree, John
   1939   Suye Mura, a Japanese Village. Chicago: University of Chicago Press.
Foster, George
   1963   The Dyadic Contract in Tzintzuntzan, II: The Patron-Client Relationship. American Anthropologist 65:1280-1294.
   1965   Peasant Society and the Image of Limited Good. American Anthropologist 67:293-315.
   1972   The Anatomy of Envy: A Study in Symbolic Behavior. Current Anthropology 13:165-202.
Gallini, Clara
   1973   Dono e Malocchio (Gift and Evil Eye). Palermo: S.F. Flaccovio editore.
Galt, Anthony
   1974   Rethinking Patron-Client Relationships: The Real System and the Official System in Southern Italy. Anthropological Quarterly 47:182-202.
   1980   Social Stratification on Pantelleria, Italy. Ethnology 19:405-425.
Garrison, Vivian, and Conrad Arensberg
   1976   The Evil Eye: Envy or Risk of Seizure? Paranoia or Patronal Dependency? *In* The Evil Eye. C. Maloney, ed. pp. 286-328. New York: Columbia University Press.
Geertz, Clifford
   1973   The Interpretation of Cultures. New York: Basic Books.
Herzfeld, Michael
   1981   Meaning and Morality: A Semiotic Approach to Evil Eye Accusations in a Greek Village. American Ethnologist 8:560-573.
Kenny, Michael
   1960   Patterns of Patronage in Spain. Anthropological Quarterly 33:14-23.
Lévi-Strauss, Claude
   1962   La Pensée Sauvage (The Savage Mind). Paris: Plon.
Maloney, C.
   1976   The Evil Eye. New York: Columbia University Press.
Mills, C. Wright
   1961   The Sociological Imagination. New York: Grove Press.
Morris, Desmond, Peter Collett, Peter Marsh, and Marie O'Shaughnessy
   1979   Gestures: Their Origins and Distribution. New York: Stein and Day.
Moss, Leonard, and Stephan Cappannari
   1976   Mal'occhio, Ayin ha ra, Oculus Fascinus, Judenblick: The Evil Eye Hovers Above. *In* The Evil Eye. C. Maloney, ed. pp. 1-15. New York: Columbia University Press.
Needham, Rodney
   1978   Primordial Characters. Charlottesville: University Press of Virginia.
Paine, Robert
   1971   A Theory of Patronage and Brokerage. *In* Patrons and Brokers in the East Arctic. R. Paine, ed. pp. 8-21. Toronto: University of Toronto Press.
Parsons, Ann
   1969   Expressive Symbolism in Witchcraft and Delusion: A Comparative Essay. *In* Belief, Magic and Anomie: Essays in Psychosocial Anthropology. pp. 177-203. New York: Free Press.
Rappaport, Roy
   1971   The Sacred in Human Evolution. Annual Review of Ecology and Systematics 2:25-44.
Reminick, Ronald
   1976   The Evil Eye Belief Among the Amhara. *In* The Evil Eye. C. Maloney, ed. pp. 85-101. New York: Columbia University Press.

Roberts, John M.
    1976   Belief in the Evil Eye in World Perspective. *In* The Evil Eye. C. Maloney, ed. pp. 223-278. New York: Columbia University Press.

Sapir, Edward
    1958   Symbolism. *In* Selected Writings of Edward Sapir in Language, Culture and Personality. David Mandlebaum, ed. pp. 564-568. Berkeley: University of California Press.

Schoeck, Helmut
    1969   Envy, A Theory of Social Behavior. New York: Harcourt Brace and World.

Spooner, Brian
    1976   The Evil Eye in the Middle East. *In* The Evil Eye. C. Maloney, ed. pp. 76-84. New York: Columbia University Press.

Teitelbaum, Joel
    1976   The Leer and the Loom—Social Controls on Handloom Weavers. *In* The Evil Eye. C. Maloney, ed. pp. 63-75. New York: Columbia University Press.

Verger, A.
    1966   Pantelleria nell'antichita' (Pantelleria in Antiquity). Oriens Antiquus 5:249-275.

Westermarck, Edward
    1926   Ritual and Belief in Morocco, Vol. 1. London: Macmillan.

Wolf, Eric
    1966   Peasants. Englewood Cliffs, NJ: Prentice-Hall.

Submitted 20 February 1981
Revised version received 11 September 1981
Accepted 25 September 1981

womb as oasis: the symbolic context of Pharaonic circumcision in rural Northern Sudan

JANICE BODDY—*University of Toronto*

Throughout 1976 and part of 1977 I conducted ethnographic research in a small Sudanese village (Hofriyat, a pseudonym) located on the Nile some 200 km downstream of the capital city, Khartoum. Before I arrived in the area I was aware that Hofriyati females underwent genital mutilation in childhood, and I had read several descriptions of that operation (Barclay 1964; Widstrand 1964). Nothing, however, adequately prepared me for what I was to witness, as described herein. Initially I felt numbed by what appeared to be the meaninglessness of the custom; yet, as time passed in the village, I came to regard this form of female circumcision in a very different light. In the present paper I discuss my growing appreciation of its significance, for it is only in understanding the practice, its meaningfulness for the women who undergo it, and its embeddedness in village culture, that those who are presently committed to its eradication (see Assaad 1980; el-Saadawi 1980; Hosken 1979; Morgan and Steinem 1980; participants in the "Khartoum Conference," W.H.O. 1979) might approach the problem with the sensitivity it demands.

villagers and the village

The people of Hofriyat are Muslim. They are organized into several overtly patrilineal descent groups, only a few of which are corporate in any real sense. Furthermore, villagers are relatively endogamous: people marry within the patrilineage when possible and practical, otherwise they marry close kin of varying degrees and prefer as spouses people who live nearby. Along with most of the population of Northern Sudan, Hofriyati speak a dialect

---

This paper represents an effort to understand why Pharaonic circumcision of females persists in the Sudanese village of Hofriyat despite numerous attempts to effect its eradication. After a brief consideration of the custom's proposed origins and functions, its rich symbolic context is examined in some detail. Here it emerges that female circumcision is intricately related to a wide variety of local customs and beliefs, all of which appear to be informed by several related idioms stressing the relative value of "enclosedness." The paper suggests that for those who have undergone it and who advocate its continuance, Pharaonic circumcision is an assertive, highly meaningful act that emphasizes feminine fertility by de-emphasizing female sexuality. [genital mutilation, circumcision, symbolism, women, Sudan, gender]

Copyright © 1982 by the American Ethnological Society
0094-0496/82/040682-17/2.20/1

of Arabic that contains numerous remnants of earlier vernaculars, principally Nubian and Bejawi (Gasim 1965).

The geographical area in which the village lies straddles two ecological zones; it is a region wherein true desert gradually begins to give way to semidesert acacia scrub, with an average annual rainfall in the vicinity of 5 cm. Rainfall, however, is unpredictable. Some years the area receives far less than 5 cm, other years (about one in five) it receives considerably more, as much as 15 cm. Thus, the region is marginal with respect to cultivation undertaken at any distance from the river. More than rain, it is irrigation and the annual inundation of the Nile on which farming in the area depends. Arable land is a limited commodity, confined to a narrow strip bordering the Nile, and is insufficient to support the entire population of the village. Therefore, younger men regularly leave in order to seek work in the country's larger towns and cities, while their families, typically older men, children, and womenfolk, remain behind in the village.

in the field: 12 june 1976

It is the height of the desert summer, a season of intense heat and daily sandstorms. It is also the season of purification (*ayām el-ṭahūr*). Schools are closed, boys and girls are home for vacation; gradually their fathers are returning to the village, on vacation from the working year spent in Khartoum, Kassala, or Port Sudan. Now is the time, I am told, when circumcisions will be performed: boys and girls have time to recover from their respective operations without losing time at their studies, and fathers have time to host the necessary festivities and religious ceremonies and to bask in the achievement of becoming the fathers of men.

For male children, the pomp and ceremony of circumcision is rivaled only by that of their weddings. It is a major social step toward full adulthood. For little girls, the unpleasant prospect of circumcision is not balanced by the achievement of womanly social status: a girl remains a girl until she is married. Her circumcision is celebrated by the briefest and most subdued of ceremonial feasts: morning tea. There are no religious festivities associated with the event, as there are for boys. The operation, however, renders her marriageable; undergoing it is a necessary condition of becoming a woman, of being enabled to use her one great gift, fertility.

It is the twelfth of June, a day that promises to be as hot and as demanding as any yet experienced. I am to witness the circumcisions of two little girls. Zaineb calls for me at sunup; it seems we are late. We run to a *ḥōsh* (courtyard) in the interior of the village. When we arrive, we find that Miriam, the local midwife, has already circumcised one sister and is getting ready to operate on the second. A crowd of women, many of them grandmothers (*ḥabōbat*), has gathered outside the room, not a man in sight. A dozen hands push me forward. "You've got to see this up close," says Zaineb, "it's important." I dare not confess my reluctance. The girl is lying on an *angareeb* (native bed), her body supported by several adult kinswomen. Two of these hold her legs apart. Then she is administered a local anesthetic by injection. In the silence of the next few moments Miriam takes a pair of what look to me like children's paper scissors and quickly cuts away the girl's clitoris and labia minora. She tells me this is the *laḥma djewa* (the inside flesh). I am surprised that there is so little blood. Then she takes a surgical needle from her midwife's kit, threads it with suture, and sews together the labia majora, leaving a small opening at the vulva. After a liberal application of antiseptic, it is all over.

The young girl seems to be experiencing more shock than pain and I wonder if the anesthetic has finally taken effect. The women briefly trill their joyous ululation (zagharūda) and we adjourn to the courtyard for tea. While we wait, the sisters receive the ritual ornaments (jirtig) that will protect them from harm as they recuperate.

a note on terminology

The operation described above is a modified version of "Pharaonic circumcision," a term widely employed both in the literature and by Sudanese themselves (ṭahāra far'owniyya). As villagers explain it, the custom is quite ancient, dating from the time of the Pharaonic Egyptians, though this point is questioned by historians, archaeologists, and medical experts alike (Barclay 1964:238; Huelsman 1976:123). Another phrase used in reference to this procedure, "infibulation," is perhaps technically more accurate, since the vaginal orifice is partially occluded by skin that is clasped or fastened together. Throughout the present paper I use the terms "Pharaonic circumcision," "female circumcision," and "infibulation" synonymously, with the acknowledgment that other forms of female circumcision exist, of course.

the operation prior to 1969

Seeing an infibulation, even in this modernized, "sterile" form, was an experience I had been dreading. Yet my virtual lack of emotional reaction then, and a few days later when I was permitted to photograph another of these events, horrified me more than the circumcisions themselves. It was all so matter-of-fact. However, the relative indifference with which my village friends treated the phenomenon only temporarily diffused its effect. For one night after the last of the operations had taken place, when I was as alone as one can be in the field, I suddenly felt the impact of what had taken place. I became determined to find out why this severe form of circumcision is practiced; why, in the face of orthodox Islamic disapproval and the contravening legislation of at least two modern Sudanese regimes,[1] it persists.

Granted, there have been recent improvements in the midwife's techniques. The operation today is less radical, somewhat more sterile, and, owing to the use of benidj (anesthetic), less painful than it was for local women circumcised before 1969. I remember sitting transfixed in alarm as my informants graphically recounted their own experiences. Before Miriam received government training in midwifery, female circumcisions used to be performed by diyat el-ḥabil ("midwives of the rope").[2] A circular palm mat with its center removed was so placed that it fit over a freshly dug hole in the ground.[3] The girl was made to sit on the mat at the edge of the hole. Her adult female relatives held her arms and legs while the midwife, using no anesthetic and having no apparent concern for sterile procedure, scraped away all of the external genitalia, including the labia majora, using a straight razor. Then she pulled together the skin that remained on either side of the wound and fastened it with two thorns inserted at right angles. These last were held in place by thread or bits of cloth wound around their ends. (Fresh acacia thorns produce numbness when they pierce the skin and may have helped to relieve the pain.) A straw or a reed was also inserted, posteriorly, so that when the wound healed there would be a small opening in the scar tissue to allow for elimination of urine and menstrual blood. The girl's legs were then bound together and she was made to lie on an angareeb for a month or more to promote healing. According to my informants, whatever the length of her recovery, it had to be less than 40 days in order to distinguish it from time spent in confinement after childbirth. When the wound was thought to have healed sufficiently the thorns were removed and the girl unbound.

explanation

To date, historical and functional explanations of this practice have been highly speculative. Many, though not all,[4] are based principally on the testimony of male informants and so risk being labeled one-sided or chauvinistic. I do not attempt to redress such shortcomings in this essay, nor to present a sexually balanced view, for most of my informants are women. Nor is it my purpose to account for the custom's remote historic origins, for even if they could be located, it is questionable whether they would contribute substantially to our understanding of its present significance. Here I wish merely to provide an interpretation of the context of Pharaonic circumcision as it is now practiced in one village in Sudan.

With little exception, arguments offered thus far are intellectually unsatisfying when taken in and of themselves, yet together they form a complex rationale that may operate (consciously or unconsciously) to sustain and justify the practice. Various authors, for example, have suggested that Pharaonic circumcision was designed to ensure chastity and to protect young women from rape (Barclay 1964; Trimingham 1965). Others (Hansell and Soderberg reported in el-Safi 1970; Dr. R. T. Ravenholt reported in Morgan and Steinem 1980) consider it to be a primitive form of birth control. And it has been argued that infibulation is thought to make women more attractive sexually, that the vaginal orifice is made smaller in order to increase the male's sexual pleasure (Barclay 1964; Trimingham 1965). According to Barclay (1964:239), it is a common belief among male Arab Sudanese that local women are "oversexed," a condition that circumcision is intended to control. Last, and least convincing, there are those who maintain that infibulation originated among desert nomads as a hygienic practice designed to prevent vaginal infection where sanitary conditions, owing to a scarcity of water, were less than ideal (Cederblad 1968).[5]

To take up the last point first, even if it could be proven that the custom had originated in the attempt to control vaginal disorders, the sanitation argument does not explain why the custom should persist under improved conditions. It does not explain why riverain sedentaries perform Pharaonic circumcisions when there is an abundance of water at their disposal and when it is customary, if not mandatory, to bathe at least once a day. Moreover, there is no evidence to suggest that the practice does not do the opposite of its proposed intent, for urinary tract infection and problems with both micturition and menstruation are common complaints among village women.

The notion that female circumcision of any kind, whether Sunna (*khafd* or "reduction" of the clitoris), clitoral excision, or Pharaonic, increases male enjoyment in intercourse is widespread both in Sudan and in Egypt (Assaad 1980:13; Ammar 1954:120). With regard to the case at hand, there are several points to be considered. First of all, the tremendous success of regional brothels, staffed by purportedly uncircumcised Ethiopian women and Southern Sudanese, must at least weaken this view (but does not obviate it entirely), especially since these establishments are patronized by married men (having direct or occasional access to women) and unmarried men alike. The growing male acceptance of recent innovations in the circumcision technique also undermines the pleasure argument. In the village where I lived there is a relatively large group of women who were circumcised before 1969 and who have never been married.[6] Most of these women are over the age of 20, an age considered late for marriage. Yet, many younger sisters and cousins of these women, circumcised after that date in the less radical manner, are presently married. Since it is customary for elder daughters and their female parallel cousins to be married before younger sisters and parallel cousins, men are now marrying,[7] —and what is more, saying that they prefer to marry—women who have been less severely mutilated. My female informants suggested the reasons for this preference to be religion (dīn) and an expected improvement in sexual relations over the experiences of their longer-married kinsmen.

Indeed, men who consider themselves religious often advocate adopting the Sunna (orthodox) form of female circumcision wherein only the prepuce of the clitoris is excised. I was informed by friends in Khartoum that many Western-educated Sudanese are now having their daughters "pseudocircumcised." In the latter operation, the girl is first given a Sunna circumcision and then loosely infibulated. Apparently the infibulation is reversible and is performed only so that the girl might save face before her traditionally circumcised cohorts at boarding school.[8]

By far, the majority of those who insist that Pharaonic circumcisions continue to be performed are not men but adult women, and notable among these are the ḥabōbat (grandmothers).[9] Any account of the practice falls short of the mark if it fails to consider why this should be so. One of the arguments mentioned earlier does suggest that circumcision is relatively advantageous to women as a form of birth control. Indeed, while this may be a latent function of the custom, as Hayes (1975) suggests, there is no evidence from my own fieldwork to support the view that limiting the number of one's children is its actual purpose. Most women in the village who have been stably married for 10 or 15 years became pregnant at least six or seven times during that period. Of these, women who tend to miscarry or to bear stillborn infants have been pregnant most often.

By contrast, I was frequently consulted on the subject of contraception. Women nurse their babies for as long as two years, yet there is a relatively short postpartum taboo on sexual activity (two to three months). It is believed that if a woman becomes pregnant too soon after the birth of her last child, the child she is nursing will sicken and die. These circumstances, coupled with the relative fecundity of village women, probably account for the fact that several of them approached me for information about birth control pills and injections, saying that they wished to space their children further apart.

virginity, fertility, and sexual complementarity   Of all the explanations for Pharaonic circumcision, those referring to the preservation of chastity and the curbing of sexual desire seem most persuasive, given that in Sudan, as elsewhere in the Muslim world, a family's dignity and honor are vested in the conduct of its womenfolk (Barclay 1964; Hayes 1975; Trimingham 1965; see Ammar 1954; Assaad 1980; el-Saadawi 1977 for Egypt). As significant as this point appears to be, however, it may represent a confusion of causes with effects.

What infibulation *does*, though this is not necessarily its original purpose—nor even, perhaps, what it is intended to do in Hofriyat today—is ensure that a girl is a virgin when she marries for the first time. It does control her sexuality and makes it less likely that she will engage in extramarital affairs. A young girl both dreads and eagerly awaits her wedding day: she welcomes the elevation in status while fearing what it implies, namely, having to endure sexual relations with her husband. My informants told me that it may take as long as two years of continuous effort before penetration can occur. For a man it is a point of honor to have a child born within a year of his marriage, and often, the midwife is summoned in secret, under cover of darkness, to assist the young couple by surgically enlarging the bride's genital orifice, a service for which she charges an exorbitant fee.[10]

Because they find it so painful, most of the women I talked to said that they avoid sex as often as possible, encouraging their husbands to sleep with them only when they wish to become pregnant. Sexual relations do not necessarily become easier for the couple over time. When a woman gives birth, the midwife must be present not only to cut through the scar tissue and release the child but also to reinfibulate her once the baby is born.

After each birth, then, a woman's body is restored, at least superficially, to its condition prior to marriage. During her 40-day confinement period, she is re-presented to her husband as a bride and given gifts of clothing and jewelry similar to those she received at her wedding, though smaller in scale. Moreover, a divorced or widowed woman may undergo reinfibulation in anticipation of remarriage, thus renewing, like the recently delivered mother, her "virginal" status. According to Hayes (1975:622), the notion of virginity assumes special significance in Northern Sudan. As she so succinctly remarks with regard to Pharaonic circumcision, "in Sudan, virgins are made, not born."

> The concept of virginity in Sudan is an anomaly to the Western world. Virginity, from our point of view, is a physical condition which is absolutely (and irrevocably) changed by a specific behavior. Virginity in Sudan can be thought of as a social category, in the sense that the physiological manifestation can be socially controlled (Hayes 1975:622).

While I am in basic agreement with this statement, I feel it requires qualification. I submit that, for Sudanese women, the social category "virgin" has somewhat less to do with sexual abstinence than it has to do with fertility. Although infibulation acts to control female sexuality, this is not its avowed purpose.[11] My friends stated that it is performed on young girls in order to make them clean (*naẓeef*), smooth (*na'īm*), and pure (*ṭahir*) (this last intended result furnishes the colloquial term for circumcision in general: *ṭahūr* [signifying cleansing or purifying]). Women say a girl who has not been purified through circumcision may not marry, and thus may not bear children and attain a position of respect in her old age. Circumcision prepares her body for womanhood, whereas marriage provides her with the opportunity to advance her position through giving birth, especially to sons.

Explanations for infibulation found in the literature apparently confuse the sexuality of women with their ability to bear children where these aspects of womanhood ought to be distinguished (the promiscuity argument). Conversely, perhaps they tend overly to dissociate the sexuality of males from their ability to impregnate women (the pleasure argument). Male fertility is closely associated with concepts of virility, as the following incident will illustrate. Once I overheard a man talking about his beautiful *bit 'amm* (FBD) whom he wished he had married. Although this woman and her present husband had been married for over a year, she had not yet conceived. Said the man, "By God, if I had married her, she would have had twins by now!"[12]

As I attempt to demonstrate in subsequent pages, infibulation neither increases, nor for that matter limits, male sexual pleasure (this is irrelevant here) so much as it ensures or socializes female fertility. By removing their external genitalia, women are not so much preventing their own sexual pleasure (though obviously this is an effect) as enhancing their femininity. Circumcision as a symbolic act brings sharply into focus the fertility potential of women by dramatically de-emphasizing their inherent sexuality. By insisting on circumcision for their daughters, women assert their social indispensability, an importance that is not as the sexual partners of their husbands,[13] nor, in this highly segregated, male-authoritative society, as their servants, sexual or otherwise, but as the mothers of men. The ultimate social goal of a woman is to become, with her husband, the cofounder of a lineage section. As a respected *ḥabōba* she is "listened to," she may be sent on the *ḥadj* (pilgrimage to Mecca) by her husband or her sons, and her name is remembered in village genealogies for several generations.

In this society women do not achieve social recognition by becoming like men, but by becoming less like men physically, sexually, and socially (see Assaad 1980:6). Male as well as female circumcision rites stress this complementarity. Through their own operation, performed at roughly the same age as when girls are circumcised (between five and ten years), boys become less like women: while the female reproductive organs are covered, that of the male is uncovered, or, as one Sudanese author states, "unveiled" (el-Safi 1970:65). Circumcision, then, accomplishes the social definition of a child's sex (see Ammar 1954:121ff.; Assaad 1980:4ff.; Kennedy 1970) by removing physical characteristics deemed appropriate to his or her opposite: the clitoris and other external genitalia, in the case of females, the prepuce of the penis, in the case of males. This last is emphasized by a custom now lapsed in Hofriyat wherein one of the newly circumcised boys' grandmothers would wear his foreskin as a ring on the day of his operation.[14]

After circumcision, young boys are no longer permitted to sleep with their mothers and sisters, but must accompany their older brothers in the men's quarters. Similarly, a young girl is increasingly restricted to association with womenfolk and is expected to assume greater domestic responsibility once she has been circumcised. Indeed, the most notable feature of village life is this polarization of the sexes, most marked between men and women of childbearing age. To the outsider it almost appears as though there are two virtually separate, coexisting societies that only occasionally overlap. Men and women generally do not eat together, they occupy separate quarters in the family compound, and they associate with those of their own sex in segregated areas at ceremonies and religious events. Further, while men have ultimate authority over women, this is often far less actual than supposed. In everyday affairs, women are more strictly governed by the ḥabōbat than by their male kin, and when it comes to a matter of direct control by her husband, the Hofriyati woman is expert in the art of passive resistance.

The nature of male authority is itself instructive. A woman is legally regarded as being under the control and care of her father and, after his death, of her brothers for as long as they live. When she marries she also becomes accountable to her husband, but her immediate male kin retain moral responsibility for her welfare. Theoretically, a measure of both economic and moral responsibility passes to her adult sons should she become widowed or divorced. What these men share is the right to allocate, and in the case of her husband, to use, the woman's reproductive potential.

Through marriage a man acquires access to his wife's fertility, and she, the means to activate it. Children are the capital on which male and female careers are built but at the same time kept separate, since marriages themselves are fragile and, for men, may be polygynous. It is only through marriage that men and women might inaugurate their respective, yet mutually dependent, social careers.

interpretation

Given polarization and heightened complementarity of the sexes as outlined above, what is it specifically about Pharaonic circumcision that, as I claim, enhances a woman's socially defined feminity, her potential fertility? If, as I suggest, the minimization of a woman's sexual enjoyment and the covering of her reproductive organs is a symbolic act, what then is the nature of this symbolism, its meaning and its context?

The question is best approached by first returning to informants' statements regarding the purposes of this custom and taking these statements to be accurate. When questioned, both men and women responded, with an opacity that frustrates many fieldworkers, that girls are circumcised because "it is our custom" (*'adatna*) and "it is necessary" (*ḍurūri, lazim*). As mentioned earlier, however, my closer female friends volunteered somewhat more exegetically that the custom was intended to make women pure (*ṭahir*), clean (*naẓeef*), and smooth (*na'īm*). As I began to learn the various uses and associations of these qualities, gradually piecing together what I was observing and what I was being told, it became increasingly obvious that there was a certain fit between this practice and others. A wide range of activities, concepts, and what villagers call their customs (*'adat*) appear to be guided by a group of interrelated idioms and metaphors, sometimes explicitly formulated, but more often not. These idioms are, as I perceive them, components of an informal logic of everyday life (Geertz 1973:10ff.). In Hofriyat, they are processes and qualities relative to things and events. They underlie both ritualized and nonritualized behavior, providing a number of overlapping contexts that inform social discourse.

To determine adequately the symbolic context of female circumcision in Hofriyat, one must trace further applications of the qualities that define it: purity, cleanliness, and smoothness. An interpretation of these qualities leads to further associations, until one is faced with a complex network of relations in which certain basic idioms predominate. Such an interpretive analysis is much like the weaving and tying of an elaborate macrame: some threads must be left dangling in places, only to be caught up again at a later point and reworked into the whole. With this caution to the reader, I proceed.

purity, birds, and fertility

The only situation other than male and female circumcision and female ritual purity in which I consistently heard people use the descriptive *tahir* (pure) was in reference to certain types of birds. Among domestic birds, pigeons are considered *tahir* while chickens are considered *waskhan* (dirty). The former are *tahir*, Hofriyati say, because they splash around in water when it is set out for them and they reside above the ground in large tins which people suspend from the rafters of their verandas. Their meat, referred to as *lahma nazeefa* (clean flesh), is a delicacy and pigeon broth a local panacea.[15] Chickens, by contrast, are regarded as filthy creatures that scratch in the dust, eat their own excrement, and generally make a mess of people's courtyards. Their meat is almost never eaten, as it, too, is considered dirty. Yet chickens are kept by villagers because they produce eggs, which are considered "clean food" (*akil nazeef*), food that "brings blood" (*byjeeb dum*).

Young unmarried girls who dance at wedding parties are often referred to as *hamāmat masheen fi sūq* (pigeons going to market).[16] The girls consider themselves on display for prospective husbands, as it is usually at such affairs that arrangements for subsequent marriages are initiated. The dance performed by women at these parties is a slow and rhythmic forward step with arms extended. It is referred to as *ragees bi rugaba* (a dance from the neck), as it consists primarily of moving the head forward and backward in the controlled manner, as my informants describe it, of a little bird or a pigeon walking along the ground.

Wild water birds, like those found along the Nile, are considered clean, though for the majority of villagers, inedible. Until very recently, people had the cheeks of their younger daughters marked with a small scar in the shape of a rounded "T." This is referred to by village women as *derab al-ter* (bird tracks, like those left by water birds walking along the beach). It is considered a mark of beauty, a feature that greatly adds to a woman's desirability.

One can thus outline a rather strong metaphoric connection between young circumcised girls (and, for that matter, older women) and birds associated with water. Both are *nazeef*; both domesticated water-linked birds and girls are *tahir*. Girls are sometimes referred to as birds and in some circumstances they are said to act like birds. Inversely, birds of this particular category behave like humans since they "bathe."

While I was in the village, I rented a *hōsh* from one of the local women. Gathering dust in the ceiling corners of the main room were four ostrich eggshells, each of which was decorated differently from the rest. As I began visiting other households in the area, it became apparent that my room was typical in this respect. Questions as to the significance of these objects met with suppressed giggling from my female companions. They explained that these are *manāẓir,* visions or views, things to look at. The idiom of "seeing" is strongly developed in Hofriyat. Someone is thought to absorb qualities of what is seen; correspondingly one might effect changes in something or someone by emitting visual influences (this is the *'aiyn ḥarra* [evil or "hot" eye]). Now, although the actual designs of these objects may be significant in themselves, they are highly variable and, according to my informants, subject only to the creative impulse of the painter; they may be painted by men or by women. When prodded further as to their significance my friends said that ostrich eggshells and similarly shaped gourds (now more commonly used) are so placed because the woman who sleeps in that room wishes to become pregnant. These objects are, however, permanent fixtures in the majority of homes; they are not put up and taken down at a woman's whim. They are not, in other words, signals in some sexual semaphore designed to dampen or to rally a husband's consummate attention. Rather, they are, if I may be permitted so Freudian a statement, fertility objects. One informant said, "We look at them because we want sons" (*āwlad,* which also means "children" in a general sense).

As fertility symbols these objects figure in a number of contexts. First, a man's testes are euphemistically referred to as his "eggs," of which the massive ostrich egg is considered an exaggerated specimen. Furthermore, though villagers themselves make no such explicit connection, it is noteworthy that the object is something associated with birds. Of course, only the shell of an ostrich egg is used for decoration; the egg itself is removed by making a small puncture in the shell and draining off the contents. Ostrich eggshells and their latter-day counterparts, gourds of similar size and form, are prized for their shape, their smooth rounded surfaces, and their creamy white color.

The quality "whiteness" usually is associated with concepts of cleanliness and purity. White foods are generally classed as "clean" and are thought to "bring blood," to increase the amount of blood in the body.[17] In Hofriyat these are eggs, goat's milk, goat's milk cheese, cow's milk, fish, rice, sugar, and white flour. Of these, only goat's milk and sugar may be considered staples; all are, to some extent, scarce or limited and expensive. There is another group of foods considered to be clean. These are also expensive and are usually purchased only on special occasions or for guests. Some of the most common are tinned fish, tinned jam, oranges, bananas, guavas, and grapefruit. These food are generally associated with Europeans, Egyptians, and Lebanese, that is, with people having light—or as villagers say, "white"—skin. They are thought of as being especially clean because they are all, so to speak, "contained" or enclosed and protected from dirt and dryness.

Hofriyati are very conscious of skin color. White skin is clean, beautiful, and a mark of potential holiness. I, being Caucasian, was repeatedly told that my chances of getting into heaven, should I choose to become Muslim, were far greater than those of the average Sudani. This is because the Prophet Mohammed was white and all white-skinned peoples are in the favored position of belonging to his tribe (*gabeela*). Ranked in order of desirability, the skin color of villagers ranges from "light," or *aṣfar* (yellow), to *aḥmar* (red, somewhat darker than *aṣfar*), to *akhdar* (green, darker still), to *azrag* (blue) or "dark." The term *aswad* (black) is usually reserved for Southern Sudanese and "Africans," people who in earlier times could be enslaved.

One context in which the concepts of whiteness as desirable in skin coloring, cleanliness, purity, and smoothness figure prominently is that of women's cosmetics. Immediately before her wedding a young girl goes through an elaborate regimen of physical preparation for the first time in her life. To begin with, all of her body hair must be removed, excepting that on her head. This is done using a combination of sugar, lime juice, and water, boiled until a thick, sticky concentrate remains. When it cools, the toffeelike substance is spread over the skin and, like depilatory wax, quickly pulled away, taking the hair with it. I am told that women cannot use razors for this purpose as do men, who shave their pubic hair. Women must experience "heat" and "pain" (ḥarr) when they depilate, whereas men use a "cold" (barid) method of hair removal. It should be noted that infibulation, too, is referred to as ḥarr, that heat and pain generally are associated with acts of feminine purification.

After her skin has been cleared of hair, the prospective bride takes a smoke bath (dukhāna). If such does not already exist, a small hole is dug in the kitchen floor or other appropriate spot indoors. It is then filled with fragrant woods and lighted. The girl removes her clothing, wraps herself in a special blanket (shamla) made of goat or camel hair, and sits over the hole, taking care to envelop the rising smoke. She may sit this way for as long as two hours or more, adding wood from time to time and gossiping with her friends. The bath is considered a success if, when she emerges, the top layer of her skin can be sloughed off, exposing a lighter and smoother surface beneath. To remove this dead layer she massages herself with a concoction of smoked dough made from millet flour and powdered aromatic woods, known as dilka. When all traces of dilka have been rubbed away, she oils herself and applies perfume. Then her hands and feet are stained with henna, the purpose of which is both to cool and to ornament the extremities.

These preparations, which may take several days to complete, are intended to make her skin soft, smooth, clean, fragrant, and desirably lighter in color. (In fact, some women go to the extent of powdering themselves with packaged vanilla custard in order to improve the cast of their skin.) After such treatment, performed for the first time when she becomes a bride, and henceforth whenever she wants to attract the sexual attentions of her husband, a woman's body shares several qualities with the ostrich egg fertility object: both are smooth, both are clean and "white," and both are pure. What is more, the shape of the ostrich egg, with its tiny orifice, corresponds to the idealized shape of the circumcised woman's womb. So, too, the cleanliness, whiteness, and enclosedness of valued edibles evoke images of the bride and of fecundity.

A distinctive feature of objects herein described as "enclosing" is their ability to retain moisture. Similarly, a bride's cosmetic routine is supposed to prevent her from perspiring. Human sweating and the smell of sweat are considered gauche at all times, but at a wedding they are especially despicable. What is more, the association between moisture retention and "pure" and "purified" women is photo-negatively expressed by the term for prostitute, sharmūṭa (literally, "that which is shredded or in tatters"). But in local parlance sharmūṭ (masculine form) is meat that has been cut into strips and hung to dry. There is thus an implicit association between prostitutes and dried meat or flesh.

All of the above relations, which should become more firmly established as we progress, combine to signify that on the day of her wedding a young girl finally reaches a peak of potential and appropriate fertility, defined in terms of the qualities "whiteness, "smoothness," "cleanliness," "purity," "enclosedness," and "imperviousness."

the alternative fertility object: division of labor, fluids, reproduction, and enclosedness

We now turn to the web of symbolic relations that spin out from the alternative fertility object, the egg-shaped gourd (gar'a). Such gourds may be used in place of ostrich eggs only after they have been preserved by drying in the sun. One knows that a gar'a is ready to be decorated and hung in a room if, when it is shaken, its seeds can be heard to rattle inside. The vocabulary of cultivation and of farming in general provides a figurative lexicon for most things having to do with human reproduction and, to a certain extent, with village social structure. The progeny of a man or a woman is referred to as his or her djena (fruit) or *zuriy'a* (crop, that which is sown). A man's immediate descendants, the lineage section of which he is head, is also his *zuriy'a*.

As such, the fact that the appropriately shaped gourd contains seeds in an enclosed space is exceedingly significant. To begin with, native theories of conception have it that the fetus is formed from the union of a man's semen, spoken of as his seed, with his wife's blood. Sexual intercourse causes the woman's blood to thicken or coagulate and she ceases menstruation until after the baby's birth. While pregnant, a woman nourishes her husband's future "crop" within her.

These ideas also relate to those concerning parents' respective contributions to the body of their child. Women told me that although young people learn differently in school these days, a child receives its bones from its father and its flesh and blood from its mother. While an adequate description of village social structure is beyond the scope of the present paper, certain of its characteristics are relevant to the symbolic interpretation given here. Just as the skeleton structures the body, so do endogamous patrilineal descent groups structure the village. But endogamy, though preferred, is not always possible in practice. What is more, adherence to endogamy is not a great concern of people entering into second or subsequent marriages. The upshot of all this is that sisters frequently marry into lineages unrelated or only distantly related to each other. And, no matter what their respective descent affiliations, the children of such women are considered close relatives. Women thus serve to link together the various named descent groups in the village. People who belong to different patrilineages, yet acknowledge relationship, say that *bain nehna lahma wa dum* ("between us there is flesh and blood"). If it is through men that the social order receives its structure, its rigidity (its bones), then it is through women that it receives its fluidity and its integration (its blood and its flesh).

There are several other contexts in which fluids and moisture figure prominently as markers of femininity. The most important of these, for our present purpose, has to do with division of labor by sex. While cultivation is thought primarily to be men's work, fetching water from the wells for household consumption is traditionally considered women's work. Thus it is through their individual labors, farming and getting water, that men and women provide the household with materials for its staple food, *kisra*. *Kisra* is made by first mixing *dura* flour with an almost equal amount of water. Then the batter is spread thinly over a seasoned griddle and the waferlike product is removed when dry.

Now *kisra* batter is mixed by hand in a special type of container called a *gūlla*. This is a squat, rounded pottery jar, about the size of an average pumpkin, having an opening at the top slightly larger than a woman's fist. It differs from water jars (singular: *zīr*) in that the latter are far larger, capable of holding 40 l of water or more. *Zīrs* are longer than they are round and are made of a porous clay that permits sweating, hence cooling of the water they contain. *Gūllas*, on the other hand, must be nonporous; they must not allow anything inside of them to seep out. This feature likens them to other objects herein described as moisture retentive: foods that are contained and the cosmetically prepared body of the infibulated bride, all of which evoke the further positive qualities of cleanliness, purity, femininity, and fecundity.

Significantly, besides serving as a container in which flour and water are mixed for *kisra*, the *gūlla* has another function, relative to childbirth. If a woman miscarries when she is only a few months pregnant, the expelled matter is treated like menstrual blood and put down the latrine. However, should she require the services of a midwife to open her up, a different method of disposal is called for. The fetus is first wrapped in a cloth, as for a corpse; then it is placed in a *gūlla* and buried somewhere within the confines of the *ḥōsh* (the house enclosure). The symbolism of this act is made more explicit when one considers what is done in the case of a stillbirth. If a baby is born but fails to breathe, its body is wrapped in a cloth and buried without ceremony just against the outer wall of the ḥōsh. But, should an infant expire having taken even one breath, then normal funeral procedure must be followed and the child buried in the graveyard on the outskirts of the village.

Both the gūlla and the ḥōsh appear in this context as symbols for the womb. In the case of the gūlla, it is an object of daily life in which the fruits of men's and women's labors are mixed. The mixture when baked produces kisra, the staple food, that which sustains life. It is important to note that only women mix and bake kisra.

Similarly, in the womb are mixed a man's seed and a woman's blood: substance and fluid, like grain and water. This mixture when formed reproduces life, and hence also sustains it. Again, only women, through their fertility, perform this reproductive task. There is, symbolically, no more fitting receptacle for an aborted "mixture" of male and female contributions than the gūlla, the impervious container of unbaked "life."

There is a certain level of exegesis involved in this interpretation. One of my informants thinks that the gūlla might be used for this purpose because in its shape it resembles the beyt el-wilāda (the womb; literally, the house of childbirth) and because in its size it corresponds to the belly of a pregnant woman. The "house" metaphor is significant and we will return to it in the conclusion to this paper.

Earlier I stated that the ḥōsh, the walled enclosure of a household area, also symbolizes the womb. More accurately, it symbolizes an initial stage in the process of becoming human. The miscarried fetus has not, strictly speaking, been born; it does not emerge with a wholly developed human body. Its progress is halted in the womb and it must be disposed of within the ḥōsh. The stillborn child emerges fully developed, but it does not breathe; its progress is halted or fixed at the point of birth. As it has emerged from the womb, so it is buried against the outer wall of the compound. The child who breathes but then dies is indeed fully human, for breath is the essence of life. A child who has breathed is placed with other humans who have lived, who have passed from the ḥōsh and the village to the grave. Significantly, women, who are associated with birth and with the ḥōsh in this and several other contexts, are not permitted to be present at a burial.[18] Such is the responsibility of men. Women may visit the graveyard, but only after the funeral has ended. The symbolism of village special organization in customs having to do with unsuccessful pregnancy thus not only expresses the physical relationship between mother (womb) and child but also describes the unsuccessful emergence of an individual into society. The child who dies at birth skips over the social phase of being, going directly from the ḥōsh to the grave.

further associations of the ḥōsh: enclosure and cleanliness, purity and sociality

Generally speaking, all enclosed areas in the village are considered clean and protected places. Ḥōsh yards are swept daily, as are the floors of its rooms and inside verandas. Clean spaces, spaces which are inside, are social areas. They are areas of relative safety, where one is least likely to become possessed by malevolent spirits (djinn aṣwad [black djinn]), hence to be driven mad. Djinn frequent open spaces such as the desert, ruins, and rubbish heaps. The insides of ḥaishan are considered relatively safer than village paths, which in turn are relatively safer than the surrounding countryside.

Yet social spaces are not always bounded by high walls. While these are desirable, some homes in the village do not have walled-in courtyards surrounding them. Instead, the open area immediately adjacent to such a structure is marked off by a ring of stones or by a thorn fence (zarība). However humble its boundaries, though, such an enclosure is regularly swept smooth to maintain the distinction between it and unmarked space.

The village, too, is bounded: to the west by farmlands and the river, to the north and south by other villages, and to the east by the desert, *el-khalla* (the emptiness). The graveyard is located on the westernmost fringe of the desert, between the village and "emptiness." Thus, as one moves eastward from the river to the desert, there is a shift from conditions of relative fecundity and abundance to those of relative sterility, with humans poised between the two.

This in-between space, social space, is organized concentrically. At the hub is the *ḥōsh*, the extended family and the place where life begins. Surrounding the *ḥōsh* in the village are neighbors and kinsmen, considered one and the same by local people: they are called *nas gareeb* (those who are close) or *gareebna* (our relatives). In nearby villages are distant relations and affinal kin. Beyond this, one soon arrives at the periphery of the known social world.

It is appropriate to mention here that social space is also relatively bounded in an ideological sense. People marry *gareeb* (close). They ought to marry within the patrilineage, preferably a FBS or FBD, but given demographic limitations they try to marry as "close" as possible (that is, other kin in a declining order of preference). Thus, it is not surprising that the best or most prestigious marriage is also the closest: between bilateral parallel cousins whose parents are parallel cousins. While it is stated by informants and in the literature that patrilateral parallel cousins are preferred spouses, my evidence indicates that matrilateral parallel cousins and cross cousins are considered exceedingly close. If for some reason one must marry a more distant relative, he or she ought yet to observe the preference for territorial endogamy: neighbors are "close" by definition. Moreover, all villagers acknowledge a plethora of consanguineal and affinal ties to all other villagers. Social space as expressed through kinship and marriage thus replicates the social organization of physical space: both are based on the principle of relative enclosure within a circumscribed "area."

enclosure of physical space: the human body

The above considerations lead us back to some earlier relinquished threads in our argument. Significant with respect to the concept of relative enclosure are several associations in another domain, that of the human body. With respect to established notions of aesthetic propriety, a human face, male or female, is considered beautiful if it is characterized by a small mouth and by narrow nostrils. What is more, body orifices are places where potentially dangerous *djinn* might abide. Burial customs dictate that all such orifices, including spaces between fingers and toes, be washed, perfumed, and stuffed with cotton before the corpse is wrapped and taken to the cemetery. This is to ensure the expulsion of any lingering *djinn* and to prevent the soul of the deceased from reinhabiting its mortal remains. Thus, while orifices of the human body are necessary for sustaining life, they are dangerous, not aesthetically pleasing if large, and not to be left open after death.

The idiom of closure is further dramatized by certain features of folk medicine as practiced in the village. Remedies are often based on the assumption that pain and swelling are caused by things coming apart or opening. One common cure for a headache, or "open head" (*rās maftuḥ*), is first to wrap a band of cloth around the head, then to tighten this band by twisting it with a key or a piece of wood. Alternatively, the head may be closed by the application of hot irons to four equidistant points on the skull, starting from midforehead. Pulled tendons and ligaments are also treated by "fire" (*nār*): hot irons are placed at either end of the affected area so that what has come apart may be fused together again by heat. The associations of heat, of fusing together, of closing, and of the aesthetic preference for small body orifices once again call to mind the practice of infibulation.

the ḥōsh, the womb, and sexual differentiation: full circle

Throughout the course of this analysis, the idiom of relative enclosure emerges predominant. The ḥōsh, the womb, and many more objects and actions of daily life; beliefs about the human body, reproduction, imperviousness, and the fertility potential of brides; the organization of space and of social relations; all that I have outlined above appear over and over again in contexts that play upon this theme. These contexts culminate in further symbolic associations of the ḥōsh, the infibulated (enclosed) womb, and sexual differentiation.

As noted earlier, the sexes are spacially as well as socially segregated. They occupy opposite sides of the dancing ground at ceremonies and are housed and fed in different households during communal feasts. The ḥōsh, too, is spacially divided into men's and women's quarters, having separate entrances for each. The "front" door (no specified orientation) is known as the men's entrance and is used by official guests and strangers. The men's room (diwān) generally is located in the front part of the courtyard near this door. The back door is known as the women's entrance and is for the use of women, close male kin, and neighbors. Women's quarters are situated at the rear of the compound, as is the kitchen. If the ḥōsh is considered a politico-economic unit, internal or domestic affairs are the province of women, while external affairs, such as marketing, are handled by men. Although women are not, strictly speaking, secluded, there is a general feeling that they ought to remain within the confines of the ḥōsh unless officially visiting kin.[19] Thus, there exists a fairly strong association of women with internal affairs, enclosedness, and the rear or interior of the ḥōsh, and of men with external affairs, nonenclosedness, and the front of the ḥōsh. These complementary relations provide further images with which Hofriyati think about social reproduction, a subject to which we now return.

The men's entrance to the ḥōsh is known as el-khashm el-beyt (the mouth/opening/orifice of the house). This term also refers to a group of kin. Properly speaking, a khashm el-beyt consists of several related lineages: it is subtribe. But in Hofriyat, as elsewhere in the Sudan (Barclay 1964:91), this term is used only to refer to people who live in or originate from a common ḥōsh (compound) or beyt (house), hence, to a lineage section.

Extension of anatomical terms to nonanatomical subjects, such as I have described above, is comon in Sudanese colloquial Arabic. For example, the supports of an angareeb are its "legs" (singular: kur'a). Doors and orifices through which things and people pass are "mouths" or "nostrils" (singular: khashm), and the insides of houses and other enclosed areas are "bellies" or "stomachs" (singular: buton).

From a converse perspective, however, nonanatomical terms are often applied to parts of the anatomy. Most important for our discussion, the word "house" is explicitly associated with the womb, for the womb is referred to as the "house of childbirth" (beyt el-wilāda) and the vaginal opening is its khashm (its door or mouth). Thus, an implicit association exists between the khashm el-beyt, meaning the men's door of the courtyard—and, metaphorically, one man's immediate descendants—and the khashm of the beyt el-wilāda, a woman's genital orifice.[20] The men's door literally opens into an enclosed area occupied by a man's sons and daughters, his zuriy'a. The khashm el-beyt el-wilāda, the door of the womb, also opens into an enclosed area which is more completely enclosed and purified by a woman's circumcision and infibulation. Just as the ḥōsh protects a man's descendants, so the enclosed womb protects a woman's fertility—her potential and, ultimately, that of her husband. Like the ḥōsh poised between the river and the desert, the womb of an infibulated woman is an oasis, the locus of appropriate human fertility.

Pharaonic circumcision, a custom which because of its apparent brutality cannot but horrify the Western intelligence, is for the women of Hofriyat an assertive symbolic act.

Through it they emphasize what they hold to be the essence of femininity: morally appropriate fertility, the potential to reproduce the lineage or to found a lineage section. In that infibulation purifies, smooths, and makes clean the outer surface of the womb, the enclosure or ḥōsh of the house of childbirth, it socializes or, if the phrase be permitted, culturalizes a woman's fertility. Through occlusion of the vaginal orifice, her womb, both literally and figuratively, becomes a social space: enclosed, impervious, virtually impenetrable. Her social virginity, defined by qualities of enclosedness, purity, and all the rest, must periodically be reestablished at those points in her life (after childbirth and before remarriage) when her fertility once again is rendered potent.

The practice of Pharaonic circumcision, though discouraged by orthodox Islam and also by the state, is thus deeply embedded in Hofriyati culture. It is a salient expression of interiority, an idiom that informs much of village daily life. Contravening legislation and international efforts to secure its eradication must, I think, cultivate an awareness of the custom's local significances if eradication efforts are to succeed. Indeed, it is ironic that this practice, which emphasizes female fertility at a cultural level, can be so destructive of it physiologically (Morgan and Steinem 1980:66–67). In this paradox might well lie the germ of an enlightened approach to the problem.

notes

Acknowledgments. An earlier version of this paper was presented to the Anthropology Colloquium, University of Toronto, in January 1979, and subsequently at McMaster University, the University of Waterloo, and the University of Western Ontario. I wish to thank the members of these various audiences for their comments and encouragement. I am especially grateful to Drs. Nadia Abu Zahara, Ken Burridge, Michael Lambek, and Judith Shapiro for their many helpful suggestions and criticisms of that draft. Responsibility for the final version is, of course, my own. Funding for research in Sudan was provided by a Canada Council (now Social Sciences and Humanities Research Council of Canada) Doctoral Fellowship. Professor P. L. Shinnie of the Department of Archaeology, University of Calgary, greatly facilitated my fieldwork in its initial stages. I am most endebted, however, to the women of Hofriyat, whose friendship, patience, grace, and wit made research among them a pleasure.

[1] The Anglo-Egyptian Condominium government outlawed it in 1945, as did the May (1969) Revolution government headed by President Nimieri.

[2] This refers to a method of child delivery no longer practiced in Hofriyat, where a woman about to give birth would support herself by grasping onto ropes suspended from the main ceiling beam of a room.

[3] This apparatus is also basic to smoke-bathing (later discussed) and to rope-delivery (see note 2).

[4] Hayes (1975) is the notable exception here. In Egypt, el-Saadawi (1977) and Assaad (1980) have investigated female genital operations using female informants.

[5] All of these explanations are common currency in the Western community in Khartoum and among educated Sudanese who are frequently hard pressed to account for the practice.

[6] This group consists of 31 of 121 resident adult females between the ages of 16 and 55, or 25.6 percent, taking age 12 as the last possible year for the operation to be performed. This is considered rather late, the average age at circumcision being somewhere between 5 and 10.

[7] The objection that this merely reflects a breakdown in traditional marriage patterns consequent upon increasing modernization does not hold. Patrilateral parallel-cousin marriages and marriages between other classifications of close kin (e.g., page 694) occur as frequently today (1977) as they did before 1969.

[8] Often, however, girls whose fathers wish to preserve them from the more severe operation are "kidnapped" by their grandmothers and Pharaonically circumcised nonetheless.

[9] It has been suggested to me by several people that the ḥabōbat are so adamantly in favor of Pharaonic circumcision because they need to justify having experienced the mutilation themselves. While I have no doubt that this is one reason for the persistence of the custom, I think it insufficient as a complete explanation of it. The cultural context, described within, is supportive of the operation. Infibulation is considered a positive change in a woman's body; it is not something negative, as the term "mutilation" implies. This, of course, is the perspective of village women and may differ from that of village men.

[10] Lest it be thought that the *ḥabōbat* as a group have a vested economic interest in seeing the custom maintained, it should be mentioned that midwives are few and in the past inherited the profession from their mothers or maternal aunts.

[11] It is certainly possible (even probable) that men do not share this view of female circumcision and its intended purpose. As Barclay (1964) and Trimingham (1965) suggest, their conception might well lean more toward the maintenance of chastity and sexual honor than toward infibulation as a means of enhancing fertility, which I argue is the feminine perspective. The two, chastity and "quality" fertility, are quite simply different sides of the same coin, for the only offspring considered socially and morally viable are those born of lawful marriages, most appropriately contracted between close kin.

[12] Ammar (1954), however, does show that circumcision has to do with fertility. He states: "The belief is that on his or her circumcision or wedding, a person could be deprived of fertility and potency, and hence great care must be taken to avoid the evil eye, and to avoid those who are sterile and desire fertility..." (1954:122).

[13] Women rarely object, and often prefer, that their husbands frequent brothels, so long as they do not spend too much money in such establishments.

[14] Apropos of this complementarity, Ammar (1954:121) notes that in Silwa, Upper Egypt (where clitoral excision is practiced): "In the colloquial language of the village, circumcision of the boy is sometimes referred to as 'cutting his pigeon' while in the case of a girl it is described as 'cutting her cockscomb'." The association of "pigeon" with the "feminine" foreskin is striking in its similarity to metaphors expressive of femininity in Hofriyat, discussed below. Further, in Silwa, circumcision and fertility are ritually associated with bread, Nile water, and eggs (Ammar 1954:117ff.), all of which are prominent symbols having like significances in Hofriyat.

[15] So pure are pigeons (*hamāmat*) considered to be that persons of limited means might substitute a pair of these birds for the obligatory sacrificial ram at the *'Id el-Aḍḥa* (the Islamic Great Feast) or, for that matter, whenever animal sacrifice is called for.

[16] All phrases are reported as given. No effort has been made to "correct" grammar, to make it consistent with rules of classical or modern literary Arabic. The reader ought to be aware, however, that most intensive contact was with women in Hofriyat. I was frequently struck by differences in speech characteristic of the adult male population.

[17] Much of what follows appears to be based upon an ancient humoral approach to disease. Body fluids figure prominently in the assessment of relative health; likewise, heat and cold are significant qualities of various symptoms, treatments, and preventatives.

[18] Males, on the other hand, are not permitted to witness childbirth.

[19] Even so, a woman, when outside her *ḥōsh*, is still "enclosed," for then she must wear her *tōb*, a garment consisting of 9 m of cloth wound around the body and covering the head.

[20] I must add that I do not recall hearing people refer to the women's entrance to the *ḥōsh* as a *khashm*. It was always simply referred to as *el-warā'* (the back) or as *el-bāb el-warā'* (the back door).

references cited

Ammar, Hamed
   1954   Growing Up in an Egyptian Village. London: Routledge and Kegan Paul.
Assaad, Marie Bassili
   1980   Female Circumcision in Egypt: Social Implications, Current Research, and Prospects for Change. Studies in Family Planning 11(1):3–16.
Barclay, Harold
   1964   Buuri al Lamaab: A Suburban Village in the Sudan. Ithaca: Cornell University Press.
Cederblad, M.
   1968   A Child Psychiatric Study of Sudanese Arab Children. Copenhagan: Munksgaard.
Gasim, Awn al-Sharif
   1965   Some Aspects of Sudanese Colloquial Arabic. Sudan Notes and Records 46:40–49.
Geertz, Clifford
   1973   The Interpretation of Cultures. New York: Basic Books.
Hayes, Rose Oldfield
   1975   Female Genital Mutilation, Fertility Control, Women's Roles, and the Patrilineage in Modern Sudan: A Functional Analysis. American Ethnologist 2:617–633.
Hosken, Franzeska P.
   1979   The Hosken Report: Genital/Sexual Mutilation of Females. Lexington, MA: WIN News.
Huelsman, Ben R.
   1976   An Anthropological View of Clitoral and Other Female Genital Mutilations. In The Clitoris. T. P. Lowery and T. S. Lowery, eds. pp. 111–161. St. Louis: Warren H. Green.

Kennedy, John G.
 1970 Circumcision and Excision in Egyptian Nubia. Man (NS)5:175–191.
Morgan, Robin, and Gloria Steinem
 1980 Genital Mutilation: 30 Million Women Are Victims. Ms. March: 65–67, 98, 100.
Saadawi, Nowal el-
 1977 Woman and Psychological Conflict. Cairo: el-Mu'assasa el- 'Arabiya lil- dirassat wa'l-nashr.
 1980 The Question No One Would Answer. Ms. March: 68–69.
Safi, Ahmed el-
 1970 Native Medicine in the Sudan: Sources, Conception, and Methods. Khartoum: Khartoum University Press.
Trimingham, J. Spencer
 1965 Islam in the Sudan. London: Oxford University Press.
Widstrand, Carl Gosta
 1964 Female Infibulation. Varia I, Occasional Papers of Studia Ethnographica Upsaliensia 20: 95–124.
W.H.O. (World Health Organization)
 1979 Pratiques Traditionelles Affectant la Santé des Femmes et des Enfants. Rapport d'un Séminaire Tenu à Khartoum du 10 au 15 Février 1979. Alexandria: Eastern Mediterranean Office.

Submitted 24 April 1981
Accepted 21 July 1981
Revised version received 14 April 1982

something borrowed: wedding cakes as symbols in modern Japan

WALTER EDWARDS—*Cornell University*

Nowhere in all the volumes filled with photographs of quiet temple gardens and crowded city streets, flooded rice fields and modern factories, bar girls and baseball stars, kimonoed geisha and half-naked sumo wrestlers; nowhere among all the images that the West has taken for itself of Japan, will the reader find the scene I am about to describe. Its central object is so alien to our notion of what is Japanese as to have gone, if not unnoticed, at least unphotographed and unpublished. Yet, it has become an established feature of a major modern ritual in which virtually all Japanese take part at some point in their lives.

The scene is a modern wedding reception, which we may interpret easily enough as the contemporary version of the traditional wedding feast that in prewar times often lasted three days. The central object is something entirely new. It is a wedding cake, of the kind one might expect to find at any American church wedding: three-tiered, frosted in white, topped with the inevitable miniature figures of a bride and groom in Western wedding dress. Behind it stand the real groom and his bride—perhaps also in Western dress, or perhaps in traditional wedding kimono—his hand steadying hers as she guides a beribboned sword into the cake. Cameras flash and the guests applaud. As Japanese sensitivity to word play prohibits (for reasons I will examine later) the use of the word "cut" at weddings, the emcee is forced to announce the event in a stilted circumlocution that smacks of the highly formal Chinese-style language: "The entering-of-the-sword into the wedding cake has been performed." The bride and groom return to their seats and the celebrations continue, the cake forgotten. It is not divided and shared by all present, nor are pieces preserved—by freezing, as is the modern American custom—by the bridal couple as souvenirs of the event. More often than not, and as if to confirm our suspicion that it is all show and no substance, the Japanese version of the wedding cake, it turns out, is inedible.[1]

The incorporation of new—and especially borrowed—elements into existing rituals presents a problem for symbolic analysis: if the additions are to be understood as meaningful rather than random, it must be shown that the incorporated element has been coherently integrated into the already existing system of symbolic meanings. In order to understand one example of a borrowed element, the Western-style wedding cake in modern Japanese weddings, this paper begins with an examination of the symbolic distinctions operative in a variety of contexts of Japanese culture. It concludes that the cake can be seen as coherently integrated in terms of these distinctions into the wedding ritual, as a symbol of fertility. [symbolic anthropology, semiotics, marriage rites, ritual change, Japan]

Copyright © 1982 by the American Ethnological Society
0094-0496/82/040699-13$1.80/1

wedding cakes in modern Japan

Wedding cakes became common among the more cosmopolitan urban Japanese in the 1920s and 1930s, but it was not until after the Pacific War, and really only within the last 20 years, that they have attained their present universal popularity. This recent incorporation into the wedding ritual presents a problem for symbolic analysis. If such syncretic additions are to be understood as meaningful rather than random, it must be shown that the incorporated element has been coherently integrated into the already existing system of symbolic meanings. This is precisely what Monica Wilson (1972) has attempted in a similar study of change in marriage ritual among the Nguni groups of southern Africa, where certain elements of European weddings have been introduced through contact with missionaries beginning in the 19th century. Wilson explains the incorporation of these new elements by showing that they expressed values that were already part of the indigeneous culture, or were relevant to the contact situation. The white wedding gown, for example, was understood and adopted as a symbol of virginity because the Nguni, like the Europeans, valued virginity in the bride. Wedding cakes, by contrast, were adopted but symbolically reinterpreted to express "traditional ideas about the dichotomy between lineages and the control of senior relatives over fertility" (Wilson 1972:195).[2] Other elements such as Western-style clothes and new forms of dance were part of a new set of symbols of status or prestige that grew out of the contact situation.

While Wilson's analysis makes a strong case for the view that elements are adopted because they are meaningful, it does not examine the mechanisms by which ritual symbols derive their meaning. Failure to deal with such questions leaves her at a loss to explain why certain symbols are selected and not others. She is accordingly perplexed by the fact that the custom of throwing grain at the bride was not adopted, despite the importance of fertility in the traditional rites, and can merely suggest that "perhaps the symbolism was never grasped" (Wilson 1972:197). She might just as well ask why white should be perceived as a symbol of virginity by the Nguni (or by Westerners, for that matter), thus facilitating the adoption of the wedding gown. In the end she is forced to relegate a large part of the process of the selection of symbolic elements to chance: "What particular symbols are retained, or borrowed, or transformed depends upon what catches the imagination" (Wilson 1972:200). I can only agree with Wilson that because of the role contingent factors play in the development of ritual forms, there will always be a certain residue of material that symbolic analysis is unable to account for. I take the position, however, that we can reduce that residue by extending the analysis beyond merely discovering the connections between symbols and values which give them meaning, to an examination of precisely what it is that makes those connections possible in the first place. This paper, by means of a semiotic perspective, undertakes such an examination of the wedding cake and other elements of modern Japanese wedding rituals.[3]

theory and method

The method I propose to use follows that developed by Lévi-Strauss (1969) for the analysis of systems of myth and ritual. It treats these systems as being analogous to language; their elements derive meaning from an underlying grammar or code that, due to its unconscious nature, remains largely hidden from both the conscious perception of the ritual participant and the direct observation of the analyst. The heart of this code is seen to consist of the distinctions the culture defines for itself as meaningful and the connections it makes between these distinctions and the elements of myth and ritual. A hypothesis about the meaning of an element must therefore make assumptions on two separate levels simultaneously: first, that a certain distinction exists in the code, and second, that it is connected with the element under consideration in a certain way. An assertion that a white gown symbolizes virginity, for example, can be restated as an assumption that the culture treats sexual purity versus defilement as a meaningful distinction for brides, as well as an additional assumption that it recognizes a connection between white, as opposed to some other color or colors, and this notion of purity. Neither assumption may be granted validity on a priori grounds alone, however, since the logic of the distinctions and the connections involved is likely to be peculiar to the culture in question, rather than universal. We can find that in Japan, for example, traditional custom also dressed the bride in white, yet virginity was not considered important. It is more plausible to see white in this instance as connected not with purity but with death: not only was white the color worn by the corpse and female relatives of the deceased at funerals (Yanagita 1957:191), there were also a number of other practices normally associated with death that occur in the wedding ceremony along with the white bridal robe. Together these have been interpreted as marking the passage of the bride out of her status as a member of her natal family.[4]

The problem of reading the connections between ritual elements and the underlying code is compounded by the fact that such elements are often composed of a number of independent aspects, each of which may conceivably be connected with the code in a different way. We cannot automatically assume, for example, that it is the *whiteness* of the wedding dress, rather than its size, shape, or mode of manufacture, that provides it with meaning. It is usual, moreover, as Victor Turner (1967:50ff.) demonstrates, for ritual elements to manifest the property of polysemy, or "multivocality"—to have a wide range of different or even contradictory meanings, at different levels—often by virtue of connections that various aspects provide.

Given that the distinctions of the code and the ways in which elements can be related to it may be idiosyncratic, and moreover that the code cannot be directly observed by the analyst, the problem becomes one of how to verify the assumptions about the code that any hypothesis necessarily involves. The only means available to the anthropologist, who is limited to working with observable phenomena that he believes to be the product of the code, is to search for regularities in those phenomena that can support his assumptions about the code and hence about the meaning an element can derive from it. The basis of the method, if it is to be successful, is sound ethnography, since the search for material necessary to determine the meaning or meanings of any single element may take the analysis far out of the original context and require an examination of all the instances in which that element occurs. Accordingly, I begin this investigation of the wedding cake with a look at another custom—the celebration of Christmas—also recently adopted by the Japanese, with the hope that in the process I will be able to establish not only the meaning or meanings that the code may give the wedding cake but also some of the broader and more basic characteristics of the Japanese symbolic code itself.

cakes and Christmas

Like the wedding cake, the celebration of Christmas first became common in Japan in the early decades of this century, and its popularity has continued to increase in the postwar years (Plath 1963). Due in part to its temporal proximity to New Year's Day, the major Japanese holiday, Christmas has not taken on the importance it holds in the West, and the aspects of it that have been adopted remain correspondingly fewer in number. While business centers of towns may be given over to Christmas decorations with reindeer and Santa Claus, not to mention the ubiquitous playing of "White Christmas," "Silent Night," and a few other well-known carols, Christmas has managed to penetrate the domestic sphere in a limited fashion only. Christmas cards and trees have not replaced the traditional New Year's cards and decorations, and gift giving, if practiced, is normally restricted to household members, usually from parents to children. The counterpart of the Western family gathering centers not on dinner, but rather—and again primarily for the benefit of the children—on the communal sharing of a "Christmas cake." The cake is a Western-style "decoration cake," a simplified and edible version of the one found in the wedding, although it is uncertain whether the Christmas cake in Japan also derives from a Western antecedent or is of modern Japanese origin.

It would seem, then, that in Japan Christmas has become a party for children, of which the following aspects are most salient: it is seen as a Western celebration, as being for children, and it centers on a cake. It occurs at the end of the year, when adult groups, both work and recreational, are scheduling *bōnenkai* ("year-end parties"). These normally take the form of the *enkai* (Japanese-style drinking party), which provides, I believe, the contrast for Christmas. It is, first of all, for adults and not for children, not only because it is adult groups which are involved but also because one of the main goals is to promote the solidarity of the group through loosening of inhibitions as the members become progressively drunk. It is also thoroughly Japanese, since it typically takes place at a Japanese-style restaurant where guests can sit on *tatami* mats, and only Japanese-style dishes, considered best for the accompanying sake, are served. Finally, it is centered on drinking either traditional sake or modern Japanese beer.

This last aspect becomes more meaningful when we recognize that the Japanese have two broad categories for classifying tastes—*amai* (sweet) and *karai*, which is perhaps best glossed as "not-sweet," since its range of reference far exceeds that of any single English taste category. Salty foods are, of course, *karai*, as are spicy ones. Cigarettes, especially the stronger brands that smoke hot and dry, are called *karai*. Curry made with a lot of spices is also *karai*, but curry made for children, which is less spicy and contains more sweet ingredients such as fruit, becomes *amai*. Sweet and dry wines are classed as *amai* and *karai*, respectively, and the distinction may be similarly used to divide sake into *amai* and *karai* varieties. As a generic term for alcohol, however, sake is normally associated with the *karai* pole. Foods served with drinks are never sweet and the exclusion is even considered to extend to people's tastes, since men who like to drink (a trait women are not supposed to share) are said to dislike sweets. *Real* sake lovers prefer their drink *karai*; sweet sake, it is said (often disdainfully), is for women.

We may now pose Christmas in Japan as an inverted form of another kind of celebration, the *enkai*, since every element we see in the context of Christmas has its opposite in the *enkai*: children versus adults, Western versus Japanese, *amai* cake versus *karai* sake. This reading of the symbolic content of Christmas is, of course, dependent on the assumption that the elements picked out are indeed essential ones and that the distinctions they allegedly represent really exist. The regularity of the relations involved does provide a measure of confidence, however, in the basic outlines of the above interpretation, which provides us with a working hypothesis for the symbolic value of cakes in Japanese society: that cakes are connected with the "sweet" pole of the distinction *amai/karai*, a distinction that can be used to differentiate children[5] from adults or, alternatively, women from men. Whether these associations can be seen as significant in the context of the wedding is a topic to which I return, in a roundabout fashion, after first examining some additional aspects of the *enkai*.

"conjunction" as symbolic meaning

I have characterized the *enkai* as a Japanese-style party for adults that centers on sake; we might add boisterousness and solidarity as essential elements. John Embree (1939) stated of the wedding banquet—which in the 1930s was less differentiated from other *enkai* than it is today—that it was "the extreme example of a pattern whereby a social gathering begins with stiff formality and ends with orgiastic abandon" (1939:209). The pattern has changed little since then: *enkai* I attended in the 1970s also tended to begin in a sober and reserved manner, but a fairly high pace of alcohol consumption would invariably break down inhibitions, enabling the members to attain a feeling of warmth and togetherness, while having a rowdy good time in the process. The ease with which alcohol dissolves normal social restraints and its importance to the creation and maintenance of group solidarity have frequently been noted by Western observers (e.g., Befu 1971:164-165; Dore 1958:208; Plath 1964:87-88); but if we conclude that the key relation in the *enkai* is the connection between sake and solidarity, would that leave the rowdiness as contingent, as a mere by-product of the real process involved?

As the question cannot be settled within the single context of the *enkai*, it is necessary to look for possible regularities in the relations between boisterousness, sake, and solidarity in other contexts. Such an examination would support the connection between sake and solidarity, if we define the latter in broader terms as the bringing into some kind of relationship of two (or more) initially separate or opposed entities. For the sake of convenience I shall call this kind of relationship a "conjunction." One example of conjunction is marriage, which links into a single social unit two persons who were initially separate, as members of different families, as well as categorically opposed as man and woman. On the ritual level, the marriage is considered sealed in Japan by a ceremony called the *san-san-ku-do*,[6] the central element of which is the communal drinking of sake by the bride and groom, who take alternate sips from the same set of sake cups. It is certain, moreover, that this is only a single instance of the wider use of sake in rites intended to create bonds between men, or between men and gods, as when sake is offered at a Shinto altar (Befu 1968:447-448).

If we interpret the boisterousness of the *enkai* as representing the more general category of noise, then a similar connection can be made with conjunction in a variety of contexts. A worshiper at a Shinto shrine, for example, sharply claps his hands twice to call down the god before offering a prayer. This particular use of noise to establish contact with a deity seems to have a long history in Japan. The cycle of creation myths first recorded in the 8th century A.D. includes an episode where the sun goddess, offended (or in another version, frightened) by her brother's rambunctious and sacrilegious behavior, shuts herself up in a cave, leaving the world in darkness. The other gods gather outside the cave and, through laughter, loud singing, and dancing (on top of an inverted tub), manage to entice her back out (Aston 1896:40-45; Philippi 1968:81-86). In a more modern context, noise is often incorporated into the wedding ritual: if the ceremony is held at a Shinto shrine, for example, it may be initiated by the loud beat of a drum. A more unusual example occurred in the first Imperial wedding of the modern era, performed in May 1900, when the completion of the *san-san-ku-do* by the Crown Prince and his bride was punctuated by a military and naval salute. It seems entirely possible, then, to interpret both sake and noise as connected with conjunction, which it is the goal of the *enkai* to produce. Before examining the logic of the connection it will be helpful to introduce two more elements that, like noise and sake, are used in connection with the conjunction of separate or opposite units.

First, straw rope is commonly used to indicate the boundary between the sacred and the secular worlds. In Shinto shrines straw rope is placed around, or in front of, places where the gods are believed to be present. At New Year's, each house, which has been given a thorough cleaning, is decorated with a similar straw rope to signify the state of purity with which it greets the new year. The second element is paper, which is used in a similar fashion and often together with rope; pieces of white paper are often twisted into the strands of rope used in the shrines or above the main entrance of the house at New Year's. Paper may also be used alone by being attached to a stick or a branch of the *sakaki* tree and presented as an offering to the gods.

Why should elements as diverse as noise, sake, straw rope, and paper all take on the same value in ritual, by virtue of their common connection with the conjunction of discrete units or categories? It may be argued that such ritual use represents the conceptual recognition of the practical side of life, a distillation of the kinds of daily uses to which certain objects naturally lend themselves. We may certainly agree that the connection between straw rope and (ritual) boundaries can be seen as echoing the kinds of uses to which straw products were frequently put, especially by the peasant in former times. Virtually every point of contact between his body and the elements was protected by straw—a straw hat for his head, straw sandals for his feet, a straw raincoat when it rained, or a straw mat to protect his back from the sun when he worked bent over in the fields, which also doubled as a picnic mat when he stopped for lunch. It would be difficult, however, to follow this kind of reasoning for all of the ritual elements mentioned above; there seems to be no reason, for example, why percussive noises and boisterous laughter, which are nonspeech sounds, should be connected with conjunction, when in everyday life ordinary speech is so much more important for forming and maintaining social relations between men.

The interpretation taken here is that the association of these elements with conjunction derives not from their practical uses, but from the way in which they are defined in terms of the symbolic code. If we momentarily leave aside the discussion of noise, the remaining elements can be seen as simultaneously connected with opposite categories of the code, thereby incorporating into their own definitions the process of conjunction itself—the bringing together of initially separate or opposed entities. Straw rope, for example, offers a vivid image of the intertwining of natural and cultural elements: it is natural material that has been minimally processed by man, merely cut and twisted into shape. The same two categories of nature and culture can be seen as simultaneously present in paper as well, since in the traditional Japanese process of manufacturing paper, not all of the raw material used is completely broken down into pulp, leaving a certain amount of the plant fiber discernible in the surface of the paper, an effect prized for its aesthetic value. Like straw rope, then, paper presents in a visible form the components of natural material and cultural process, in a combination in which both retain their separate identities. Although sake, which is also processed natural material, does not present that material in a visibly discernible form, the material itself—rice—takes on the same ritual value when it is used alongside sake as an offering to the gods at a Shinto shrine. This use of rice to conjoin gods and men may be attributed to the duality of its role as a cultigen: as a plant it is part of the natural world, yet precisely that part which culture has most fully embraced and made its own. Like paper and straw rope, then, sake, especially through its association with rice, represents a conjunction of the opposite categories of nature and culture.

The same reading—that of combining opposite categories—cannot be given for noise, yet the ritual value of noise is difficult to deny, especially since ethnographic literature shows that noise is ritually significant worldwide and often in strikingly similar ways. There is a belief commonly held by nonindustrial peoples, for example, that the occurrence of an eclipse called for the production of loud noise (Lévi-Strauss 1969:286–289); the Japanese myth of the disappearance of the sun goddess mentioned above is often interpreted as a reference to a similar custom (Philippi 1968:81). In a bold attempt to deal with the variety of such ethnographic material in universal terms, Lévi-Strauss (1969:289) concludes that noise always marks an anomaly in the unfolding of a syntagmatic sequence, a formulation that would encompass the use of noise in Japan but, being so broad, seems to add nothing in the way of explanation. It may be possible to give a more specific interpretation, one that, although inverted, is similar to the one already arrived at for straw rope, paper, and sake. It requires us to pose an opposition between the signifying sounds of speech, which carry culturally defined meaning, and silence, as the absence of any possibility for meaning. Noise is anomalous to both categories, since it is neither silence nor composed of culturally defined significance. This perspective would allow us to pose the following similarity between noise and the other elements: straw rope, paper, and sake may all be interpreted as negating a distinction between nature and culture by combining aspects of both; noise may be interpreted as negating a distinction between signification and silence by allowing aspects of neither.

"marking" versus "doing" as symbolic functions

While treating noise, sake, paper, and straw rope as having the same ritual referents, it should be noted that it is possible to see a difference between them in ritual function or emphasis, along the lines of a distinction pointed out by Lévi-Strauss (1969:337): "Either simultaneously or alternatively, rites provide man with the means either of modifying a practical situation or of characterizing and describing it." On the whole, it may be said that noise and sake are used more often to create a conjunction, for example, to seal a marriage or call down the gods; rope and paper tend more to symbolize, or comment on, the fact of conjunction, as in the use of straw rope to mark off a place already considered sacred.

A similar use of paper and string (instead of rope) to mark a conjunction rather than create one can be seen in the context of gifts, especially those exchanged between members of different families. Such gifts play a vital role in creating or maintaining social relationships, since each gift calls for its recipient to respond in a similar fashion in a never-ending round of reciprocal giving. Most gifts are bought in department stores or specialty shops, where they are wrapped, as are all purchases, with the store's own decorative paper. If the purchase is to be used as a gift, however, an additional piece of paper—called *noshigami*—is attached; this is white, smaller than the gift itself, and on it the giver's name and the occasion for the gift are written. The *noshigami* distinguishes it from an ordinary purchase and announces the fact that it is a gift. As a final touch, the entire package may be tied up, as was formerly more common than today, with a kind of decorative string, called *mizuhiki*. This string is itself made of paper that is colored either red, white, black, silver, or gold. I have already suggested that *mizuhiki* bears a symbolic similarity to straw rope, and this suggestion can be supported in two ways. Both have the same ritual emphasis of marking, rather than making, a conjunction, since it is the gift that creates or sustains a social relationship while the *mizuhiki*, along with the *noshigami*, point to the gift, and through it, to that relationship. There is also a structural similarity between *mizuhiki* and straw rope, in that both represent in visible form the mixing of two separate categories, that is, nature and culture for the rope and different colors for *mizuhiki*, since two strings of different colors are normally used together is a prescribed fashion: red and gold, red and white, or silver and gold, with gifts for auspicious occasions; white and black or white and silver for those connected with funerary or memorial rites.

If it can be accepted that the role of the *noshigami* and *mizuhiki* can be differentiated, as marking or announcing a situation, from that of noise, sake, or, we might add, the gift, which is to create or modify a situation, then certain facts about *noshigami* and *mizuhiki* can be explained. Lévi-Strauss, in making the distinction, which might be glossed simply as "marking" versus "doing," points out the complementarity of the two emphases: in traditional systems they would often be no more than two aspects of the same process. But in societies where, as he puts it, "the power of magical thought is tending to weaken" (Lévi-Strauss 1969:338), the outlook for the survival of the two functions is not the same. Lévi-Strauss asserts that the "doing" aspect does not survive, while the "marking" one does, but only as a vestige. In light of the material that has been examined so far, and with the aid of a little speculation, I believe we can modify that assessment slightly and provide insight into why the survival patterns of the two functions are different. When the "doing" functions of ritual come into confrontation with modern scientific notions of causality, they will not survive; witness the fact that the custom of creating a din during an eclipse ("to frighten away the animal or monster that is about to devour the heavenly body"), reported for primitive societies throughout the world, was also recorded formerly in Europe, where it has since died out (Lévi-Strauss 1969:287). But, and here we have to modify Lévi-Strauss's position, where such customs do *not* confront science—which can no more "create" the social relationship of marriage, for example, than can sake—those customs may indeed survive, and survive in an unreduced form. This would explain the survival of the uses of sake, noise (at weddings, parties, and Shinto shrines), and the gift described above.

Different factors will affect the "marking" elements, provided that at some point these are seen as no longer having any "doing" function. If *mizuhiki* is no longer considered to tie anything, metaphorically or physically, then it functions only as a signifier of the fact of tying. It may, therefore, without losing its ability to signify, undergo a process that I shall call "reduction," due to its often taking the form of reducing the signifier from a three-dimensional to a two-dimensional object. This is precisely what is happening to the *mizuhiki*: nowadays it is frequently "reduced" to a picture of the tied strings printed on the *noshigami*. The *noshigami* itself is in part the result of such a process; originally a slice of dried shellfish—called *noshi*—was attached to gifts not connected with funerary or memorial events to denote that the occasion did not call for abstention from eating fish (Befu 1968:445–446). This was later reduced to a stylized piece of origami which was meant to symbolize the *noshi*. The actual origami—also called *noshi*—is now used only on very elaborate occasions, as in the presentation of the betrothal gift; for most events it has been further reduced to the printed image of the origami on the *noshigami*. The word *noshigami* itself derives from this association (*noshi* + *kami* [paper]), although it is now also used to refer to the paper that is attached to funerary gifts, on which the image of the *noshi* does not appear. It would be a mistake, however, to see such linguistic changes or reductions in physical dimensions as indications that the ritual element has lost its meaning and become purely decorative. For it is still the printed images of the *noshi* and the *mizuhiki*, or the *mizuhiki* alone, that differentiate *noshigami* from ordinary paper and mark the fact of the gift; they also still function to mark differences between different types of gifts: for example, black and white *mizuhiki* and no origami images for funerary or memorial gifts, images of origami and red and gold (or some other auspicious combination of colors) *mizuhiki* tied in a special knot for wedding gifts.[7]

a second look at the wedding

Another example of the "marking" role of *mizuhiki* and paper occurs in the *san-san-ku-do*, introduced above. In the modern Shinto version of the ritual the sake is poured for the bride and groom by two young girls serving as shrine maidens, each of whom holds a vessel containing sake. Both vessels are decorated with *mizuhiki* and a piece of origami representing a stylized butterfly, one male and the other female.[8] Sake from both vessels is poured into the same cup, which is then shared by the bride and groom in succession. The *san-san-ku-do* seems to combine all of the aspects of ritual elements examined thus far. Sake has, as was noted above, a "doing" function, since the sharing of sake by the bride and groom is considered to create the marriage bond. But it also has a "marking" function, since it is mixed from two separate vessels, which are linked with the opposition of male and female.

It is, of course, conjunction that is thus marked, because marriage joins separate social units, the opposed categories of male and female, and also of nature and culture, since marriage is a culturally constrained biological union. The origami butterflies can be seen as marking both the male/female and the nature/culture oppositions; the latter doubly so since the butterflies are, first of all, made out of paper (culturally processed natural material) and also, as origami, are conventional representations of natural forms. Moreover, they are closely connected with children—the product of such culturally constrained biological unions. The fact that the sake vessels decorated with the butterflies are held by young shrine maidens appears to be the logical continuation of this association with children from the days before the locus of the wedding shifted from the home to Shinto shrines sometime in the 20th century, when the sake was poured by two small children who were themselves sometimes called, by extension from the vessels they held, the male and female butterflies.[9] The association with children is also supported by the general attitude of the time, when such home weddings were the norm, that a marriage was really made permanent by the birth of children,[10] which would also enable us to understand the "doing" function the children have in the ritual, for it is they who mix and serve the sake, which "makes" the marriage. Finally, the *mizuhiki,* which is wrapped around the handles of the sake vessels, can be seen as being used in the same way it is used with the gift: to mark the tying of a social bond.

It should be mentioned, in this context, that the linguistic resemblance that English gives to the tying of social bonds and the physical tying of string is also found in Japanese. The reason for the prohibition on the word "cut" at weddings is the phrase *en o kiru* (literally, "cut the connection"), which is a frequently used metaphor for the severing of social bonds. The same phrase can be turned into a metaphor for marriage by substituting *musubu* (to tie) for *kiru* (to cut).

We are now prepared to address the problem raised at the beginning of this paper concerning the incorporation of the wedding cake into the Japanese marriage ceremony. The problem may be restated as follows: from the point of view of symbolic analysis, can the cake be seen as coherently related to the distinctions of the underlying code and as functioning in the manner of other ritual elements, as "marking" or "doing" something in the ritual? Or is it only randomly related in terms of symbolic content and its presence due entirely to the working of some external factor, such as the tendency to emulate Western forms, or economic opportunism on the part of the hotels and reception halls? I have no doubt that external factors of this sort are always at work, but they cannot operate entirely free from constraints imposed by the symbolic system, and there will be a tendency for those elements that "make sense" in terms of the symbolic code to be chosen over those that do not. We do not see, for example, the Japanese adopting the custom of throwing rice at the bride, no doubt due to the influence of the traditional attitude toward rice, which still has a vital ritual function as an offering to both the gods and the ancestors and is treated in everyday life with such respect that, as one observer remarked, "there is no forgiveness for anybody who wilfully [sic] throws away a handful of rice" (Rabbitt 1940:191).[11] No such traditional attitudes can be found regarding cakes, but this does not prevent us from taking the position that the wedding cake "makes sense" in terms of the symbolic code by articulating with the code in the following manner.

It will be recalled that the sword used for cutting the cake is "marked" with ribbons, which are tied in a bow.[12] In other contexts we have interpreted rope, string, and tying as marking conjunction; the same reading here would see the ribbons as pointing to the conjoining of male and female—especially since both bride and groom clasp the sword hilt together—and of nature with culture. The latter assertion is more compelling when we recall the highly suggestive circumlocution for "cutting the cake," mentioned above. The key phrase—*nyūtō* (literally, "entering-of-the-sword")—is linguistically marked in two ways: by its formal, Chinese-style construction, even though the term itself is apparently of 20th-century Japanese origin,[13] and by the fact that it is used only in the context of the cutting of the wedding cake. This reduces the ambiguity of the possible phallic interpretation, since the only occasion when it is used is one in which sexual symbolism could be meaningful, provided we dare gloss marriage as the social sanctioning of coitus. Such an interpretation—that the cutting of the wedding cake is a metaphor for reproduction in Japan[14]—may be supported by the fact that, as previously noted, the cake itself is capable of referring to children through the opposition *amai/karai* and by the notion, no less strong in Japan today than in former times, that the purpose of marriage is to produce children. It also provides us with a way of dealing with the fact that the cake is inedible: since its function here is to *signify* reproduction and children, as a "marking" rather than a "doing" element, it may be subject to the same process of reduction that has changed the *noshi* from a real piece of shellfish to the printed image of a piece of folded paper, without losing its ability to signify.

conclusion

If the wedding cake does represent children and fertility in Japan, it is not necessarily the result of a symbolic "reinterpretation," since a brief look at the history of the wedding cake suggests it has played a similar role in Western culture. The modern, large cake evidently evolved in the 17th century from smaller cakes or biscuits which, at English weddings, were broken over the bride's head, a custom perhaps descended from a similar one practiced in Roman society (Scott 1953:238). This was related on the one hand to a widespread complex of rites in which the breaking of eggs, plates, pots, spoons, branches, or even furniture was intended to facilitate or symbolize the breaking of the hymen; and on the other to a group of rites in which contact with fruit, nuts, grain, or grain products was considered to bring fertility and prosperity (Westermarck 1921, II:457–464, 470–484). Thus, the crumbs of the broken cake were gathered up and eaten by the guests to ensure the bride's fertility or, alternatively, to bring fortune and plenty to those who consumed them, a notion that seems to have survived in the form of the modern English folk custom that holds that a girl who keeps a piece of the cake in her pocket until the couple's honeymoon is over will soon marry (Baker 1977:113).

We may have no way of knowing if these symbolic aspects were evident to the Japanese from the first examples they observed of the wedding cake. This would depend on when the cake was first introduced and by whom, how it was perceived and presented by those who introduced it, how it happened to have been first copied, spread, and commercialized by the Japanese, information that may not be recoverable historically and that is dependent on too many contingent factors for theoretical analysis to reconstruct. Whether the Japanese treatment of the cake as a fertility symbol stems directly from Western tradition or was arrived at independently is irrelevant from one point of view: that which holds that any treatment as a fertility symbol would not have been possible had there not been a way for the cake to be perceived as a fertility symbol in terms of the Japanese symbolic code. I have tried to show that such a point of view is tenable, that we can construct a model of the workings of the code that would make treatment as a fertility symbol understandable. By working out such models, which would allow us to show which forms are or are not capable of integrating with the code, we can ultimately reduce the residue of material that we must simply leave as beyond the ability of symbolic analysis to explain. In this respect, at least, changes in ritual form are not random: it is not simply a question of "what catches the imagination," but rather, given the range of forms that historically contingent factors produce, which of those forms *could* catch the imagination.

notes

Acknowledgments. I wish to thank James A. Boon, David Holmberg, Bernd Lambert, and Robert J. Smith for helpful comments on earlier drafts of this paper.

[1] The section that receives the sword may be real cake, but the rest is made of permanent construction materials.

[2] In traditional Nguni weddings, separate feasts were held at the homes of the bride and groom, with members of the two lineages competing in dancing on both occasions. The wedding cake was integrated into this pattern of competition: "The two families vied with each other to provide a magnificent cake and, first at the homestead of the bride and then at that of the groom, bride's friends and groom's friends danced separately, each grouped round their cake, which was carried by one of the women dancers" (Wilson 1972:194–195). After the cakes were cut, proper distribution by the mothers of the bride and groom of pieces of each cake to kin was considered important for fertility. Although Wilson regards both the connection with fertility and the fact that two cakes are involved as due to changes made by the Nguni, there is reason to question whether either aspect actually represents a change. A custom of separate bride's and groom's cakes formerly existed in parts of Europe and has survived to the present or very recent past in certain places in the New World (Baker 1977:111–112). The connection in Western tradition between wedding cakes and fertility is discussed later in this paper.

[3] It is also an attempt to suggest a needed correction in the bias toward the exotic, noticeable in Western approaches to Japanese culture—a bias visible in, for example, any photographic treatment of Japan. If the appeal of the exotic lies, as I believe it does, in its ability to point out to us the arbitrary nature of cultural forms (by presenting radical alternatives to our own), then there is an understandable loss of interest when cultural forms converge through modernization or cultural borrowing. Familiar looking forms are arbitrary nonetheless, being based on codes of convention that may just as easily be discovered through analysis of the commonplace and the ordinary, or the just plain disappointing—such as a Western-style wedding cake that turns out to be "fake."

[4] Yanagita (1957:177) notes that the customs observed at the departure of the bride from her home, of breaking the teacup she last used and building a fire at the gate, are similar to those performed at funerals after the removal of the coffin, in order to prevent the dead from returning. Erskine (1925:39–40) adds that the departing bride reversed the lap of her kimono, also in the manner of a corpse, because "according to the Japanese tradition the bride, upon leaving her father's home to enter a new family, dies to her old family ties, that is, to her father's family."

[5] That the association between cakes and children goes beyond the context of Christmas is shown by Embree's (1939:180) account of the naming ceremony performed on the third day after the birth of a child. This featured a "tray of formal congratulatory cake" which was made in the shapes of "*tai* fish, pine, plum, and bushy-tailed tortoise, the traditional Japanese symbols of good fortune and long life, and into the shape of Momotaro coming out of a peach." This last motif is discussed in note 14.

[6] The *san-san-ku-do* is normally performed before the reception and therefore before the cutting of the wedding cake.

[7] Popular manuals of ritual etiquette (e.g., Iida and Fujioka 1979) help to preserve such distinctions.

[8] The vessels were formerly more frequently used in ceremonies and banquets but are now found only in the wedding. The use of the butterfly as decoration stems from its alleged ability to counter the ill effects of liquor. In the case of the wedding ceremony these decorations are specifically called *ochō-mechō* ("the male and the female butterfly") and are sometimes explained as symbolizing togetherness and marital constancy, after the habit of butterflies of flirting about in pairs (Casal 1940:121).

[9] In some accounts the sake is reported to have been served by an elderly woman or by the go-between (e.g., Norbeck 1954:183).

[10] Embree (1939:182) wrote, for example, that "the birth of a child is a much more certain sign of a permanent marriage than is a wedding ceremony. Indeed, a marriage is often not put in the village office records until after a child is on the way."

[11] This attitude may be slowly changing in the postwar era, however, as the position of rice as the major part of the diet has been steadily declining.

[12] The same use of ribbons may be observed in Western weddings, where the sword or knife used to cut the cake may be decorated with "bows, wax orange blossoms, and a festoon of white satin ribbons" (Baker 1977:114). The Japanese have added a characteristic twist, however, since ribbons of two colors (red and white) are normally used together.

[13] The word itself—*nyūtō*—occurs in popular manuals on ritual etiquette (e.g., Iida and Fujioka 1979) but has not yet found its way into modern dictionaries (e.g., Masuda 1974; Nihon Daijiten Kankōkai 1976).

[14] This interpretation bears a close resemblance to an episode in the highly popular folk tale "Momotaro," which opens with a childless elderly couple finding an enormous peach. When the husband goes to cut it open—with a large kitchen knife—out comes a little boy, whose adventures comprise the rest of the tale. (This similarity was pointed out to me by Morio Hamada.)

references cited

Aston, W. G., transl.
  1896 Nihongi: Chronicles of Japan from the Earliest Times to A.D. 697. London: K. Paul, Trench, Trubner.
Baker, Margaret
  1977 Wedding Customs and Folklore. Totowa, NJ: Rowman and Littlefield.
Befu, Harumi
  1968 Gift-Giving in a Modernizing Japan. Monumenta Nipponica 23:445–456.
  1971 Japan: An Anthropological Introduction. San Francisco: Chandler.
Casal, U. A.
  1940 Some Notes on the Sakazuki and on the Role of Sake Drinking in Japan. Transactions of the Asiatic Society of Japan (Series 2) 19:1–186.
Dore, Ronald Philip
  1958 City Life in Japan: A Study of a Tokyo Ward. Berkeley: University of California Press.
Embree, John F.
  1939 Suye Mara: A Japanese Village. Chicago: University of Chicago Press.
Erskine, William Hugh
  1925 Japanese Customs: Their Origin and Value. Tokyo: Kyōbunkan.
Iida, Eiichi, and Shū Fujioka
  1979 Kankonsōsai no Jiten. Tokyo: Seitōsha.
Lévi-Strauss, Claude
  1969 The Raw and the Cooked: Introduction to a Science of Mythology. New York: Harper & Row.
Masuda, Koh, ed.
  1974 Kenkyūsha's New Japanese-English Dictionary. Tokyo: Kenkyūsha.
Norbeck, Edward
  1954 Takashima: A Japanese Fishing Community. Salt Lake City: University of Utah Press.
Nihon Daijiten Kankōkai
  1976 Nihon Kokugo Daijiten. Tokyo: Shōgakukan.
Philippi, Donald, transl.
  1968 Kojiki. Translated with an introduction and notes by Donald L. Philippi. Tokyo: University of Tokyo Press.
Plath, David W.
  1963 The Japanese Popular Christmas: Coping with Modernity. Journal of American Folklore 76:309–317.
  1964 The After Hours: Modern Japan and the Search for Enjoyment. Berkeley: University of California Press.
Rabbitt, James A.
  1940 Rice in the Cultural Life of the Japanese People. Transactions of the Asiatic Society of Japan (Series 2) 19:187–258.
Scott, George Ryley
  1953 Curious Customs of Sex and Marriage. London: Torchstream.
Turner, Victor
  1967 The Forest of Symbols: Aspects of Ndembu Ritual. Ithaca: Cornell University Press.

Westermarck, Edward
　　1921　The History of Human Marriage. 3 vols. London: Macmillan.
Wilson, Monica
　　1972　The Wedding Cakes: A Study of Ritual Change. *In* The Interpretation of Ritual: Essays in Honour of A. I. Richards. J. S. La Fontaine, ed. pp. 187-201. London: Tavistock.
Yanagita, Kunio
　　1957　Japanese Manners and Customs in the Meiji Era. Charles S. Terry, transl. Tokyo: Ōbunsha.

Submitted 31 July 1981
Accepted 1 September 1981
Revised version received 27 October 1981

"comets importing change of Times and States": ephemerae and process among the Tabwa of Zaire

ALLEN F. ROBERTS—*University of Michigan* and *Albion College*

Ephemeral phenomena, especially irregular ones like comets, are often neglected by anthropologists, since their brevity would appear to reduce their relevance to and impact on society as long-term process. The study of ephemerae, with that of anomalies and monsters, has been deemed a "bootless sort of wisdom" by many over the centuries.[1] Yet, in the apparition of comets as viewed and understood by the Tabwa of Zaire, an opportunity exists to reflect upon how elements of thought available from explanations of more usual and regular events may be assembled to describe a startlingly different phenomenon. Several issues of theoretical and philosophical importance may be raised as a consequence.

The Tabwa of southeastern Zaire live along the shores and upon the plateaus southwest of Lake Tanganyika. The vegetation of their area, in most places the distanced trees and high grass of *Brachystegia* woodland, does not obscure their view of the heavens (as might the canopy of denser forest). Yet Tabwa, like most other Central Africans, seem to have paid little attention to the stars (although cf. Roberts 1981). The swathes of comets, by contrast, intrigued many Tabwa as they have mankind everywhere over the years (see Lagercrantz 1964). Several turn-of-the-century accounts of comets as perceived by Tabwa exist in

---

The study of spectacular 19th-century comets, as perceived by the Tabwa of Zaire, provides an opportunity to consider the process of symbolization. Firsthand written accounts discovered in archives are complemented by present-day informants' exegeses. The comet was felt to augur—perhaps to cause—great misfortune. Its symbolism is one of transition and transformation; the prosopopoeic comet was made the subject of allegory, a story form in which multiplicity of interpretive levels allows narrators and audience to reflect upon social analogies of the "pristine volitility and freedom" and the "pure possibility" the apparition was taken to represent. The discussion leads to an understanding of why, as one very old man had it, the comet was Jesus bringing Europeans the astounding technology and other powers that allowed them to conquer and dominate the Tabwa with such ease. No single interpretation of great changes of Times and States suffices to capture them for the apprehension of all people at all times; so must the symbols marking the advent of transition and transformation be multireferential as the creative impulse is given play. [non-Western astronomy, symbolic analysis, religious change, cosmology, Tabwa, southeastern Zaire]

Copyright © 1982 by the American Ethnological Society
0094-0496/82/040712-18$2.30/1

missionary literature; more material was gleaned during four years of fieldwork among Lakeside Tabwa.

Some of the most spectacular comets known were visible to 19th-century Tabwa. The Sungrazer of 1843 (I) extended a third of the way across the sky and had two pronounced tails; Donati's Comet of 1858 had a bright nucleus and a scimitar tail; that of 1861 (II) stretched across two-thirds of the sky; Coggia's Comet of 1874 (III) was seen even in full moonlight; the Sungrazers of 1880 (I), 1882 (II), and 1887 (I) were especially brilliant.[2] These years also saw successive invasion of Tabwa lands by Ngoni raiders at mid-century, Swahili slaver/traders, Nyamwezi elephant hunters, and others who would vie for politico-economic advantage with resident Tabwa chiefs. First European travelers visited in the late 1860s (Livingstone) and 1870s (Cameron, Thomson, Stanley); and in the 1880s an outpost of the International African Association, soon ceded to Missionaries of Our Lady of Africa (White Fathers), was established among Tabwa at Mpala. Tabwa associated these epochal events with comets of the same years. The brilliance of the comets, to follow an image apt to both Tabwa and our own thinking, became that of the events so imported. Perhaps the opposite was also true and the "charged atmosphere" of the historical moment intensified the "brilliance" of the comets (Cassirer 1953:72; Daniel Moerman 1981:personal communication).

A problem of methodology arises as one seeks logical links between information that is scores of years old and that currently known to informants. Perils await he who may propose meanings for symbols without sufficient attention to "temporal embeddedness," or he who may assume symbolic association to be synonymous with "meaning"—a conundrum of no mean measure! The subject of comets as perceived by Tabwa is one of archaeoastronomy. Whereas the richness of the data leads the anthropologist to wish this were an all-too-rare opportunity to trace the transformations of a symbol over the course of the century that Tabwa have been in contact with literate observers (see Ohnuki-Tierney 1981:462), no truly spectacular comets have appeared since just after the turn of the century. Kohoutek let us down![3] "Songs and snatches" are all that are available for analysis, leaving conclusions drawn to be somewhat speculative. This not-so-very-distant past can be reconstructed through data from missionary diaries, letters, and reports; oral traditions as offered and explained by Tabwa today must be exploited as well, to gain a more complete understanding of what comets may have meant to earlier Tabwa.

Contemporary accounts of 19th-century comets discovered in Zairian archives were discussed with key Tabwa informants, several of whom offered exegetical detail of their own.[4] Most people did not recognize the term "comet" in their own language, or if they did, could give no more detailed explanation of what one is than one might expect of, say, Americans, if asked a similar question. No one contacted was able to provide a coherent account known to or accepted by all other Tabwa listening or later exposed to the thoughts. As a subject of archaeoastronomy, they were obliged to reconstruct what might have been meant, according to a logic *they* believe consistent with that of their ancestors. Their inability to reconstruct the "right" explanation with which everyone would agree is in part a function of being divorced from the actual events by nearly a century or more, in part one of a tendency among Tabwa loath to agree among themselves in conversation concerning *any* topic, so great is their enjoyment of controversy and debate. But if lack of consensus exists at one level, there is another level where ambiguity and paradox themselves have a place and where "edification by puzzlement" (Fernandez 1965:912; 1980; Stromberg 1981:544–545) is a vital part of the dynamic logic.

It is at this second level that ideas and associations stated by Tabwa informants (those of early writers and my own), while retaining their integrity through the course of our analysis, must be incorporated into a structure consonant with, but generally independent of and unavailable to, Tabwa thinkers (Lévi-Strauss 1963:217-218). This Tabwa cosmological structure has a high degree of coherency and is closely related to the cosmological structures of neighboring peoples (see Roberts 1980, 1981, in press a on the Tabwa; Heusch 1972 on the Luba; Willis 1972, 1981 on the Fipa).

Tabwa called 19th-century comets Kang'inaleza ("the little mother of God") or Kang'inalolo ("the little mother of chiefs"). The comet's name bears an obvious paradox: mothers are for Tabwa what they are for everyone—the essence of love and nurturance; yet *this* "little mother" portends death and disaster. In particular, when a comet appears it is felt that a great chief will perish. But with the death of one chief, another is "born" as a successor begins his own reign. The "little mother," I would suggest, foretells *transition* and *transformation*. It is associated with the period *between* states, rather than with the states themselves. It signals not the "child born" (the new chief, the new state of affairs), but the *bearing*.

Tabwa call an interregnum *kisama*. It is a time of elaborate confusion. My oxymoron is deliberate, for in *kisama,* even as those burying the chief kill, break, or seize for ransom all in their path, in their seeming chaos a " 'pregnant' moment" is created in which "whole series of occurrences are epitomized and phases of reality that are temporally widely separated ... connected and linked for historical conception and understanding" (Cassirer 1953:27-28). Turner's (1970:98) discussions of liminality prove apposite to its context, as *kisama* is, truly, a period of "primitive hypothesis," one of "pure possibility whence novel configurations of ideas and relations may arise," after which a new reign begins. The comet announces through its references to the unbounded the impending, sanctioned confusion of the interregnum. The comet as a symbol of separation and an agent of transformation shares features with what Hermann Usener has called a "momentary deity" (in Cassirer 1953:19).[5]

Usener's momentary diety is the first phase of an evolution of religious thought. The triggering is of "stark uniqueness and singleness" that "exists only here and now, in one indivisible moment of experience." It "overcomes a man in sheer immediacy, with emotions of fear or hope, terror or wish fulfillment: then the spark jumps somehow across, the tension finds release, as the subjective excitement becomes objectified, and confronts the mind as a god or a daemon." Yet there is a retention of the "pristine volatility and freedom" of the phenomenon (Cassirer 1953:33); made a symbol, its "paradoxical form expresses the inexpressible without betraying it' " (Heinz Politzer cited in Crossan 1976:250).

In most anthropological circles, it is unfashionable to consider the origin and evolution of religious concepts (although the same is done in the guise of studying "the symbolization process"). Following Durkheim (1966), 19th-century theories of animism and naturism propounded by Usener, Max Müller, and others have been dismissed from our discourse and indeed, from our knowledge. What for Usener might be a "momentary deity" is for Durkheim (1966:103) merely a "momentary variation" of the "regularity which approaches monotony" synonymous with nature. Producing only "equally momentary impressions," such "variations" could not "serve as a basis for these stable and permanent systems of ideas and practices which constitute religions." Certainly, most would agree with Durkheim (1966:103) that "we misunderstand what the religious sentiment really is, if we confound it with every impression of admiration and surprise"; few would be so naive as to assume that in speaking of comets or other ephemerae, we are assuming for them "a veritable creation *ex nihilo*" (1966:106). Yet, just as Durkheim (1966:42) finds that "the new is a part of nature just as well as its contrary," so can an examination of Tabwa perceptions of comets—which, by their accounts, burst upon the senses—hint at the nature and direction of *noticing* or "pointing," which must precede the function of denoting or naming (Cassirer 1953:29; Ohnuki-Tierney 1981:457).

While many (Westerners included) have been surprised by the apparition of unexpected comets (Brown 1974:81), comets do not "shoot" or otherwise move rapidly (as do meteors and bolides). Indeed, some comets have been seen for extended periods (e.g., Comet 1811 [I], visible in the Southern Hemisphere to the naked eye for about ten months; Chambers 1910:140). A comet's apparition, then, may be a singular and startling event, but it lingers; and in the 19th century, a series of spectacular comets must have allowed beliefs concerning them to be routinized.

To the double meaning of "the little mother" mentioned above is added another, since other events, although important, were *not* so presaged. While for Cassirer and Usener a momentary deity evolves into a generality (a special god, *Sondergötter*) associated with "some rustic activity" (Cassirer 1953:19; cf. Weber 1963 [1922]:10–19), comets are not common or predictable and so cannot invariably herald change, except, perhaps, in distant afterthought as time and event are collapsed. The very unpredictability of the comet in the natural realm is what makes it such a useful vehicle for contemplation through its ready analogy to events in the social one. Death is the predictably unpredictable foil of order, a surprise, yet one that happens to us all. The continuity of kinship is predicated upon the discontinuity of particular lives. The unpredictability of the comet leads to an easy analogy with the nature but also to the cause of death—often sorcery perpetrated by close kinsmen or neighbors with whom one has had lifelong relations of positive intimacy. If not one of Usener's "special gods," repeated (although astronomically different) comets *did* come to symbolize such capriciousness in social life, unexpected but inevitable.

Some of Usener's insight, however outmoded in its overall sweep, proves useful to our apprehension of the "sudden perception of an objective relation" that is metaphor (Herbert Read cited in Empson 1966:2), as the mind moves from noticing to denoting to connoting to assuming that the phenomenon in question imports some likely condition or outcome. This progression is similar to that most recently discussed by Ohnuki-Tierney (1981) as the "phases of symbolization" and is reminiscent of the much earlier distinction drawn by Mill (1956 [1843]) and Spencer 1976 [1866] between denotation (Ohnuki-Tierney's phases A-C) and connotation (phases D-F). Attempting to dissect the process of symbolization into its constituent parts (roughly following the progression of the subheadings of this paper) presents difficulties, given the historical nature of the data. Rather, the phases are condensed as presented in written sources or as known now, and the sense of wonder is mixed with these later, complex phases of symbolization, including causation. These texts might be considered analogous to the icons Ohnuki-Tierney discusses as the last phase of symbolization.

The following exegetical material captures the excitement of the event of apparition. It also allows an understanding of how useful the phenomenon was to prove to Tabwa—like us all—trying to understand through its analogy the nature of their own existence in a world of social as well as cosmic surprises.

the sanguine comet's baleful glare (Virgil)

At first glance, the various accounts seem confused, a jumble of images. "They saw with stupefaction something in the east which shone like the moon, but which was not the moon. The thing had a sort of head, luminous like the Morning Star, but much larger than this latter, for it was fat *(grosse)* like the moon, and [yet] it was not the moon" (Colle 1935:466).[6] One has the impression of a narrator groping for a proper image.

> This head scintillated and whirled, "one would have said [it was like] a 'pande' shell," (that is, a spiral). Firey flames were emitted all around it. She was round, had numerous, diversely-colored, parallel lines, one would say like the sun's rays. Her light was almost as bright as that of the sun, and on moonless nights, one could see as one can with a full moon.... Those who saw her compared her to the rainbow, but a rainbow white and red only, altogether unique in the sky, long and curved like the bow of a hunter; for under the spiral of fire, there descended a long curved tail.... On one side it had a little wing, and on the other side too, long like those of the nightjar, white on all sides [and] enveloped in mist *(fumée)* like the rain clouds. The plumes of fire resembled two trails of stars, which consumed themselves by burning like the sun (Colle 1935:466–467).[7]

The familiar phenomena—moon, sun, fire, and rain—are conjured, yet none quite suffices to capture the brilliance of the great comet. As a Tabwa friend told me, "It was like a bullet, people didn't know *what* it was"; that is, it "exploded" upon their senses. Rather than being a function of contradiction, "indecision, linguistic incompetence, or critical misapprehension," however, this account may be seen as an "obedient reflection of the multiplicity imaged in and by" the comet (Crossan 1976:274).

Such wealth of detail deserves scrutiny. The comet is like the moon and its "whirling" is evocative of the spiral of the conus shell disks, called *"pande"* or *mpande*. The two, moon and shell, are of a paradigm, as is most clearly shown in a set of Tabwa myths about the construction of a tower to reach the heavens, in which they are interchanged without altering the story structure (Roberts 1980:416–430). The *mpande* shell is a particularly important symbol, since, as I have suggested elsewhere (Roberts 1980:96–101), its flat spiral or concentric circles are a representation of the chief's descent, expanding outward from the emergence of the primal ancestor from a deep pool or hole in the ground (the center of the shell disk, often where a hole is practiced) to the limits of time and space imposed upon the Tabwa-centric universe (cf. Shorter 1972:104). There are other dimensions to the symbol as well.

At birth, every Tabwa is given a "belt," which is kept throughout life and inherited. The object may change and need not be a belt, although figuratively called that. To succeed someone is "to wear the belt" of that person. Life is eternal in that the "belt" is always inherited (except in the case of executed sorcerers; see Roberts in press a), but finite in that each individual is born and dies. Descent is a succession of "belts" over time, each generation encompassing that of all those preceding. The image that results, reproduced by the *mpande* shell disk as discerned by Tabwa observers, is of an expanding set of concentric circles ("belts") or a flat spiral.

With this in mind, it is not difficult to understand why there was equivocation in the comparison between the "head" of the comet and the conus disk by Colle's Tabwa informant. The shell is used to celebrate the continuity of a line of chiefs; in earlier days, only chiefs could possess or display them. As a lunar symbol and one evoking kinship and descent, it must be opposed to the comet that brings death and destruction and is called "the devourer of chiefs" (Colle 1935:466). Although a celebration of continuity, the shell is also a metonymic recognition of the discrete units of its composition: the lives of succeeding chiefs represented by the turn of its spiral. Paradoxically, for there to be continuation, there must be discontinuity. Life is posited upon the assumption of death. The comet, like an *mpande* shell, celebrates both succession (discontinuity) and kinship (continuity).

The comet was *like* these lunar referents, but was not limited to them. It was also sunlike in its brilliance and in the constancy with which it reappeared in the same place, night after night (Colle 1935:467; Kaoze 1909:43), a feature like the sun's own unchanging, repetitive nature (and opposed to the moon's varying phases and positions in the sky at nightfall).[8] Colle (1935:467) notes that many dared not look at the comet, as "it entered into their eyes, as does the sun he who stares at it." A praise for the Supreme Being known to Tabwa and neighboring Luba peoples, and equating God with sun, is "the sun at which one cannot stare" (Van Caeneghem 1956:53). The comet, then, would be of a set with both God and the sun.

An implicit relation, verbalized by a Tabwa informant, is that "a sorcerer is the sun, and the sun is God," an equation based on the belief that a sorcerer seeks God-like transcendence of cultural and natural laws, with effects on the community as devastating as those of an overstrong or uncontrolled sun on growing crops. The comet's apparition spells death (like a sorcerer's actions) and in some of its attributes it appears "solar," a refraction of an otiose deity that itself might be seen as "a unification of infinite diversities" (Deng 1973:50).

The comet is also compared to the rainbow. Both comets and the rainbow, for my informants, are red, and everything they fall upon is reddened, withers, and dies. Red is the color of shed blood, hence frequently metonymic for the transitions of violence and death. The rainbow both signals and "causes" the end of the rainy season; its power to dessicate makes it of a set with the sun, the advent of whose moment (the dry season) the rainbow ensures.

Colle's informants said the rainbow is red and white. These two colors are most often opposed, as are war and peace, death and life, famine and bounty; and so they do not appear together in many contexts. Where they do, one may expect this coexistence of itself to be significant. As Turner (1970:99) notes, the "coincidence of opposite processes and notions in a single representation characterizes the peculiar unity of the liminal: that which is neither this nor that, and yet is both." One context where both colors are found is on *mwamba* shrine objects, clay representations of the rainbow made as offerings to the afflicting spirit of that name. This dichromatism reflects the Tabwa perception of the rainbow as possessing both qualities, both members of the opposed pair: being both destructive and necessary to life, the rainbow is the two-way transformer between the states. As a symbol, the comet likewise foreshadows the impending liminality of interregnum or other transitions.

Such multiplicity of meanings for a single phenomenon is consonant with Kaoze's (1909:43) insistence that the great comets appear for seven days, or Colle's (1913, II:718) that the Sungrazer of 1843 (I) appeared for nine days every month for two successive years. A song about the comet ends in the refrain, "Ohee! She is invisible!" (Colle 1913, II:718). A body must be *present* to be invisible, a paradox recognized by Tabwa. If it may be assumed that "seven days" or "nine" are spans accurate in terms of meaning, if not necessarily in absolute chronology, then one may speculate that at issue here is the visibility of the comet, conditioned by concurrent phenomena. Specifically, all but the most spectacularly bright comets are invisible in competition with moonlight. Before moonrise, after moonset, and as moonlight wanes and ceases at the new moon, the comet "appears." In the last case it does so for a few days (perhaps "seven"), to disappear again until the next month's darkest nights. This suggests an opposition between the comet's and the moon's light.

Sun and moon may be opposed in Tabwa cosmological thought, as they are in that of neighboring people. The sun is continuity, lack of restraint, heat, dryness and the dry season, sterility, famine, and disease; the moon, by contrast, is periodic, measured, cool, wet and the rainy season, fertility, bounty, and health. Lunar heroes struggle with and often vanquish solar ones in myths, bringing to the universe order, cycles of succession, and, for neighboring Luba whose precolonial political organization was more complex than that of the Tabwa, the state (Heusch 1972; Reefe 1981). The essence of chiefship is grasped by Tabwa through a lunar metaphor. As sun and moon may be opposed in the cosmos, so may comet and chiefship.

Outside activities and travels are conducted in full moonlight, and in general, lunar phenomena are "beneficient" according to Tabwa thought. As the neighboring Luba have it, moonlight "illuminates" the Earth, the verb *kutokezya* being employed. This carries the sense "to whiten, to render clear, clean, cloudless, calm; to purify or make happy" (Theuws 1954:50). Lest one assume the symbolism to be univocal, a Tabwa proverb has it that "someone has been fooled by the moonlight" (Kaoze and Nagant 1973:756), reminding us of midsummer nights' dreams when the marvelous reigns. In general, though, a primary distinction is drawn between auspicious moonlight and the inauspiciousness of its lack.

Ndubilubi, the tenebrous two or three nights of the new moon, is a time of fear and wonder for Tabwa, when large numbers of fish and game may be seen that always seem to elude their stalkers. The prosopopoeic moon is an *ndozi* or sorcerer then, it is said, preventing man's success in the chase. Even as the moon is itself invisible during *ndubilubi* to all save those with the singular ken of the practitioner (hence another name for these days, *kamwonanganga* [the one seen by the practitioner]), it tantalizes Tabwa fishermen and hunters. Ferocious beasts and pernicious serpents, by contrast, pose a very tangible threat as they "wander about excessively" during *ndubilubi.* For those few days, the ophidian manifestations of Earth spirits—immense snakes that "sparkle like the stars"—descend from the mountain lairs where they have lain in peaceful repose, to afflict all imprudent passersby. That is, what "should" be seen (the moon itself and the sources of danger its light illuminates) is not; while that which "should not" (e.g., lions and serpents that can be avoided if seen under normal circumstances) is. The transitional quality—the liminality of the moment between light and darkness—is one of a set with other cultural and natural phenomena "betwixt and between," sorcery in the social setting being a prominent member. The striking brilliance of a comet at such an *ordinarily* inauspicious time of reversals must be a doubly baneful portent. Its disappearance as auspicious moonlight again illuminates the Earth proves an especially alarming analogy with sorcerers who may inhabit a same or adjacent household and whose nefarious side is masked by one of ordinary congeniality.

A descriptive association from Colle and other primary sources is between the streaming tail of the comet and the feathers of the nightjar. Old Kizumina sang for us in KiTabwa about the comets of the past: *kang'-inalolo wa kamwene pa kapili, kavwele mintetenga* ("You have seen Kang'inalolo on the hill, it is wearing streaming feathers").

Such feathers, it was explained, are like those of pennant-winged nightjars *(Macrodipterix vexillarius),* crepuscular birds that migrate southward to Central Africa, to breed there from September to November (Williams 1964:159; Reynolds 1980:26). This time, in turn, is marked by *kansensebwa,* a wind blowing from the north only then, which brings the first rains. It may be said that the arrival of the nightjars, their breeding, and their being most evident at twilight (the limen between light and dark), coincides with or "brings" the transition to the rains of October. That the comet's "feathers" should be "enveloped in mist like the rain clouds" bespeaks this relationship. Yet, in the sentence following, the same are called "plumes of fire . . . which consumed themselves by burning like the sun." Is this mixed imagery of rain and sun as confused as it may appear?

A return to Tabwa ideas concerning the rainbow provides an answer. It is said that the rainbow dries or "burns" the rains of late spring and thus ushers in the dry season. Tabwa believe the rainbow to be the breath of an immense serpent emitted from the ground, through holes in parched forest clearings or those of termitaries. The serpent is mentioned in another context: the bushfires set late in the dry season to clear the land of debris and to aid in hunting in vacant fields and mountains. Medicines are put in the woods at a place thus destined to become the center of the holocaust; fires are set that, once caught by the four cardinal winds, are brought to a center—that of the medicines. Animals are forced to congregate there as the pyrrhic circle closes. As they perish, the swirling column of smoke is Nfwimina (the great serpent) standing on its tail. The smoke of such fires is deemed to bring the first rains. In other words, Nfwimina terminates the rains with its multicolored breath (the rainbow) and then ensures their return at the end of the opposite term (the dry season). Again, the rainbow is a transformative agent of dual "valence."

A final point reinforces the comet's association with the rainbow. At dawn, the comet "vanished" *(s'évanouir)* like a wisp *(fumée)*" (Colle 1935:467). In this, it is like the rainbow, said to be ethereal, like *funta* (the fog of the rainy season) or *lunsilila* (the haze of the dry). With such phenomena, if one sees them before himself and then goes to that place, he will find nothing there; so it is with the rainbow. Many told us of having tried to reach the place where they saw the rainbow descending, only to find it forever before them, as if in retreat. The comet was an intangible; yet it, like the rainbow, was a sign of transition that could not be ignored.

brandish your crystal tresses to the sky (Shakespeare): the comet personified

There is a second set of images in these same accounts. Not only did the comet have a "head," as above; it "undoubtedly had eyes and ears, but because of the distance, we didn't see them." Furthermore, it had

> the appearance of a human, a body, a chest [and] arms, all which scintillated. She had no legs, for she seemed to emerge from a hole twisting about from the waist, and was the size of a child.... In the middle of her chest she was whiter than the whitest cloth.... Our fathers called this brilliant thing "little mother, girl," for she did not vary, every day she was the same, without *aging*, always beautiful, always radiant *(plein d'éclat),* surpassing the splendor of all the stars (Colle 1935:466–467).

In this last regard, Schmitz (1903:316) wrote that a longer name for the comet is Kang'inaleza Kansimwonamitenge. He translated the second word as "the one who has not been inside the house of men," offered that this refers to the belief that the comet is a "virgin," and compared "her" to Mary. Kaoze (1909:41), too, noted that the comet is "like a youngster, because it was truly beautiful."

That the "virgin" is not a whole person, but one visible from the waist up, may be explained by the tail of the comet extending below the horizon, "into the Earth." This division (or transition) is more significant a trait than such a matter-of-fact explanation might denote, however. In two myths dealing with the origin of death, the opposition of states is contained in or made manifest by the same person (Colle 1913, II:522–523, 519). In both, an aged woman, the senior wife of Kyomba (the first named man), seeks rejuvenation. In strict seclusion, she begins to remove her old skin to reveal a new one, "fresh as that of a baby," as one account has it; in the other, she became "a beautiful, totally-white girl, *toute fraîche,* one would say she had just been born" (Colle 1913, II:523, 519). The comparison with the lovely, never-aging childlike Kang'inalolo, whose "chest... was whiter than the whitest cloth," is unmistakable. The metamorphosis of the old woman is interrupted, however, by bumptious second wives. In the one story, the old woman has yet to remove the skin from her head and is thus divided between old and new; her demise results from this incompleteness. Both the woman seeking transformation and the one interrupting the process are striken, and death is introduced to the human condition thereafter.

The comparison between the aged woman seeking rejuvenation through the removal of her skin, and the manner in which snakes are thought to do this, is made manifest by other

Tabwa myths in which a serpent receives immortality from God *(Institut Apostolique* 1882:27). Immortality, in turn, is one trait of a set with other linear, uncontained, unrestrained members personified by the rainbow-breathing solar serpent, Nfwimina.

The *kizimba* (activating agent; Richards 1969) of Nfwimina may be employed in potent medicines by Tabwa practitioners and specifically in "stopping the sun" *(kusimika jua)*. This is effected to prevent rain and bring the sun to remain stationary at its zenith, that it may cause an enemy's fields to wither. Such is blatant sorcery. Given the difficulty of obtaining such a rare substance through combat with Nfwimina itself, a transformation is sought. One possible source is in the execution of a *musala:* an amenorrheal woman, referred to as a "woman-man" because of this. Luba-ized Tabwa describe the rainbow as the union of two opposite-sexed serpents (Colle 1913, I:353), which, as both male and female, is neither one nor the other, but oddly both. So is the *musala,* and it is she who makes the strongest *nkula,* the crimson powder of *Pterocarpus* bark used to signify violent intent (Roberts 1980:233–257).[9] The *musala* and the old woman seeking immortality are closely linked. Furthermore, the contradictions that each embodies are like those of the comet, half-emerged from a "hole," whose exposed head and torso are opposed to her unavailable loins.

This opposition, in turn, allows consideration of an issue raised in Willis's (1972; 1981:189–191) studies of the Fipa. The Fipa live directly across Lake Tanganyika from the Tabwa, and my Tabwa informants agree with Willis's Fipa ones that Fipa commoners are Tabwa immigrants (Willis 1964:342), long separated. In discussing Fipa notions of sovereignty and descent, Willis has discerned an important pair of opposed, "dominant symbols," which he terms "head" and "loins" respectively.[10] Of a paradigm with "head," he finds the Twa lineage of chiefs (who do *not* trace their ancestry to Tabwa), authority, seniority, masculinity, intellect, patrilateral kin; and at the most abstract level, becoming, contingency, and change. "Loins" is of a set with the Milansi commoners (the distant Tabwa relatives), submission, "juniority," feminity, sexuality, reproduction, maternity, matriliny; and abstractly, being, transcendence, and continuity (Willis 1972:316, 318). This structure is common to Fipa and Tabwa thought and is closely related to that of Luba as well (see Heusch 1972:53–56 on the personified rainbow's severed head). "The little mother of chiefs," the comet, is only the first member of this opposition, however, hence quintessential "head." Just as the division of the old woman seeking rejuvenation spelled her doom, so must any occasion when only half of the head/loins opposition is present (and particularly only the former, with its references to hunting, warfare, and authority without subjects, among other things).

That this imbalance should be so fraught with danger is even clearer from other ethnographic detail. Schmitz (1903) wrote that the "beautiful child" (the comet) was a "virgin." The name he cites contains more information than Schmitz reveals. In typical Bantu fashion, Kansimwonamitenge is a collection of word particles (*ka-* [little], *-si-* [not], *-mw-* [third person personal pronoun], *-ona-* [to see]). The final *-mitenge-* may refer to "roofs" (Van Acker 1907:67), but probably refers more specifically to the temple of the same name of the defunct Butwa society, an organization once widespread throughout Tabwa and societies adjacent to the south. Some authors have reported that within the dark, windowless recesses of the *lutenge,* all manner of sexual excess took place. Others qualify this, noting that "the essential goal of Butwa is the initiation to puberty" and "teaching and accustoming the young to their relations with the opposite sex" (Brelsford 1974:30; Colle 1912:195; Gouldsbury and Sheane 1911:260). I have suggested elsewhere (Roberts 1980) that the design of the secret hut of the myth mentioned above, to which the old woman repairs seeking rejuvenation, is of a paradigm with the *lutenge*. Death originates at the center of the former, replaced by sexual license in the latter. Kang'inalolo, the prosopopoeic comet, "has not seen the [inside of] Butwa temples," and so Schmitz might conclude "she" is a virgin. But in her second name there is implicit reference to sex and violence.

This recognition is important to understanding a taunt in which the comet is evoked. "Unmarried girl so spruced up and proud, have you seen Kang'inaleza? We have seen her on the hill, surrounded by her friends." Colle explains that the "friends" (masimba) are the rays or tail of the comet. Alphonse Kiwele, an early Tabwa cleric, explained to Father Colle that when a young person who had dressed for a dance swaggered or sashayed (dandiner) through the village, the elders would call this out. Colle (1935:466) adds (as if this were a conclusion) that "Kang'inaleza is all that is the most beautiful" (see also Van Acker 1907:49).[11] Such is true, and the older people are making a comparison between the young person and one more attractive still. But the comet presages great misfortune, and their irony is directed at the less salubrious consequences of pride, vanity, and egotism. The Tabwa myth of the chief who would seize the moon by building a tower to the heavens is a more explicit tale (although one of opposite sexual symbolism, some might say) in which these qualities are given physical representation; the tower crumbles, bringing death to the hubristic.

Kang'inalolo has a divided self. The exposed portion of her body is so "white," so beautiful, that she is called a "virgin"—one nubile, one desired. Her loins are hidden, though, and so such emotions are fatuous. Instead, through her relation to the rainbow, the immediate message she brings is one of sterility and impending disaster.

some say that thou dost never fail to bring some mischief in thy tail (Lattey)

This explains something of what Kang'inalolo *is*. We may now examine what Tabwa say or have said "she" imports and what measures man may take in response.

Above all, 19th-century (and earlier?) comets are remembered for the chiefs said to have died soon after their appearances. The comet is called Kang'inalolo, "the little mother of chiefs." *Kilolo* (chief)[12] is probably derived from the verb *-lola* (to be awake, to see, to lead to, to mean; Van Acker 1907:45; White Fathers 1954:354). Sight, perception, and meaning, then, are personified in the chief, *kilolo*. There may be a pun in this name for the comet, however, for a derivative verb, *-lolesha*, means "to covet" (or look at something overintently, with envy or unseemly attention), and *lolo*, a noun, is "a confirmed thief" (White Fathers 1954:355)—that is, one who not only covets, but *takes*. The comet, Kang'inalolo, may be the "little mother of chiefs" or the "little mother/thief," one who "steals" lives. This adds to the pregnancy of the paradox and is similar to the chief's own dual nature as "father of his people" and the greatest sorcerer in the land.

According to Colle (1935:467), another name for the comet is Kapata Makolo, which he translated as "the destroyer of chiefs." His gloss is inadequate. *Makolo* are indeed "chiefs," a term derived from the sense of the verb *-kola* as "a scraping together" of subjects. *-Kola* also refers to intoxication, poisoning, or severe coughing ("scraping out" the throat) and provides the root for the name of the rainbow, *mukola mvula*. This latter not only "scrapes away the rain" (*mvula*; White Fathers 1954:263), and thus causes it to cease according to Tabwa, but is associated with all manner of disease and disaster, as above (cf. Heusch 1972). This, like Kang'in'alolo, is a multidimensional name, then.

The other word in the same name, *kapata*, is only figuratively "to destroy," as Colle would have it. *Kupata*, the verb, is "to stick in the throat," as may a bone or food, a meaning it has in Kiluba and CiBemba as well. In the latter languages, it can be "to have bad luck" (as one does who chokes!), but also "to have difficulty in talking due to a thick tongue" (from stroke?), hence "to be muddled" as well as "to be susceptible to all kinds of disease" (Van Acker 1907:52; Van Avermaet and Mbuya 1954:502-504; White Fathers 1954:593). The pun inherent in the word *makolo* is thus reinforced: coughing on the one hand, choking on the other. The data allow no clear explanation of this name as a whole, although some speculation is possible.

Tabwa and Luba preserved relics—generally the skulls—of their antecedents. Verbeke (1937) has written that for Luba, only the crania of chiefs dying violently would be kept in this way; if the man died peacefully, his skull would be replaced by the skull of one of his brothers ritually executed for the purpose. Red *nkula* powder would be employed to stuff the nose and throat of the victim, that he might suffocate (Verbeke 1937:54; cf. Verhulpen 1936:94). Heusch (1972:42-46) is correct in suggesting that the use of *nkula* here evokes Nkongolo Mwamba, the primal Luba monarch and personified rainbow. The same relation exists in Tabwa thought between the substance and Nfwimina, the rainbow-breathing serpent, as mediated by the *musala* (woman-man) who grinds the bark into powder. Here it is as though the sacrificial victim, associated with the moon and rains through his chiefship (in ways outlined by Heusch), were being forced to ingest the rainbow itself, in its surrogate substance. The "rainbow" ends the "rains" as the chief's substitute succumbs. Might not the verb *kupata* in KiLuba refer to this? That the *dipata* is the seat of Luba chiefship (at least for the Luba Samba), where the baskets containing these same relics are kept (Van Avermaet and Mbuya 1954:501), would suggest such an important association. By this reasoning, the comet's name or praise, Kapata Makolo, might be better translated as "the stifler of chiefs."

To be stifled is ultimately to perish; but to a less extreme degree, it is to be *silenced*. The chief was "speechless" before the apparition of the comet and would hide in his house at night to avoid looking at its brilliant, perilous light (Colle 1935:467). The play between speech and light is one of great importance to Tabwa thinking, for it is believed that at death one's speech *becomes* light.

Consider two Tabwa proverbs. "The chief is his people" *(sultani ni watu)* is a commonly made statement of the leader's identification with those dependent upon him. "The chief is the belt which preserves the people of the public place" (Kaoze and Nagant 1973:757) requires more explanation. *Nsaka* (the public place) is derived from the verb *kusaka* in KiTabwa, meaning to surround a cultivated field or other place with a thorn hedge or ditching, to protect it from animals or other intruders. *Nsaka* (or *lusako*) itself may refer to the hedge or other device, or more figuratively to the space enclosed (Van Acker 1907:56-57; White Fathers 1954:547). *Nsaka* may also be the meeting ground before the chief's residence. In explaining the term, informants pointed to the place's use in the evenings, when young people assemble to hear stories told by the elders, the chief predominant among them. A fire is lit and all sit within its glow. *Kizingo* (belt), in the same proverb, has among its meanings "circle," and in this case one may guess it to be that of light thrown by the fire lit for the event. The meeting ground is bounded, as one would expect an *nsaka* to be, given its other meanings, only by the firelight. Definition is from the center to the periphery, as opposed to other *nsakas* that are surrounded.

Those who congregate in the *nsaka* do so for the transmission of knowledge. The center of attention is the speaker, the chief who "is" the heritage he conveys, just as he "is" his people. Speech and light combine in the *nsaka*. Kaoze does not translate *kizingo* as "circle," however, but chooses the more specific referent "belt." Earlier, the "belt" was discussed in terms of Tabwa descent; it is metonymic for a human lifetime, encompassing an individual's time on Earth from birth, when it is received, until death, when given to an heir. Here the "belt" refers to the firelight before the chief's residence. A chief's "belt" encircles not only his own life, but those of his subjects with whom he is identified. The stories told around the fire are the wisdom of his time. The chief's "belt" is his reign: it is those who lived when he did, and what they knew and did.

Kaoze (1909:93) offers an unexplained, tantalizing datum: when the comet appeared, a fire would be lit in the *nsaka*. As an omen (or "cause") of the chief's demise, the comet must be opposed in some manner, that its baneful nature be held in check. The terrestrial and wordly light of the chief is to counteract that of the heavens, that the chief's words *not* become light through his death. Reference to quintessential "loins" (the "belt," continuity, kinship, life, and fertility) is made to oppose the "severed head" of the comet. In saving the chief, the people save themselves, as they conceive of their social life in his person.

The above is of accord with the notion that the comet is like a rainbow. The redness and transformative power of the one is as lethal as that of the other. Tabwa chiefship, like Luba, is endowed with and understood through lunar symbolism and is opposed to the rainbow and the solar serpent producing it. The death and burial of Tabwa chiefs was, in earlier days, performed in an idiom of the seasons; the wet-season hero, the chief who has protected and ensured the fecundity and well-being of his people, was buried by "grandchildren" acting as heroes of the dry season. The skull of the chief would be preserved while the rest of the corpse was buried in a grave under or beside a water body or course. This division, head/body, was, at least sometimes, augured by and in the comet's disjointed appearance, as was the momentary victory of solar principles over lunar ones.

The lethal breath of the solar serpent Nfwimina is displayed as the rainbow, and it reddens, dries, and exterminates all upon which it falls. The time most associated with the rainbow, when rains are still heavy but on the wane, is one of *kimina* or pestilence, smallpox, and malaria. Should a woman carelessly leave her cooking pots upside-down on the ground then, Nfwimina's breath will contaminate them and her family will suddenly die. Measles and coughs may afflict youngsters, again as products of Nfwimina's breath. Given the relation drawn between the rainbow and the comet (one of whose names contains references to severe coughing, choking, strokes [?], and susceptibility to disease), little wonder is it that the appearance of the comet, too, is said to have heralded epidemics of smallpox and cholera (cf. Langercrantz 1964:322). Again, the relation posited between rainbow (that "dries" so severely) and comet is consonant with the Tabwa observation that the comet announced (or "brought") famine. More figuratively, referring to the Tabwa song of Kang'inalolo sung to a vain young woman, a further verse ironically asks the "little mother" what one will eat at her home and concludes "I weep, I weep like a slave, as at their home, if one says 'we eat well here,' they will laugh" (Colle 1913, II:718; my translation from the KiTabwa). Vanity may be associated with sterility, as above, and is of a set with the disregard of household responsibilities devised to ensure the maintenance of a family and to avoid starvation (especially of nurslings).

Finally, having said something of the transformative nature of the rainbow (stopping and returning the rains), we can make sense of Schmitz's assertion that people believed the comet to bring both grief and riches. Nfwimina is also called "the mother of wealth" by Tabwa and is associated with the gold and other resources the colonists exploited in Tabwa territory. The inverse is the comet's own attractiveness, at once captivating and perilous. A derivative noun, *makola,* from the same root as are names for the rainbow *(mukola mvula)* and the comet *(kapata makolo),* can mean "beauty" in KiTabwa (Van Acker 1907:37), underscoring this relationship. Life is not, and never has been, easy for Tabwa. Those too weak to farm, fish, and otherwise "keep their end up," may perish. Those who prove remarkably successful, who become "wealthy" and above, hence outside, the norm, are strongly suspected of sorcery.

If for the Tabwa, speech (viz., verbal communication) becomes light at an individual's death, then *this* great light, the comet, is communication inverted, muffled, or muddled.

Rather than uniting men, it divides them through the discontinuity of death. Death is not absolute separation for Tabwa, but a change of state. A new sort of communication is possible and necessary between the spirit and its survivors, initiated by the former through affliction, recognized and made comprehensible by the latter through dreams, possession ceremonies, and divination (see Davis-Roberts 1980; Nagant 1976). While announcing the *discontinuity* of death, then, the comet presages the continuity to be established with the new spirit.

farewell, dear comet, rainbow of my soul (Molière)

Our discussion of Tabwa cometary lore is not quite complete. Kapata makolo, "the stifler of chiefs," was a name for a comet as above. It is also a term for "pistol," according to the KiTabwa/French dictionary of Van Acker (1907:52). My own informants used a related image, comet as "bullet," but there are important historical dimensions outstanding. More than any other "technogen," the pistol or gun must symbolize the momentous change in Tabwa life and culture effected by 19th-century intrusives, both African and European (see Headrick 1981). Specifically, a particularly well known tale concerns the establishment of European presence and power with the collision of two great egos, those of Tabwa chief Lusinga and the International African Association expedition leader Emile Storms, who created an outpost at Mpala in 1883 (very shortly after the spectacular Sungrazer Comet of 1882 [I], a "truly remarkable event for all the niggers of Tanganyika"; Vyncke 1887). Lusinga was intrigued by Storms's brace of pistols and wished to obtain these and other firearms to pursue his slaving. Storms reacted to his belligerent demands by having him assassinated and decapitated. This latter act (with Lusinga's skull sent to Belgium for study by anthropologists!) ironically recapitulated the ordinary division of head and body practiced at a Tabwa chief's death. Rather than the skull being preserved and venerated by a successor, however, thus underscoring the perpetuity of the line, the skull was lost to the conqueror, the ascendant power.

Kizumina, whose elder brother witnessed the above drama, offered another story about the comet. This—our last here—demonstrates the manner in which a symbol of discontinuity, one that foretells separation, is especially apt as the vehicle for allegorical parable.

Kang'inalolo appeared before he was born, Kizumina told us, but the elders *(wakubwa)* explained that it fell in Europe and was Bwana Yesu, Jesus Christ. They in Africa had seen it climbing skyward and had called it Kang'inalolo; but in Europe people said it was Jesus arisen from the dead and going to Heaven *(alifufuka, alikwenda binguni)*. Jesus did not come to where the Tabwa live. Had he done so, he would have brought them knowledge of Europeanness *(maarifa ya kizungu)*. He did not, though, and so the Tabwa have been overlooked, left behind *(tumechelewa)*.

Kizumina, dead in 1978 at about 100 years of age, had a long history as an irascible opponent of the missionaries and their alteration and/or destruction of Tabwa culture as he understood it. In other words, this is a tale of a believer, not of Christianity as a devout church-goer (he was never baptised), but as one who knew the oppressive profundity of change occasioned by those implementing Christian/colonial beliefs in the various arenas of social life, economic and political as well as religious (see Roberts 1979, 1982, in press b). Kizumina knew the "change of Times and States" as intimately as any (his lineage being denied the chiefship since colonial times). The comet was the vehicle by which this transformation was imported and, in a sense, caused. The possibility for syncretism between the great star at Christ's birth, Biblical images of Christ's resurrection and ascension, and the comet are obvious enough; but the comet is not just what it might appear objectively: it is Kapata Makolo, "the stifler of chiefs." Kizumina's tale, I would suggest, is an "allegorical parable" and retains paradox at its heart, multiplicity of meaning as its message (Crossan 1976:277).

Kizumina's tale is a pointedly political one, given our knowledge of the radical reduction of prerogative suffered by indigenous chiefs during the years of colonization (and more specifically that experienced by Chief Mpala, Kizumina's own close kinsman) and our understanding of the symbolism ascribed to the comet. Chiefship itself, as it had evolved and was known before the European occupation, was stifled by the new power, in the present case wielded by the White Fathers. From their fortified mission at Mpala, they would dominate all overt aspects of social life from 1885 until around 1970, when expatriot priests withdrew and many church-related activities were suspended (see Roberts 1982).

The idiom of the comet, informed by implicit reference to the rainbow, Nfwimina, the *musala,* and the other transformative agents discussed here, contains much more information than Kizumina's brief tale would seem to yield. This great transition from traditional to colonial society, and its attendant reformulation of culture, is placed in a set of comprehensible members. The twist is that whereas comets for Tabwa were portentious and followed by all manner of disaster, here the comet is not, or is not only, Kang'inaleza, it is Jesus Christ, bearer of "the knowledge of Europeanness" (the economic and political status recognized as superior by Tabwa) to those among whom he "fell." Nonetheless negative to Tabwa, the comet is supremely *positive* for colonizing Europeans. Judging from other stories of the sort,[13] this is a relation of indirect proportion in a world in which all forces are in some ultimate balance: that is, as Tabwa fortunes and independence have declined, so have European ones risen. This, then, would be the greatest "change of Time and State" of the century known to Kizumina.

conclusion

Nineteenth-century comets as perceived by Tabwa provide us with an opportunity to reflect on the symbolization process more generally, with the caveat that the paucity and condensation of available accounts make the choice of data for "earlier" phases ("noticing" the "momentary deity"), as opposed to "later" ones (the connotation of comet as portentious), somewhat arbitrary. More useful is the recognition that ambiguity—"a phenomenon of compression" (Empson 1966:31)—is inherent to the event of a comet's apparition, as first understood and then considered an agent of transformation.

The comet has proven useful to Tabwa as they reflect upon the epochal years before and just after the turn of the century. Just as no single interpretation, no single sweeping statement, is sufficient to sum up the effects of an event such as the death of a great chief or the advent of the Europeans, so must the omens and symbols heralding and marking the moment be multireferential in nature. The apparition of a comet, marked by the "sheer immediacy," "pristine volatility and freedom" of a "momentary deity," by its liminal nature allows for, indeed demands, a recognition of the "pure possibility" of many levels of interpretation, from psychological to sociological to philosophical to theological, all of which make sense unto themselves and each of which adds to the sense of all others. The momentary deity then becomes an apt subject or vehicle for allegory, a form "whose plurality of interpretive levels indicates that the original is itself a metaphor for that multiplicity" (Crossan 1976:273-277). The paradox of the comet captured the fact that the surprising, the unclear, the inchoate in *social* life can be grasped by reference to a singular, if ephemeral, phenomenon in nature.

notes

Acknowledgments. Anthropological fieldwork conducted in southeastern Zaire from late 1973 until late 1977 was funded by the National Institute of Mental Health (# 1-F01-MH-55251-01-CUAN), the Committee on African Studies and the Edson-Keith Fund of the University of Chicago, and the Society of the Sigma Xi. Sincere thanks are extended to Jane Bachnik, John Comaroff, Lawrence Fisher, Keith Hart, Kalunga Mwela-Ubi, Don Merten, Daniel Moerman, Genevieve Nagant, Randall Packard, Jonathan Post, Christopher Davis Roberts, and Roy Willis for helpful comments as this paper has developed; and to Tabwa friends "Nzwiba," Mumba, "Mumbioto," and the late Kizumina Kabulo for their insight and information. I am indebted to Professor Emeritus Freeman Miller for lively discussions of the aspects and visibility of 19th-century comets in southeastern Zaire; to Dr. Tobin Siebers for reminding me of Cassirer's discussion of Usener's "momentary deity"; and to Dr. Donald Pitkin for introducing Cassirer's discussion to me years ago. All responsibility for the present work remains my own, despite such generosity. In memory of Clarissa and Allen Parrette.

[1] The reference is from the Platonic dialogue *Phaedrus,* in which Socrates tells a young admirer that as the Delphic precept has it, he must know himself and not concern himself with such "extraneous matters" as "gorgons, pegasuses and countless other strange monsters" (in Cassirer 1953:1). The quotation in this paper's title is from Shakespeare's *Henry VI,* part 1.

[2] Among the many works devoted to comets, Chambers's (1910) and Brown's (1973) are useful for the novice, while Vsekhvyatskii's (1964) monumental study remains the specialist's "bible."

[3] As Dan Moerman (1981: private communication) has noted, Comet Kohoutek of late 1973 did nothing of the sort: "What let us down was a philosophy of nature based on mechanism and extrapolation which went seriously awry, or, perhaps, is always seriously awry." Even had Kohoutek been as spectacular as expected, younger Tabwa separated by generations from past comets might have postulated different sorts of associations with its apparition than did their ancestors; one is reminded of Gombrich's examples of locusts or lions "drawn from life" by artists centuries ago, having forms radically different from the way Western artists would represent them nowadays (cited and discussed in Ohnuki-Tierney 1981:456–457). It is likely that people would have consulted the same established sages that I did, and general conclusions might have been consonant with older ideas as exposed here.

[4] Three men and a woman with whom C. D. Roberts and I worked closely for several years provided greatest input concerning comets. True intellectuals interested in the world around them and in their cultural heritage, three of the four are renowned diviner-healers, the other (now deceased) a traditional political leader and "man of memory," as Reefe (1981) would say.

[5] Cassirer develops these ideas from Usener's (1896) *Divine Names: An Essay Toward a Science of Religious Conception,* as he discusses the relation between myth and language.

[6] Colle (1913) is most famous for his writings on the eastern Luba-ized Tabwa, whom he calls "Baluba"; here he presents exegesis from the central lakeside Tabwa, gathered around Baudouinville (Moba) at the turn of the century. Colle's and Kaoze's accounts share many phrases, suggesting a common inspiration.

[7] The gender of the pronouns here is feminine in Colle's French, because the comet is called "little mother"; pronouns show no gender in Swahili or in KiTabwa.

[8] The appearance of the comet must change in time and aspect, as it follows its orbit and the Earth its own. That a comet is often first seen as it begins to rise at dusk or set at dawn, its tail extending "upwards" from where the sun has gone or will reappear, further underscores the comet's solar associations.

[9] *Pterocarpus* wood is burned on moonless nights, since its resins make an especially bright fire. In this, it is like the comet which allows one "to see as one can with a full moon" (as in Colle 1935:467). It might be said that the *nkula* powder the *musala* amenorrheal woman grinds from *Pterocarpus* bark replaces the menses (called "the little dry season" by Tabwa) she never sees.

[10] "Loins" is an ambiguous word in English, referring to the area between ribs and pelvis, "the region of the thighs and groin," or "the reproductive organs" (Morris 1969:767). *Unnsana* (loins) in KiFipa is "the lower abdomen and lower back in both men and women" and includes the genitalia of both sexes (Willis 1972:316; 1981: personal communication); it is, then, as ambiguous as our own word "loins." Rather than a reference to the sexual organs, however, from the Tabwa case it is suggested that the "loins" in question is the area of the waist (lower abdomen and lower back) encircled by one's *belt.* The descent reference, then, would be that of the navel/umbilicus and not the sexual organs. The Fipa used a belt (*unnkowa*—a word one would suspect to be related to the KiTabwa *mukowa* for "clan") trimmed with lion skin—"a symbol of kingship"—"metonymically to represent achieved rank in the indigenous administrative structure" (Willis 1981: personal communication), which would seem to underscore this association.

[11] In his earlier work, Colle (1913, II:717–718) recorded a Tabwa song, the three verses of which include both this line and the one Kizumina sang for us in 1976, cited above.

[12] This term once may have referred more specifically to a chief's subordinate or replacement (see Van Acker 1907:45; cf. White Fathers 1954:102 and Van Avermaet and Mbuya 1954:360). KiTabwa shares a "basic language correspondence" of 90 percent with CiBemba and one of 71 percent with KiLuba (Werner 1971:10; Reefe 1981:73-78), allowing some confidence in this sort of etymological speculation.

[13] A paper in preparation, tentatively entitled " 'Sinister Caricatures': The Anthropophagic Other for Europeans and Africans in the Belgian Congo," addresses issues of the kind. The strength of one group, be it European *or* African, was felt to be sapped, literally consumed, by the other.

references cited

Brelsford, Vernon
   1974   African Dances of Northern Rhodesia. *In* The Occasional Papers of the Rhodes-Livingstone Institute, 1-16. No. 2. Manchester: Manchester University Press.
Brown, Lancaster
   1974   Comets, Meteorites and Men. New York: Taplinger.
Cassirer, Ernst
   1953   Language and Myth. Suzanne Langer, transl. New York: Dover.
Chambers, George
   1910   Story of the Comets Simply Told for General Readers. London: Oxford University Press.
Colle, Pierre
   1912   Le Butwa (Société Secrète Nègre). La Revue Congolaise 3:195-199.
   1913   Les Baluba. 2 vols. Brussels: Albert Dewit.
   1935   Apropos d'Apparitions. Grands Lacs 51(10):466-468.
Crossan, John
   1976   Parable, Allegory and Paradox. *In* Semiology and Parables: Explorations of the Possibilities Offered by Structuralism for Exegesis. Daniel Patte, ed. pp. 247-281. Pittsburgh: Pickwick.
Davis-Roberts, Christopher
   1980   *Mungu na Mitishamba:* Illness and Medicine among the BaTabwa of Zaire. Ph.D. dissertation. Department of Anthropology. University of Chicago.
Deng, Francis
   1973   The Dinka and Their Songs. London: Oxford University Press.
Durkheim, Emile
   1966   The Elementary Forms of the Religious Life. New York: Free Press.
Empson, William
   1966   Seven Types of Ambiguity. New York: New Directions.
Fernandez, James
   1965   Symbolic Consensus in a Fang Reformative Cult. American Anthropologist 67:902-929.
   1980   Edification by Puzzlement. *In* Explorations in African Systems of Thought. Ivan Karp and Charles Bird, eds. pp. 44-59. Bloomington: Indiana University Press.
Gouldsbury, C., and H. Sheane
   1911   The Great Plateau of Northern Rhodesia. London: Edward Arnold.
Headrick, Daniel
   1981   The Tools of Empire: Technology and European Imperialism in the 19th Century. New York: Oxford University Press.
Heusch, Luc de
   1972   Le Roi Ivre, ou l'Origine de l'Etat. Paris: Gallimard.
Institut Apostolique Africain des Pères Blancs
   1882   Près du Tanganika par les Missionnaires de Son Eminence le Cardinal Lavigerie. Anvers: H. Majoor.
Kaoze, Stefano
   1909   Manuel Kitabwa à l'Usage des Missionnaires. Algiers: Maison Carrée.
Kaoze, Stefano, and Genevieve Nagant
   1973   Proverbs Tabwa. Cahiers d'Etudes Africaines 52, XIII (4):744-768.
Lagercrantz, Sture
   1964   Traditional Beliefs in Africa Concerning Meteors, Comets and Shooting Stars. *In* Festschrift fur Ad. E. Jensen. Tome 1, pp. 319-329. Munich: Klans Renner Verlag.
Lévi-Strauss, Claude
   1963   Structural Anthropology. New York: Basic Books.
Mill, John Stuart
   1956[1843]   A System of Logic. London: Longmans, Green.
Morris, William, ed.
   1969   American Heritage Dictionary of the English Language. New York: Houghton Mifflin.

Nagant, Genevieve
   1976   Famille, Histoire, Religion Chez les Tumbwe du Zaire. Thèse du Troisième Cycle. Department of Anthropology, Ecole Pratique des Hautes Etudes.
Ohnuki-Tierney, Emiko
   1980   Phases of Human Perception/Conception/Symbolization Processes: Cognitive Anthropology and Symbolic Classification. American Ethnologist 8:451-467.
Richards, Audrey
   1969   Land, Labour and Diet in Northern Rhodesia. London: Oxford University Press.
Reefe, Thomas
   1981   The Rainbow and the Kings: A History of the Luba Empire to 1891. Berkeley: University of California Press.
Reynolds, John
   1980   Nightjars, Experts at Camouflage. Swara 3(1):25-27.
Roberts, Allen F.
   1979   "The Ransom of Ill-Starred Zaire": Plunder, Politics and Poverty in the OTRAG Concession. In Zaire: The Political Economy of Underdevelopment. Guy Gran, ed. pp. 211-236. New York: Praeger.
   1980   Heroic Beasts, Beastly Heroes: Principles of Cosmology and Chiefship among the Lakeside BaTabwa of Zaire. Ph.D. Dissertation. Department of Anthropology, University of Chicago.
   1981   Passage Stellified: Speculation upon Archaeoastronomy in Southeastern Zaire. Archaeoastronomy 4(4):27-37.
   1982   Enclave of Order, Seat of Dissent: The Establishment of a "Christian Kingdom" in Central Africa, 1885-95. Ms. Files of the author.
   in press a   Anarchy, Abjection and Absurdity: A Case of Metaphoric Medicine among the Tabwa of Zaire. In The Anthropology of Medicine. Lola Romanucci-Ross, Daniel Moerman, and Lawrence Tancredi, eds. Amherst: Bergin.
   in press b   "Insidious Conquests": War-time Politics along the Southwestern Shore of Lake Tanganyika. In Black Men in a Whiteman's War. Melvin Page, ed.
Schmitz, Bruno
   1903   Une Dame Céleste. Missions d'Afrique (Pères Blancs). pp. 315-320.
Shorter, Aylward
   1972   Chiefship in Western Tanzania. London: Oxford University Press.
Spencer, Herbert
   1976[1866]   First Principles of a New System of Philosophy. New York: Appleton.
Stromberg, Peter
   1981   Consensus and Variation in the Interpretation of Religious Symbolism: A Swedish Example. American Ethnologist 8:544-559.
Theuws, Theodore
   1954   Textes Luba. Bulletin du Centre d'Etudes des Problèmes Sociaux Indigènes 27.
Turner, Victor
   1970   The Forest of Symbols. Ithaca: Cornell University Press.
Usener, Herman
   1896   Götternamen, Versuch einer Lehre von der religiösen Begriffsbildung. Bonn: F. Cohen.
Van Acker, Auguste
   1907   Dictionnaire Kitabwa/Français/Kitabwa. Musée Royal du Congo Belge, Annales, Serie V, Ethnographie-Linguistique. Tervuren.
Van Avermaet, E., and Benoit Mbuya
   1954   Dictionnaire Kiluba-Français. Musée Royal du Congo Belge, Annales, Sciences de l'Homme, Linguistique 7. Tervuren.
Van Caeneghem, P.
   1956   La Notion de Dieu Chez Les Baluba du Kasai. Academie Royale des Sciences Coloniales, Sciences Morales et Politiques, Mémoire N.S. IX, 2.
Verbeke, F.
   1937   Le Bulopwe et le Kutomboka par le Sang Humain Chez les Baluba-Shankaji. Bulletin des Juridictions Indigènes et du Droit Coutumier Congolais 5(2):52-61.
Verhulpen, E.
   1936   Baluba et Balubaïsés du Katanga. Anvers: Eds. de l'Avenir Belge.
Vsekhvyatskii, Sergei
   1964   Physical Characteristics of Comets. Jerusalem: The Program for Scientific Translations. (Also available from the Office of Technical Services, U.S. Department of Commerce, Washington, DC.)
Vyncke, Amaat
   1887   Correspondence to Cardinal Lavigerie from Kibanga, 15 August 1887. General Archives of the White Fathers, C. 19-396. Rome.
Weber, Max
   1963[1922]   The Sociology of Religion. Boston: Beacon.

Werner, Douglas
  1971 Some Developments in Bemba Religious History. Religion in Africa 4(1):1-24.
White Fathers
  1954 Bemba English Dictionary. Cape Town: Longman.
Williams, John
  1964 A Field Guide to the Birds of East and Central Africa. London: Collins.
Willis, Roy
  1964 Traditional History and Social Structure in Ufipa. Africa 34:340-352.
  1972 The Head and the Loins: Lévi-Strauss and Beyond. In Reader in Comparative Religion. William Lessa and Evon Vogt, eds. pp. 313-322. New York: Harper & Row.
  1981 A State in the Making: Myth, History and Social Transformation in Pre-Colonial Ufipa. Bloomington: Indiana University Press.

Submitted 4 December 1981
Revised version received 5 March 1982
Accepted 14 March 1982

a trinity of Christs:
cultic processes in Andean Catholicism

M. J. SALLNOW—*London School of Economics and Political Science*

A universalistic religion must extend its role of divine intermediation across geographical and cultural frontiers. Yet at the same time it must retain anchorages in the diverse sociocultural systems it overarches. In other words, it must subsist on forms of religious expression that are essentially local. Some local cults it rejects, but others it attempts to regulate, or at least to establish a rapprochement with them. Often it cloaks them with its own universalistic symbolism and assimilates them to a greater or lesser degree, subjecting them to a process of theological systematization and refinement to render them compatible with orthodox doctrine and liturgy. The religious elite thereby harnesses popular religious enthusiasm. This process of officialization, however, frequently stimulates the emergence of new forms of local religious expression to replace those appropriated. Furthermore, while officialization entails a progressive universalization of local cults, its inevitable corollary is their subsequent reparochialization, for as they are adopted or imposed elsewhere they pass to a greater or lesser extent into the local religious vernacular. Elite control is therefore partial at best. Universalistic religions may themselves succeed one another via imperialism or colonialism; the process then becomes more convoluted, for each religion must adapt to an indigenous pattern of ritual and belief itself fashioned through an interplay between its predecessors and the local cults they in their turn have domesticated and transformed.

This model is here applied to a study of religious processes in the central Andes of South America. It is inspired principally by the work of Robert Redfield (1941, 1956) on great and little traditions but draws heavily on the ideas of other writers on the same theme: Marriott (1955) on universalization and parochialization in Hinduism; Christian (1972, 1981) on local religion in Spain; and Vrijhof (1979) on official and popular Christianity. The model is not necessarily appropriate to all universalistic religions, nor to every region penetrated by Catholicism, the tradition with which I am chiefly concerned. The dynamics of religious change in the central Andes, however, clearly exemplify the process outlined. I aim to show

---

This article uses historical and contemporary ethnographic data to elucidate the patterns of religious processes in the central Andes. It focuses on three neighboring Catholic shrines in a Peruvian rural locality. The interrelated devotional histories of these shrines are shown to exemplify processes evident in both the precontact and postcontact epochs whereby popular cults, patterned according to an indigenous Andean cosmology, are variously officialized, stifled, or controlled by emergent cultural elites. [Peru, Andes, Quechua, Catholicism, religious change]

Copyright © 1982 by the American Ethnological Society
0094-0496/82/040730-20$2.50/1

ultimately how these processes give rise to varied transformations of a uniquely Andean cosmology.

My ethnographic focus is a cluster of nominally Christian shrines in the San Salvador locality of the Cuzco region, southern Peru. By lifting these shrines out of the wider, regional shrine system in which they are embedded and by examining their respective devotions in detail, I attempt to unravel their particular structural and ritual interrelationships, thus adumbrating the characteristics of the shrine system as a whole. We perceive in this system a number of continuities with both Incaic and pre-Incaic religious processes. The better to demonstrate these continuities, I begin with a brief sketch of Andean religious history.

the historical background

For some four centuries before the Inca expansion in the mid-1400s, the central Andes enjoyed a temporary respite from military-theocratic imperialism. It was a period of interregnum between the Huari-Tiahuanaco empires on the one hand and those of the Inca and Spanish on the other, and was characterized by a high degree of regional and ethnic autonomy coupled with extensive interregional commerce (Lanning 1967:141). This autonomy was manifested in both the political and the religious spheres. The preeminence of the two great shrines of Pachacamac, on the coast just south of modern Lima, and Tiahuanaco, near Lake Titicaca in the high altiplano, persisted unassailed throughout this period and into the Inca and Christian epochs, although Tiahuanaco itself was unoccupied from about the 12th century. At the other extreme were the myriad *wak'as*, tutelary and origin shrines of communities and local groups, many associated with natural features such as caves, springs, lakes, mountain peaks, and rock outcrops.[1]

In between there were regional shrines, often local *wak'as* that had expanded their spheres of influence beyond their homelands to become the foci of ethnic nationalisms. The expansion of such a cult's dominion over neighboring peoples was frequently represented in myth in terms of a journey undertaken by the deity to annex or conquer the local *wak'as* and to establish new client shrines. Hierarchies were established between regional and local shrines, invariably utilizing the idioms of siblingship or descent. A feature of these kin-based hierarchies was their tendency to group shrines into sets of five (Avila 1975:52ff.). These pentadic hierarchies were locally focused, with the relations and rank order of deities varying from area to area (Avila 1975:73). As we shall see, the number 5 recurs constantly in Andean religion and cosmology; Pease (1968:66) has suggested that it symbolizes the totality of the cosmos, being composed of the four cardinal points plus the center. Few regional cults during this period achieved long-term stability; most waxed and waned depending, inter alia, on their oracular reputations, the wealth and power of their priesthoods, and—most importantly—on the shifting oppositions and alignments between tribal groupings. Shrine hierarchies were thus inherently unstable, subject to revision as certain *wak'as* rose in status and others declined.

The rise to transcedence of the Inca over this ethnic-religious mosaic brought about a refocusing of relations on the imperial capital of Cuzco. The solar cult of the Inca tribe was at once universalized and relocalized by establishing in every major settlement throughout the empire a counterpart of Qorikancha, the Cuzco Temple of the Sun. Monthly sacrifices were performed in many of these provincial temples to match those in the capital (Jiménez de la Espada 1965, I:161). While Quechua, the Inca tongue, became the lingua franca of the empire, ethnic loyalties were mobilized rather than suppressed, and cults of local and regional shrines were allowed to continue alongside the imperial religion. Indeed, some acquired new vigor. A 16th-century myth from Huarochirí, in the north-central highlands, tells of the apparition to a woman working in the fields of a *wak'a* called Llocllayhuancu. The *wak'a* claimed to be the son of Pachacamac, saying that he had been sent by his father to protect the people of the area—in the face, it seems, of Inca encroachment. At first a small chapel was built for him, but as his cult spread this was replaced by a large temple (Avila 1975:89).

In view of the esteem in which Pachacamac was held by the Inca, the attribution of the new *wak'a*'s parentage was astute, to say the least. For while Qorikancha and the other holy places of the Inca tribe now took official precedence among the shrines of the empire, the major provincial shrines were respected, even feared, by the Inca. Temples of the sun were built at Lake Titicaca and at Pachacamac, and in various ways the conquerors sought to establish a modus vivendi with the provincial centers of priestly power. From time to time these shrines, together with their priests, the ethnic lords, and their military commanders, were collocated in the imperial capital—not for the chief calendrical celebrations of Inca political power, but for the extraordinary ritual of Qhapaq Hucha (Duviols 1976). This was staged to mark a major event or crisis—a military victory or defeat, the coronation or demise of the emperor and the like. After a mass immolation of children and livestock the provincial *wak'as* converged on the capital to be allocated new ranks among themselves. In place of the many inconsistent ethnocentric shrine hierarchies, there was now but one official ranking system, legitimated by the center and revised at each Qhapaq Hucha to take account of shifts in the balance of power among the ethnic sovereignties of the empire. This stage of the ceremony was also an opportunity for the Inca to negotiate with the representatives of the more powerful shrines, concluding military treaties and fiscal contracts without which their political dominance would have been seriously threatened (cf. Rostworowski de Diez Canseco 1976).

Not only ritual organization but also Andean mythology and cosmology were rewrought under the influence of Inca culture to a pattern fitting to an expanding empire. The Inca origin myth was amplified so as to incorporate the origin stories of subject peoples. Inca political dominance was construed according to the key opposition between center and periphery, between stability and chaos, conceptualized in terms of the opposition between the category of Inca, associated with Cuzco, the mountains, sun, and fire, and that of Viracocha, associated with Lake Titicaca, the coastal sanctuary of Pachacamac, and with water in general. Viracocha was the Andean creator god, displaced to the margins by the Inca in the person of the ninth ruler, Pachacuti (Zuidema 1962; Pease 1973; Urbano 1974). "Pachacuti" means "transformer of the world" (Imbelloni 1946). His suzerainty, usurped from his father, Viracocha's namesake, ushered in the latter half of the fifth world, or age—that of Inca Runa (Inca People; Ossio 1973:190–191). The number 5 recurs elsewhere, in the system of five age classes of the census, and in the quinquepartition of each of the two moieties of the imperial capital (Zuidema 1964:213ff.). Inca myth and belief thus reposed upon autochthonous categories and concepts that had their origins in earlier epochs, now skewed in favor of Inca dominion.

In 1532 the Inca yielded to the Spanish invaders. The Catholic Church entered the New World under the patronage of the Spanish throne, for by 1508 King Ferdinand had wrested from successive popes most powers concerned with Church government, appointments, and finances in the Spanish Indies (Mecham 1966 [1934]:13ff.). However, while the Crown exercised total control over secular clergy, its control over the religious orders was more circumscribed; while seculars vowed obedience to the episcopate, which was itself in the monarch's thrall, regulars pledged obedience to a general in Rome and to his provincials overseas. The Crown made several attempts to curb the autonomy of regulars, but without success (Pike 1964:6).

Royal protection and sponsorship ensured that the colonial Church—or at least the diocesan establishment—devoted its energies more to political maneuvering than to spiritual proselytization, and in the Andes Catholicism was slow to take root (Vallier 1970:25; Kubler 1946:343). The cults of the sun and of the rest of the imperial pantheon all but disappeared, in part because of their relatively recent imposition on the subject peoples but also for want of the durability that only a literate great tradition can have. Other pagan cults, however, continued more or less openly. The latter half of the 16th century was punctuated by a number of nativistic messianic movements; one of the most widespread, the Taki Onqoy, is particularly interesting for its prophecy that the wak'as of the conquered Indians would unite, not at Cuzco, but at Lake Titicaca and Pachacamac (Millones 1973:87).

Effective conversion was not accomplished until 1660, when the belated campaigns against idolatry—spearheaded by the Jesuits—came to an end (Duviols 1972). According to Marzal (1977), the mid-17th century saw the crystallization of a new, syncretic Andean religion. Certainly around that time the Iberian complex of village patron saints and fiesta sponsorship was established in the colony, the patronal devotions partly displacing the cults of the local tutelary spirits. While the cults of the regional shrines were suppressed during the campaigns against idolatry, some quickly reemerged in a new guise, typically as devotions focused on shrines commemorating apparitions of Christian personages at or near the pre-Hispanic sacred sites. Significantly, two of the major shrines in the viceroyalty—both of the Virgin Mary—were established at Copacabana, on the shores of Lake Titicaca, in 1583 (Ramos Gavilán 1976), and at Pachacamac in 1601 (Vargas Ugarte 1947, II:106). In the course of the 17th century, Christ, rather than the Virgin, began to figure more prominently in such shrine devotions, mirroring a devotional shift that had begun slightly earlier in Spain and that may have been linked to a general Christocentric emphasis in response to the rise of Protestantism (Christian 1981:182–184).

During both the colonial and the republican eras, new shrines continued to be founded on the basis of religious visions or other theophanies, the incidence of which seems to have been correlated with periods of major social dislocation.[2] Whereas patron saints were usually localized versions of universal Christian advocations, each of these apparitional shrines possessed an intrinsic uniqueness by virtue of its geographical site and often explicit pagan associations. They were thought to have thaumaturgic powers: their divinities could intervene directly in the lives of devotees, and they became the foci of more or less extensive pilgrimage catchments. Some of these pilgrimage centers passed into the hands of the religious orders, for whom they became both powerful instruments of proselytization and lucrative sources of revenue. To this day Catholicism in the Andes, at least in the rural areas, has remained largely extrasacramental, resting not on the priestly bestowal of grace through the sacraments but on public and private devotionalism, by its very nature more or less refractory to sacerdotal control.

the local setting

The microregion of San Salvador straddles the Vilcanota Valley, the principal transport artery and agricultural belt of the Cuzco region (Figure 1). However, the microregion is ill-favored in terms of both topography and location. Not only is there a dearth of alluvial bottomland for commercial cereal production in the locality, but its collateral position relative to Cuzco ensures that it is bypassed by city-bound traffic and thus deprived of external commercial stimulus. For both these reasons the microregion is economically underdeveloped, and this has conduced to a marked degree of ethnic polarization and

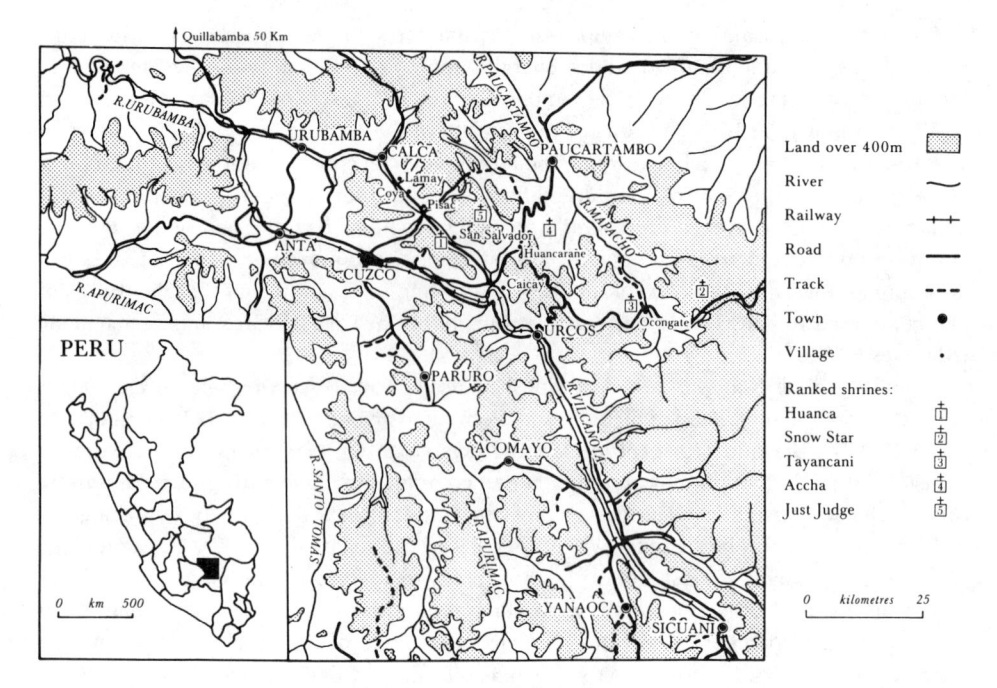

Figure 1. Map of Cuzco region.

political encapsulation (cf. Bailey 1969:144)—the features of what Aguirre Beltrán (1967) has called a "refuge region."

The locality is focused on the nucleated mestizo village of San Salvador, lying on the bank of the river in the fertile lower *keshwa* (cereal) zone at an altitude of 3000 m. The village is one of numerous *reducciones* (reductions) created by Viceroy Toldeo in the 1570s in an attempt to concentrate the scattered indigenous population of the colony in settlements laid out on the Iberian grid pattern. Throughout the colonial period the locality was subject both politically and ecclesiastically to the nearby village of Pisac, but in 1873 it became a district and a parish in its own right.

Agriculture is the primary means of livelihood in the district. In 1972 the population numbered 4000, of whom one-quarter lived in the village itself (Peruvian National Census 1972). The remainder lived either as labor-tenants on haciendas[3] or as subsistence peasants in hinterland "Indian" communities, each of which exercises traditional collective rights to a territory, generally in the mountainous upper *keshwa* (tuber) and *puna* (pasture) zones. These communities are politically subordinate to the municipal authorities in the district capital, with community mayors *(alcaldes)* traditionally fulfilling the intercalary role. In the last 20 years, however, most communities in the district have been legally registered and now elect administrative committees responsible to a government bureaucracy, thus loosening somewhat their links of political dependence with the district capital.

The religious patron of the parish is the eponymous San Salvador del Mundo, Christ Savior, a universal advocation honored in San Salvador as elsewhere in Christendom on the feast of the Transfiguration, 6 August. Each of the larger communities in the district is a subordinate chapelry of the parish, with its own patron saint drawn—with one exception—from the standard liturgical inventory. Two shrines in the district stand outside this familiar nested hierarchy of parish and community devotions. One is the shrine of Christ of Huanca (Señor de Huanca), housed in a sanctuary on the valley slopes 2 km northwest of the village; the other is the shrine of Christ the Just Judge (Señor el Justo Juez), located in the chapel of the mountain community of Occoruro some 10 km to the northeast. The titular fiestas of these two shrines are celebrated separately but on exactly the same day, 14 September, the feast of the Exaltation of the Cross; Christ of Huanca attracts some 15,000 pilgrims, Christ the Just Judge around 500. With three Christological shrines in such close proximity, we are faced with the question: Why this apparent devotional replication?

Christ of Huanca

The shrine of Christ of Huanca is situated in the lower *keshwa* zone on the eastern slopes of the mountain of Pachatusan. It consists of a large crag jutting from the mountainside, on which has been painted a mural of Christ tied to a column and undergoing scourging. Around the crag has been built a large temple, one of a cluster of buildings that includes sleeping quarters for pilgrims and a small monastery for the Mercedarian Fathers who manage the shrine. Behind the shrine complex, in an area called the Park of Siloam, are three rivulets known respectively as the waters of Christ, the Virgin, and the Devil, the first two reputedly possessing miraculous healing properties. Two or three Mercedarian priests are in permanent residence, while for the September fiesta several others come across from the order's monastery in Cuzco. Because the shrine is run by a religious order it is technically outside parish jurisdiction, a source of much contention over the years between the shrine guardians and the Pisac priests.

Christ of Huanca's official mytho-history tells of three separate apparitions (Márquez Eyzaguirre 1937, I:40ff.). The first is said to have taken place in May 1675. Diego Quispe, an Indian laborer in the goldmines of Yanantin on the summit of Pachatusan, decided to run to freedom in order to escape punishment for some misdemeanor. He took refuge in a small cave on the mountainside, intending to travel to his home village of Chinchero under cover of darkness. As night fell, the cave was suddenly suffused with a glow, and on a rock at the back of the cave Diego saw the figure of a man, stripped and bleeding from the blows of a whip. The Indian was so overcome that he lost consciousness. The figure appeared to him in his sleep, saying that he wanted the spot to become a font of salvation and love. He instructed Diego to return, after first telling his parish priest about the incident and making his first communion. A few weeks later Diego, his family, and the priest from Chinchero visited the spot, where they witnessed the second vision of the flagellated Christ. The priest informed the Mercedarian Fathers, to whose estate the land pertained, and they in turn notified the Bishop of Cuzco. A commission was set up to verify the reports, and the Mercedarians were given permission to paint a mural of Christ on the rock, recording all the details of the original vision. A modest thatched chapel was built around it and the cult was launched. In the beginning, however, pilgrims were few in number and came from the immediate locality only.

The third apparition took place in 1717 in Bolivia.[4] Pedro Valero, a wealthy mine-owner living in Cochabamba, fell ill of a terrible disease resistant to all known cures. A strange doctor arrived in the city and cured him simply by giving him water. He told Pedro that his name was Emmanuel and that, as payment, Pedro should visit his home in Huanca, Cuzco. A year later, loaded with gifts of gold and silver, Pedro set out to find his curer. Eventually, after several months of vain searching, he came to Huanca and discovered the chapel, now abandoned and ruined. Hidden behind a tangle of weeds was the mural, the features of the tortured Christ corresponding exactly to those of his mysterious doctor. The date was 14 September 1719. Once agaqin the Bishop of Cuzco was notified and a new commission of investigation was formed. As a result the devotion received official diocesan sanction and its popularity has been growing ever since.

Local tradition reiterates the main themes of this official myth but states that the image appeared miraculously on the rock to Diego Quispe and that no artist's hand was involved. It also makes a significant addendum having to do with the converse of miraculous theophany—miraculous disappearance. A woman pasturing her flocks in the vicinity is said to have been visited by angels, who told her that the image of Christ and his torturers would eventually disappear and that when this happens, the Day of Judgment will have arrived. In popular tradition the cult thus acquires a millenial flavor. Many observers have testified to the fact that the image is indeed fading away (cf. Barrionuevo 1969:211–212).

The official myth draws a strong contrast between the two visionaries of Christ of Huanca. The first was a poor Indian mine-worker—Quispe is a stereotypical Indian name—while the second was a wealthy mine-owner, his surname denoting Spanish rather than Indian descent. The transformation of social status correlates with a shift in the theodicy of the shrine. For Diego Quispe the tortured divinity represented deliverance from what probably would have been an identical punishment: the message of Christ taking on himself the sins and sufferings of the world is obvious and direct. Pedro Valero's devotion was more overtly instrumental: votive offerings in return for miraculous healing, albeit portrayed as symbolic rebaptism.[5] The transformation also correlates with a change in the ecclesiastical standing of the cult. The first apparitions, though they were brought to the attention of the religious authorities, did not attract widespread devotion; indeed, the story suggests that by 1719 the cult had all but collapsed. It required a visionary of higher social status than Diego Quispe to secure full ecclesiastical recognition of the devotion and thence to relaunch it in its present form. The myth states, in other words, that while the cult originated from the vision of an Indian, it owes its present popularity to a seer who nowadays would be classed as a mestizo and who, moreover, made a pilgrimage of some 900 km bearing gold and silver for his benefactor.

There is little doubt, however, that the importance of the area as a sacred site predated the Christian apparitions. It is likely that the monolith itself was originally venerated as a *wak'a*, for in pre-Hispanic times monoliths known as *wanq'as (huancas)* were believed to be the wraiths of conquerors and culture heroes and to regulate the fertility of surrounding fields (Duviols 1979). Furthermore, the mountain on whose slopes the shrine is situated, the massif of Pachatusan—literally, "stanchion of the world"—was of singular importance in Inca astronomy and mythology. At 4840 m it is the tallest mountain in the vicinity of Cuzco and its summit is directly due east of the Temple of the Sun in the imperial capital. It thus lay on one of the four principal *ceques*, straight lines radiating outward from Cuzco to its surrounding shrines. This *ceque* was the sight-line for observing the sunrise at the equinoxes (Zuidema 1977:233). It may be significant, therefore, that the fiesta of Christ of Huanca is held in September and that its octave, the day on which the rites are formally concluded, falls on the vernal equinox itself.[6]

Pachatusan recurs several times in Inca mythology, often in connection with hidden gold. One story tells how the Inca ruler ordered 300 tributaries laden with gold to be buried inside the mountain in order to allay a frost that was destroying the crops (Santacruz Pachacuti 1950:254). The Christian myth retains this association with precious metals, while today the locals will confide that the interior of the mountain is an enormous goldmine. Indeed, Pachatusan is still an important pagan deity, for as the highest peak in the area it is the most powerful of the local tutelary *apus*, or mountain spirits (see below). Attitudes toward the *apu* are ambivalent: for the people of Soncco, 20 km to the north, the mere utterance of its name is inauspicious (Wagner 1978:82). Although there is by no means a straight identification of the *apu* of Pachatusan with Christ of Huanca, the manifold pagan associations of the mountain clearly conduced to the establishment of a Christian shrine within its ambit.

The cult of Christ of Huanca soon began to distance itself from its demotic origins, however, thanks to a steady process of officialization at the hands of the Mercedarian priests. It seems that in the decades immediately following the first apparitions, the shrine did indeed attract only local interest. A diocesan letter indicates that it was not until 1693 that the Bishop of Cuzco granted permission for mass to be celebrated in the chapel at Huanca, stipulating that it must be low, not sung, and expressly prohibiting Easter services so as not to encroach on parochial rights (Márquez Eyzaguirre 1937, II:160). Following diocesan recognition in 1719, the shrine began to attract wider attention: Bueno (1951:108), in his geography of the viceroyalty first published in 1768, refers to the "great gatherings of devotees" at Huanca. The 18th century probably saw a steady increase in the popularity of the shrine as the Mercedarian priests advertised its healing powers to the faithful. Several of the buildings and cult objects date from this period (Márquez Eyzaguirre 1937).

As with the pilgrimage centers of medieval Europe, however, Huanca had to be able to offer papal indulgences to maintain devotion to the shrine once its miraculous luster began to fade. Ironically, the appeals to the Vatican to this end were stimulated in part by the persistent hostility of the Pisac priests toward the custodians of Huanca. The Mercedarian clergy had a direct line of communication to the pope through their general in Rome, and in 1801 Pius VII granted a plenary indulgence for attendance during the fiesta novena (Márquez Eyzaguirre 1937, II:202-203). Despite papal support, Huanca was still subjected to interference by the Pisac clergy, who prevented the Mercedarian priests from receiving fees for masses in the sanctuary and attempted to bring them under parochial jurisdiction (1937, II:205) Faced with this continuing opposition, and apparently receiving little support from the Bishop of Cuzco in defense of rights conferred on Huanca by his own office, the Mercedarians again appealed to Rome. Pius VIII supported them, stating in a papal brief of 1829 that it was "his will to segregate and make independent Señor de Guanca where without the intervention of the parish priests they might freely summon the dues of sung masses and perform all the public offices of Holy Week and of the other feasts of the year" (1937, II:207). In 1842 Gregory XVI bestowed further indulgences on the sanctuary, while in 1930 Pius XI united Huanca to the Lateran Basilica in Rome, thus granting it *ad instar* all the indulgences and spiritual benefits conceded to the Basilica (1937, II:217-219).

In their assiduous propagation of the Huanca cult, the Mercedarian Fathers have directed their attentions to the counterparts of Pedro Valero, the second seer, rather than those of the humbler Diego Quispe. In 1931, under a particularly energetic chaplain, the brotherhood *(hermandad)* of Christ of Huanca was put on a formal footing, and there are now branches of the brotherhood in towns and villages throughout the Cuzco region and beyond. Members tend to be drawn from the mestizo rather than the Indian ethnic stratum. They pledge themselves to an annual payment to the shrine and underwrite the cost of sleeping quarters and other facilities for the respective branches. In the 1930s, too, a motor road was built to the sanctuary from San Salvador, the express purpose being to encourage the attendance of townspeople deterred by the taxing climb (Márquez Eyzaguirre 1937, II:304). Building at the shrine complex continued apace, and in 1965 a new temple for the sacred image was finally completed.

The official brotherhood now constitutes the foundation of the Huanca cult. For the greater part of its history, however, the shrine has been a focus for the "traditional" form of Andean pilgrimage commonly associated with Indian folk religion. This devotional style prevails today at many other shrines in the Cuzco region. It entails the escort of a portable icon *(lámina)* from the home chapel to the chosen shrine by a sponsored community-based group *(nación)* that includes ritual dancers and musicians as well as "lay" pilgrims. Prestige commensurate with the expenditure incurred accrues to those who occupy offices *(cargos)* in the group: pilgrimage of this kind is in fact referred to as *tipo cargo* (*cargo*-type). As in all

Indian rituals, the consumption of alcohol on the journey and at the shrine is de rigueur. In the 1920s, however, in an attempt to encourage a more sober, contemplative form of devotion, the Mercedarian priests decreed that thenceforth all dancing and drinking at Huanca was prohibited. This effectively banned Indian pilgrims from engaging in their traditional devotional practices. Two hundred and fifty years after Diego Quispe's vision, the cult had been finally purged of its Indian origins. But the traditional devotion quickly found an alternative outlet, as will be shown presently.

Today, Huanca is patronized mainly by devotees with claims, or pretensions, to mestizo status. They tend to be drawn from the ranks of the lower-middle and working classes in the towns and from those of the small farmers and petty traders in the countryside. Although most are bilingual, they tend toward Spanish rather than Quechua as their habitual tongue. Geographically, the catchment for the September fiesta is interdepartmental, even international, with pilgrims not only from the department of Cuzco and neighboring Andean departments but also from Bolivia, Chile, and Argentina. Sick, injured, and disabled pilgrims feature prominently among the throng; those who gain the ear of one of the priests might be allowed to touch the image itself, but the rest settle for an ablution in the holy waters of the Park of Siloam. Piles of ex-*votos*—crude models of arms, legs, and other parts of the body for which pilgrims seek a cure—testify to the continuing belief in the healing powers of the divine "doctor."

The fiesta follows a similar program each year. There are daily masses and rosary services during the novena, with nightly sessions of self-flagellation for those who so choose. Sometimes a confirmation service is held on the afternoon of the 14th, presided over by the Archbishop of Cuzco. Then comes the climax of the proceedings. Two solemn processions, the men following a statue of Christ of Huanca and the women of the Virgin of Sorrows, take different routes through the shrine complex and converge in front of the sanctuary. Christ of Huanca is accompanied on the journey by costumed pilgrims representing Christ carrying the cross, his assistant Simon of Cyrene, Roman soldiers, and executioners complete with hammer, nails, and a pair of severed, pierced hands. Participants in the processions wear crowns of thorns in imitation of Christ. When the two groups have reunited, with darkness closing in around the sacred eyrie, there is a long sermon in which the votaries are exhorted to maintain their faith and devotion to the shrine. As the sermon reaches its crescendo, the assembled pilgrims fall to their knees, many sobbing uncontrollably. Most leave later that night or the next day, but some stay on for the octave, when daily masses and rosary services are repeated.

The chaplain of the sanctuary was somewhat embarrassed by the theatrical nature of the Huanca cult, by its overt iconolatry, and especially by the conspicuous forms of public penance in which some of the devotees indulge. He stressed to me that the clergy did nothing to encourage these practices and that they stemmed from the naïveté of certain pilgrims, particularly the peasants (*campesinos*). These people, he claimed, have two conceptions of God, the God who loves and the God who punishes, and it is the latter that takes precedence. He pointed to the absence of drinking and dancing as a feature that distinguished Huanca from other, less sublimated shrine devotions.

The religious activities at the Huanca sanctuary are not the only attraction for visitors to the September fiesta, for coinciding with the pilgrimage is a major regional fair held just across the river from San Salvador. The fair is one of a number of such annual events held on different sites throughout the area, many of them similarly coinciding with pilgrimages to apparitional shrines. They differ from the hundreds of daily and weekly markets in the scale of their operations, in the highly variegated trade that they embrace, and in their festive and recreational diversions. At the fair in San Salvador there is a bewildering variety of foodstuffs from all the ecological zones of the region; one can also buy earthenware vessels, ploughshares and rubber sandals from the specialist artisan communities to the southeast, and livestock of every description. In addition there is an assortment of industrial manufactures. Stallholders pay a tariff to the municipality, and the district governor oversees all livestock sales. The flurry of commercial activity in the village is short-lived, but for about ten days San Salvador ceases to be an economic backwater and becomes the cynosure of the whole of the southern Peruvian Andes.

To summarize: the Huanca shrine displays many pre-Hispanic religious continuities and owes its present, Christian form to an Indian seer. But the cult has undergone a continual process of officialization on the part of the religious order which controls the shrine. This process has included de-emphasizing in the shrine's mytho-history its lowly, Indian origins; lobbying the Vatican for papal recognition and support; courting the more orthodox devotees, who also happen to be the wealthier patrons; and prohibiting the practices associated with traditional Andean pilgrimage. This relatively successful strategy of officialization has had a remarkable consequence: the establishment nearby of a second apparitional shrine whose cult preserves the popular devotional forms of Andean Catholicism and of whose existence the priests at Huanca, significantly, professed complete ignorance.

Christ the Just Judge

This shrine, Christ the Just Judge, is situated on the borders of the upper *keshwa* and *puna* zones in the community chapel of Occoruro. It consists of a statuesque boulder, painted and garbed to represent an austere Christ sitting in judgment upon mankind. Its part-time staff comprises peasants from the community; the parish priest visits only occasionally, to celebrate mass during the major fiestas. Unlike the Huanca shrine, which is independent of the parish, that of Christ the Just Judge is not only a pilgrimage center but also the religious patron of a dependent community. This dual status affects local ceremonial, as we shall see presently.

The origin myth of Christ the Just Judge is part of local oral tradition. The commonest version sets the date of the apparition some 300 years ago, making it roughly contemporaneous with that of Huanca. A young woman from the community of Ccamahuara, immediately adjacent to Occoruro, was pasturing her flock in the *puna* when she came across a boulder with the figure of a man imprinted on it. She recognized the figure as a *taytacha*, the Quechua term used to refer to all manifestations of Christ. The figure told the woman that he wanted to be moved to the chapel in Ccamahuara, and she ran to tell her family. Some people from Occoruro heard of the incident and preempted the Ccamahuarans by removing the boulder to their own community chapel, where it has remained ever since, displacing the official community patron of the Virgin of Bethlehem. As news of the miracle spread, pilgrims and dancers began to gather at the shrine.

While the boulder may have been an ancient *wak'a,* the purported antiquity of the Christian cult in this myth is not vouched for by other sources, one of which sets the date of the miracle as late as the 1940s (Casaverde Rojas, Sánchez Farfán, and Cevallos Valencia 1966:97). The apparition undoubtedly postdated the ban on drinking and dancing at Huanca, and the commemorative fiesta—timed to coincide exactly with that of Huanca—became a new local focus for sponsored pilgrimage.

The two shrines of Huanca and the Just Judge are linked in local tradition via a rank ordering of five miraculous christological shrines, in a manner redolent of pre-Hispanic practice. It is said that this group of five brother *taytachas* had traveled from place to place, each brother stopping to rest at the spot where his shrine is now located. The shrine hierarchy represents the order of fraternal seniority and corresponds to the supposed thaumaturgic powers of the shrines. Huanca features first in this hierarchy, followed by Christ of the Snow Star (Señor de Qoyllur Rit'i), a major Indian shrine near Ocongate some 70 km to the east, and Christ of Tayancani, another shrine in the same area said to be the same personage as Christ of the Snow Star (see Ramirez 1969). Next comes Christ of Accha, a minor shrine near Huancarane, and finally Christ the Just Judge (see Figure 1).

Similar shrine sets are reported from elsewhere in the central Andes, but their composition varies from place to place. Thus the important regional shrines of Huanca and the Snow Star also figure in the shrine pentad given by a native of the province of Acomayo, to the south of Cuzco; but the three other miraculous shrines in the set are local ones, closer to his homeland (Valderrama Fernandez and Escalante Gutierrez 1977:67–71). In the Pampa de Anta area west of Cuzco, meanwhile, Huanca is again regarded as the senior brother—this time of a trio—but his younger siblings are Christ of the Earthquakes (Señor de los Temblores), a famous and much revered image in Cuzco Cathedral, and Christ of Inquillpata, a regional shrine in the immediate locality (Núñez del Prado 1970:100). While Huanca thus occupies a prominent position in ethnocentric shrine hierarchies throughout the region, in each it is linked diacritically to other major pilgrimage centers and to local apparitional shrines of lesser renown.

A similar pattern of mutually inconsistent but overlapping hierarchies characterizes relations between *apus* (mountain spirits; cf. Morissette and Racine 1973:178). *Apus* are usually male, complementing the generalized female principle of Pachamama, "earth mother" (Mariscotti de Görlitz 1978). No public cult attaches either to the *apus* or to Pachamama in the San Salvador locality, but invocations are made to them extempore by individuals and more formally during domestic livestock ceremonies. These pagan deities tend in the main to be held responsible for the fertility and general well-being of humans, crops, and livestock, while Christian apparitional shrines are typically supplicated in order to effect some improvement in the temporal or spiritual fortunes of individual devotees. In a given locality, the *apus* of the immediately surrounding hills are ranked beneath more powerful regional *apus* of wider renown. The chief *apu* of the Cuzco region is generally given as Ausangate, a mountain peak associated with the nearby Christian shrine of Christ of the Snow Star in the same manner as Pachatusan is associated with Christ of Huanca. Here, however, we encounter another inconsistency, for while local cosmology in San Salvador places Huanca above the Snow Star in the shrine hierarchy, it places Ausangate above Pachatusan in the *apu* ranking. Clearly, shrines and *apus* are associated but not identified with each other; indeed, they may sometimes be in competition (Gow 1976).

Today the annual fiesta of Christ the Just Judge is attended by about 500 pilgrims divided among 20 or so contingents (*naciones*), the majority from upland peasant communities within a 25-km radius. "Indian" as opposed to Western dress predominates. Each contingent comes with its portable icon (*lámina*), its troupe of ritual dancers, and its band of musicians. The most popular dance style is that of the *wayri ch'uncho,* regarded as typically Indian; music is provided by traditional Andean pipes and flutes. Prayers, sermons, and general social intercourse are conducted in Quechua; indeed, most devotees are Quechua monolinguals. Apart from a brief visit by the parish priest on the 14th to celebrate mass, there is no ecclesiastical supervision. There are no *ex-votos* and no indulgences, and while individuals attend in order to supplicate the shrine for personal favors, as strong a motive for many is the acquisition of prestige and the fulfillment of social obligations by assuming an office (*cargo*) in a contingent. Although the shrine is treated with respect the occasion is definitely a festive one, with none of the lugubriousness of the activities at Huanca. There is no trading in Occoruro beyond the provision of victuals for the visitors, though many pilgrims call at the fair in San Salvador. In terms of ritual participation, however, the two fiestas are mutually exclusive: I met no one who attended both. Huanca is predominantly a mestizo devotion, the Just Judge an Indian one. The ethnic specialization of apparitional shrines, evident in some degree throughout the central Andes, is here cast into sharp local relief.

The competitive relationship in the foundation myth of the Just Judge between the communities of Ccamahuara and Occoruro is translated into a cooperative one in the running of the fiesta, Ccamahuara's special role being symbolized by its distinctive iconic representation at the shrine—a large cross as against the *láminas* of the other *naciones*. The people of the two communities claimed that their fiesta, with its music and dancing, though as yet a minor event compared with that of Huanca, was nevertheless a far more splendid affair. Their enthusiasm in the 1970s for a project to drive a road through the area was prompted in part by a desire to make the shrine more accessible so that it might begin to compete with its counterpart in the valley. They regularly petitioned the shrine itself for help with the road project, "for the benefit of all the *taytacha's* children."

Christ Savior

The third christological shrine in the locality is the parish patron, Christ Savior. The advocation was assigned to the village at its foundation in the 16th century, though the present plaster image is relatively recent. Like most other local patron saints, it is thought to exert an abiding tutelage rather than to possess any intrinsic miraculousness. Its fiesta on 6 August is one of three annual rituals in which icons from the dependent chapelries are brought to San Salvador. At Christmas the community *niños* (dolls representing the Christ child) converge on the parish church; at the fiesta of Holy Cross on 3 May, the community crosses; and at that of Christ Savior, the community patrons.

The patronal fiesta resembles hundreds of other festivals held in rural parish seats throughout the central Andes. An office-holder from the village shoulders the principal expenses of the event. The visiting saints, accompanied by the community authorities, attend mass, the congregation being drawn exclusively from the parish. Afterward the saints are borne in procession around the plaza, Christ Savior bringing up the rear. They then return to their home chapels. As the quintessential ritual of the center, the fiesta may be seen as integrating the separate religious identities of the various communities into a bounded microcosm whose symbolic framework is congruent with the political structure of the district.[7]

There is, however, one conspicuous deviation from the stereotype. Occoruro is represented at the fiesta not by Christ the Just Judge, but by its former patron, the Virgin of Bethlehem. Occoruro's supralocal status as the site of a miraculous shrine is thus disregarded by the ritual, which accords recognition only to its official local status as a subordinate chapelry of the parish. The exclusion of the Just Judge, Occoruro's de facto patron, from the parish fiesta of Christ Savior amounts to a ritual screening of the official ecclesiastical domain from the devotional field of miraculous shrines—a field in which the Just Judge far outshines its parochial superior in religious renown.[8]

analysis

We may now review and systematize the data on the three shrines by first examining the extrinsic features of the devotions (Table 1). Christ Savior is the patron of the parish, having a fixed, ethnically heterogeneous congregation. Christ the Just Judge is the patron of a dependent chapelry but is also an apparitional shrine with a vicinal Indian catchment. Christ of Huanca is a regional shrine independent of the parish altogether and has a spatial-

Table 1. Extrinsic features of devotions.

	Christ of Huanca	Christ the Just Judge	Christ Savior
Ecclesiastical status	Independent of parish	Dependent chapelry	Parish center
Date of fiesta	14 September (Exaltation of the Cross)	14 September (Exaltation of the Cross)	6 August (Transfiguration)
Span of catchment	Interdiocesan	Interparochial	Parish
Ethnic appeal	Mestizo	Indian	Heterogeneous
Commercial activities	Regional fair	Services to pilgrims	None

ly extensive, predominantly mestizo catchment. The fiesta of Christ of Huanca, not that of the parish patron, is the pretext for the regional fair in San Salvador, while in Occoruro commercial activities amount to the servicing of pilgrims' needs only.

The oppositions and contrasts suggested by this sociostructural comparison of the devotions are heightened when we consider the characteristics of the shrines themselves (Table 2). Here a clear pattern emerges, with Huanca and the Just Judge opposed to each other on one axis but together counterposed to Christ Savior. Iconologically, Huanca and the Just Judge are diametrically contrasted, the one representing the punished Christ submitting to his torturers, the other the punishing Christ sitting in judgment upon mankind. These two images of Christ, suffering mortal versus omnipotent judge, are frequently juxtaposed in Christian theology: in the Middle Ages they were the dominant conceptions of God, for "only by imitating Christ the man could one placate Christ the judge" (Sumption 1975:135; see also Richardson, Pardo, and Bode 1971). The parish shrine of Christ Savior offers a third, soteriologically more central variant: that of the loving redeemer, promising salvation to all mankind. This shrine is thus opposed to both Huanca and the Just Judge as salvation is opposed to punishment. We are reminded here of the observation of the priest at Huanca concerning the two Andean folk conceptions of God, the God who loves and the God who punishes.

Another set of contrasts, especially significant in the Andean context, emerges at the level of material form. Huanca is a painting on an immobile crag, the Just Judge a movable boulder; but both, as exemplifications of the "living rock" so pervasive in Andean religion, contrast with the manufactured effigy of the Savior. The contrasts may be pursued further at the level of Christian eschatology. Here, Huanca and the Just Judge are again linked: both are miraculous theophanies, the one fading and the other permanent, the eventual disappearance of the tortured Christ of Huanca heralding the *dies irae* of Christ the Just

Table 2. Iconology of shrines.

	Christ of Huanca	Christ the Just Judge	Christ Savior
Advocation	Christ suffering	Christ judging	Christ saving
Material form	Rock: painting on a crag	Rock: statuesque boulder	Manufactured effigy
Theophany	Miraculous appearance, but fading	Miraculous appearance; permanent	Atemporal
Theogony	Senior brother in shrine pentad	Junior brother in shrine pentad	Unrepresented
Thaumaturgy	Stressed: most powerful in shrine pentad	Stressed: least powerful in shrine pentad	Unstressed

Judge By contrast the shrine of Christ Savior, the bringer of eternal salvation, is atemporal. Finally, in the local fraternal hierarchy of miraculousness, Huanca is regarded as the senior brother and the most powerful shrine, the Just Judge as the junior and the least. Christ Savior, on the other hand, does not figure in the hierarchy at all, and its thaumaturgy is wholly unstressed.

These homologous structural relationships are the components of a concentric dualism: the contrast between the Christs of the parish church and of the two pilgrimage centers literally enshrines the key opposition between center and periphery. As Lévi-Strauss (1968) has shown, concentric dualism—as distinct from the diametric variety—is inherently transformational, concealing a set of ternary relations better represented by a pole and axis. Figure 2 portrays the three shrines according to this representation.

This synchronic analysis of shrine patterning enhances our understanding of the diachronic process of religious change. It was suggested that this proccess consists in part of the progressive officialization of local cults leading to the genesis of new forms of religious expression. The foregoing indicates that novel devotions in San Salvador have emerged, not randomly, but in such a way as to generate distinct symbolic affinities and contrasts. In the 17th century, the symbolism of the miraculous theophany of Huanca—an "icon of subversion," to use Leach's (1972) terminology—departed determinately from that of the official parish shrine of the Savior, the "icon of orthodoxy."[9] As a particularistic advocation of the same divine figure, it established a set of harmonic oppositions between the two shrines that could serve to differentiate their respective devotions. Three centuries later the symbolism of the miraculous theophany of Occoruro, as a new icon of subversion, departed determinately from that of both Huanca and the Savior, giving rise to a more complex set of contrasts. It too was a particularistic christological advocation, but one that served on the one hand to differentiate the two ecclesiastically peripheral centers from the parish shrine and on the other to distinguish these two centers from each other. Over the centuries, the various symbolic oppositions have been transiently attached to diverse social and institutional cleavages within the Catholic cult—between regular and secular clergy, between clergy and laity, and between mestizo and Indian devotees. Symbolic production in the popular Catholicism of the locality, then, has proceeded dialectically, generating topographically distinctive variants of universal Christian iconography.

While San Salvador may be unusual in having three such sharply polarized shrines in such close proximity, the limited data available suggest that similar patterns of symbolic coding may be detected between shrines elsewhere in the Andes at both the local and regional levels. Documentation is beyond the scope of this paper. Suffice it to say that the structural links elucidated between the three chosen shrines are but elements of an extensive, spatially unbounded network of symbolic relationships that are subject to continuous historical ramification as the cultic processes of Catholicism unfold. The imported Chris-

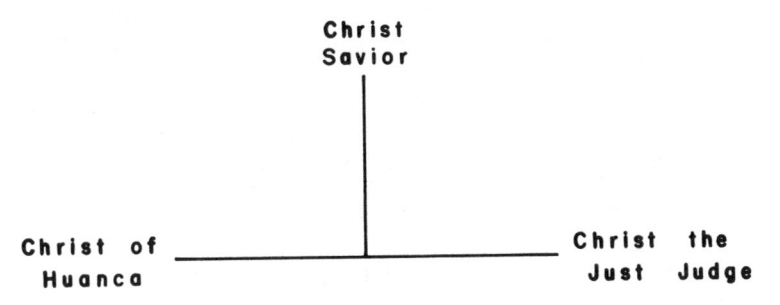

Figure 2. Iconological relationships between shrines.

tian tradition, however, while exhibiting its own peculiar brand of symbolism, has everywhere had to adapt to the contours of native religion. Contemporary ritual and belief reveal a syncretism not merely of symbolic content but also of structural form, in an underlying persistence of pre-Hispanic cosmological models.

We noted that during the four centuries or so of regional autonomy in the central sierra before the Inca conquest, shifting political and ethnic configurations were matched by a volatile religious culture. Shrines constituted the parameters for conceptualizing both social and physical space, the ritual ascendancy of this or that cult being reflected in ethnocentric shrine hierarchies typically utilizing a pentadic kinship idiom. The multiple contours of this sacred geography were constantly shifting as new shrines emerged and old ones advanced their reputations or declined into oblivion. The fluid, regionalized pattern of central Andean society to which this model gave expression served as the backdrop not only to the Inca empire but also to earlier military theocracies.

This indigenous model still manifests itself today. Christian apparitional shrines are invariably associated with natural environmental features, and in some cases a direct continuity can be traced with pre-Hispanic sacred sites. Shrine hierarchies share a range of formal and cultural characteristics with their pagan forebears. Both display variations across space and through time. Common cultural features include myths of foundation by itinerant deities; the pretext of divine efficacy for assigning rank; the use of kinship idioms for expressing shrine interrelations; and a predilection for pentarchical sets. The typical careers of both Christian and pre-Hispanic apparitional shrine cults conform to an identical syndrome, as a comparison of the cults of Huanca, Occoruro, and Llocllayhuancu clearly demonstrates. Llocllayhuancu's apparition, incidentally, seems to have coincided with Inca activity in the area. Christian apparitions, too, it seems, tend to occur during periods of political uncertainty. In a variety of ways, then, contemporary devotions attaching to Christian apparitional shrines adhere to cosmological models and ritual processes dating from the pre-Incaic epoch.[10]

As the Inca extended their sway across the Andes, they imposed on the multiform sacred geography a centripetal model of politico-religious control, focused on Cuzco and replicated locally throughout the empire. The major provincial shrines, however, represented potential rallying points of disaffection and even of revolt. They were absent from the calendrical, political rituals of the metropolis but were mollified and regulated at the extraordinary ceremony of Qhapaq Hucha, without which they might have posed a serious threat to Inca dominion.

The Spanish appropriated this centripetal model of politico-religious control, and today in San Salvador, as in countless other central Andean localities, the cult of the parish patron continues to map out a pyramidal hierarchy of official community shrines. Occoruro's shrine of Christ the Just Judge, however, is an anomaly. It is Janus-faced, being at once the patron of a dependent chapelry and an independent pilgrimage sanctuary—the epitome of the challenge to the center from the periphery. At the annual parish festival the singular status of Occoruro is ritually ignored, the community being represented by its quondam official patron. The superiority of the parish patron thus passes unsullied, and ecclesiastical hierarchy prevails, carrying with it the legitimation of political dependence.

In what sense, it may be asked, did the Occoruro shrine constitute a *challenge* to the center? For the Inca, provincial shrines sometimes posed a real threat either of the refusal of military assistance or of outright secession. It might be argued that in comparison the "threat" of Christ the Just Judge to the authority of the parish center was purely figurative.

Cults of apparitional shrines, however, frequently possess a political dimension: through their detachment from prevailing political and ecclesiastical structures they constitute domains in which local social hierarchies are temporarily abrogated and in which new social oppositions and alliances may be generated and novel social processes unfold (Sallnow 1981). The Occoruro shrine is the focus of both conflict and coalition not premised by local patterns of political dependency. Two examples will suffice.

In the past, on the pre-Lenten feast of Compadres, an annual battle known as the *tinkuy* was fought in the mountains above Occoruro between hinterland communities of the adjacent districts of San Salvador and Pisac. Similar battles still take place elsewhere in the central Andes (e.g., Gorbak, Lischetti, and Muñoz 1962). The ostensible aims are said to have been to slay one's adversaries and to capture their women, the event being bound up with beliefs concerning blood sacrifice, fertility, and propitiation of the *apus*. Today the battle has been transformed into an apparently irenic ritual; indeed, according to one tradition the transformation was prompted by the miraculous appearance of Christ the Just Judge (Casaverde Rojas et al. 1966:97). Preparations are still as for war, however, and before the ritual the participants come to light candles before the shrine to invoke its protection on the "battlefield."

A week earlier, on the feast of Compadres, the shrine annually imparts a less divisive blessing. On that day the community authorities of Occoruro and Ccamahuara gather at the chapel for the sacralization of the political insignia of the *alcaldes* (community mayors). The *alcaldes* are officially installed during the Christmastide ceremonies in San Salvador. Whereas these ceremonies, with their collocation of community *niños* before the parish patron, symbolically elaborate the dependence of the hinterland communities on the district capital, the Compadres ritual bespeaks interdependence between peripheral communities themselves. The occasion is not simply a ritual one but a pretext for the reaffirmation of bilateral interests. Joint collective work sessions are planned and matters of mutual concern discussed. In 1974, with the social and economic reforms of the Velasco government beginning to take effect in the area, formal speeches were made advocating the full organizational union of the two communities so as to create a more effective political lobby. In that year, too, the community authorities of Ampay, in Pisac district, participated in the ritual. Their presence derived, it seemed, from the fact that Ccamahuara and Ampay were the prime movers in the interdistrict community coalition seeking government assistance for the building of a road through the area, linking Pisac and Huancarane (see Figure 1). Local peasants regarded the road as essential for the general development of the area and in particular for the nurturing of Occoruro as a pilgrimage center. They also realized that it would severely dislocate the district of San Salvador, further isolating the district capital—where, not surprisingly, opinion was opposed to the project. Some Ccamahuarans anticipated the day when, thanks to the road, their community would grow in commercial importance such that it might challenge the authority of San Salvador and eventually become a district in its own right.

The hope seems a vain one. By 1980, though the various communities had collaborated extensively on the preliminary earthworks, government help was still not forthcoming. This example and the preceding one illustrate, however, that the Occoruro shrine can serve as a focus for intercommunity activities of an egalitarian nature both within and across district boundaries. In other words, through its partial independence from the parish, it provides a religious arena for the redefinition of social relations untrammeled by formal allegiances to the politico-religious center. As such it may indeed constitute a mute challenge to the center, for it stands as a virtual catalyst of novel, even subversive, political alliances.

conclusion

This paper has attempted to show how the pattern of contemporary Catholic devotion in a central Andean locality may be seen as the outcome of a continuous historical process whereby successive religious elites have sought to impose their dominion and to domesticate and control local religious expression. The process has assumed a distinctively Andean form, each religious tradition submitting to indigenous sociocultural paradigms while simultaneously bequeathing a cultural legacy of its own. An analysis of the histories of Christian apparitional shrine devotions revealed the manner in which syncretic theophanies, once enshrined, are subjected to a progressive officialization, stimulating the dialectical emergence of new apparitional shrines. Such shrines partake in the same opposition between the controlled center and the subversive periphery as had characterized Inca politico-religious hegemony over the ethnic patchwork of the central sierra. It was further apparent that the folk model of ritual interrelations between apparitional shrines betrays the persistence of a cosmology that predates the Inca epoch and that derives from the waxing and waning of cults in the highly regionalized, ethnically fluid society that constituted the foundation for successive transient empires. The dialectics of the Catholic cult in the central Andes thus unfold within a framework fashioned in the course of earlier universalistic religious ventures.

notes

Acknowledgments. This article is based on fieldwork in 1973–74 and 1980, financed by a Foreign Area Fellowship from the Social Science Research Council (United States), the Staff Research Fund of the London School of Economics, the Social Science Research Council (United Kingdom), and the Radcliffe-Brown Fund of the Association of Social Anthropologists. I am grateful to the officers of all these bodies for their support. Previous versions of this article were presented to the Intercollegiate Anthropology Seminar of London University, the Anthropology Seminar at the University of Sussex, and the symposium on Plurality in Religion at the 1981 IUAES Intercongress, Amsterdam. In all cases participants offered useful criticisms. I should also like to thank Richard Werbner for seminal comments on earlier drafts. The map was kindly prepared by the Drawing Office of the London School of Economics.

[1] Quechua words are rendered according to standard modern orthography, except in the cases of proper names of people and places with established Hispanicized transcriptions.

[2] The evidence for this correlation is scanty but suggestive. The 17th-century spate of religious visions may have been connected with the emergence of the hacienda system (Keith 1971), while the apparent outbreak this century may be due to renewed market penetration in the rural areas. Escobar (1967:63) links a miraculous apparition in the Puno region in 1957 with anxieties among peasants about possible loss of land due to an irrigation project. It should be pointed out that very few religious apparitions lead to the establishment of cults; usually such stirrings are vigorously quashed by local clergy, as another example from Escobar (1967:63) illustrates.

[3] In 1973 the Velasco government's agrarian reform law began to take effect in the area, leading to the expropriation of some of these haciendas and their conversion into state-controlled cooperatives.

[4] There is some disagreement concerning the date of the third apparition. Marzal (1971:226–227) utilizes a source that places it in 1775. Since Márquez Eyzaguirre's account purports to be the official history of the shrine, I here follow his chronology, which also accords better with independent contemporary sources.

[5] The idea of pilgrimage as symbolic rebaptism was widespread in medieval Christianity (cf. Sumption 1975:129).

[6] The ritual significance of 14 September throughout the Andes might, however, derive from its having been set aside by the 16th-century extirpators of idolatry as the day on which a special Christian festival was to be held in a town following the destruction of its *wak'as* (Arriaga 1968:255).

[7] Such congruence is not inevitable. For instance, in the village of Chuschi, Ayacucho department, the convergence of saints' images still maps out the relations of ecclesiastical dependence established during colonial times, despite four of the seven communities concerned having since been transferred to an adjacent district (Isbell 1978:63).

[8] Similar ritual contrivances are encountered elsewhere in the central Andes. For example, the sworn patron of Cuzco, the miraculous image of Christ of the Earthquakes, does not take part in the parade of the city's saints at Corpus Christi, but has its own fiesta celebrated during Holy Week.

[9] For Leach, an "icon of orthodoxy" corresponds to the pattern whereby a worshiper approaches a divinity via a hierarchy of human intermediaries, and an "icon of subversion" to the direct manifestation of the deity to the devotee.

[10] Apparitional shrines in Christian lands commonly display systemic continuities with earlier organizational models. In Mexico, for example, their pilgrimage catchments tend to correspond to pre-Hispanic political, ethnic, or economic units (Turner 1974:179).

references cited

Aguirre Beltrán, Gonzalo
    1967   Regiones de Refugio. Mexico: Instituto Indigenista Interamericano.
Arriaga, Pablo Joseph de
    1968   La Extirpación de la Idolatría en el Perú (1621). In Biblioteca de Autores Españoles (Cont.) 209, pp. 191-277. Madrid: Ediciones Atlas.
Avila, Francisco de
    1975   Dioses y Hombres de Huarochirí (1608). José María Arguedas, transl. Mexico: Siglo XXI.
Bailey, F. G.
    1969   Stratagems and Spoils: A Social Anthropology of Politics. Oxford: Basil Blackwell.
Barrionuevo, Alfonsina
    1969   Cuzco, Magic City. Lima: Editorial Universo.
Bueno, Cosme
    1951   Geografía del Perú Virreinal (Siglo XVIII). Lima: Daniel Valcárcel.
Casaverde Rojas, Juvenal, Jorge Sánchez Farfán, and Tomás Camilo Cevallos Valencia
    1966   Wifala o P'asña Capitán. Folklore (Cuzco) 1:83-102.
Christian, William A.
    1972   Person and God in a Spanish Valley. New York: Seminar Press.
    1981   Local Religion in Sixteenth-Century Spain. Princeton: Princeton University Press.
Duviols, Pierre
    1972   La Lutte contre les Religions Autochtones dans le Pérou Colonial. Lima: Institut Français d'Etudes Andines.
    1976   La Capacocha. Allpanchis 9:11-57.
    1979   Un Symbolisme de l'Occupation, de l'Aménagement et de l'Exploitation de l'Espace: Le Monolithe "Huanca" et sa Fonction dans les Andes Préhispaniques. L'Homme 19:7-31.
Escobar, Gabriel
    1967   Organización Social y Cultural del Sur del Perú. Mexico: Instituto Indigenista Interamericano.
Gorbak, Celina, Mirtha Lischetti, and Carmen Paula Muñoz
    1962   Batallas Rituales del Chiaraje y del Tocto de la Provincia de Kanas (Cuzco-Perú). Revista del Museo Nacional de Lima 31:245-304.
Gow, David D.
    1976   The Gods and Social Change in the High Andes. Ph.D. dissertation. Department of Development Studies, University of Wisconsin, Madison.
Imbelloni, José
    1946   Pachacuti IX (El Inkario Crítico). Buenos Aires: Editorial Nova.
Isbell, Billie Jean
    1978   To Defend Ourselves: Ecology and Ritual in an Andean Village. University of Texas, Institute of Latin American Studies. Austin.
Jiménez de la Espada, Marcos, ed.
    1965   Relaciones Geográficas de Indias (1557-86). 3 vols. Biblioteca de Autores Españoles (Cont.) 183-185. Madrid: Ediciones Atlas.
Keith, Robert G.
    1971   Encomienda, Hacienda and Corregimiento in Spanish America: A Structural Analysis. Hispanic American Historical Review 51:431-446.
Kubler, George
    1946   The Quechua in the Colonial World. In Handbook of South American Indians, Vol. 2. Julian H. Steward, ed. pp. 331-410. Washington, DC: Bureau of American Ethnology.
Lanning, Edward Putnam
    1967   Peru before the Incas. Englewood Cliffs, NJ: Prentice-Hall.
Leach, Edmund
    1972   Melchisedech and the Emperor: Icons of Subversion and Orthodoxy. Proceedings of the Royal Anthropological Institute 1972:5-14.

Lévi-Strauss, Claude
   1968   Do Dual Organizations Exist? In Structural Anthropology. Claire Jacobson and Brooke Grundfest Schoepf, transls. pp. 132-163. Harmondsworth, UK: Penguin.

Mariscotti de Görlitz, Ana Maria
   1978   Pachamama Santa Tierra. Berlin: Gebr. Mann Verlag.

Márquez Eyzaguirre, Luis G.
   1937   Huanka Rumi: Historia de las Apariciones del Señor de Huanka y de su Célebre Santuario. 2 vols. Arequipa: Editorial La Colmena.

Marriott, McKim
   1955   Little Communities in an Indigenous Civilization. In Village India. McKim Marriott, ed. pp. 171-222. Memoirs of the American Anthropological Association, No. 83. Menasha: American Anthropological Association.

Marzal, Manuel
   1971   El Mundo Religioso de Urcos. Cuzco: Instituto de Pastoral Andina.
   1977   Una Hipótesis sobre la Aculturación Religiosa Andina. Revista de la Universidad Católica (NS) 2:95-131.

Mecham, J. Lloyd
   1966 [1934]   Church and State in Latin America: A History of Politico-Ecclesiastical Relations. Chapel Hill: University of North Carolina Press.

Millones, Luis
   1973   Un Movimiento Nativista del Siglo XVI: El Taki Ongoy. In Ideología Mesiánica del Mundo Andino. Juan M. Ossio, ed. pp. 95-101. Lima: Ignacio Prado Pastor.

Morissette, Jacques, and Luc Racine
   1973   La Hierarchie des Wamani: Essai sur la Pensée Classificatoire Quechua. Recherches Amérindiennes au Quebec 3:167-188.

Núñez del Prado, Juan V.
   1970   El Mundo Sobrenatural de los Quechuas del Sur del Perú, a través de la Comunidad de Qotobamba. Allpanchis 2:57-120.

Ossio, Juan M.
   1973   Guaman Poma: Nueva Corónica o Carta al Rey. Un Intento de Aproximación a las Categorías del Pensamiento del Mundo Andino. In Ideología Mesiánica del Mundo Andino. Juan M. Ossio, ed. pp. 153-213. Lima: Ignacio Prado Pastor.

Pease, Franklin
   1968   Religión Andina en Francisco de Avila. Revista del Museo Nacional de Lima 35:62-76.
   1973   El Dios Creador Andino. Lima: Mosca Azul Editores.

Pike, Frederick B.
   1964   Introduction. In The Conflict between Church and State in Latin America. Frederick B. Pike, ed. pp. 3-27. New York: Alfred A. Knopf.

Ramirez, Juan Andrés
   1969   La Novena al Señor de Qoyllur Rit'i. Allpanchis 1:61-88.

Ramos Gavilán, Alonso
   1976   Historia de Nuestra Señora de Copacabana (1621). La Paz: Editorial Universo.

Redfield, Robert
   1941   The Folk Culture of Yucatan. Chicago: University of Chicago Press.
   1956   Peasant Society and Culture: An Anthropological Approach to Civilization. Chicago: University of Chicago Press.

Richardson, Miles, Marta Eugenia Pardo, and Barbara Bode
   1971   The Image of Christ in Spanish America as a Model for Suffering: An Explanatory Note. Journal of Interamerican Studies and World Affairs 8:246-257.

Rostworowski de Diez Canseco, María
   1976   Reflexiones sobre la Reciprocidad Andina. Revista del Museo Nacional de Lima 52:341-354.

Sallnow, M. J.
   1981   Communitas Reconsidered: The Sociology of Andean Pilgrimage. Man (NS) 16:163-182.

Santacruz Pachacuti, Joan de
   1950   Relación de Antigüedades deste Reyno del Pirú (1615). In Tres Relaciones de Antigüedades Peruanas. Marcos Jiménez de la Espada, ed. pp. 205-281. Asunción: Editorial Guaranía.

Sumption, Jonathan
   1975   Pilgrimage: An Image of Mediaeval Religion. London: Faber & Faber.

Turner, Victor W.
   1974   Dramas, Fields and Metaphors: Symbolic Action in Human Society. Ithaca: Cornell University Press.

Urbano, H. Osvaldo
   1974   La Representación Andina del Tiempo y del Espacio en el Fiesta. Allpanchis 7:9-48.

Valderrama Fernandez, Ricardo, and Carmen Escalante Gutierrez
   1977   Gregorio Condori Mamani, Autobiografía. Cuzco: Centro de Estudios Rurales Andinos.

Vallier, Ivan
   1970   Catholicism, Social Control and Modernization in Latin America. Englewood Cliffs, NJ: Prentice-Hall.

Vargas Ugarte, Ruben
   1947   Historia del Culto de María en Iberoamérica. 2 vols. Buenos Aires: Editorial Harpes.

Vrijhof, P. H.
   1979   Official and Popular Religion in 20th-Century Christianity. *In* Official and Popular Religion: Analysis of a Theme for Religious Studies. P. H. Vrijhof and J. D. J. Waardenburg, eds. pp. 217–243. The Hague: Mouton.

Wagner, Catherine Allen
   1978   Coca, Chicha and Trago: Private and Communal Rituals in a Quechua Community. Ph.D. dissertation. Department of Anthropology, University of Illinois, Urbana-Champaign.

Zuidema, R. T.
   1962   The Relationship between Mountains and Coast in Ancient Peru. *In* The Wonder of Man's Ingenuity. Mededelingen van het Rijksmuseum voor Volkenkunde, Leiden, no. 15. pp. 156–165. Leiden: E. J. Brill.
   1964   The Ceque System of Cuzco: The Social Organization of the Capital of the Inca. Leiden: E. J. Brill.
   1977   The Inca Calendar. *In* Native American Astronomy. A. Aveni, ed. pp. 219–259. Austin: University of Texas Press.

Submitted 31 July 1981
Accepted 21 October 1981
Revised version received 26 February 1982

signs in the social order: riding a Songhay bush taxi

PAUL STOLLER—*West Chester State College*

The lord whose oracle is at Delphi neither speaks nor conceals, but gives signs
—Heraclitus

When a Western visitor to Songhay country rides a bush taxi, he or she is suddenly thrown into a social universe in which many of the advantages of being a "prestigious" European are rudely pushed aside. No matter a person's status in the pecking order of Songhay society, riding a bush taxi in Songhay country is a rude initiation both to the uncomfortable conditions of public travel in the Republic of Niger and to the "hardness" of Songhay social interaction.

I took my first bush taxi ride in the fall of 1969 when I had been in the Republic of Niger a scant three weeks; I was going to depart for the town of Tera and my first teaching post. Arriving at the bush taxi depot early, I fully expected the taxi to leave on schedule. I waited impatiently for nearly 30 minutes before I asked someone in French about the hour of departure. The man to whom I had directed the question seemed to be organizing the loading operation. He smiled at me and said, *"toute de suite."* Reassured, I sat down under a tree and bought two oranges. One hour passed. City taxis came into the bush taxi depot and deposited more passengers bound for Tera. Young men took the baggage of these passengers and hoisted them atop the bush taxi. In my inchoate Songhay I asked the old woman sitting next to me about the hour of departure. "Who knows," she said. "In a little while." After two hours of waiting I noticed that a man, who appeared to be working on the engine of the bush taxi, was leaving the depot. Beside myself, I asked him where he was going. "To the autoshop. We need a new part." When I asked him when he would be back, he said, characteristically, *"toute de suite."* Another hour passed before the Songhay mechanic returned from the autoshop. He looked at me and said, "You should buy some

---

In any field of experience anthropologists are confronted by spates of signs, many of which they fail to perceive. By way of an analysis of the mundane activities associated with riding a Songhay bush taxi in the Republic of Niger, this article probes the reflexive process through which anthropologist and ethnographic other learn to interpret the signs that comprise the discourse of social action. Having been confronted repeatedly with the signs of the other's universe, anthropologists may not only gain a new awareness of the sociocultural systems they seek to uncover but may also realize the limitations of their knowledge. Through what Dilthey called the hermeneutic, anthropologists will be more able to proceed profoundly and accurately toward an understanding of those signs that give substance and order to the complexities of social universes. [ethnology, hermeneutics, fieldwork, Sahelian ethnography, Niger]

Copyright © 1982 by the American Ethnological Society
0094-0496/82/040750-13$1.80/1

meat before we get started." About 30 minutes later, another man, who had been scurrying about the depot all morning, announced that the taxi was about to depart and that all the passengers for Tera should board the taxi.

Bush taxis in the Songhay view of things are either converted Pugeot 404 pickup trucks, the carriers of which have two wooden planks secured to the floor for passenger seating, or larger vehicles called *mille kilo,* which are more like buses. Our vehicle for the ride to Tera was of the *mille kilo* variety. Along with the other passengers I picked up my bags and moved toward the vehicle that would transport us and our baggage to our destination. As I approached the *mille kilo* three or four young boys attempted to help me with my things. When I resisted their efforts, exclaiming that I could handle my own bags, they said something to me in Songhay that I did not comprehend and then attempted to help the elderly Nigerian gentleman just ahead of me with his things. He gave them his bags and gave each of them a few francs for their efforts. Inside the bus, the man who had announced our departure was telling people where they should sit. He suggested to the generous elderly gentleman that he sit next to the driver. When he saw me, he suggested that I sit next to the elderly gentleman. I said that it would be better for an old woman to sit in front of the taxi: "I'll sit in the back of the taxi like everyone else." The man looked at me strangely and told me to move on. The other passengers already seated in the back of the taxi greeted me and either giggled or laughed. Meanwhile, I squeezed myself between two young mothers, both of whom were nursing their children. The noontime heat made the air hot and stuffy in the crowded *mille kilo,* and the baby to my left vomited on me. The driver started the engine and we began our trek to Tera, a voyage of some 190 km which, due to frequent flat tires, engine breakdowns, social visits, and police stops along the way, took more than ten hours to complete.

I was too overcome by the heat, filth, and discomfort, not to mention my own ignorance of the Songhay sociocultural world, to understand what was occurring all around me. As in the case with the oracle of Delphi, no one was "speaking" to me and no one was concealing anything from me; rather, I found myself immersed in an alien universe of signs that I did not comprehend.[1]

When I returned to Songhay country in the Republic of Niger in 1976 to conduct anthropological fieldwork, I continued to use public transportation. After having taken bush taxis exclusively for a two-year period, I was no longer angered and irritated by long delays, engine failures, flat tires, or vomiting babies; in fact, I rather enjoyed talking with the friends I had made during all those many stops along the bush taxi route. Besides, I had gotten to know the drivers, apprentices, and the personalities of the bush taxi depot. Still, I did not "read," in the sense of Ricoeur (1979), bush taxi interaction as deeply as I might, for I was still only beginning to learn about Songhay society from the Songhay perspective.

Now, more than ten years after my first disconcerting bush taxi ride, I realize that the complex interactions that form the totality of Songhay bush taxi interaction correspond to deep-seated Songhay beliefs about the nature of the Songhay social world. Much as in Geertz's (1973) Balinese cockfight or Basso's (1979) Apache jokes about whitemen, riding a bush taxi, a thoroughly mundane social event, can be "read" as a set of symbolic actions that reinforce a corresponding set of Songhay cultural conceptions. This paper is therefore not only about the dynamic mesh that connects bush taxi interaction to Songhay culture, or the mundane to the profound, but also about the reflexive process in which anthropologist and ethnographic other learn to interpret the discourse of social action. It is through what Dilthey (1976) called the hermeneutic, I suggest, that anthropologists, like the seasoned interpreters of the oracle of Delphi, will be more able to proceed profoundly and accurately toward an understanding of those signs that form the foundations of sociocultural life.

bush taxi interaction in its social context

In the more than ten years since I took my first bush taxi ride in Songhay country, I have learned that the identities involved in any bush taxi interaction are all tied in one way or another to the history of the Songhay Empire. Some of the passengers in a *mille kilo* headed toward Tera, for example, are bound to be of noble blood *(mamar hamey)*, being the patrilineal descendants of Askia Mohammed Touré, the founder of the third and last dynasty of the Songhay Empire. The taxi drivers, the apprentice drivers, and the taxi loaders, by contrast, are likely to be (1) patrilineal descendants of prisoners of precolonial wars, which makes them former slaves *(benyey;* see Olivier de Sardin 1975, 1976); or (2) members of ethnic groups (Zerma, Wogo, Kurtey, Fulani, Hausa) who were conquered but not completely assimilated by the Songhay warriors (foreigners, *yeowy*).

In many ways the past intersects with the present when the members of these separate, but putatively unequal, social groups interact in any number of mundane social events including, of course, riding a bush taxi. This intersection of past and present seems to occur because "ideal" behaviors in everyday and ritual life are associated substantively with a Songhay's social grouping. Nobles, for example, are still considered to be separate and exclusive of both former slaves and foreigners. One reason for this is the ongoing practice of preferred endogamous marriages (patrilateral parallel cousins) within noble families. In the social arena of everyday behavior, nobles reinforce their exclusivity, and hence their prestige, through their comportment. They often dress in white robes and walk with wooden canes—two signs of chiefly authority. If they speak at all, they do so laconically. Should they wish to speak at length to a person of another social category, they employ a spokesperson to represent them (see Stoller 1978). Following a model similar to that of the Fulani (Riesman 1977), Songhay nobles are expected to be in absolute control of their actions and emotions *(maigatarey)*.

Former slaves and foreigners, by contrast, stand in complementary opposition to the nobles. While the restraint and laconicity of the nobles is considered dignified and prestigious, the emotionality and talkativeness of former slaves and foreigners is associated with undignified and stigmatized behavior. A noble would probably not lose his temper, and hence "face" (Goffman 1967), even in the most dire of circumstances. The former slave or the foreigner, by contrast, might well display his emotions openly and not lose "face," even in public contexts. These "ideal" behaviors that correspond to the major social groupings of Songhay society by no means account fully for the dynamics of Songhay social interaction. The culturally denoted expectations of ideal noble/nonnoble interaction, however, have a major bearing on which kind of social activities a son of Askia, as compared to a son of a prisoner of war, might engage in. Nobles to this day do not deign to engage in commercial activity; they would rather be represented by an intermediary (see Stoller 1978). Former slaves and foreigners, by contrast, have participated fully in the money economy, which was introduced into the rural areas of Songhay country some 50 years ago and today forms the foundation of the local economy. The noble, therefore, might well be a passenger on a bush taxi, but former slaves and foreigners are almost always the drivers, loaders, or owners of transport vehicles.

The foregoing description suggests that the structure of Songhay society is relatively static, the ideal behavioral expectations of the noble/nonnoble dyad having produced and maintained unequal and exclusive social categories. While the correlation of structure with both cultural categories and ideal behavioral expectations may account for the outcomes of some encounters in which Songhay are members of different social categories, it can tell us little about the encounters of people within one social category. The close "reading" of the set of symbolic interactions below suggests that in Songhay social interaction within nonnoble social categories, notions of status and role are not rigidly fixed by "ideal" cultural categories and behavioral expectations.

loading bush taxis in Bonfebba

Men load cargo and people into bush taxis every Friday in the village of Bonfebba, which is situated on the east bank of the Niger River in Songhay country. On Friday, which is market day, traders and travelers from the west bank, known in Songhay as *haro banda* (behind the river), come to Bonfebba by dugout to participate in market activities or to travel by bush taxi to such urban centers as Tillaberi and Niamey[2], which are located to the south. While the cast of characters who participate in the loading of a bush taxi may change from week to week, the mechanics of bush taxi loading remain fairly constant. A bush taxi cannot be loaded, obviously, if there are no passengers or cargo. But if there is cargo and if passengers do appear, then they must come in contact with people associated with bush taxis at market towns. There is the *coxeur,* who collects money from the passengers and who directs the actual loading of the taxi. The *coxeur* typically has one or two assistants who place the small cargo in the taxi and tie the more bulky cargo onto the taxi's roof. The assistants to the *coxeur* often hire their own assistants. The passenger, therefore, often comes in contact with the *coxeur*'s assistants' assistants. Each taxi, of course, has a driver, someone who has obtained his driver's permit and who knows very well how to repair automobile engines. The driver always has his personal assistant, who is called the *apprentice.* To become a driver one must serve a several-year apprenticeship.

All of the people associated with the loading of a bush taxi maintain some notion about the status and expectations of their social role. As we shall see from the description of the actual interaction involved in loading a taxi, however, the notion of status and the expectations it carries is negotiable.

Soga *(coxeur):*	Hey, everyone, hey! Come here. Tillaberi people. Loga people. Niamey people. Come here quickly. We must go. We will not wait.
((Passenger A presents herself to Soga.))	
Soga:	Where are you going, woman?
Passenger A:	I'm going to Tillaberi.
Soga:	Hand over the money, 600 francs.
Passenger A:	((laughs)) There is not enough [money]. Lower your price.
Soga:	((looking around)) Zakarey? Where is he? ((sees Zakarey, his assistant)) Come here!
((Zakarey arrives at the taxi.))	
Soga:	Zakarey, put the bags on top [of the bush taxi].
Zakarey:	Okay.
Soga:	((talking to the woman, Passenger A)) Go over there to wait, woman.
((Soga goes into the market to look for passengers. Passengers B, C, and D present themselves.))	
Soga:	Where are you going?
Passenger B:	Niamey.
Passenger C:	Tillaberi.
Passenger D:	Karta.
Soga:	The one going to Karta, 750 francs. The one going to Tilla, 600 francs. The one going to Niamey, 950 francs.

((The passengers give Soga the money without an argument; they know the standard prices.))

Soga: Zakarey. Go and fetch Boreyma. We need two people to carry the passengers' things.

((All of the passengers, nine in total, are waiting around the bush taxi while Zakarey and Boreyma, another assistant, hoist goods and personal baggage up to the roof of the taxi. The driver is nowhere in sight.))

Passenger C: When are we going to go? It is necessary that I arrive in Niamey before noon.

Soga: Patience man. Patience. ((looking around the market)) Okay. Everyone get into the bush taxi. . . . Boreyma, show the people where they should sit.

((Soga inspects the seating arrangement.))

Soga: It is no good. Alfa Abdoulaye! You must not sit in the back. Come here. Sit in the cabin [i.e., next to the driver in the most comfortable seat].

Passenger D: Where is the driver? We must go.

Soga: Patience. ((looks for the driver)) Good. He is coming now.

((The driver arrives and greets Soga, Zakarey, Boreyma, and a few of the passengers. He opens the hood of the bush taxi and looks under the taxi to inspect the suspension and the tires.))

Soga: Has everyone paid?

((Soga looks into the taxi and counts the money he has collected.))

Driver: Okay, Soga. How much [money] do you have?
Soga: There is 6500 francs.
Driver: In God's name, it is not enough, Soga.
Soga: It is enough!

((The driver gets into the taxi. Soga explains to him where each person is going and how much they had paid.))

Boreyma: ((pointing to a man in the back of the taxi)) Soga, you forgot that man.

Soga: ((in a loud voice)) I did not forget anyone. You [Boreyma] are a donkey. . . . ((looking at the driver)) Is it good?

Driver: It is good.

((The driver goes through the money and takes out 500 francs in 100-franc coins and gives them to Soga.))

Soga: ((screaming)) It will not do! It will never do! There is not enough money. You give some more.

Driver: ((smiles at Soga)) The owner does not agree, you know.

((The driver closes the window of the taxi. While Soga and Boreyma try to force open the window, the driver starts the engine and drives away.))

Soga: That man [the driver] is not easy [i.e., hard]. He is not good.
Zakarey: Where is my cut?
Boreyma: And mine?

((Boreyma grabs Soga while Zakarey searches his pockets.))

Zakarey: It is the money that we want. Hand it over.
Soga: ((gives them each 100 francs)) You get 100 francs.
Boreyma: It is not enough! It is not enough!
Zakarey: Soga, you, too, are a donkey. You must increase [our cut].

Soga: ((smiles at Zakarey and Boreyma)) If you are not agreed [to the amount], go and look for work again [i.e., somewhere else].[3]

In this interaction, Soga the *coxeur* is the focal point. By following closely what Soga does and says, one can uncover interactional patterns not uncommon in everyday Songhay life. To begin with, neither the owner nor the driver, the two most highly ranked social identities in the transport pecking order, are present for the entire interactional sequence. During most of the interaction, therefore, Soga the *coxeur* is in authority. Soga, in his interaction, attempts to maintain his social prestige as *coxeur*, as reflected in his use of language that is laced with requests and demands.

Since Soga knows the owner's prices, he will not (1) bargain with the woman, which would reveal his weakness, or (2) load the baggage on the roof of the taxi, which would be a symbolic reflection of inferior status. For the physical labor involved in loading the taxi, Soga hired, on his own initiative, two assistants. Soga's language to both his assistants and to his passengers—his requests and his demands—have an implicational force suggesting that he perceives that he is in authority and is maintaining his social prestige.

Soga's authority is diminished greatly, however, when the driver returns to the taxi. As soon as the driver arrives Soga makes his first request for information other than the destination of the passengers, asking if everyone had paid. The driver ignores this and asks the *coxeur* how much money he had collected. When Soga tells him the amount, the driver replies that the *coxeur* is short. Here the implication is that (1) Soga might have pocketed the money, a veiled insult, or (2) the driver, knowing that 6500 francs is the correct amount, is making trouble for Soga so as to shame the *coxeur* in public while asserting his own prestige as driver. Boreyma, sensing the driver's motive, tries to take advantage of the situation by asserting that Soga has forgotten to collect money from one passenger, a rather direct challenge to Soga's competence and authority. Soga, reacting to Boreyma's assertion and wishing to maintain face, insults his assistant, calling him a donkey; he then asserts that he has forgotten no one. The driver accepts this and gives Soga 500 francs for his work. Soga becomes angry with the driver for paying a *coxeur* so little money—an insult to his competence and skill as *coxeur*. But the driver absolves himself; the owner, the ultimate, albeit absent, authority, is the person who sets the prices for passage, for cargo, and for *coxeurs*. Despite the near-violent protests of Soga and his assistants, the driver leaves Bonfebba, having used this brief interaction scene to reinforce his authority at the expense of Soga.

The give and take of Songhay bush taxi loading is not complete, however. Soga's assistants want their money. They begin therefore to play the kind of game Soga played only a minute earlier with the driver. Soga, once again in authority, must be firm. He gives each assistant 100 francs and suggests that if they are not happy with this amount, they should search elsewhere for work. Here, Soga's pattern of language use reverts back to its strong full tone of assertions and demands and not the pleading questions of angry but powerless assertions. Beneath the surface encounters of the bush taxi interaction, however, there appears an ethos of "hardness," examples of which are expressed throughout the interaction. Soga harshly ignores the woman who cannot pay the required price for the trip to Tillaberi; he tells her to go and sit under a tree, and no one comes to her aid. The taxi driver expresses little sympathy toward Soga when he gives the *coxeur* an unsuitable fee for his services; instead, he expresses his contempt for Soga and his assistants by rapidly shutting his taxi window, literally closing himself off from his social inferiors. Soga also treats his assistants crudely, barking orders at them as though they were donkeys. Soga's assistants attempt to insult him in public. The result of all of this "hardness" is that people are either shaming others or being shamed in public contexts. Indeed, from brief exposure to this typical slice of Songhay bush taxi interaction, we confront a Songhay social arena—the marketplace—that is not only "hard," but crude and harsh as well.[4]

The results of this interpretive analysis of Songhay discourse present us with an ethos of "hardness." But is the expression of "hardness" found only in market contexts? Are there cultural roots to that which is expressed in the market? And if there are cultural roots to Songhay market discourse, how do we proceed to uncover these deeper levels of meaning?

deep and surface readings of bush taxi interaction

To uncover the deep meanings of bush taxi interaction, the analyst must understand how elements of interaction express meanings at various levels of cultural significance. Readers of bush taxi interaction must therefore attempt to understand "not another person, but a project, that is, the outline of new being-in-the-world" (Ricoeur 1979:79). Put another way, the deep reader of Songhay bush taxi interaction must come to understand what people are "saying" to one another and how this "saying" corresponds to those signs that make the world comprehensible.[5] To approach a more profound "reading" of bush taxi loading, we must journey beyond the analysis of surface discourse and attempt to see how this discourse "reverberates" (Bachelard 1964) in the pit of Songhay being.[6] If we wish to "seize the reality of an image" (Bachelard 1964:xv) to see how it "reverberates" in the pit of (Songhay) being, we must consider the metaphorical aspects of symbolic expression.

The analysis of metaphor is "perhaps the most perplexing, vexed and intractable question in the whole philosophy of language" (Edie 1976:151). Despite the embryonic state of metaphorical theory, we can say that metaphors are tropes that, by linking two seemingly unrelated semantic domains, forge a new meaning (Sapir 1977:6). Further, the metaphor may also juxtapose "elements of a concrete image in order to formulate some set of more abstract relationships" (Beck 1978:83). Indeed, metaphor appears to be a central cognitive mechanism that can provide the organizing images that render experience intelligible (Fernandez 1976:100–102). It is for this reason that elements of metaphor can be found in ordinary discourse: "Metaphor permeates all discourse, ordinary and special, and we should have a hard time finding a purely literal paragraph anywhere..." (Goodman 1963:80). Johnson and Lakoff (1980:454) suggest, moreover, that metaphors "structure what we perceive, how we get around, and how we relate to one another." Metaphors therefore seem to structure the relationships among many of the objects, concepts, and/or social others we confront in our experience.

bush taxis, metaphors, and Songhay proverbs   It is clear that people do not speak entirely in metaphors. In the sentence, "The chairman ploughed through the meeting," the word "ploughed" is the only metaphorical element in an otherwise literal sentence (Black 1962). Returning to the bush taxi interaction, it is equally clear that the interactants are not speaking in metaphors. If we reread the bush taxi sequences presented above, however, we can isolate a number of relationships structured through metaphors. If we then juxtapose those relationships to a number of corresponding Songhay proverbs and idiomatic expressions, we can interpret the interaction more deeply.

Consider, first of all, the relationship between TIME and PATIENCE, which finds expression in the following items from the interaction as well as from a number of Songhay proverbs and idioms.

example 1   Q: When are we leaving?
A: Patience, patience.

example 2   Q: When is the driver coming?
                A: In a little while. Have patience.
example 3   Old men have patience.
example 4   Men without patience die young.
example 5   Youth are always in a hurry; they have no patience.

These statements consider time on two levels. Time is considered in a chronemic manner, as in examples 1 and 2, in which the request for information as to when X is coming or when X is going is answered not by a distinct time (noon, 3:30) but by the exhortation "patience." This answer reflects the more fundamental relationship in Songhay thought between time-in-life and patience. "Old men have patience," hence they understand the meaning of time, for "men without patience die young" and "youth are always in a hurry" (i.e., they lack patience). The metaphorically structured statements about time that I have isolated, however, seem not to reference—even tangentially—Songhay beliefs about time and wisdom, age and wisdom, or the sweep of time from the mythic origins of Songhay to the present. Beliefs about time and wisdom and age and wisdom seem to be more connected to the metaphoric elements found in proverbs. Notions of Songhay mythic time are even further removed from surface discourse; they are embodied in the symbolic movement of such rituals as possession dance, magic rites, and circumcision. Symbolic "motion thus becomes a metaphor, one's time being enacted within another, distilling myth, incarnating it in the process of being enacted" (Armstrong 1980:77–78). The surface discourse of the bush taxi interaction therefore presents to the analyst an opening to deeper levels of metaphoric interpretation.

The second metaphoric relationship that I have isolated in the bush taxi loading sequence concerns MEN and DONKEYS. In the slice of interaction presented above, Soga says to Boreyma:

example 6   You [Boreyma] are a donkey.

Later in the interaction, Boreyma returns the compliment. There are other statements in Songhay speech in which human activities are understood (unfavorably) in terms of donkeys.

example 7   Your head and a donkey's head; it is the same thing.
example 8   You are the son of a donkey.

From these examples, which can serve as real or ritual insults (see Stoller 1977), we understand that the activities of human beings who are slow-witted are seen in light of donkeys. But the observation of human beings interacting with donkeys and a perusal of Songhay proverbs sheds more light, it seems, on the relationship of MEN and DONKEYS. Donkeys have no dignity in the natural order. Songhay throw stones at donkeys and sometimes beat them over the head with *batons* for no apparent reason. Donkeys are abused and are expected to work incessantly, as is suggested by the following proverb.

example 9   Even while the donkey is resting, there is a load on its back.

By juxtaposing a number of relevant Songhay proverbs to the analysis of the symbolic expression found in the bush taxi interaction, we flesh out the relationship of men to donkeys. In everyday language, Songhay are not likely to use sentences that highlight the similarity of the behavior of some men to that of donkeys.

The third metaphoric relationship I have isolated concerns MEN and ROCKS. In everyday language, and in the bush taxi interaction, men and their behaviors can be conceived in terms of rocks, that which is hard, not easy to move, or intractable.

example 10 The man is *not easy* [hard].[7]
example 11 His hands are *hard*.
example 12 He has inner strength (*fula*); he is *not easy*.

To be hard is a desirable quality in Songhay social life: one is respected if he or she is tough, resolute, and successful in asserting his/her will, just as the taxi driver asserts his will in his interaction with Soga. Despite his "hardness," however, the driver does not want to be held responsible for the low wages he gives to Soga and his assistants. He therefore tells them that the owner is the one who sets the prices; someone external to the immediate context, the driver is "saying," is responsible for your grief and misfortune. A hard man is capable of mercy if mercy does not jeopardize his social position. The ethos of "hardness" is therefore not limited to market discourse; it is anchored to an important conception of Songhay social life, a conception that, at its foundation, is metaphorically structured.

nonlinguistic metaphors and Songhay symbolic interaction

Analysts such as Thompson (1974), Fernandez (1976), and more recently Beck (1978), have discussed the fact that metaphors can be nonlinguistic as well as linguistic and that scholars of symbolic expression in society would profit by paying as much attention to the nonlinguistic as to the linguistic aspects of metaphor. The examination of the linguistic data of the bush taxi loading in Bonfebba does provide us with some significant insights. We do get the connection of time and patience, men and donkeys, and men and rocks. The more substantive statements of these metaphoric relationships are brought forth in proverbs (example 9) and idiomatic expressions (examples 3, 4, 5, 12, and 13) that were not directly expressed during the bush taxi loading.

Proceeding deeper than the interpretation of the metaphoric relationships based on the interactive sequences or on Songhay proverbs and idioms, we arrive at the threshold of metaphorically structured symbolic interaction. Here, the total comportment of the interactant is considered as a whole. The analysis of the bush taxi interaction has already suggested to us that the relationships of men and rocks (i.e., "hardness") is metaphorically structured. What about the notion of money and hardness? If one relies on strictly linguistic data, he or she would not isolate a relationship between money and "hardness"; but if we consider the total scope of symbolic expression, the relationship between money and "hardness" stares us in the face. Soga, for example, is "hard" in his interaction with the passengers. He uses short, curt sentences with them and will not negotiate prices. Indeed, the driver acts "hard" when he deals with Soga. In both cases, "hardness" as a set of behaviors is associated with money and its handling.

Probing still deeper into the Songhay world of meaning, we see that "hardness" and social negotiation are interconnected. There are a number of instances in which Soga's assistants attempt to exceed the limits of their social role. Boreyma does just this when he suggests that Soga, a professional *coxeur*, has forgotten to collect money from one man. Soga realizes this affront and puts Boreyma in his place by calling him a donkey.

In general, this kind of social negotiation and attempt at status manipulation is highly characteristic of the Songhay marketplace; it pervades the loading of a bush taxi. Passengers, for example, must be seated in symbolic patterns. If the appropriate pattern is violated, as when the Islamic cleric had been seated in the rear of the taxi, clearly a position designated for someone of a lesser social status, the situation must be corrected in a "hard" way. The driver's interaction with Soga, moreover, is a clear case of social negotiation—the driver inflates his status at the expense of Soga, who before the arrival of the driver had been "hard" and in control.

Despite the aura of social negotiation, the people associated with loading a bush taxi go only so far. While Boreyma, Soga, and the driver manipulate Songhay symbolic expression to gain as much momentary prestige as possible, when all is literally said and done, no one has progressed. The driver still maintains his superior position vis-à-vis Soga, who remains in a position superior to Boreyma and Zakarey. The absent owner controls the entire group; he sets the prices and the payment schedules. Correspondingly, the social interaction of bush taxi loading exhibits negotiation, but the rights and duties of many of the roles remain by and large fixed—controlled, as they are, by external forces. This extremely important conception of Songhay everyday reality concerning the fixedness of the social order is not referenced in everyday language, but through the deep "reading" of experience day in and day out.

Foreigners and former slaves cannot become nobles; *coxeurs* do not become drivers. There are, of course, exceptions to this pattern in the commercial sector: some assistants do become *coxeurs;* apprentices become drivers; some drivers become owners. But these upward transitions are rare, in the Songhay view of things, and the odds are in favor of role stagnation rather than role transformation. The notion of fixedness corresponds to the Songhay notion that life in general is controlled by forces outside the self. One's putative progress in life in the commercial sector depends on the whims of another (in the case of Soga, on the whims of the driver and the absentee owner). Fixedness, therefore, is a central concept of the relation of self to the Songhay social world.

With the notion of fixedness, we are again confronted with a static representation of the Songhay social order. If the Songhay's fate is ascribed at his or her birth, then his or her social category is fixed. This static representation of the Songhay social order seems inaccurate, however. As we have seen, Songhay actors in the public arena of a social event manipulate symbolic expression to inflate their public status, however fleetingly, at the expense of the social other. Perhaps it would be more fitting to say that Songhay fixedness seems to represent a set of invariant brackets within which social negotiation takes place. Former slaves cannot become nobles, but if they are crafty negotiators in the commercial sector, they can become noblelike (see Stoller 1980).

Moving another step deeper into the Songhay scheme of things we can appreciate fully the connection of social negotiation to "hardness." In the past nobles were "hard" warriors *(wangari);* today their comportment is a demonstration of the noble attribute *fula,* inner strength and intractability. Similarly, former slaves and foreigners demonstrate the "hardness" of Songhay social interaction, challenging one another if only for a brief moment of social prestige, as in Boreyma's challenge to Soga. Generally speaking, the "harder" a person is, the more prestige he or she gathers; and the more prestige he or she gathers, the more noblelike he or she becomes. These, then, are the cross currents in Songhay society. The social order is arranged in ascribed and generally exclusive social categories of unequal rank; the nobles are exclusive of the foreigners and the former slaves; and human interaction in this ascribed social order is characterized by a high degree of social negotiation. Former slaves will sometimes challenge the "face" of the nobles, and they sometimes win a momentary victory (see Stoller 1981). The former slaves' victorious encounter with a son of Askia is illusory, however, for when all is said and done, not much has changed. The former slave can never claim to have the blood of the Askias running in his veins.

reading and metaphoric linkages

"Reading," in the interpretive sense I am using here, is an essential attribute of the process of gaining and integrating knowledge; as I have attempted to demonstrate in this article, it is a subjective action the depth of which is shaped by our set of experiences. In my own case, my first "reading" of Songhay bush taxi interaction had little to do with the Songhay and more to do with my own set of admittedly ethnocentric predispositions. Anthropologists, for the most part, are keenly aware of their cultural blindness when they are first exposed to another culture. The accumulation of knowledge through fieldwork, however, enables most of us to focus our vision of the other culture. Fieldwork experiences, however exceptional they might be, do not guarantee a deep comprehension of another culture. Deeper readings of bush taxi interaction, for example, must correspond to deeper experiences in the Songhay world, for "we must say that the meaningful patterns which a depth-interpretation wants to grasp cannot be understood without a kind of personal commitment similar to that of the reader who grasps the depth semantics of a text and makes it his own" (Ricoeur 1979:100). This commitment, it seems to me, is not to use what one can discover about the Songhay or any other group to prove or disprove a universal truth, but to attempt to understand the ethnographic other from his or her perspective.

The commitment to which Ricoeur speaks obliquely is more than the anthropologists' attempt to master the language of the people he or she is studying. As any sociolinguist would suggest, there is more to learning a language than studying its phonology and grammar. To be able to use a language one must immerse oneself in both *langue* and *parole* and learn both linguistic and sociolinguistic rules (see Albert 1972; Hymes 1974). Going one step further, one could say that for deep "readers" to make the text their own, they must begin to grasp the metaphoric linkages, the "reverberations" that are expressed in discourse.

> It is perhaps the emergence of expressivity that constitutes the marvel of language.... There is no mystery in language. The most poetic, most "sacred" language operates with the same semic variables as the most banal word of the dictionary. But there is a mystery of language. It is that language says, says something, says something of being. If there is an enigma of symbolism it resides entirely at level of manifestation where the equivocity of being becomes said in discourse (Ricoeur 1967:71).

As I have begun to learn more about Songhay language, in Ricoeur's sense, the better I am able to place the symbolic interactions of such mundane activities as loading a bush taxi into deeper perspectives. This vantage has revealed to me the full significance of "hardness" and its relation to social negotiation. Perhaps the importance of a hermeneutical approach to anthropological inquiry is, however, that as a process it continually reveals to the anthropologist the limitations of his or her knowledge. After more than 40 years of commitment to the Songhay world, Jean Rouch is still learning about the vagueries and the metaphoric complexities of the Songhay cosmos. Such commitment is probably beyond the expectations or hopes of American anthropologists who must compete for dwindling research funds. Without this commitment to "language," or to deep "reading," which may take years to develop, how can we be sure that what we claim to know is indeed knowledge? As one of my Songhay teachers suggested to me: "If you listen to us, you will learn much about our ways. But to have vision, you must grow old with us." As the discipline of anthropology proceeds from crisis to crisis, it might be beneficial to remember the aphorism of Heraclitus and confront fully those signs we encounter daily in the field.

notes

Acknowledgments. For their advice about the deeper "readings" of Songhay social life, I thank Jean Rouch and Sohanci Adamu Jenitongo of Tillaberi, Niger. I would also like to thank Paul Riesman and the anonymous reviewers of this journal for their comments. The research on which this article is based was made possible through monies provided by a Fulbright-Hays Doctoral Dissertation Research Fellowship (G00-76-03659), a Wenner-Gren Foundation For Anthropological Research Grant-in-Aid

(#3175), and a NATO Postdoctoral Fellowship in Science for the academic year 1979-80. I thank the institutions that granted me these funds for their generous support. I also wish to thank S. E. Colonel Seyni Kountché, President of the Republic of Niger, for granting me authorizations to conduct ethnographic research in Niger. Thanks are also due to Mrs. Lucille Mitchell who typed and retyped the manuscript.

[1] This paper is a hermeneutical analysis of the nature of anthropological understanding. My use of the term "sign" should therefore not be taken as an intrinsic part of a strict semiological analysis of Songhay bush taxi interaction. Here, I use the term "sign" to denote the presence of a fact, condition, or quality not immediately evident to an observer.

[2] Tillaberi and Niamey are the major urban centers of the westernmost regions of the Republic of Niger. Most of the passengers boarding at Bonfebba, however, pass through Tillaberi enroute to Niamey, a city of more than 250,000, which is also the capital of the Republic of Niger.

[3] While I have presented a corpus of interactional data in this paper, my presentation and analysis of it do not fit within the conventional parameters of conversational analysis (see Schegloff, Jefferson, and Sacks 1977; Labov 1973; Sudnow 1972). Here, interactional data are not seen as data sources from which rules and/or structures can be induced but rather as indications of deeper symbolic and metaphoric relationships that are central to a deeper comprehension of the complexities of Songhay social life. In this light, my analysis is more akin to some of the earlier works of Goffman (1971, 1974).

[4] Paul Riesman pointed this out to me.

[5] "Saying" refers to metacommunicative action. As Bateson (1972), among others, has pointed out, the utterance of a simple sentence may carry any number of metacommunicative messages, some of which are "deeper" than others.

[6] Bachelard uses the term "reverberations" in his discussion of poetics. He suggests that the impact of a poem, for example, lies not in its referential content, but in how this referential content carries a message that strikes a resonant chord (reverberates) in the reader. In a similiar vein, the signs one confronts in Songhay bush taxi interaction can precipitate "reverberations" in a person immersed in this field of Songhay experience.

[7] In the Songhay language there exists a set of expressions such as *Ni manti fala* (literally, "You are not easy"), which means in the context of its use, "You are hard." Similarly, there are idioms such as *hal manti moso* (literally, "until not a little"), which means "a whole lot" or "very much." One therefore finds a sentence such as *A ga ba ni hal manti moso* (literally, "I like you until not a little"). In the context of its use, however, this sentence means "I like you a whole lot."

references cited

Albert, Ethel
    1972   Cultural Patterning of Speech Behavior in Burundi. *In* Directions in Sociolinguistics: The Ethnography of Communication. J. J. Gumperz and D. Hymes, eds. pp. 72-106. New York: Holt, Rinehart and Winston.

Armstrong, Robert Plant
    1980   Review Essay of African Art in Motion: Icon and Art in the Collection of Katherine Coryton White. Studies in Visual Communication 6(2):77-82.

Bachelard, Gaston
    1964   The Poetics of Space. New York: Orion Press.

Basso, Keith
    1979   Portraits of "The Whiteman." New York: Cambridge University Press.

Bateson, Gregory
    1972   Steps to an Ecology of Mind. New York: Ballantine Books.

Beck, Brenda, E. F.
    1978   The Metaphor as a Mediator Between the Semantic and Analogic Modes of Thought. Current Anthropology 19:83-88.

Black, Max
    1962   Models and Metaphors. Ithaca: Cornell University Press.

Dilthey, Wilhelm
    1976   The Development of Hermeneutics: Selected Writings. H. P. Rickman, ed. and transl. Cambridge: Cambridge University Press.

Edie, James
    1976   Speaking and Meaning: The Phenomenology of Language. Bloomington: Indiana University Press.

Fernandez, James W.
    1976   The Performance of Ritual Metaphors. *In* The Social Use of Metaphor: Essays on the Anthropology of Rhetoric. J. David Sapir and J. Christopher Crocker, eds. pp. 100-132. Philadelphia: University of Pennsylvania Press.

Geertz, Clifford
   1973   Deep Play: Notes on the Balinese Cockfight. *In* The Interpretation of Cultures. pp. 412–455. New York: Basic Books.
Goffman, Erving
   1967   Interaction Ritual: Essays on Face to Face Behavior. Chicago: Aldine.
   1971   Relations in Public. New York: Harper & Row.
   1974   Frame Analysis. New York: Harper & Row.
Goodman, Nelson
   1963   Languages of Art. Indianapolis: Hackete Publishing.
Hymes, Dell
   1974   Foundations in Sociolinguistics: An Ethnographic Perspective. Philadelphia: University of Pennsylvania Press.
Johnson, Bruce, and George Lakoff
   1980   Conceptual Metaphor in Everyday Language. Journal of Philosophy 78(8):453–487.
Labov, William
   1973   Language in the Inner City. Philadelphia: University of Pennsylvania Press.
Olivier de Sardin, Jean-Pierre
   1975   Captifs Ruraux et Esclaves Imperiaux du Songhai. *In* l'Esclavage en Afrique Precoloniale. Claude Meillassoux, ed. pp. 99–135. Paris: Francois Maspero.
   1976   Quand Nos Pères Etaient Captifs. Paris: Nubia.
Ricoeur, Paul
   1967   Le Problème du "Double" Sens Comme Problème Hermeneutique et Comme Problème Semantique. Cahiers Internationeaux de Symbolisme 6:56–71.
   1979   The Model of the Text: Meaningful Actions Considered as a Text. *In* Interpretive Social Science. Paul Rabinow and William Sullivan, eds. pp. 73–103. Berkeley: University of California Press.
Riesman, Paul
   1977   Freedom in Fulani Social Life: An Introspective Ethnography. Chicago: University of Chicago Press.
Sapir, J. David
   1977   The Anatomy of a Metaphor. *In* The Social Use of Metaphor: Essays on the Anthropology of Rhetoric. J. David Sapir and J. Christopher Crocker, eds. pp. 3–33. Philadelphia: University of Pennsylvania Press.
Schegloff, Emanuel, Gail Jefferson, and Harvey Sacks
   1977   The Preference for Self-correction in the Organization of Repair in Conversation. Language 53(2):361–382.
Stoller, Paul A.
   1977   Ritual and Personal Insults in Songrai Sonni. Anthropology 2:31–37.
   1978   The Dynamics of Bankwano: Communication and Political Legitimacy among the Songhay (Republic of Niger). Ann Arbor: University Microfilms.
   1980   The Negotiation of Songhay Space: Phenomenology in the Heart of Darkness. American Ethnologist 7:419–431.
   1981   Social Interaction and the Management of Songhay Sociopolitical Change. Africa 52(3):765–780.
Sudnow, David, ed.
   1972   Studies in Social Interaction. New York: The Free Press.
Thompson, Robert Farris
   1974   African Art in Motion: Icon and Art in the Collection of Katherine Coryton White. Berkeley: University of California Press.

Submitted 7 August 1981
Accepted 10 November 1981
Revised version received 9 February 1982

taskonomy: a practical approach to knowledge structures

JANET W. D. DOUGHERTY—University of Illinois, Urbana
CHARLES M. KELLER—University of Illinois, Urbana

Ethnoscientific research has contributed significantly to the comparative study of man's classification of natural phenomena (Berlin, Breedlove, and Raven 1973; Berlin and Kay 1969; Rosaldo 1972; M. Brown 1978; Bulmer 1968; Hunn 1976). In a few cases, exemplified by Frake's (1961) analysis of Subanun disease, research in this tradition has focused on other phenomena, adding a new dimension to our understanding. Extensions of this classificatory framework to artifactual material have been particularly problematic (Brown, Kolar, Torry, Triiong-Quang, and Volkman 1976; Rosch, Mervis, Gray, Johnson, and Boyes-Braem 1976).[1] Currently, a diversification of research strategies is developing in the field of cognitive anthropology which builds on the earlier work and establishes a new focus on conceptualization rather than on language. Broad directions for modification of the traditional ethnoscience include attention to time (Gatewood 1978), process (Randall 1976, 1980; Lave 1980; De La Roche, Faust, and Murtaugh 1980), function (Hunn 1980), and variability in human behavior (Hays 1976, 1980; M. Brown 1980). Taskonomy draws on all of these, emphasizing particularly process and function, to account for the productivity evident in even the most prosaic human behavior. Our concern here is with everyday behavior and its relationship to language, not with the system of labeled categories as isolated from that behavior. As such, our emphasis is cognitive, not linguistic.[2]

Our discussion is intended to demonstrate three main points, two of them substantive, one methodological. Beginning with the premise that information is organized for much of everyday activity on the basis of goal-oriented tasks and strategies (Schutz 1964, 1971; Miller, Galanter, and Pribram 1960; Schank and Abelson 1977), it is shown that (1) everyday activity requires recognition and manipulation of distinctions not codified in naming; (2) a

---

The New Ethnography spawned studies in cognition focusing on reference, naming, and the relations among labeled categories. Building on this research, we examine the connections between labeled categories and everyday behavior. In day-to-day situations, standard labeled segregates are often aspects of taken-for-granted knowledge. A task at hand differentially focuses an individual's awareness as strategies for action in the situation are constructed. Knowledge is thus selectively focused and organized in response to constraints of the task. The basic units in this organization are the notions (often unlabeled) of particular processes and things and the complexes of relevant features that people focus on. These units and their interrelations are flexible constructs subject to continual modification as the task at hand changes. [ethnomethodology, ethnoscience, preindustrial technology, New Ethnography, cognition]

Copyright © 1982 by the American Ethnological Society
0094-0496/82/040763-12$1.70/1

task at hand determines features of relevance for conceptualization; and (3) as strategies for action, organizations of knowledge are particularistically oriented, and the processes of organization are productive.

As individuals behave they create and recreate organizations of aspects of their knowledge relevant to a task at hand. The pragmatic orientation of such everyday behavior is well illustrated in technological activity, characterized as a set of categories and plans to achieve a given end (from Bock 1969:269). The investigation of cognition described here is based on the technological activity of blacksmithing, which involves the heating and shaping of iron. It draws upon the blacksmithing expertise of Keller, which includes an apprenticeship in 1976 and four subsequent years of practice, and upon observations and interviews with blacksmiths of the American Southwest over a five-year period.[3] The mode of analysis we develop is not unique to blacksmithing. Any mundane project and attendant strategies will play a similar role in establishing relevance for conceptual organization.

task-oriented constellations of knowledge

In investigating the knowledge of blacksmithing, it soon becomes evident that there are numerous ways in which relevant knowledge is organized and reorganized, and, initially, that the place of the naming system within this complex of conceptual organizations is not clear. Lists of the names of tools can easily be elicited. The labeled units include *hot punch, center punch, hardy, slitter, bending forks, file, hammer, half-round file,* and *two-pound farrier's hammer.* Materials and products can also be enumerated by name. It is difficult, however, to elicit consistent statements concerning the relationships among these units. The named categories appear to be considered as part of a taken-for-granted world that belongs within a system of open possibilities (Schutz 1971:81).

Open possibilities suggest shifting, flexible, creative organizations of knowledge. It is this very "open" quality that frustrated our initial ethnosemantic inquiries. Once extensive inventories of named categories of tools, products, and materials had been collected, we proceeded to investigate the ways in which these named units are conceptually interrelated. Interviews proceeded as follows: "Given all these tools, can you sort them on the basis of some natural groupings?" or "Of these three tools which two go together?" The consistently elicited response was, "For what?" Without a particular task as the basis for cognitive organization, the blacksmith relies on principles generally relevant to blacksmithing. For example, "things that can be used as they are" versus "things that can be used without much additional work" versus "things that were once something but are now scrap."

More specific probing for a basic organizational system based on language, such as that suggested in the work of Brown et al. (1976) or Rosch et al. (1976), seemed to push the informant to make irrelevant decisions. Questions such as, "Is a cross-peen a kind of hammer?" or "Is a sledge hammer a kind of hammer?" or "Is this [holding a claw hammer] a kind of hammer?" were considered odd by practicing blacksmiths. "Nobody talks about it that way" is a common response. These early interviews, coupled with observation of natural conversations in the blacksmith shop, failed to point to basic linguistic units and the relations of contrast and inclusion among them as primary conceptual dimensions.

Concerned by the lack of reliance on ready-made named categories, we sorted tools using a linguistic template for the organization of categories. In the context of a working shop, with the tools present, they were sorted into clusters based on their common labels. *Hammers,* including ball-peen, claw, sledges, mallets, and a variety of others were separated from *saws,* including hacksaws, coping saws, a Japanese carpenter's saw, and cross-cut and rip saws. Similar units of *tongs, clamps,* and *chisels* were segregated as well.

One blacksmith queried about the logic of this organization tried to make the point that this was only one of a large number of possible ways to think about the tools. "We could sort them into tools with wooden handles, single pieces of metal, pivoted metal tools, and multicomponent tools, too...." Without some sort of goal direction or task these sortings seem irrelevant to task-oriented blacksmiths.

The linguistic sorting is the result of applying a general classification scheme that solves the task and is consistently based on patterns of naming. Such general classification schemes may be employed by an analyst to create a context for sorting that an informant can work within if required to, even though it is not necessarily useful during specialized activity. The assumption, common in ethnographic semantics, that conceptualization frequently parallels such linguistically based clustering (Frake 1969:28; Berlin et al. 1973: 214-216; Kay 1970:19) is one we cannot make. To better understand the relationship between speech and other cognitive activity, we turn to an investigation of a system of specialized knowledge.

We discard the notion of the basic morphological/linguistic hierarchy as central to the cognitive organization of blacksmithing and, in what follows, examine the kinds of organization that do make sense to blacksmiths at work. Here we return to the notion of open possibilities—to the productive organization of information on the basis of a particular context. The first relevant (and the broadest) organizational system to emerge during our investigation is based on the proper location for each tool in the shop. Every tool has a place based on associations for common jobs, component materials, shape, availability with respect to fixed elements such as the forge and the anvil or post drill, and physical features of the shop. The location-based system is task oriented. It is used when specific tools are selected and also when tools are replaced during the task of cleaning up. To quote from a section of one interview concerning the proper location of tools in the shop:

> bending forks, crescent wrench, pliers, hacksaw go on the vise post, most commonly used hammers go on the ground by the anvil stump,.... Wire brush, bick and files with handles go on the holders in the anvil stump, other files go on the ground or in the tool box. The rivet header goes on the anvil stump. The spoon, little poker and tongs go on the rack on the forge. The sprinkler can goes in the slack tub. The mallet goes on the other stump. The graphite block goes close to where the torch is.

Tools are organized on the basis of proper location in a way that crosscuts the structures based on naming patterns. Some hammers go in one place, some in another; some files go with the rivet header on the anvil stump, others go elsewhere; bending forks, crescent wrench, pliers, and hacksaws, linguistically unrelated, are grouped together as tools belonging on the vice post. Common labels do not constrain proper placement.

The locational system of conceptual organization does involve shallow hierarchy. Within the context of putting things away or retrieving them, labeled units such as *stump tools, drill press rack tools,* and *fire tools* emerge. These are usually idiosyncratic labels for clusters of tools based on location. The names are not necessarily shared even by smiths in the same shop, but develop individually for personal, cognitive organization in the working situation, or for ease of reference during an interview with the anthropologist. Variable as the linguistic labels are, however, these names do refer to useful clusters of tools. As analysts, we might represent such organizations as taxonomic trees, as in Figure 1. But these illustrations of shallow hierarchy should be treated only as analytical conveniences. The diagrams suggest a permanence or context-free validity that is inappropriate for genuine taskonomy. The organizations of knowledge, in short, need a task-oriented contextual frame. An alternative representation, from one working blacksmith's point of view, is presented in Figure 2. This situates the clustering of tools appropriately in the context of location within a shop. Such a context-specific, locational image, and the tool assignments

```
        FIRE TOOLS                    STUMP TOOLS

      poker    spoon      hardy   old file used for hot rasping   wire brush

                     DRILL PRESS RACK TOOLS

   drill bits   extension cords   vise grips   C clamps   squares   one electric drill
```

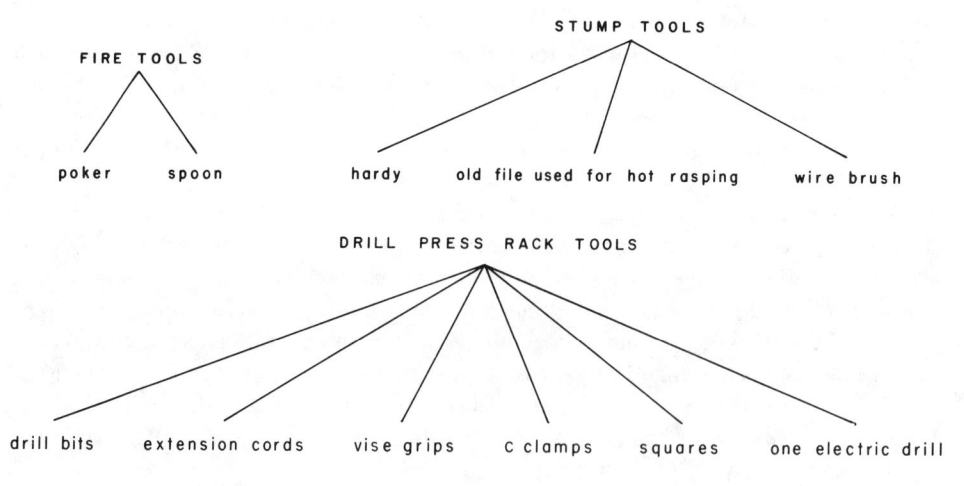

Figure 1. Illustrative hierarchies representing interrelations among clusters of tools kept at particular shop locations.

within it, while messier than the taxonomic trees, more closely reflect the smith's conceptual organization and the project-oriented (locational) relevance of this body of knowledge.

The locational clustering of tools is unique among organizations of tools for the smith in two ways. First, it is the only organization that includes all the tools in the shop at a given point in time. Second, it provides a consistent framework out of which the smith selects items for other task-specific constellations. This locational scheme is not constant, but may be revised as the tool inventory or other relevant variables change.

What about other conceptual schemes? We suspected that another broad organizational system might be based on the primary function of tools. Outside the context of any particular job, tools might be classified by their primary function. *Hardy, chisel, hacksaw, cut-off saw,* and *cutting torch* are among the tools primarily used for cutting; *tongs, clamps,* and *vise* are primarily used for holding; *hammers* and *wooden clubs* are primarily used for pounding. An abstract system of classification based on such functional distinctions can be produced by a knowledgeable smith. Similar classification schemes are commonly reproduced in the organization of merchandise in hardware stores.

Like the linguistic hierarchy, however, this system is too general for the everyday activities of a blacksmith (although it may be relevant to the owner or employee of a hardware store). This classification system broadly based on function is inappropriate for the blacksmith in two ways: (1) It is artificially comprehensive in its attempt to incorporate a total universe of blacksmithing tools. (2) It is at the same time artificially narrow in its failure to incorporate the materials, processes, and products associated with the primary functions of smithing. In other words, it is inadequate to explain the productivity and variation typical of tool use because it focuses only on the categories of tools themselves (see Agar 1974).

Our continued investigations led us to characterize knowledge structures as constellations of conceptual units arising in response to a task at hand. The basic principles of such organizations are functional relations. Like Agar (1974), we see the task or process orientation as of primary importance in the organization of complex systems of knowledge; unlike Agar (1974), we draw attention to the significance of unnamed conceptual distinctions as an important part of such systems or constellations. These constellations are held together only while immediately relevant (Fillmore 1978 hints at the importance of such contextual associations in his discussion of frame semantics).[4] A Santa Fe blacksmith aptly

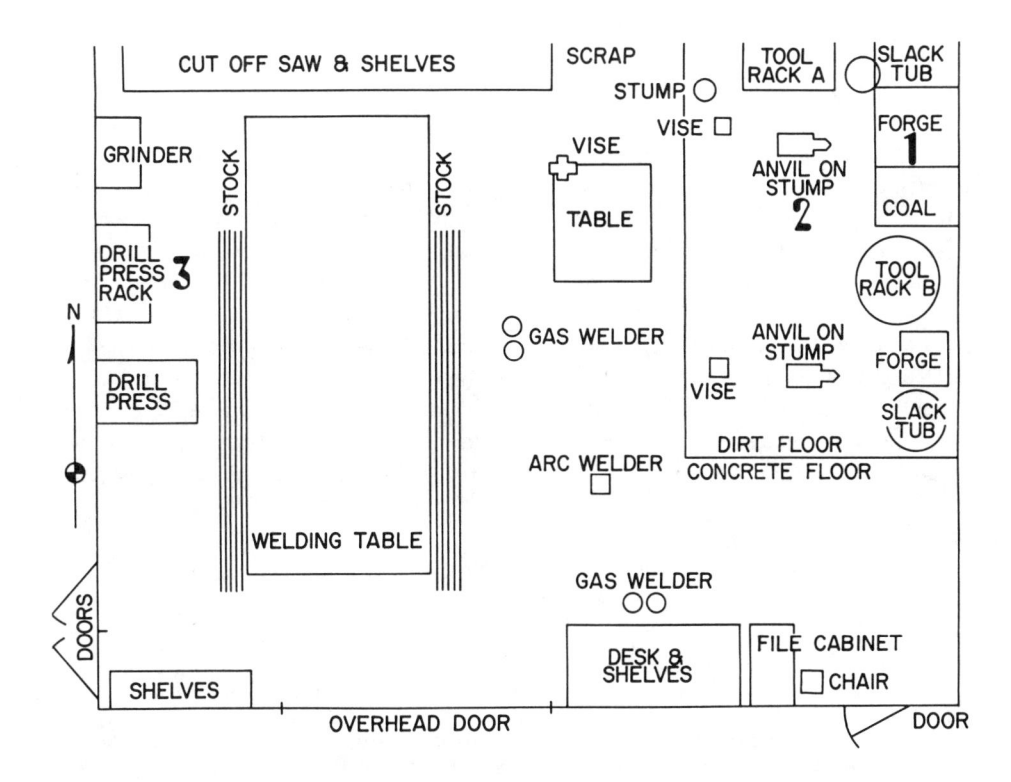

Figure 2. Sketch map of blacksmith's shop indicating three prominent sites for tool storage. The tools clustered at each site may be located or retrieved by reference to the following working definitions: (1) *fire tools* (poker, spoon); used for tending fire, kept on forge; (2) *stump tools* (hardy, an old file used for hot rasping, wire brush); frequently used when working on the anvil, kept on the anvil stump; (3) *drill press rack tools* (drill bits, extension cords, vise grips, C clamps, squares, one electric drill); used with the drill press or with the nearby grinder or cut-off saw, and tools not kept elsewhere that can be hung easily.

refers to this productive organization and reorganization as follows: Having decided what shape you want the iron to take, "as you are standing taking a nice good heat, ... plan the next step. What tools do you need? Are they in reach?" Each step requires a constellation of tools in association with materials, processes, and a notion of the desired end point. The first-order concern is to decide what shape the metal is to take and what materials are appropriate; following from that is a consideration of means and implements.

One example of a constellation derives from a common goal for the blacksmith of increasing the length and/or width of a section of iron by decreasing its thickness, referred to as *drawing out*. One set of means to this end is *fullering,* a process that involves making regular depressions in a hot iron rod and subsequently hammering down the intermediate ridges to produce a narrower rod of greater length than the original. With this goal in mind, and with fullering as the selected process, a relevant constellation includes raw material selected on the basis of the job, a particular hammer or hammers, either an anvil horn or fuller depending on the blacksmith's preference, the dimension of the material, possibly a pair of tongs matched to the dimensions of the iron rod, and a wire brush to remove the scale from the metal.

A more complex example is evident in making a fleur-de-lis. In this task a rod is pointed and spread to a picket point. The tip of the picket point is cut with a hot chisel and the sections below drawn out and bent to form the arms. This involves first using the hammer and anvil and selecting a hot chisel (either straight or curved) and a pair of pliers. The piece would be hot rasped after the picket point was made and wire brushed after each heat. Each microepisode requires a unique association of notions of process, materials, implements, and desired end point, embedded within the larger conceptual constellation of making a fleur-de-lis. The constellation derives from the sequence of operations through which the smith goes and the tools and materials incorporated into those operations.

Making a *collar* requires a different constellation. The procedure is roughly as follows: A length of iron sufficient to encircle the elements to be collared is cut. The elements to be collared are supported with open space surrounding the point of attachment. With a small anvil and hammer at hand, the end of the iron collar is heated in the flame of a cutting torch and bent, using the anvil and hammer. The bend must be such that the end of the collar covers about half of the width of the iron to be collared. Then the collar end is tacked to the point to be collared with an arc welder to hold it in place. The collar is heated and bent around until the ends overlap on the back of the piece to be collared. The overlap is cut off with the cutting torch and the collar is hammered down. The seam of the collar is finally closed with an arc welder.

The final constellation to be illustrated is specific to a particular task of twisting a pair of brackets to hold a hand rail. Here we quote an apprentice smith.

> I used half-inch rod and heated and hammered the center so it was semi-square. I heated it again and quenched the end and clamped it in the vise. I grabbed the opposite end with a small pipe wrench and walked around to give the twist. It was a nice soft twist because of rounded shoulders from semi-squaring the rod. I reheated the rod and straightened it with a big wooden club on a stump. That way by using soft stuff the twist wasn't distorted. Quenching was to keep the vise from mashing the round part when it was clamped. Then I heated it again and bent it with a fork to a 90° angle [to finish the bracket].

Enumerating such constellations of knowledge could go on. The process of formation is productive, and novel circumstances lead to novel constellations. The blacksmith's knowledge must include detailed representations of the features of processes, products, materials, and tools that mutually influence one another in the creation of unique constellations oriented to particular tasks.

Such constellations of knowledge are fundamental. The knowledge organized into constellations is not retrievable from a morphological/linguistic hierarchy, nor from a general classificatory system based on primary function. Constellations of knowledge, such as that for drawing out an iron rod or making a fleur-de-lis, account for productive behavior by providing an overriding notion of ends and means, which in combination with appropriate materials provide a basis for the selection and interrelating of a set of tools. Each element of a constellation is related to and influences each other element in nonhierarchical fashion. Constellations are ephemeral, being pulled together and held in mind only as long as appropriate for a given task. There will be individual variation in the formation of constellations oriented to a given end and situational variation in the specific materials and tools incorporated into a sequence of operations. Any individual tool or material may occur in multiple constellations.

Some constellations recur as the situations for their use recur, and these may become established "recipes" (see Goodenough 1963). The blacksmith's knowledge includes recipes for typical procedures such as fullering; typical sequences of operations oriented to a specific end product, such as making a fleur-de-lis; and typical arrangements, such as proper location. While such recipes may come to be relied on habitually, like more productive constellations they may be modified and oriented to particular characteristics of a task at hand. In the example of twisting brackets described above, general recipes for the process of twisting and for the requirements of brackets form the basis of a unique task-specific constellation.

noncorrelation of named classes to conceptual units

No one set of features consistently informs decisions involved in the production of constellations. Features are selectively focused on as a task demands. As Randall (1976:552) points out, a particular situation directs the selection of "a contrast set of characteristics that is both sufficiently general to achieve a practical and safe result and sufficiently specific to accomplish one's purposes efficiently." Relations of contrast are crucial in the formation of constellations of knowledge, but the specific dimensions of contrast constantly shift as the overriding notions change.

This productivity is not reflected in naming. For example, a particular hammer may be selected for some task on the basis of the shape and size of its face. A small round face marks sharp depressions in hot iron and spreads the metal equally in all directions; a long narrow face makes sharp straight depressions and spreads the metal perpendicular to the axis of the peen; a hammer with a round face of a particular radius might be chosen to match the curve of a place on the horn of the anvil to produce matching depressions on opposite faces of the hot iron; a flat hammer face produces a flat surface. Weight of the hammer also enters into the decision making, becoming a crucial feature for selection if a piece of iron is to be driven into a cavity or if a very large dimensioned material is being shaped. Such differences, crucial to the everyday processes of blacksmithing, are not consistently correlated with labeled classes of hammers.

Similarly, the smith is not constrained by a given inventory of tools, but is largely free to create new tools as the need arises. For example, tongs are manufactured to hold standard stock endwise and sideways. If a special shape stock is used, or a standard size significantly modified, the blacksmith can reforge the jaws to create a new set of tongs. The discontinuities evident in a tool inventory at any given point in time are not perceived as fixed boundaries within which one must work, but as the arbitrary result of tools assembled for past tasks.

In other cases, tools need not be manufactured for novel situations, but objects intended (and named) for some other purpose may serve a blacksmith's needs.[5] In making a gun spring, for example, one smith used a small sardine can for a tempering container, and the can well served the needs of the task. Another illustration of this kind of improvisation appears in Pirsig's (1975:50–51) *Zen and the Art of Motorcycle Maintenance*. The author offers to tighten his friend's motorcycle handle bars using a piece of an aluminum beer can as shim stock. Although the friend indignantly refuses the offer, the aluminum can is perfect as stock for shims.

Named classes then are inadequate as the sole guide to the conceptual units relevant to everyday behavior. The members of a named class can be described by numerous features, relatively few of which are crucial to class definition. In the course of performance attention will be focused differentially on specific features appropriate to the strategies for action, regardless of the importance of these features for category definition. By the very standardization crucial to naming, the named classes fail to reflect the productivity evident in behavior.

other task-oriented conceptual organizations

As we have argued, specific task orientations provide the meaningful features in line with which constellations as conceptual organizations are developed. The nature of the task then determines the nature of the relevant features. Tasks of identification usually require recognition of morphological/perceptual features, while other tasks, such as those we have ben discussing, tend to rely on features functionally related to specific activity. The latter have been illustrated in the discussion of constellations.

Knowledge relevant to blacksmithing also includes perceptually based systems of classification. These systems hold across a wide range of contexts for blacksmithing. They are less subject to particularistic orientation than the constellations discussed above. The more standardized of these classification systems provide guidelines for decisions which recur across task-oriented contexts. Two such classification schemes are focused on color, reflecting distinctions of temperature, malleability, and hardness.

The color spectrum relevant for normal foraging of iron ranges from *grey* through *low red* to *orange, light yellow,* and *white*. As the iron is heated it gradually reaches an incandescent red described as low red. From this point the metal is glowing and its color moves through the indicated, named spectrum as its temperature increases. The color tells the smith how malleable the iron is. If it is overheated a molecular change takes place; the iron burns and is no longer workable. If it is worked at too low a temperature, the metal will become brittle and crack. This classification of the color spectrum as a reflection of temperature and malleability allows the blacksmith to monitor his working conditions. The knowledge is relevant to forging in general. One smith, advising his apprentice, commented, "A blacksmith who works between a bright orange and a low red usually can work faster because he doesn't have to leave the iron in the fire so long." Such knowledge, applicable across a wide range of contexts, is amenable to standard linguistic expression.

A second classification of colors is associated with tempering, a process of reducing the hardness and brittleness of carbon steels used in the manufacture of cutting tools so that the tools will have the requisite strength and resiliency. The tool is first heated to a medium red (between low red and orange in the spectrum described above) and quenched in water or oil. The rapid cooling hardens the metal, leaving it brittle. The surface of the metal is then polished or filed until it is white and shiny. This polishing facilitates the reading of the tempering colors. The tool is heated again slowly, and the gradual reheating reduces the brittleness of the metal. As the temperature of the iron rises slowly, the surface changes color from *pale straw* to *dark straw* to *yellow brown* to *brown* to *iridescent peacock* to *blue, green,* and *grey*. When the desired color, indicating the desired hardness, appears on the working part of the tool, it is quenched again to retain this state. These colors reflect cooler temperatures than the normal forging spectrum. The tempering colors are too quickly bypassed and too subtle to be read during normal forging.

Like the normal forging spectrum, the tempering colors apply consistently across contexts. As a result, it is advantageous for the linguistic coding of the spectrum to be consistent for one smith from one task to another and across smiths. These systems of classification are associated with control over the malleability of iron. This is a task orientation common to all situations of forging. The conceptual structure embodying this knowledge can therefore remain constant. Because of the consistent nature of relevant distinctions, standardized names—in this case color designations—are useful.

A similar reliance on consistent morphological features occurs again (as might be expected) in a domain where recognition is the primary task orientation: that of coal and its by-products as it burns. Coal is the fuel used in forging. Before it is burned, the coal is referred to as *green coal*. The burning process produces *coke, clinker,* and *ash,* each of which must be identified and distinguished from the green coal in the forge pan so that each can be treated appropriately. Green coal appears black, angular, dense, and shiny. It is hard to ignite, does not produce as much heat as coke when it burns, and is very smoky.

Coke is the coal from which certain gases have been driven by the heat of the fire, concomitantly producing other changes. Coke appears dark, grey, rounded, porous, and dull. It ignites with reasonable ease and burns hot, with little smoke. In the forge the fire consumes coke (produced from burning the green coal) and produces clinker and ash. The green coal around the fire is continually being converted to coke, which is periodically fed into the fire to replace that which has been burned.

Clinker is lighter grey than coke, frequently accumulates at the bottom of the fire in a spongy, sticky mass, and has glassy inclusions. When a large mass of clinker has formed, its presence is revealed by an ineffective fire and by a mass at the base of the fire that glows yellow in contrast to the bright orange of the coke. Clinker often cements together pieces of ash and impurities into a mass that blocks the flow of air into the fire. In some forges it is possible to rotate a shaker and allow the clinker and ash to fall into an ash dump; in others it is necessary to clean the fire by removing ash and clinker with a spoon, leaving just enough glowing material to avoid extinguishing the fire. Ash is a light grey, gritty material that has not been consolidated by clinker. It is blown up out of the fire by the blast of air from the blower and falls back into the coke and coal mixture around the fire. If it is not removed periodically, it accumulates to the point that the fire's effectiveness is reduced as a result of the low density of fuel in the forge.

Here, features of color, shape, size, texture, density, and shine are consistently employed in distinguishing coal and its by-products. Identification of these elements is crucial to the maintenance of an effective fire. As a result, the organization of relevant knowledge is constant across contexts. Because the task of identification remains constant, the relevant features for making distinctions can remain consistent across contexts. As with the functionally oriented constellations of knowledge discussed earlier, the nature of the task determines the features of relevance. The broad contextual applicability of the perceptual distinctions makes useful, standardized labels for the conceptual units: *green coal, coke, clinker,* and *ash.*

conclusion

The set of named classes, and the interrelations among these names, cannot be taken to indicate a basic conceptual organization or a fixed set of units within which the blacksmith is constrained to operate. Labeled concepts do not provide a privileged, acontextual background system that is differentially tapped during the process of smithing. (If there is such a neutral framework for the blacksmith it is the locational classification.) Named classes reflect only one possible way of interrelating a variety of basic elements relevant to blacksmithing.

Reliance on distinctions encoded by common labels occurs for the knowledgeable smith in two cases: (1) when a task occurs across a broad range of contexts, and (2) when the smith is attempting to communicate to a less informed other. In the first case, a set of distinctions will be consistently relevant; and, as in the case of the color spectrum or coal distinctions, these concepts are likely to be consistently named. In the second case, the smith must use labels shared in common with the nonsmith, but the inference that such named distinctions reflect consistently salient conceptual distinctions for the practicing smith is not justifiable.

Named distinctions reflect classes with broad contextual relevance. As such they must be sidestepped or further specified in any specific activity for which the named units fail to encode dimensions of context crucial for the task-oriented project of the moment. What leads to highly effective means of blacksmithing is flexibility in classification. There is no one basic structure to which we can turn as the key to the practice of blacksmithing. Blacksmithing, like other behavior, is characterized by productivity.

We offer an anti-Whorfian argument that is very different from the universalist conclusions previously derived from ethnoscientific work (Berlin and Kay 1969; Berlin et al. 1973). Our investigation leads us to argue that everyday technological activity requires attention to individual processes, entities, features, and their potential relationships in the constant production of new constellations of knowledge. There is a set of named distinctions reflecting elements of the universe that are generally taken for granted: *ball-peen, hammer, half-round file, small sardine can.* Tasks require attention to particular attributes of the members of these classes in the production of new categories that crosscut these named classes (for related results see Burnham and Clark 1955; Lantz and Stefflre 1964).

It is the particular characteristics of a task, of a set of procedures, and of individual implements and materials that are the focus of awareness. The named class to which an object belongs for purposes of standard reference in general classification schemes has little influence over its occurrences in other constellations of applied knowledge. It matters little whether a wooden club (common in blacksmiths' shops but usually unnamed) is linguistically grouped with hammers because it pounds, or is separated from them because it does not have a transversely attached head. What does matter, when an iron rod needs to be pounded, are features of relevance oriented to the particular tasks: the relative softness or lightness of the wooden club, or the radius and curvature of a hammer face.

Recipes may result from habitual constellations; these may be individual or culturally specific, but they are not dependent on primary linguistic designations. Japanese and American smiths given the task of producing a fleur-de-lis, or collaring design elements together, would probably approach these tasks differently. They would do so not because they label their tools differently, but because their customary approaches to forging differ.

Finally, we must constantly beware of imputing to the minds of others the categorical or cognitive relationships that we construct from data elicited from such others. In *Argonauts of the Western Pacific,* Malinowski (1961:229-230) warns the ethnographer against systematizing conceptual organizations, for "this represents neither the native's mind nor any other form of reality." It is well known, and generally accepted, that organizations of knowledge postulated on the basis of elicited responses to directed interviewing must be carefully interpreted in the study of cognition. Freedman (1970:169), in discussing Siassi kinship, argues that "the contemporary [Siassi] patriline is merely an ethnographical artifice." In her autobiography, Mead (1972:199) reports taking individuals through complete census materials: "They could respond to a genealogical tree with a systematic kinship statement. But it turned out that this was not the way in which they used kinship at all." And Randall (1976:545) reports the surprise he encountered from informants when they were faced with the logical implications of the knowledge he elicited from them concerning marine food chains. As Schutz (1964:72-73) points out, everyday behavior is characterized by apparent inconsistency and contradiction (see also Leiter 1980:6-7). Human behavior is not simple; the cognitive systems underlying behavior are complexly rational. We have tried to take one step toward understanding the task-oriented, practical creativity that this complexity generates.

notes

[1] Cecil Brown (1979:407) argues that the principles of taxonomic organization he focuses on do not have clear implications for "cognitive reality."

[2] This is not to deny the importance of linguistic research in anthropology, but to point up its relevance to our own interest in cognition and productive behavior.

[3] Keller worked with three key informants, all of whom are self-employed professional blacksmiths, and participated in observation and discussion with at least seven other blacksmiths at blacksmithing

conventions or workshops. Interviewing in these contexts was informal discussion directed with Keller's research goals in mind. Dougherty interviewed Keller as a blacksmith using a more formal format and at some length.

[4] The data that suggest our constellations are derived from interviews with smiths. The descriptions are necessarily incomplete and, as a result of the requisite verbalization, tend to overemphasize labeled units. This is unavoidable because of the research procedures and because our task is written communication. Nonetheless, the flexibility and particularistic emphasis of elements within the task-oriented constellations is clear.

[5] In this context, note 8 in Brown et al. (1976:84) is enlightening. Kolar found that informants were capable of generating unusually large numbers of labels for tools after observing that "almost anything could be a tool."

references cited

Agar, Michael
   1974   Talking About Doing: Lexicon and Event. Language in Society 3:83–89.
Berlin, Brent, Dennis E. Breedlove, and Peter Raven
   1973   General Principles of Classification and Nomenclature in Folk Biology. American Anthropologist 75:214–242.
Berlin, Brent, and Paul Kay
   1969   Basic Color Terms: Their Universality and Evolution. Berkeley: University of California Press.
Bock, Philip K.
   1969   Modern Cultural Anthropology: An Introduction. New York: Knopf.
Brown, Cecil
   1979   Variability, Cognitive Reality and Principles of Classification and Nomenclature. American Ethnologist 6:407–408.
Brown, Cecil, John Kolar, Barbara J. Torry, Tipawan Triiong-Quang, and Phillip Volkman
   1976   Some General Principles of Biological and Non-Biological Folk Classification. American Ethnologist 3:73–85.
Brown, Michael
   1980   Intracultural Variability in Andean Food Classification. Paper presented at the 79th Annual Meeting of the American Anthropological Association, Washington, DC.
   1978   From the Hero's Bones: Three Aguaruna Hallucinogens and Their Uses. In The Nature and Status of Ethnobotany. Richard Ford, ed. pp. 119–136. Ann Arbor: University of Michigan Press.
Bulmer, Ralph
   1968   Karum Classification of Frogs. Journal of the Polynesian Society 77:333–385.
Burnham, R. W., and J. R. Clark
   1955   A Test of Hue Memory. Journal of Applied Psychology 39:164–172.
De La Roche, O., Katherine Faust, and Michael Murtaugh
   1980   Building an Atlas of Everyday Problem Solving Events. Paper presented at the 79th Annual Meeting of the American Anthropological Association, Washington, DC.
Fillmore, C.
   1978   The Organization of Semantic Information in the Lexicon. In Parasession on the Lexicon. Papers from the Chicago Linguistic Society. D. Farkas, W. M. Jacobsen, and K. W. Todrys, eds. pp. 148–173. Chicago.
Frake, Charles
   1961   The Diagnosis of Disease among the Subanun of Mindanao. American Anthropologist 63:113–132.
   1969   The Ethnographic Study of Cognitive Systems. In Cognitive Anthropology. Stephen Tyler, ed. pp. 28–41. New York: Holt, Rinehart and Winston.
Freedman, Michael P.
   1970   Social Organization of a Siassi Community. In Cultures of the Pacific. T. C. Harding and B. J. Wallace, eds. pp. 159–179. New York: Free Press.
Gatewood, John
   1978   Fishing, Memory and the Stability of Culture Complexes. Ph.D. dissertation. Department of Anthropology, University of Illinois, Urbana.
Goodenough, Ward H.
   1963   Cooperation in Change. New York: Russell Sage Foundation.
Hays, Terence
   1976   An Empirical Method for the Identification of Covert Categories in Ethnobiology. American Ethnologist 3:489–507.
   1980   Looking for Culture Amidst Diversity: Old Assumptions and the New Ethnography. Paper presented at the 79th Annual Meeting of the American Anthropological Association, Washington, DC.

Hunn, Eugene
   1980   Towards a Utilitarian Model of Folk Biological Classification. Paper presented at the 79th Annual Meeting of the American Anthropological Association, Washington, DC.
   1976   Toward a Perceptual Model of Folk Biological Classification. American Ethnologist 3:508-524.

Kay, Paul
   1970   Some Theoretical Implications of Ethnographic Semantics. Current Directions in Anthropology 3(3) Part 2:19-31.

Lantz, D., and V. Stefflre
   1964   Language and Cognition Revisited. Journal of Abnormal and Social Psychology 69:472-481.

Lave, Jean
   1980   The Cultural Shaping of Mundane Problem Solving Methods. Paper presented at the 79th Annual Meeting of the American Anthropological Association, Washington, DC.

Leiter, K.
   1980   A Primer on Ethnomethodology. London: Oxford University Press.

Malinowski, B.
   1961   Argonauts of the Western Pacific. New York: Dutton.

Mead, Margaret
   1972   Blackberry Winter. New York: Morrow.

Miller, G. A., E. Galanter, and K. H. Pribram
   1960   Plans and the Structure of Behavior. New York: Holt, Rinehart and Winston.

Pirsig, Robert M.
   1975   Zen and the Art of Motorcycle Maintenance. New York: Bantam Books.

Randall, R.
   1980   There's More to Social Behavior Than Naming Things: Some Notes on the Relations between Verbs and Problem Solving. Paper presented at the 79th Annual Meeting of the American Anthropological Association, Washington, DC.
   1976   How Tall Is a Taxonomic Tree? Some Evidence for Dwarfism. American Ethnologist 3:543-553.

Rosaldo, Michelle Z.
   1972   Metaphors and Folk Classification. Southwestern Journal of Anthropology 28:83-99.

Rosch, E., Carolyn B. Mervis, Wayne D. Gray, David M. Johnson, and Penny Boyes-Braem
   1976   Basic Objects in Natural Categories. Cognition Psychology 8:382-439.

Schank, R., and R. Abelson
   1977   Scripts, Plans, Goals and Understanding. Hillsdale, NJ: Erlbaum.

Schutz, A.
   1964   Collected Papers II: Studies in Social Theory. The Hague: Martinus Nijhoff.
   1971   Choosing among Projects of Actions. Collected Papers, Vol 1. The Hague: Marinus Nijhoff.

Submitted 9 January 1981
Revised version received 4 September 1981
Accepted 10 November 1981
Final revisions received 9 July 1982

"commitment" in American marriage: a cultural analysis

NAOMI QUINN—*Duke University*

An enduring question in anthropology has concerned the nature of culture. Cognitive anthropology inherited from its parent school, ethnoscience, its own distinctive answer to this question: culture is shared knowledge. One chronicler of the modest intellectual history of cognitive anthropology, Roger Keesing, sets this history in perspective when he suggests that far outlasting ethnoscientific absorption with systems of folk classification has been "a new and important view of culture as cognition" in which "cultures are seen as systems of knowledge" (Keesing 1974:77). This view is most explicit in the various writings of Goodenough, especially in his now familiar passage also cited by Keesing:

> A society's culture consists of whatever it is one has to know or believe in order to operate in a manner acceptable to its members. Culture is not a material phenomenon; it does not consist of things, people, behavior or emotions. It is rather an organization of these things. It is the form of things that people have in mind, their models of perceiving, relating, and otherwise interpreting them (Goodenough 1957:167).

Whatever it is that one does have to know or believe to pass oneself off as a member of one's culture, however things, people, behavior, and emotions may be organized in the mind, whatever people's models of perceiving, relating and interpreting these things may be—all remain unspecified in Goodenough's definition. Rather, the definition unfolds an ambitious theoretical program.

Cognitive anthropologists began to turn from their original questions about the taxonomic and paradigmatic structure of categorization systems to broader concerns with the organization of knowledge. They began to contemplate the various kinds of structures that must be posited to account for all that people know: for example, in Goodenough's (1971) discussion of the interaction among propositions, beliefs, values, rules, recipes, routines, and customs; in D'Andrade's (1972) treatment of the organization of belief systems; and in a variety of proposals for recognition of the primary or vital role of particular conceptual

---

On the basis of syntax, metaphorical usages, formulaic language, and the senses of utterances, it is argued that American interviewees use the key word "commitment" in the context of marriage both in a general, superordinate sense and in three subordinate polysemous senses, of PROMISE, DEDICATION, and ATTACHMENT. These three polysemous senses are related in a culturally shared scenario for American marriage—the story of the speech act that initiates it, and the entailments of this act: a state of intentionality, and an emotional relationship to another person. [American marriage, knowledge structures, scenario word, polysemy, cultural knowledge, goals]

Copyright © 1982 by the American Ethnological Society
0094-0496/82/040775-24$2.90/1

structures such as propositions (Kay 1973), events (Frake 1977), and structured sequences of behavior settings (Frake 1975). Most recently, some of these anthropologists and their students are directing detailed research efforts to questions about the organization of knowledge and are pressing toward a unified theoretical statement. In these pursuits, cognitive anthropology converges with other fields in a newly fashioned multidisciplinary effort called cognitive science, which takes the issue of the representation of knowledge as a central concern. In delineating the role of culture in the organization of knowledge, this branch of anthropology now finds itself in a position to make a unique contribution.

This paper deals with one structure, here called a "scenario word," which plays a part in organizing knowledge. It assumes that one important way in which cultural understanding comes to be shared, and the way in which the knowledge embedded in scenario words is shared, is through learning to speak a common language. This is, of course, an unabashedly Whorfian claim. But the following analysis benefits from lexical semantic theory that postdates Whorf considerably and that permits a more precise description of how words can organize understanding.

data

The present paper emerges from research on people's understandings of an important everyday concern: their own marriages. In this research a small number of individuals (husband and wife in 11 marriages) were interviewed separately and extensively about their marriages (a rough average of 15–16 hour-long interviews per person).[1] The analysis here rests on that portion of the interview material that has been transcribed to date—the first 8 hours with each interviewee. Occasional segments from later interviews were also transcribed and analyzed when they were identified as containing relevant material.

The interviews themselves were patterned as closely as possible after ordinary conversations, the interviewer following the conversational lead of the interviewee and providing each interviewee the maximum opportunity to say all he or she had to say on the topic. Thus, the interviews contain substories (about the interviewee's marital experiences) in what Linde (1981) has called the individual's "life story"; that is, they focus on the place of marriage in the interviewee's life. While the interview context is somewhat unusual, the stories the interviewee tells in this context are similar, but not identical, to what transpires in naturally occurring conversations with one's friends, family, and spouse. What is told to the interviewer, then, in Linde's (1981:7) words, is one "cross-section of a speaker's life story." While this cross-section certainly does not reveal all that a given individual thinks about his or her marriage, it is representative of how that individual thinks.

What people know about an interpersonal relationship such as marriage is hardly systematic. A range of knowledge is brought to bear on a diverse set of cognitive tasks such as interpreting another's behavior, selecting and monitoring goals, and decision making and planning, which arise in various contexts. Yet some of this knowledge has to do with broad understandings of the nature and point of the relationship itself, and it is this knowledge on which the current research focuses.

Certain abstract words such as "commitment," "relationship," "fulfillment," and "love," which recur across the transcripts of different individuals, play an important role in understanding the point and nature of marriage. This paper offers an analysis of interviewees' use of the word "commitment" (and its verb form, "commit"), a word that is employed by a majority of the spouses interviewed and that occurs a total of 283 times in 90 interviews. Note that "commitment"/"commit" are italicized in the excerpts that follow so as to flag each occurrence for the reader. "Commitment" became the object of analytic attention because of the frequency of its use in this material and because of a seeming paradox in the manner of its use. Interviewees took for granted the interviewers' grasp of the meaning of this word and resisted requests to define it more closely. Yet, inspection of the following interview excerpts should convince the reader that "commitment" can mean different things to different interviewees.[2]

1W-3 It really made me think. I had to set there and think, "Gah." You know, "Am I really doing the right thing? Do I really love him enough to *commit* myself?" With this other guy over here that I thought I loved at one time telling me not to do this [GET MARRIED].

2W-5 I think it's harder for the *commitment* to break down than it is for the relationship and that's what causes a lot of bitterness and heartache when you break up with someone.

6H-11 But it just kind of occurred to me that I was going to propose to her when I saw her next. This—that I was going to make a *commitment,* you know.

5H-3 I think she is very *committed* to making our relationship and marriage work well. I think she works harder at that than I do.

5W-1 When I was dating anybody, they had to be completely *committed* to me, or finished. I didn't care, I wasn't waiting around for them to say, "Some day," or anything, they had to—right on the line.

6W-1 And as soon as I could convince them that the *commitment* was there, although the marriage was not, then they were very happy. And they—the more they saw us together then they realized that we really were quite committed to each other and that we would make the same type of effort to make it work whether we were married. When we finally told them we were going to get married my father said, "It's about time." And my mother said, "Why? It's been going so beautifully. Why?"

These statements suggest, but do not begin to exhaust, the variety of usage in our interview material.

approach

It will be argued in detail that three alternative syntactic patterns of striking regularity in these data, and certain metaphorical and other linguistic features highly consistent with this syntax, mark three distinct senses of the word "commitment" as it is used in the context of American marriage. These three polysemous senses are themselves subordinate to a fourth, more general sense reflected in other usages. The superordinate sense encompasses all of the subordinate senses rather than differentiating among them. These three subordinate senses are that of PROMISE (or PLEDGE); that of DEDICATION (or DEVOTION); and that of ATTACHMENT (or BOND, or TIE). Here, upper case has been used to indicate that these are not words but *concepts*—basic or underlying meanings—most closely captured in the American English word or words so capitalized. Whether these concepts are themselves decomposable into other concepts, or whether they constitute primitive notions in an American folk psychology, is not addressed here. Because the words "promise," "dedication," and "attachment" come closest to saying what these concepts mean, there has come to be a partial mapping of syntax and metaphor belonging to these words onto the word "commitment." When used in each different sense, "commitment" takes the usage of another English word closest to that sense.

There is, however, more to the argument, which goes on to say that these three subordinate senses of "commitment," and no others, occur in the context of American marriage because of the way in which they are related to one another. This claim leans on an approach to word meaning suggested by Fillmore (1977a; 1977b) and Langacker (1979). Fillmore (1977a:59; 1977b:84) asserts that "meanings are relativized to scenes" so that "when you pick up a word, you drag along with it a whole scene" (1977b:114). Illustrating this notion with verbs from the domain of commerce, he argues

> that a word like buy or pay activates the scene of the commercial event; that everybody who understands the word knows what are the various components and aspects of such an event; and that a speaker's linguistic knowledge of the verb includes that knowledge of the grammatical ways in which the various parts of the event can be realized in the form of the utterance (1977a:73).

He goes on to sketch a cognitive basis for this view of word meaning:

> Now when I say that meanings are relativized to scenes, what I mean is that we choose and understand expressions by having or activating in our minds schemes or images or memories of experiences within which the word or expression has a naming or describing or classifying function (1977a:74).

And even more explicitly,

> I am using the word *scene* in this discussion in a technical sense that includes its familiar visual meaning, but much more as well. I mean by it any coherent individuatable perception, memory, experience, action, or object (1977b:84).

These scenes include, as well as individual memories,

> schemata of concepts, stereotypes of familiar objects and acts, and standard scenarios for familiar actions and events that can be spoken of independently of given individuals' memories of experiences (1977b:126).

Langacker (1979:10-11) carries his approach to a consideration of nouns, speaking of an "established functional assembly" akin to Fillmore's standard scenario and illustrating this notion with the word "orphan":

> It tells a whole story in a single word, a story based on a functional assembly of kin relations and the life cycle.... This is an established functional assembly because people know that death occurs and often reaches both parents while their offspring is still relatively young. The word orphan designates an entity that plays a particular role in this conceptual complex.... Not only is its designation restricted to the person in the offspring role, but it is further restricted to that person in a particular time frame, subsequent to the death of the parents but prior (say) to maturity (1979:10-11).

A parallel analysis of the word "commitment" is argued here. The three subordinate senses of "commitment," PROMISE, DEDICATION, AND ATTACHMENT, are related as different aspects of one interpersonal relationship. "Commitment" differs from "orphan" in being a story, not about a social status and the circumstances of a life cycle that surround it, but about a social institution, the speech act (PROMISE) that initiates it, and the entailments of this act: a state of intentionality (DEDICATION) and a relationship to another person (ATTACHMENT). Unlike the commercial event analyzed by Fillmore, but like "orphan" in Langacker's example, the story of "commitment" is told in a single word. By contrast to "orphan," the word "commitment" has a more complex structure that is reflected in its variant usages. Finally, like both "orphan" and the terms for commercial transactions, "commitment" can be considered part of what Langacker calls an "established functional assembly" because American English speakers share the usages of this word, usages that carry shared understanding of a "scenario" that includes the speech act and its standard entailments for American marriage. In other words—words an anthropologist might choose—"commitment" embodies cultural knowledge. While the linguists cited above are primarily concerned with how this knowledge is employed in word understanding, the present application of their approach points mainly in the other direction, to the role of words that contain such knowledge, in the understanding of experience. Parenthetically, however, the present analysis has an important implication for linguists' understanding of polysemy: that polysemous senses of the same word, seemingly arbitrary when taken out of all the different contexts of its use and grouped together, demonstrate their relatedness within the specific contexts in which usage has evolved.

analysis

Eleven unhelpful cases of the quotative use of "commitment" (as in "I guess that's what I mean by 'commitment'") and another 31 cases in which the word's referent is only tangential or wholly unrelated to marriage (e.g., commitment to career, children, leisure activities, causes, or issues) were set aside. Of the remaining 241 cases amenable to analysis, 32 take a global or superordinate sense of the word "commitment" in reference to marriage, while 195 can be argued to take one of the three more particular or subordinate senses of the word; 12 additional cases seem to combine two subordinate senses. Two last cases will be explained as variants borrowed from usage more typical of contexts outside of marriage. The analysis rests on four kinds of evidence: (1) syntactic regularity; (2) metaphorical usage; (3) formulaic language; and (4) sense of utterance. As will be seen, these criteria for assignment overlap in many of the actual usages to be examined. The persuasiveness of this analysis must be judged on the weight of all these pieces of evidence taken together.

Usage of "commitment" in its superordinate sense affirms the appropriateness of this notion in the context of marriage, without further specifying its entailments. For example,

7H-2 That's when any *commitment* could be proven. Or shown in a real-life situation as opposed to being always saying, "I love you, I love you."

5H-4 So, therefore, what the *commitment* meant and all that was in too much flux then to really make any kind of projections.

Adjacent usages, or the sense of the entire utterance, may clarify what particular aspect of "commitment" the interviewee had in mind, as in the statement (see 6H-2, below): "I think the marriage *commitment* is slightly different and that it is a commitment to grow old together...." Other superordinate usages appear to be left general in order to convey the full force of all that marital commitment involves. Similar to the following example, such usages often make clear that commitment is central to what marriage is all about:

2H-1 We felt strongly enough about each other and we were both oriented towards marriage as, you know, a way of life. The thing to do, whatever. And, so that was for us the expression of *commitment*. You know, were we willing to get married and accept whatever, you know, the legal and social aspects that go along with getting married?

three broad syntactic patterns Each of the three subordinate senses of the word is more specific. These different subordinate senses correlate with three alternative patterns of syntax that help to distinguish them. An idea of the regularity and distribution of this syntactic patterning can be gained from the fact that in these data, 101 cases can be unambiguously assigned to one or another of the three syntactic patterns—38 to PROMISE, 17 to DEDICATION, and 46 to ATTACHMENT.

Using the convention that X and Y are persons, the agent and beneficiary respectively, and *a* is a thing that takes the patient role, these three patterns may be represented as follows:

1. *X* makes a commitment/it is a commitment to *Y* to do *a*/that *X* will do *a*.
2. *X* is committed/it is a commitment to *a*/to doing *a*.
3. *X* has a commitment/is committed/commits self to *Y*.

While these three patterns have been displayed here in the present tense singular in the interests of legibility, it should be understood that the verbs can and do take the variety of tenses grammatically permitted in these constructions and that person, as well, may be singular or plural. In the monogamous world of American marriage, the plural is limited to the dual. Since commitment is never self-reciprocal in these statements, as indicated by the convention of distinguishing person *X* from person *Y*, it follows that the husband is the only person who can take the beneficiary role when the wife is agent, and vice versa. When person is dual in those constructions of types 1 and 3 in which both *X* and *Y* figure, the automatic result is reciprocity between *X* and *Y*. Actual usage can and does vary between nonreciprocality and reciprocality; that is, interviewees may say either "I made a commitment to her" or "We made a commitment to each other."

Below, each of these three patterns is illustrated in turn.

examples of syntactic pattern 1

2W-7 Basically, that kind of a leap was saying that we were making a *commitment* together, that we were going to stay together, that we were going to try and make a go of our relationship permanently. For all intents and purposes. You know, I've explained, I think, already our idea of permanence is not permanent, permanent, permanent.

7H-1 I guess we looked at ourselves, each other, a little more seriously. I felt that we had made the—a real *commitment*. I mean even more so than we had before because we had exchanged—we had—we'd said to each other in front of all our closest friends and family at that ceremony, we had written the ceremony ourselves.

6H-2 I think the marriage commitment is slightly different and that it is a *commitment* to grow old together, have children, and, you know, intermix, and so forth.

4W-1 And I think the other thing that's changed has been our—just our *commitment* to communicate; our *commitment* to work things out and to share. And I think that makes a big difference.

5H-7 Perhaps part of our *commitment* to continually evaluate where we are is some sort of awareness of that phenomenon. That the greatest liability to our relationship is to not work on trying to get a good sense of where we are. If I let her alone and don't try and she leaves me alone, we might satellite far enough away so we're not sure what's in between us.

4H-1 I'd say that we got serious sometime after we made the *commitment* to get married. Once we got married that was a *commitment* to at least figure out how to get serious.

6W-1 But there was the commitment, we really at that point, once E. had said there was always a place with me, I knew that he meant it and he waited until he was sure, and he waited until he knew that he would not be swinging my decision, that I had already come to that decision myself too. And so right then we both had made a *commitment* but it just seemed so—we were so happy together that the arguments were not worth breaking up over.

3H-1 More, you know, fleeting kinds of relationships, that were three months to nine months to a year kind of relationships that—where both parties knew there was not much hope for permanence and it was just a nice solid attachment. But that it probably wasn't going to last forever. And now suddenly you're in a situation where you're saying, well, you know, this may last. This may be a permanent situation. Am I willing to make that *commitment*? She certainly was. It was more a question of whether I was willing because I was the one who was much more reticent, I guess, about being tied into one relationship than she was.

7W-1 He said, "I hear you're engaged." "Yeah, I guess I am." I mean there was a whole—I really didn't like the word, I didn't like—mainly it was that I made this *commitment* and I wasn't really yet ready to make that *commitment*.

2H-2 You know, were we willing to get married and accept whatever, you know, the legal and social aspects that go along with getting married? And make the *commitment* to each other and then worry about where we were going to get jobs and where we were going to school. So—was the—in other words was—the choice was, was that more important, what we had, what we felt for each other than, you know, career circumstances?

8W-5 Well, she's young, she's just going to be twenty-one, and she has not been ready to make a *commitment*. Now C., the boy, has been ready to make a *commitment* ever since they came back from Spain. As far as he was concerned, he was ready to, you know, get engaged or do whatever it was to show that this is a—but she has not been ready to say this is it.

1H-4 Well no, that was a problematic relationship because it wasn't—that—it wasn't *even*, it wasn't even. Because I was much more—well, I was more enthusiastic about her than she wa—well I was willing to make a *commitment* to *her* more than she was willing to make a *commitment* to me. So that was a problematical aspect to it of the whole time.

examples of syntactic pattern 2

2W-1 The word "commitment" strikes a chord in me. You know, like it just—it goes fairly deep. It feels like, if I'm *committed* to something, I'm going to—I feel strongly about it. I feel strongly enough that I'm not going to let it go easily, be it a relationship, a cause, a friendship—something that I believe in. I take my beliefs seriously and I act on them. I don't like to say one thing and do another.

3W-12 To cherish me and the children and the relationship. I think he feels totally *committed* to doing that. At least as much as I feel *committed* to doing that. I've never felt like he would be more willing than I was to say, "Oh, let's just break it up." Or anything like that. I've never felt that.

6H-2 By the time the communication really had broken down and both people were *committed* to entirely different and conflicting things. A total flip flop of where they had been. Which in our case didn't happen, fortunately.

4W-1 I would say it's a *commitment* to our marriage, a *commitment* to wanting to make our marriage work, wanting to put the effort into making it work. I think it's very easy to—I think it's very easy for people to let a marriage slide. Just slide right down the tubes. There's so many odds against it anyway.

5H-7 And I think now it's much more a *commitment* to making certain that we're pretty clear where each of us are in our growth, in our lives, in our living, not—what I don't feel, in what you asked is, not to keep the relationship together but because

6W-1   we have a relationship. I *truly* could conceive of us in our evolution of things, feeling that an ongoing relationship, living together, does not make sense. When we're at a point in growth and who we are or because of another person or another opportunity that seems to be there, that says, okay, you know, we need not and we probably should not perpetuate this.

6W-1   I guess just a *commitment* to making our life very happy together and me making his life very happy and trying not to do things that would consciously hurt him and his—the same for me.

examples of syntactic pattern 3

1W-1   And what's to say you're too young to be married, just because you're *committed* to someone, I mean, you know, and you—if you love them enough what difference does it make if you're married or not married?

2W-2   I sat down and I tried to—I said, "Look, I really just—I need the emotional support of sleeping with him. We feel married already. We have the *commitment* to each other. Please, you know, let us do that."

7H-1   You know, you choose someone to live with who, in the same way as a marriage partner, is stimulating to you, who shares interests with you. It's not like you're married to them in the same sense. You're not—you don't have that kind of *commitment* because you just—they can move out anytime or you can move out.

3W-7   I think when we met, okay, I was a junior in college. He was the first boyfriend that I had that I really considered a boyfriend in a long-term kind of way. I had gone out with a lot of other guys and sometimes they had been my boyfriend for a while but none in terms of, "Hey, this is somebody I really want to settle down with who also think—feels that way about me." And to settle into that—also that kind of sexual relationship where you—you know, you're fairly *committed* to each other and this is the—you assume—

. . . . . .

Yeah. And, that like I say I think I fell in love with him in the ter—in the sense of being really not interested in anyone else once that came along.

6H-12   That was stability and it was, you know, a loving kind of person that was not afraid to express that. And that she was *committed* to me and—I don't know, it is hard to reconstruct it.

5H-4   And none of us had a clear enough conception of the series of *commitments* that we had to one another, to make many projections down the pike.

5W-2   I wanted D. to be *committed* to me but, I don't think I expected his commitment. There were other people that I dated that it took several months for me to feel that I wanted them to be *committed* to me, but because I slept with D. so early, I don't know whether I pressured him, I don't know if that's really the right word. But I was concerned that he care about me, because this was really an important thing.

4H-5   At the very beginning of these tapes I remember saying how T. and I felt a deep commitment to marriage and family. I have no *commitment* whatsoever to my parents that I can—not—I'm sure I have some *commitment*. But limited commitment to my parents.

6W-5   In G.'s position, especially if she is a little gun-shy, she said she couldn't go through the hurt she's been through, again, I think that what living with B. would do is just make her very confident about her marriage. That she wouldn't go in with any nervousness at all, with any apprehension that it might fall apart. That she could—they would have the *commitment* and the devotion to each other already. And I think that makes marriage fun rather than scary.

2H-2 Because she, you know, was very much concerned about being on the job market and all the things that went along with that. And having, you know, knowing that she was going to move. And she wanted to know, you know, was I that serious about the relationship? Did I want it to continue? Was I willing to, you know, *commit* myself to her?

Now, while some of these 101 usages exhibit the full syntactic pattern that they exemplify, others are abbreviated in the sense that one or another optional element of the syntactic construction is omitted from the particular utterance. Thus, for example, in constructions of the first type, *X, Y,* and *a* are optional, resulting in utterances such as the following:

7H-2 I wouldn't have made a *commitment* to a woman who didn't fit that kind of general image (*a* omitted).

6H-2 I guess it's [MARRIAGE] the *commitment* that now it's no longer just games and you can drop it, you know. You mean to be together—period (*X* and *Y* omitted).

2H-2 I definitely wanted to make such a commitment ... (*Y* and *a* omitted).

Optional elements can be indicated notationally by means of parentheses. Thus, the examples above can all be subsumed under the general pattern

1a. ((*X*) makes/it is) a commitment (to *Y*) (to do *a*/that *X* will do *a*).

The omissions are interesting in and of themselves because they reflect the speaker's choice of a perspective from which one or another element of a situation may be put into the foreground (Fillmore 1977a). In one context it may be the beneficiary of a commitment who is salient and therefore foregrounded by the speaker, as in the first example above; in another context the nature of the commitment may be at issue; or, in still another, the act of making it. Other elements of the situation are taken for granted and may be deleted from the utterance. Thus, much variability in the use of the word can be accounted for by the concerns that lead speakers, both by selecting one or another subpattern (e.g., *X* makes a commitment ... versus it is a commitment ...) and by making or not making deletions optional in that subpattern, to foreground different aspects of their commitment. At the same time, this feature of language creates a problem in classifying certain usages of "commitment" that are so abbreviated by deletion that they cannot be unambiguously assigned to one syntactic pattern or another. The undeleted syntactic elements are ones shared by two patterns.[3] There are nine such ambiguous cases.

Strikingly, however, the assembled usages rarely cross these syntactic patterns. Interviewees do not, for example, say such things as "We made a commitment to working at our marriage" (a combination of syntactic pattern 1, which uses the verb "make," and pattern 2, which takes the gerundive), or the reverse, "We are committed to communicate with each other" (pattern 2, followed by pattern 1). Nor do they make such statements as the more normal sounding "We had a commitment to marriage" (a combination of pattern 3 with pattern 2) or "We made a commitment to our marriage" (patterns 1 and 2 combined). While readers may feel that some or all of the above are perfectly good English, in fact they simply are not said in these interviews. By comparison with the 101 usages that conform unambiguously to one of the three syntactic patterns, and the nine additional ambiguous cases, only 4 usages mix syntactic patterns. Two of these rare mixed constructions are contained in the following segment:

4H-1 ... both of us have deep *commitments* to the concept of marriage based on our backgrounds and upbringing. We couldn't have given that up once we made the *commitment* to it.

Here, the first usage combines elements of patterns 2 and 3, while the second usage combines features of patterns 1 and 2. Of course, were it common for speakers to mix syntactic patterns in this way, then it would certainly be unreasonable to assign abbreviated usages to one or another of the three patterns on the basis of a single syntactic element that the usage shares with that pattern, in such cases as "We had made a real commitment" or "You don't have that kind of commitment."

The fact that such mixed constructions occur at all, and the fact that they do not seem to violate our sense of grammaticalness, are both compatible with the theory of polysemous meaning underlying this analysis. These three specific senses of the word "commitment" are, after all, closely related to one another, and to the superordinate sense of the word, as parts of a single scenario for marriage. It should not be surprising, then, that these senses can and do "run together," intermingling in particular utterances as they do, and more rarely, in a single usage of the word. Brugman (1981:8-9) has borrowed from prototype theory to suggest, in the analysis of a different kind of polysemous word—"over"—that within the supercategory of the word will be cases that exist on the edge of two subcategories—that is, between two subordinate senses. Since both senses are named by the same word, the issue of grammaticalness does not arise.

The present analysis, unlike Brugman's, is based on frequencies of actual usage rather than intuitions about grammaticalness. What requires explanation is the finding that speakers so infrequently use the word "commitment" to apply simultaneously to two of its specific senses, even though the syntactic constructions that resulted would be grammatical. That such mixing of its subordinate senses does not ordinarily occur in natural discourse about marital "commitment" may have the following explanation. These distinct subordinate senses of the word have arisen in the first place, we can suppose, to mark out the culturally recognized components of an experience (Brugman 1981:107). So long as speakers continue to agree that these are indeed the separate components into which the experience can be meaningfully segregated, they will tend to use that word in these separate focal senses in order to make, and not obscure, these culturally important distinctions. At the same time, as Brugman (1981:107) stresses, these different aspects of experience go by the same name, rather than different names, because they are related.

Thus, to restate the claim being made, when interviewees offer such statements as "We made the commitment to get married" and "We were making a commitment together, that we were going to stay together," they are using "commitment" in the sense of PROMISE. When they say, "We are deeply committed to marriage and family" or "It's a commitment to wanting to make our marriage work," they are using the word in the sense of DEDICATION. And when they say such things as "We were really committed to each other" and "Was I willing to commit myself to her?" they are using "commitment" in the sense of ATTACHMENT. While the three patterns of syntactic regularity distinguish many usages of "commitment," other usages can be assigned to one or another sense on the basis of additional, minor syntactic patterns to be considered next.

other evidence for three polysemous senses What are here called minor syntactic patterns contrast sharply with those already discussed in being highly infrequent; each may occur once or twice in the entire body of material under analysis here and together they account for only seven cases. These cases are, however, all the more telling for their infrequency. It is as if interviewees, instead of drawing on the syntactic constructions they habitually use with the word "commitment," are more actively mapping the syntax of other words onto "commitment" to create new constructions. Thus, for example, one interviewee says,

2W-1 Commitment was made I suppose about the same time we decided to get married, but even when I said yes to his proposal, it was more of a yes to "I want to try and make our relationship work for as long as it can." I guess that's what I mean by "commitment," making—deciding—*committing* to each other that you're going to try your best to make the relationship work, that it's worth some struggle and pain, to keep it going.

This construction, of the form

4. X commits to Y that X will do a,

occurs only once, but employs a construction very natural with the word "promise." Similarly, one could substitute "promise" for "commitment" in the following two cases, which exhibit the pattern

5. the commitment of a/doing a. . . .

2W-5 The specific commitment of living together [WOULD END].

. . . . . .

Not the commitment to support each other because as long as he's a friend of mine, he's—I would still support him. I support my friends.

5H-4 I think the *commitment* of P.'s love to me, knowing P., in some sense I thought was written in stone somewhere. That "So she loves and she will love and Amen."

Still another construction occurs in four usages of "commitment" in what appears to be its ATTACHMENT sense; the preposition "with" is used in place of "to" to yield

6. X has a commitment with Y,

as in the statement

2W-1 And I really don't believe in the institution of marriage. I don't believe it's necessary. I believe if you have a *commitment* with the person that the piece of paper, the legal thing, is not necessary.

"With" is certainly a familiar syntactic alternative to "to" in constructions, not with the word "attachment," but with the synonyms "bond" or "tie," from which this syntax seems to be borrowed.

The evidence that interviewees treat "commitment" alternatively as PROMISE, DEDICATION, and ATTACHMENT is not only syntactic, but also comes from an examination of metaphorical usage, and one usage of formulaic language, as well as from the senses of the utterances in which the word "commitment" is employed. This evidence often overlaps with syntactic criteria but just as frequently permits assignment of a usage to one or another sense of "commitment" when syntactic evidence is ambiguous or absent. In the remainder of the analysis it has proven most manageable to treat each sense of "commitment" in turn.

Lakoff and Johnson (1980) have called attention to the pervasiveness of metaphorical thinking reflected in everyday language. They would probably agree, for example, that the use of "make" in such phrases as "make a promise" or "make a commitment" turns these acts of speech into objects. It is not intended here to force a distinction between syntax and semantics in classifying such usages by their syntactic pattern rather than their metaphorical sense. It is simply a diagnostic convenience to group the multiple instances of this syntactic pattern together and contrast them with other syntactic patterns. Other usages are more varied as to syntax and can more conveniently be grouped by the pattern of borrowed metaphor that they display. Thus, certain further metaphors that are specific to the act of promising treat a PROMISE as various particular kinds of object: a promise can be "given" and "kept," "lived by" or "forgotten" (some may want to argue that forgetting a promise involves a literal meaning of "promise" as a speech event that becomes a mental construct in memory). All of these four usages typical with the word "promise" are appropriated by interviewees in the five cases below to describe marital commitment. (Since these cases are introduced here for purely diagnostic purposes, no full treatment of the metaphors which give rise to them, such as Lakoff and Johnson might provide, is attempted.)

7H-1 I think you can make a commitment from day one.

It just takes—use the word—it takes work to keep the *commitment*. Because of other factors that enter into a relationship of your life.

7H-2 To maintain it or to make it real you have to give some kind of *commitment* to that person, that you will be with them. You will stay with them, you know, through the good times and the bad times. Just like it says in those traditional vows.

4H-2 She was feeling a deep commitment, which I admire her commitment, to her mother, and she was on the verge of forgetting the other *commitment*.

3H-5 ... I mean if you're going to make a human commitment to somebody then you ought to be prepared to live by the *commitment* and to do so because you want to, not because you feel obligated to.

2H-2 Well that she was willing to, you know, make a commitment to me, in terms of marriage and, you know, being together. But she also was very much concerned about her career and what that was going to mean, what the *commitment* that she was going to give me was going to mean in terms of her career. And I think she had to know, from me, whether or not I was willing to make the same commitment. Both, you know, both for her emotional health and for her professionally.

The sense of "commitment" as PROMISE is marked not only by borrowed metaphor, but by the borrowing of what Fillmore (in press) calls "formulaic language." Two speakers seem to be mapping the expression "NOT make any promises" onto "commitment" when they say

1W-1 And he was kind of in limbo, as he told me later, you know, he was going to school, finishing up his meat-cutting school, whatever you want to call it. And he was waiting to pass his exams before he—because he would be getting a big raise. And he didn't want to—didn't make any *commitments* until he had this raise, or was sure he was going to be a meat cutter.

2W-1 For about four months at least we didn't make that commitment verbal at all. We didn't say anything to the effect, we both were essentially free to see anyone else and I think we had stated that, too. That if either one of us felt like seeing someone else that was all right at that point because we hadn't made any *commitments,* monogamous commitments or anything else, it was just—but we wanted to spend—I mean, we were both interested enough in the relationship that we wanted to spend all our time together.

These usage of "commitment" share with utterances such as "I can't make any promises, but I'll try" the conjoining of a negative verb form, the word "any," and the plural form of "commitment" distinctive of this particular formulaic expression. (Other pluralizations of "commitment" are rare in these data and almost always used in the sense of multiple ATTACHMENTS to different people.)

Interesting indirect evidence for "commitment" as PROMISE is provided by the sense of five utterances in which "commitment" is explicitly treated as an act of speech:

2W-1 For about four months at least we didn't make that *commitment* verbal at all. . . .

5H-4 I think the *commitment* of P.'s love to me, knowing P., in some sense I thought was written in stone somewhere. . . .

6W-1 And it's a very lovely, very simple ceremony. You just sit quietly and then we stand and say our vows and you can say anything. We chose the standard one which is just a very simple sentence-long *commitment*.

6W-6 The marriage itself is a public acknowledgment or a public statement of your love and *commitment* to someone. And it's also hard, I think, to promise much more than to be loving and faithful, and if you can't be then perhaps you—marriage isn't right at that time anyway.

7W-1 I think the part of me that—the 14 years in the convent, sort of took that away. I mean I made vows for life, too. I'd already made a *commitment* that was supposed to last forever and didn't. So that—in an aside I must say though that getting married was not as hard to make that lifetime commitment as celibacy. Or getting—going into the convent.

While these statements do not all differentiate between PROMISE and other speech acts that might conceivably be the basis for this usage of "commitment," they do clearly distinguish between "commitment" as a kind of speech act and the other senses of "commitment" to be discussed below.

When "commitment" is used in the sense of DEDICATION or ATTACHMENT, it seems to take on their attribute of being an internal state. In these usages the word can thus take a common metaphor for internal psychological states in American English: it can be felt (13 cases). In its PROMISE sense, a "commitment" cannot be felt; thus interviewees never say such things as "I feel a commitment to work at this marriage." They can and do say, however,

4H-5 At the very beginning of these tapes I remember saying how T. and I felt a deep *commitment* to marriage and family. . . .

Here "commitment" is being used in the sense of DEDICATION. Using "commitment" in the sense of ATTACHMENT, interviewees also make such statements as

2W-5 His is just a deeper level of the same process. He's someone that I've been able to get to a much deeper level with, the deepest of anyone that I know. But every relationship that I have is somewhere in that process. I feel very strongly—very *committed* to so many people.

Both the syntax (to *a* in the first usage and to *X* in the second) and the modifiers taken by "commitment" ("deep" and "strongly" respectively, metaphorical usages to be discussed below) permit distinction between the DEDICATION sense of "commitment" in the first case above and the ATTACHMENT sense in the second case. In four cases in which "feel" is employed, however, the remainder of the construction fails to distinguish unambiguously between these two senses. For example:

7H-2 Or the person, let's say, who solved the problem would—who's ego has been a little inflated would feel real good about themselves, you know, it would make them feel more *committed* because they did good and they feel real good for what they did.

Other metaphors are more specific to one or the other sense of the word. In its DEDICATION sense, "commitment" can be metaphorized as "deep," or "deeply felt," as in the phrase "I felt a deep commitment to marriage and family" (above) and two additional cases. Another metaphor borrowed from DEDICATION is one which treats "commitment" as requiring continuous effort; this usage of "commitment" with the verb "maintain" occurs once in the material under analysis:

4W-7 Well, it's hard to pinpoint any time or any event. It [THE MARRIAGE] simply moved slowly. I think probably a part of it moving was developing a stronger commitment or a trust that somehow it could work out in the marriage, in the relationship. That is was worth trying to develop the independence and autonomy while at the same time maintaining the *commitment* to the relationship.

The sense of "commitment" as the directed, motivated, intentional state conveyed by DEDICATION is overwhelming in the kinds of marital goals interviewees make commitments to and are committed to. Commitment is to marriage, family, the relationship—to serious goals such as raising a family and staying together:

3W-1 That [LIVING TOGETHER FIRST] was part of the process of deciding that that would happen. But I think in terms of a long-term *commitment*, it—if we had said to each other "Well we really are going to stay together for a long time, but we won't get married," that would have seemed silly to me. You know, I mean I was able to think in terms of our relationship, "Well, we'll settle down and we'll have children, we'll . . ." you know, there was some future kind of a thing, that "This is the way we're going to do it."

6H-12 Then there's two of us and then—and you have to like—and getting my degree, going through that whole thing and sticking with it, was partly a *commitment* to our relationship, you know, wan—thinking children in the future in a vague sort of way, you know, so by that point I was not—no longer feeling footloose and fancy-free either as I was when I was leaving India, you know, or wanting to be.

And commitment is to effortful goals: "to making our relationship and marriage work well"; "to wanting to make our marriage work, wanting to put the effort into making it work"; "to making our life very happy together"; "to trying to stay together"; "to continually evaluate where we are"; "to at least figure out how to get serious"; "to communicate . . . to work things out and to share"; "that you're going to try your best to make the relationship work, that it's worth some struggle and pain, to keep it going"; "that you will stay with them through the good times and the bad times"; "that it's no longer just games and you can drop it."

4H-1 That, you know, we were now a family. Just the two of us, we were a family, and that the *commitment* was to make that family work.

5H-7 And I think now it's much more a *commitment* to making certain that we're pretty clear where each of us are in our growth, in our lives, in our living. . . .

4W-1 I think that when we got married and when a lot of people get married, you think of "commitment," "Well, sure we're *committed* to staying together and blabbetty-blah. . . ." You know, the whole aura that goes along with what marriage is supposed to be. And then when you really get in it, and you find out how painful it is, and how difficult it can be, how much you have to give of yourself and feel like you're giving up and trading off and all that kind of stuff.

The third sense of "commitment," ATTACHMENT,[4] invites a number of usages all drawn on the metaphor of an attachment or bond as a physical connection between people. Interviewees use this metaphor to locate their "commitment" to their spouses on several dimensions. For example, "commitment" can vary in strength (12 cases), as in the statement,

2W-5 As you grow together the commitment grows and the more time you spend you're developing on that. You know. Beginning a relationship the *commitment* is very weak at the very beginning when you first meet someone—*commitment* is extremely weak but there's a tiny bit of commitment there to either continue the relationship, you know, make an effort on it to make that person into a better friend. You know? Or drop them altogether.

Other adjectives vary "commitment," as "attachment" can be varied, in primacy (8 cases),

4W-3 And that we don't have the usual contract that folks have which is that this is a no-no, this will ruin everything, this means you've been unfaithful, untrue, unloyal, and all kinds of bad things. And that's obviously there because of the experiences we've had, because we've learned that you don't give up your basic *commitment,* that we haven't given up our basic *commitment* with each other and to each other in the process of having cared for, loved other people. That it's still there.

5H-5 There was a primary *commitment* to me and the relationship with F. was ancillary, may deal on areas that I didn't. But was largely additive and so that made it good and okay and reasonable and all that.

in duration (4 cases),

6H-11 Well sort of ability to deal effectively with people on a certain level [IS QUITE COMMON IN AMERICA] but beyond that a real lack of commitment to other people. As persons, you know—individual kind of longstanding *commitments* to other people and, you know, I guess maybe that's why it's easier—easy to get married with somebody else, you know, and so forth and so on.

2H-2 Neither of us were afraid of permanent *commitment.* We weren't trying to play, you know, loose and keeping our options open or things like that. That w—neither of us were really interested in that.

and in type, which can be legal, as in the single case below,

1W-1 And, it's terrible, I'll say I trust him enough not to go out, yet I'm sure he trusts me but I was doing it. But we had no commitment, really. Not any kind of legal *commitment* or, it's different now, but then—.

but is overwhelmingly emotional (9 cases), as in the following segment:

3W-12 That he has a right to have a wife who has the sort of emotional *commitment* to him that many couples seem to have, and one part of me says, "Well you probably do have at least as much emotional *commitment* to him as almost anybody would have but you don't have the mindless 'I'm in love' kind of losing yourself." Pu—surrendering your judgment and perspective and stuff like that. And some part of me must keep saying to me, "That's the way you're supposed to be in love, that's why you're supposed to be married that's the ideal, you know, that's what you owe to your husband."

A number of interviewees also speak of "commitment" as something that "is there" (11 cases). Unlike "commitment" in the sense of PROMISE, an act of speech that must be made, or "commitment" in the sense of DEDICATION, an internal motivational state one is in, "commitment" as ATTACHMENT is externalized as a physical bond existing "there" between two people:

1W-2 I knew I loved him when I was in college, but I still went out with other people, for a while. But I wouldn't have done it here in Burlington, where he would have found out and it would have hurt him unless I were going to tell him. Because we kind of—I mean it wasn't a complete *commitment,* there as far as, you know, we weren't seeing anybody else. You know we were kind of together all the time.

2W-4 It's further solidifying the commitment.

. . . . . .

The *commitment's* there, but the closer together we get, the stronger the commitment gets.

4H-2 I still, at the very beginning, I said, you know, right away we knew there was a *commitment.* And this was the same thing that was basically true about all these couples. I think they all got married thinking that this was the thing, the right thing to do and it made sense for them and it was real.

Other overlapping criteria, such as the sense of the first utterance above (which makes clear that exclusivity of attachment is at issue) and the metaphor of strength in the second utterance, are invariably consistent with this interpretation of "there" as referencing an attachment between spouses.

This bond is not immutable, however. The same actions that can be performed on physical or metaphorical attachment can be performed on commitment. Not only can one actively "commit oneself" to another person in the same way one can attach oneself, one can also threaten, give up, develop, intensify, continue, solidify, utilize, and build on a commitment (12 cases), in such observations as,

2W-4 The strongest commitment I have to anyone on this earth is the commitment that I have to C.

. . . . . .

And, you know, if it came down to a friend that I had a commitment to versus the commitment to C., if I had to give up one of them, I would give up the *commitment* to the friend.

5H-4 I think it worked out that through miles of talking, with one another, on a lot of this, that it at least made sense to us and felt important to us to continue our *commitment* and our living together with one another.

Since attachment to another person is at the same time a human emotion engendered by the tie between people, it seems to take on physical properties in common with certain other feelings in American English. Not only can it be felt, but it also grows and otherwise changes in degree. "Commitment," in turn, takes on these metaphorical capacities (12 cases). Commitment can grow, strengthen, or conversely, break down, in statements such as:

2W-5 As you grow together the *commitment* grows. . . .

2W-5 I think it's harder for the *commitment* to break down than it is for the relationship. . . .

The following interview segment illustrates explicitly the concrete sense of ATTACHMENT this husband has in mind:

7H-2 In a healthy marriage or in a healthy relationship, the *commitment* will follow an upward curve. I guess, bell curve [sic]. Steadily. And then it will probably level off at a certain peak and—

. . . . . .

and it'll reach a certain peak and it'll level off. Can't keep going on forever. It can go down, but in a healthy—you reach a healthy state of relating together.

. . . . . .

I mean, yeah, between two people, you know, you only go so far. You know, without—you're not—you may be married, you know. You don't—you're not cemented together physically, you know. You can only get so close. And it's not good to get that cl—it's good to know your partner as well as you can know another human being possibly.

Finally, two further properties of attachment between persons that can be conveniently conveyed by the metaphor of physical connection are enduringness and exclusivity. When "commitment" is described in terms of either of these dimensions, this is taken as evidence for the sense of ATTACHMENT. The idea of enduringness is conveyed not only in modifiers such as "permanent," "longstanding," and "long-term" commitment (discussed above), but also in the sense of statements such as:

2W-1 . . . if I'm *committed* to something, I'm going to—I feel strongly about it. I feel strongly enough that I'm not going to let it go easily, be it a relationship, a cause, a friendship. . . .

7H-1 We may have been together for 4 or 5 years and it may seem like a long time to us, but look at people who've been married for 50 years and there you really see *commitment* or attempted *commitment*.

3W-12 It's not as much emotional *commitment* as I want to have because I would feel happy with—as I think K. deserves. I'm certainly committed emotionally but there *is* a part that I'm holding in reserve. There's that part that says, "Well there may come a time when I have to dissolve this relationship because I can't deal with it anymore." It's a realistic kind of thing.

6W-5 . . . That she wouldn't go in with any nervousness at all, with any apprehension that it might fall apart. That she could—they would have the *commitment* and the devotion to each other already. . . .

7W-1 Well, I don't know, I was uncomfortable with how we—really sharing things without some kind of *commitment* back. And there were two issues that I felt. One was living together and—I had a certain amount of savings for my dissertation and I didn't want that used for anything but me and my dissertation. Especially for someone who might not be here the next week or the week after.

The feature of enduringness that interviewees impute to "commitment" allows five otherwise uninterpretable usages to be assigned the ATTACHMENT sense of the word. Not all of the interviewees who discuss "commitment" in terms of enduringness necessarily agree that it implies permanency. Some deliberately qualify their statements to allow for the possibility that the intention of staying together permanently may not always be realized.

For other interviewees commitment raises the issue of exclusivity:

1W-2 Because once I got married that was my complete, total *commitment*. I would never, I mean, that's what I was saying, if I were to get to where I wanted to go out with somebody else I'd leave him first.

5W-1 I mean he was crazy about me. I mean I just like it when somebody's crazy about me. They have to be crazy about me and like everything about me. And he was really pretty *committed*. He didn't date anyone else. I mean as far as I know he didn't date anyone else—and I didn't.

Six otherwise ambiguous cases can be assigned the sense of ATTACHMENT because the utterances in which "commitment" is used make clear this entailment of exclusivity. Some interviewees talk about the exclusivity of commitment in terms of monogamy or faithfulness, suggesting that sexual exclusivity may be at the core of the matter. All these variable views of enduringness and exclusivity are common ways of talking about attachments to people, imported into the meaning of "commitment."

At this point it is prudent to summarize the disposition of cases. As already noted, 32 usages carry the most general, superordinate sense of "commitment." While syntax, metaphor, formulaic language, and sense of utterance may overlap, singly and together these criteria permit the assignment of 182 (of the remaining 209) usages to one or another of the three subordinate senses of "commitment." An additional 9 syntactic constructions and 4 usages of "commitment" with the verb "feel" exhibit features consistent with their assignment to a subordinate sense of "commitment" but are ambiguous with respect to which sense they are to be assigned. There are, in addition to the four cases of mixed syntax discussed earlier, another 8 usages of "commitment" that mix a syntactic pattern appropriate to one sense of the word with a metaphor appropriate to another sense. An example of this latter kind of mixed usage is:

2W-5 The relationship has changed in a way that you no longer want to be solidly *committed* to living with that person.

which seems to combine DEDICATION syntax with a metaphor of ATTACHMENT. These 8 cases can be compared with another 21 usages in which syntactic and metaphorical criteria overlap (e.g., "to the depth of commitment to doing it" or "I committed myself emotionally to him") and 14 usages in which two metaphorical criteria are concatenated (e.g., "a strong emotional commitment") to produce utterances consistent with a single subordinate sense of the word. Again, usages that combine two senses of "commitment" do occur but are in the minority. Speakers tend to, though they need not always, use the word in one or another of its distinct focal senses.

Two cases remain unaccounted for. These merit special attention because they do not fit the interpretation set out here at all; they invoke instead a sense of "commitment" common in everyday speech but virtually absent from talk about marriage: "commitment" as AGREEMENT or UNDERSTANDING. This sense is characterized by the syntax,

7. there is a commitment that X will do a,

and is represented in statements by two different interviewees:

4W-3 So that the assurance is there that J. is never going to one day just walk out the door, with anybody. And I'm never one day going to walk out the door, never say a word, never talk about anything. The *commitment* is there that we must talk about it no matter what it is. And really make some kind of effort to get an understanding of what's happening.

7W-1 But there would be some *commitment* that we were going to spend—that we intended to make it work, that we did intend to share the rest of our lives together. That was our intent. That we intended to be with each other forever.

Utterances of this form, like utterances employing "commitment" as a kind of OBLIGATION—for example, in the formulaic expressions "fulfill one's commitment" and "honor one's commitments"—and constructions of the form

8. X has a commitment to do a,

senses that seem to occur very commonly in everyday usage, are conspicuous by their absence in these interviews. These senses of "commitment," and others, simply do not seem to be part of the marital picture. Possibly these senses foregound a contractual aspect of the word that is available for the characterization of some relationships but is either inappropriate or deliberately suppressed in conceptualizing the marital relationship.

conclusion

Why are the three senses of "commitment" as PROMISE, DEDICATION, and ATTACHMENT packaged in a single word applicable to marriage? The relationship between PROMISE and DEDICATION is perhaps most transparent. In the context of marriage, a "commitment" is not just any promise, but, as reflected in interviewees's statements of goals, a promise to do something effortful and ongoing—something very difficult over the long run. It is in this sense that interviewees speak of making "such a commitment" and "that kind of commitment." To carry out such a promise engenders a particular state of intentionality, a dedication to the trying. It is as if, for those who elect to use it, the notion of "commitment" frames the kinds of goals that are appropriate to American marriage—goals of staying together, having a family and raising children, working out a relationship with one another, and making one another happy. This interpretation, that PROMISE and DEDICATION are related by virtue of their combined relationship to goals—the promise to attain certain goals entailing the intention to pursue them—is borne out by the observation that these marital goals can be couched in either the syntax of PROMISE or in the syntax of DEDICATION. Interviewees make statements of the form "We made a commitment to have a family" as readily as they make statements of the form "We are committed to having a family."

It is in the nature of these goals that they involve its makers not only in a long-term effort to keep a promise but also in a joint effort to do so, and hence in a long-term relationship with one another. Making such a commitment to someone is at the same time attaching oneself to that person for the duration of time—whether this be conceived of as "forever" or only "as long as possible"—required for pursuit of the goals to which commitment has been made. The attachment is not intellectual, as commitment to an idea can be, or contractual, as commitment to an obligation; its overriding sense is rather that of emotional attachment. In American folk psychology, two people do become emotionally attached, or grow more emotionally attached over time, as they engage in a joint pursuit of goals as important, effortful, and remote as making a family; making the marriage work; struggling to figure out what it is about or where each other is; or helping each other "through the good times and the bad times." In sum, the word "commitment" tells a complex story about American marriage.

This complex relationship in which two senses of "commitment," PROMISE and DEDICATION, entail the third, ATTACHMENT, is reflected in a number of interviewee statements about the enduringness and exclusivity of their commitment that couple these features of ATTACHMENT to the senses of "commitment" as PROMISE or DEDICATION. Thus, enduringness and exclusivity themselves figure among the goals to which a couple has made a commitment or to which they are committed to pursue. The goal of enduringness, particularly, is likely to be the logical consequence of other, long-term goals. Thus, the commitment is made "that we were going to stay together, that we were going to try and make a go of our relationship permanently"; that "you will stay with them, you know, through the good times and the bad times"; "that now it's no longer just games and you can just drop it, you know. You mean to be together—period"; "to grow old together, have children, and, you know, intermix and so forth"; "that we intended to make it work, that we did intend to share the rest of our lives together." Interviewees say, "We couldn't have given this up once we made the commitment to it, without tremendous trauma"; "You know, this may last. This may be a permanent situation. Am I willing to make that commitment?"

An occasional interview segment captures even more completely this interrelationship among original promise, subsequent effort, and the expectation of resulting attachment between spouses. It is in the juxtaposition of several usages of "commitment" in such passages, rather than within a single usage, that speakers are most likely to shift from one polysemous sense of the word to another.[5] The following interview excerpts are representative of such complex utterances. These three excerpts are reproduced in full because the discussions surrounding the word "commitment" and its several usages make one or both links between the three parts of the commitment scenario particularly explicit.

4W-3   I think we are *committed* to making our marriage work. Making the effort to do the best we can until some—unless at some point doing the best we can doesn't work—simply doesn't work, doesn't meet our needs, doesn't make anybody happy and that kind of thing. So that primary *commitment* to make the effort, to work, to work together, understand each other, I think is what I mean by our primary *commitment* to each other. There is no one else I feel that kind of *commitment* to. And I—there's no one else that J. feels that kind of *commitment* to. That's the most important *commitment* we have.

3H-5   I think that too often—that too many decisions are made without real thought; made on impulse, made on—made for reasons other than conscious decision that this is somebody you want to not just be with for the next week or the next night or the next ten minutes, but someone you want to be with for a long—extended period of time. And if you—if—it seems to me when you make a *commitment* to something like that, in human terms, when you make a *commitment* to another person, irregardless [sic] of who it is, whether it's going to be your wife, or your male lover or whoever in God's name it is, if you're going to make a human *commitment* to somebody then you ought to be prepared to live by the *commitment* and to do so because you want to, not because you feel obligated to.

8W-10 Yeah, when you said *"commitment"* that's, see, because it means something. Marriage is—these people who keep kidding themselves that living—what's the difference whether you're living together or you wrote something on a piece of paper? The difference is *commitment*.
. . . . . .
It's an emotional *commitment*. I mean you have decided definitely that this is a person that you are going to exert yourself to spend your life with. You don't feel that little loophole. That, you know, if I get mad at him, well, you know—.

Because knowledge of word use is shared, words carry culturally shared understanding; and abstract words such as "commitment," which organize complex relations among concepts, play a large role in such understanding. At the same time, word use accommodates considerable variation. The content of the PROMISE, the specific long-range goals that a couple sets and tries to meet in their marriage, are widely variable; similarly, the nature of the ATTACHMENT, for example whether it is exclusive or only primary, whether it is forever or only "as long as it can work," or whether it grows over time or not, can vary. Moreover, knowledge of language may be shared, but its use is a matter of selectivity. Usage permits one or another of the three senses of "commitment" to be emphasized or neglected in a particular marriage or a given context. Emphasis may be put on the couple's goals of marriage in one case or on the relationship between spouses, in another. Finally, by electing not to use the word "commitment," an individual or a couple may reject the "commitment model" of marriage altogether.

A final important issue raised in this analysis has to do with the relationship, not between cognition and culture, but between cognition and goals (and hence, indirectly, between cognition and behavior). In suggesting that "commitment" "frames" certain marital goals, this paper introduces a rather important claim about how goals themselves are conceptualized. The claim is that knowledge structures that organize broad understandings about people's marriages and other interpersonal relationships, about themselves and other people, and about their lives, are, at the same time, goal-defining knowledge structures. This is so because such broad understandings incorporate, among other things, understandings of what one wants out of, for example, a relationship, and how to get it. Thus, in the present case, the "commitment model" of marriage may engender expectations about what will happen to a couple in the natural course of their marriage—that their commitment to one another will grow stronger over time, for instance—and still other expectations about their own role in the outcome of their marriage—for instance, that in order to make the marriage work, they must be committed to trying to make it work.

In a book justly influential for the fresh and sweeping formulation of the organization of human knowledge that it undertakes, Schank and Abelson (1977) also relate goals to understanding. They distinguish three categories of broad understandings, which they call "themes"—interpersonal themes, role themes, and life themes—and they characterize these themes as bundles of related goals. The present analysis suggests that such a characterization is insufficient. In Schank and Abelson's (1977:140) formulation, the "theme" is a single, overarching concept of an interpersonal relationship, such as the interpersonal theme MARRIED; no notion is given as to how the goals bundled into this theme are organized by it. Here it is suggested that marital goals are organized, in part, by knowledge of the word "commitment." The particular part "commitment" seems to play is to constrain appropriate marital goals to the class of goals that are characteristically long-range and effortful. "Commitment" does not, however, fully specify the goals appropriate to American marriage.

This ongoing research reveals that another type of knowledge structure—stable, underlying metaphorical models of marriage reflected in the language interviewees use—define individuals' marital goals still further (Quinn 1981). For example, a model of marriage as a DURABLE PRODUCT allows one husband to make the metaphors "we forged a lifetime proposition"; "we have both looked into the other person and found their best parts and used those parts to make the relationship gel"; "we made that the cornerstone"; "they had a basic solid foundation in their marriages that could be shaped into something good"; "our marriage was strengthened"; "marriage is a do-it-yourself project." Not surprisingly, this husband uses the word "commitment" to mark the priority of a goal engendered by this model: he says that "the commitment was to make that family work. You know, that this was going to be a solid thing." By contrast, a second husband, whose metaphorical expressions cluster around a model of marriage as a SPATIAL RELATIONSHIP, uses the word to emphasize the priority of another goal, one consonant with this latter model. He speaks of "our commitment to continually evaluate where we are" and "a commitment to making certain that we're pretty clear where each of us are in our growth, in our lives, in our living."

Marital goals thus gain specification by the conjunction of two different knowledge structures that contribute differently to the total understanding of the marital experience. Metaphorical models define these goals and "commitment" prioritizes them. The word, in framing the kinds of goals and the degree of attachment appropriate to marriage, may influence the invention and acceptance of metaphors that adequately capture these features of the marital relationship. Interviewees, for example, are wholly disinclined to characterize marriage as A GAME, A SPORT, or any other activity that is relatively brief in duration and nonserious in intent. Reciprocally, individuals' selection of certain metaphors may dictate their use or disuse of the word "commitment" and the senses of "commitment" that they choose to emphasize. Metaphorical models of marriage as A DURABLE PRODUCT, A QUEST, AN INVESTMENT, GROWTH, A STRUGGLE, or A JOURNEY may thus encourage the emphasis of the PROMISE and DEDICATION senses of "commitment," while metaphors of marriage as A PARTNERSHIP, TWO PATHS CROSSING, MUTUAL PARENTING, BEING A UNITED FRONT, BEING A PAIR, or BEING ONE may be more favorable to selection of the ATTACHMENT sense of the word. The story of these culturally shared metaphors for American marriage remains to be told.

notes

Acknowledgments. An earlier version of this paper was read at a session entitled "New Directions in Cognitive Anthropology" at the 79th Annual Meeting of the American Anthropological Association in Washington, DC, December 1980. The research described is funded by a National Institute of Mental Health research grant, No. 1 RO1 MH330370-01. The results owe much to the skill and perseverance of Rebecca Taylor, research assistant to this project, who completed interviews with 6 of the 11 couples in the study, and a student, Laurie Moore, who completed interviews with a seventh couple. I cannot adequately thank the 22 anonymous husbands and wives who participated in the long interview process and gave us an appreciation for their unique and beautiful ways of seeing their marriages. This paper has benefited immensely from exchanges with Claudia Brugman, Roy D'Andrade, Virginia Dominguez, Janet Dougherty, Dorothy Clement Holland, Paul Kay, George Lakoff, Catherine Lutz, Daniel Maltz, and Rebecca Taylor. Of course, none of the persons named above is necessarily committed to my ideas.

[1] All interview segments in this paper have been regularized for stammers, stutters, elisions, slips of the tongue, and hesitations. Names of persons have been replaced by fictive initials and place names have been changed. Each usage of the word "commitment" under discussion is italicized; all other occurrences of "commitment" in the same segment are neither italicized nor tabulated unless they too exhibit the pattern of usage under discussion. Occasionally, when a segment is difficult to interpret out of context, the sense of the relevant portion of the preceding interview is summarized and appears in upper case, surrounded by square brackets. A line of dots between lines of interview indicates that the interviewer has interjected a comment. Dots before and/or after a segment indicate that this particular segment has been quoted more fully elsewhere in the paper. The code at the left of each segment contains, in order, an interviewee identification number, a **W** or an **H** to indicate whether that interviewee was a wife or a husband, and the number of that interview in the sequence of interviews with that individual. This information will allow the reader to compare women's usage with men's, as well as the utterances of a particular interviewee. It would have been convenient to identify interview segments in a manner allowing readers to compare each interviewee's usages with those of his or her spouse. However, disclosure of such information posed a possible breach of confidentiality since spouses themselves would then be enabled to identify their own spouses' interview segments.

[2] All interviewees are residents of one town in the southeastern United States. All are native-born Americans, but couples were selected for diversity of geographic origin within the United States, ethnic and racial identity, occupation, education, and neighborhood and social network. Efforts to attain educational and occupational diversity were not wholly successful, with college graduates and, to a lesser degree, professionals predominating. Duration of marriage ranges from 1 to 27 years, concentrated somewhat more heavily at the lower end of the distribution. All of the marriages are first marriages. Diversity, rather than representativeness, was sought. The study aims to investigate how people organize knowledge rather than how any particular organizing principle varies across sociological categories such as gender or ethnicity.

[3] For example, in the utterance,

5H-2   Oh, I think they were delighted. I think the extent of time that we were somewhat *committed,* the five year time of just kind of being in and out, bode well for them in the sense that I was not trying to sweep a young Miss off her feet, prematurely anyway. Or precipitously.

it is impossible to decide whether the couple is "somewhat committed" to each other (pattern 3) or to something, say the relationship (pattern 2). And in

5H-4   I think it worked out that J. and I both perceived that we had very little idea of, in fact, what our *commitments* to one another involved. That we did not, in many ways, know ourselves particularly well relative to relationships.

there is ambiguity as to whether these commitments are ones which each spouse had to the other (as in syntactic pattern 3) or made to one another (as in pattern 1).

[4] This sense of "commitment" would seem to correspond, roughly, to Schneider's (1968) characterization of American marriage as "for love, and forever," taken in conjunction with his famous definition of familial love, including marital love, as "diffuse, enduring solidarity." The similarity is certainly not coincidental, since Schneider, too, was working from what Americans said about mar-

riage. The present analysis is differently motivated, however. Schneider (1968:18) claims to have achieved "an account of the American kinship system *as a cultural system, as a system of symbols, and not as a 'description' at any other level,*" an account avowedly "*not* about what Americans *think,* as a rational, conscious, cognitive process, about kinship and family." I take this to mean, emphatically, that culture can be analyzed as a self-contained system independently of cognition (or conscious thought, anyway). I do not understand how culture can be treated independently of individuals' thinking about it, so I am motivated to describe the role of cultural knowledge in thought. I claim to have located certain shared knowledge (or cultural knowledge, which I am using synonymously) in the language Americans have available to think with. Thus, the present analysis specifies that ATTACHMENT is shared by virtue of being part of the structure of the word "commitment." Of course, as this analysis will show, individuals apply such shared knowledge selectively to the interpretation of their own experience.

The description of culture in isolation from cognition and its treatment as a unitary, integrated, and self-contained system is a position weakened by Schneider's method, which is neither forthcoming with data nor explicit about procedures for getting from this interview data to the final account. He defends this method by saying that "the book is the data" (Schneider 1980:124). But clearly, the extensive interviews on which the book rests are relevant, too; and were these data subjected to systematic scrutiny, they would likely yield a much more complex and variable, less integrated and self-contained picture of American cultural knowledge about kinship than Schneider has drawn freehand. Inexplicably, he justifies the lack of data in his book by equating all data with apt illustration, saying: "I might be wrong in my analysis, but I was certainly not going to cheat, and using nice little quotes and convincing little illustrations was, I thought then and think equally strongly now, a form of cheating: it pretends to documentation when it is not that at all" (Schneider 1980:124). I hope that the analysis presented here demonstrates the feasibility of doing something more systematic with these kinds of rich interview data than drawing on them selectively for apt illustrations.

[5] Interestingly, these passages, selected because they create a full marital scenario out of the different senses of "commitment," also exhibit an unusual number of mixed usages (3 out of the 12). In the first excerpt in the text, the second usage of "commitment" ("So that primary *commitment* to make the effort") refers back to the first usage ("I think we are *committed* to making our marriage work. Making the effort. . . .") to convey the connection between DEDICATION and PROMISE. The following usages, in the sense of ATTACHMENT, make clear that "that primary *commitment* to make the effort" is at the same time a "primary *commitment* to each other" and that this is an ATTACHMENT of unique strength. The mixing of an ATTACHMENT metaphor with the PROMISE construction in the second usage appears to result from a blending of that usage with the next, anticipated usage. Again, in the second excerpt, the mixed usages "when you make a *commitment* to something like that" (PROMISE syntax with that of DEDICATION, an apparent speech error that is corrected in the next phrase) and "if you're going to make a human *commitment* to somebody" (PROMISE syntax, with a modifier that seems to be more appropriate to ATTACHMENT) occur in the context of a longer scenario. In this scenario, "commitment" in its PROMISE sense is argued to entail an extended, voluntary relationship. It is as if the DEDICATION implied by "a *commitment* to something like that" and "you ought to be prepared to live by the *commitment* and to do so because you want to" and the ATTACHMENT explicit in "someone you want to be with for a long—extended period of time" creep into the sense of the word itself. Juxtaposition of different parts of the scenario that "commitment" invokes invites blending of the word's senses.

references cited

Brugman, Claudia
   1981   Story of *Over*. Master's thesis. Department of Linguistics, University of California, Berkeley.
D'Andrade, Roy
   1972   Cultural Belief Systems. Report to the National Institute of Mental Health Committee on Social and Cultural Processes, November.
Fillmore, Charles J.
   1977a   The Case for Case Reopened. *In* Syntax and Semantics, Vol. 8: Grammatical Relations. P. Cole and J. Sadock, eds. pp. 59–81. New York: Academic Press.
   1977b   Topics in Lexical Semantics. *In* Current Issues in Linguistic Theory. R. W. Cole, ed. pp. 76–138. Bloomington: Indiana University Press.
   in press   The Problem of Ungenerated Language. Cognitive Science.
Frake, Charles O.
   1975   How to Enter a Yakan House. *In* Sociocultural Dimensions of Language Use. M. Sanches and B. G. Blount, eds. pp. 25–40. New York: Academic Press.
   1977   Plying Frames Can Be Dangerous: Some Reflections on Methodology in Cognitive Anthropology. Quarterly Newsletter of the Institute for Comparative Human Development 1(3):1–7.

Goodenough, Ward H.
   1957   Cultural Anthropology and Linguistics. *In* Report of the Seventh Annual Round Table Meeting on Linguistics and Language Study. P. Garvin, ed. pp. 167–173. Washington, DC: Georgetown.
   1971   Culture, Language, and Society. Addison-Wesley Module in Anthropology. Reading, MA: Addison-Wesley.
Kay, Paul
   1973   Ethnography and Cultural Theory. *In* Drinking Patterns in Highland Chiapas. H. Siverts, ed. pp. 59–64. Bergen: Universitelsforlaget.
Keesing, Roger
   1974   Theories of Culture. Annual Review of Anthropology 3:73–97.
Lakoff, George, and Mark N. Johnson
   1980   Metaphors We Live By. Chicago: University of Chicago Press.
Langacker, Ronald W.
   1979   Grammar as Image. Paper delivered at the Conference on Neurolinguistics and Cognition, Program in Cognitive Science, University of California, San Diego, March.
Linde, Charlotte
   1981   The Life Story: A Temporally Discontinuous Discourse Type. Ms. Palo Alto.
Quinn, Naomi
   1981   Marriage Is a Do-It-Yourself Project: The Organization of Marital Goals. Proceedings of the Third Annual Conference of the Cognitive Science Society. pp. 31–40. Berkeley.
Schank, Roger, and Robert Abelson
   1977   Scripts, Plans, Goals and Understanding. Hillsdale, NJ: Erlbaum.
Schneider, David
   1968   American Kinship: A Cultural Account. Chicago: University of Chicago Press.
   1980   American Kinship: A Cultural Account, 2nd ed. Chicago: University of Chicago Press.

Submitted 20 February 1981
Revised version received 31 July 1981
Revised version received 23 April 1982
Accepted 23 April 1982

"instigating": storytelling as social process

MARJORIE HARNESS GOODWIN—*University of South Carolina*

Within the past decade, research in several different disciplines has converged on the analysis of a particular speech event—stories. Recent work in folklore has analyzed the relationships of storytelling to larger social scenes (Bauman 1972; Kirshenblatt-Gimblett 1974; McCarl 1976, 1980; Nusbaum 1976). Such "performance-centered" (Hymes 1962, 1972, 1975; Abrahams 1968, 1970, 1972; Bauman 1977) studies argue for the need to investigate the relationship between folkloristic materials, such as "storytelling events" (Georges 1969), "and other aspects of social life *in situ* . . . where that relation actually obtains, the communicative events in which folklore is used" (Hymes 1972:46). By way of contrast, analysis of features of the internal structure of stories has been the primary focus of research by sociolinguists, anthropologists, and folklorists influenced by Labov and Waletzky's (1968) studies of narrative (Brady 1980; Kernan 1977; Polanyi 1977, 1979; Pratt 1977; Stahl 1977; Watson 1973; Wolfson 1978)[1] and Goffman's (1974) notion of "frame" (Babcock 1977; Schiffren 1980; Sherzer 1980). Despite the convergence of several fields of study on the analysis of stories, few researchers as yet investigate specific texts in detail to examine how the fact that stories can be part of larger speech events embedded in social processes extending beyond the immediate social encounter[2] is consequential for the construction of a story by a speaker and its interpretation by a hearer. Such is the endeavor of this paper.

In a gossip-dispute activity called "he-said-she-said," observed among urban black preadolescent children (M. Goodwin 1980b), the activity of reporting to a recipient what was said about her in her absence constitutes an important preliminary stage. It is the point where such an event becomes socially recognizable as an actionable offense. The party talked about may then confront the party who was reportedly talking about her "behind

---

This paper investigates a particular form of storytelling, instigating, that occurs within a gossip-dispute activity called "he-said-she-said." Through the storytelling a party is informed about another person's having committed the offense of talking about her behind her back. The larger framework of the dispute provides organization for the storytelling process in several ways: (1) it provides structure for the cited characters and their activities within the story; (2) it influences the types of analysis recipients must engage in to appropriately understand the story; (3) it makes relevant specific types of next moves by recipients: for example, evaluations of the offending party's actions during the story, pledges to future courses of action near the story's ending, and rehearsals of future events at story completion and upon subsequent retellings. [conversation analysis, social organization, narrative, gossip, situational analysis, Black English Vernacular]

Copyright © 1982 by the American Ethnological Society
0094-0496/82/040799-21$2.60/1

her back." Such informing typically is accomplished through use of structured descriptions of past events or "stories"[3] (Sacks 1974) by a girl who will stand as neither accuser nor defendant. Such storytelling is called "instigating" by the children. They talk about the activity of deliberately presenting the facts in such a way as to create conflict between people in the following way:

example 1   Sha: Everytime she- we do somp'm she don't like she go and tell somebody a lie. She make up somp'm and then she always go away.

The instigator may initiate a sequence of events that leads to conflict as part of a process for sanctioning the behavior of a girl who steps outside the bounds of appropriate behavior.

Instigating possesses features of the black speech event analyzed as "signifying" by Mitchell-Kernan (1971, 1972) and Kochman (1970). According to Mitchell-Kernan (1972:165) signifying refers to "a way of encoding messages or meanings in natural conversations which involves, in most cases, an element of indirection," either with reference to "(1) the meaning or message the speaker is adjudged as intending to convey; (2) the addressee—the person or persons to whom the message is directed; (3) the goal orientation or intent of the speaker" (1972:166). Kochman (1970:157), in discussing signifying, has stated that "the signifier reports or repeats what someone else has said about the listener; the 'report' is couched in plausible language designed to compel belief and arouse feelings of anger and hostility."

The sequence of events that occurs as a result of stories being told about what was said in a story recipient's absence is parallel to the sequencing of events resulting from the "signifying" that occurs in one of the most popular of black folklore forms, "The Signifying Monkey" (Abrahams 1964:147-157; Dorson 1967:98-99). In its "toast" form the lion confronts the elephant after the monkey tells him that the elephant was talking about him. The monkey provokes the confrontation by talking about the insults against the lion delivered by the elephant. As in the "he-said-she-said," past events are reported in such a way as to lead to confrontation; however, the offenses at issue are not the more general activity of having talked about someone in her absence, but rather personal insults. The folklore form of "The Signifying Monkey" crystallizes what in everyday life is a recognizable event configuration in black culture; the positions in the he-said-she-said drama are, however, transformed into animal figures.[4]

The larger social process at issue that interpenetrates the storytelling, bringing about future confrontation through indirection, has consequences for the actions of both speaker and hearer. It not only provides organization for the internal structure of the story (for example, the characters in the story and the actions they perform); but, in addition, it influences the types of analysis the recipient must engage in to appropriately understand the story, as well as the types of responses that the recipient is expected to provide. A later section of this paper investigates such features in detail and relates them to how storytelling is constitutive of larger social processes. In the next section of this paper I discuss how this feature of reporting is relevant to general issues of description in anthropology.

the relevance of this study for cultural anthropology

Because anthropologists frequently rely on reports as primary data sources, a central concern has been how accurately the report corresponds to the initial events it describes (Bilmes 1975). Others have argued, however, that the central issue is not the correspondence between the report and the event it describes but rather the organization of the description as a situated cultural object in its own right (Sacks 1963, 1972:331-332).

In the present investigation I am concerned not with how accurately a story reflects the initial event it describes but rather with the problem of how the description of the past is constructed in the first place such that it is a recognizable cultural object appropriate to the ongoing social project of the moment. Indeed, I wish to argue, as does Vološinov (1971), that the context of reporting itself provides the description with its primary organization. Anthropologists, rather than accepting reports as instances of the events they describe, must seriously investigate the process of reporting itself. In a similar vein, as recent writers on "the anthropology of experience" such as Bruner (1980) have argued, it should be kept in mind that the *ethnographer's* "story" of events is not itself unmotivated; rather, "how we depict any segment of the sequence [past, present, future] is related to our conception of the whole" (Bruner 1980:4).

Insofar as the present study of the activity of instigating attempts to analyze what Frake (1977:5-6) describes as "the script for planning, staging, and performing" a particular cultural "scene," it is situated within an approach to the analysis of culture that advocates description of the formal procedures for constructing culturally recognizable events (Goodenough 1964, 1971). While, as Goodenough (1971:102-103) notes, "anthropologists have rarely considered simple clusters associated with one or only a few activities as the units with which to associate the phenomenon of culture," here I am explicitly concerned with such an undertaking.

Previous studies of gossip have been concerned with different endeavors—outlining gossip's social functions (Gluckman 1963, 1968; Epstein 1969; Colson 1953; Hannerz 1967; Harris 1974; Herskovits 1937, 1947; Frankenberg 1957), as well as the uses to which it is put by individuals and factions (Szwed 1966; Hannerz 1967; Campbell 1964; Cox 1970; Paine 1967); discussing its performance standards (Abrahams 1970); and arguing that its investigation "reveals how native actors examine, use and manipulate cultural rules in natural contexts" (Haviland 1977:5). While gossip is constituted by what people say to one another, in no instance have researchers described how people gossip by providing transcripts of naturally occurring gossip;[5] that is, though gossip is recognized as a form of talk, that talk is not the phenomenon anthropologists have chosen to analyze. As this analysis shows, the structure of the interactive situation itself influences the form gossip talk takes; and, indeed, to be the recipient of appropriate gossip talk one must be a potential player in the larger event, something that most anthropologists who elicit talk are not.

Ironically, it is not at all uncommon for anthropologists investigating activities constituted through talk—whether informal or rhetorical—to omit texts from their analysis (see Ben-Amos 1981:113). Yet, if "describing a culture in a way that allows one to have some confidence in a claim to have revealed a bit of reality rather than to have created a bit of fantasy" (Frake 1980:333) constitutes a goal of ethnographic description, providing texts for the scrutiny of others should be a primary rather than an incidental concern. Such texts enable the anthropologist to describe institutions such as social control mechanisms within a society as dynamic cultural processes rather than as formal static structures. The close analysis of verbal exchanges in the conflict situation of the "he-said-she-said" permits a dynamic study of the scripting and enacting of what Turner (1974, 1980) calls "social drama."

Lack of attention to what people say to one another may in part be due to a prejudice that such activities are banal by comparison with larger, more exotic spectacles or "big moments" through which societies, the social unit generally studied by anthropologists, as opposed to smaller "clusters," are felt to embody symbols which smack of their cultural core. Face-to-face talk is, however, not only one of the most pervasive, but one of the most central, types of social organization that human beings engage in. It should therefore be a central concern for anyone attempting to develop a general theory of human social organization, one that embodies linguistic and cultural competence.

It was only in the 1960s and 1970s, primarily through Goffman's (1963, 1964, 1967, 1971) insights, that small and humble forms of social organization—the routine encounters of everyday life—came to be thought of as phenomena with a ceremonial structure as important, and sometimes as intricate, as that of the most elaborate rites of passage, worthy of study *because of* their utter banality and pervasiveness. A very powerful approach to the study of the details of ordinary conversational sequences was developed by Harvey Sacks and his colleagues (Sacks, Schegloff and Jefferson 1974; Schegloff, Jefferson and Sacks 1977; Schegloff and Sacks 1973; Sacks 1974; Schegloff 1968, 1980; Jefferson 1974; Pomerantz 1978). Concurrently, philosophers and linguists, attempting to look beyond the sentence toward "pragmatics," hypothesized a theory of preconditions and postulates underlying "speech acts" (Austin 1962; Searle 1970; Grice 1969; Labov and Fanshel 1977). Thus, in recent years, anthropologists have been afforded new and rich tools for the systematic investigation of everyday talk, making possible the exploration of phenomena as diverse as how children acquire proficiency of conversational skills (Ochs and Schieffelin 1979); or how institutions such as the law (Atkinson and Drew 1979; Maynard in press), the schools (Mehan 1979; McDermott 1976), and the press (Fishman 1980) carry out their business; or how speakers and hearers jointly influence one another during the course of utterances (C. Goodwin 1981). In addition, activities seemingly unrelated to talk, such as how scientific facts are reported (Garfinkel, Lynch, and Livingston 1981; Lynch in press; Latour and Woolgar 1979), have received fruitful analysis from a perspective that includes focus on the details of the interactive organization of talk.

The importance of focusing anthropological research directly on conversational activities has been recently stated quite eloquently by Frake (1980:334):

> It is not ... just that the ethnographer must talk to people to get his work done. It is also the case that the ethnographer's work, after all, is to describe what people do. And what people do mostly is talk. Another great mystery in my life has been to understand how social scientists of all breeds have so long been able to ignore this simple fact. Yet it is through talk that people construe their cultural worlds, display and recreate their social orders, plan and critique their activities, and praise and condemn their fellows ... good ethnography requires careful listening to—and watching of—people talking to each other in the natural scenes of their social life.

The study of ordinary conversation not only focuses attention on what cross-culturally constitutes one of the most pervasive of all human activities; in addition, it causes us to examine critically the very process of reporting, which constitutes a primary vehicle for learning about culture.

characteristics of the girls' social organization

The data that form the basis of this study are the conversations of a particular group of black, working-class children from west Philadelphia, ages 7 through 13, whom I recorded for a year and a half as they went about their play activities on the street. These children, who for purposes of reference will be called the "Maple Street group," live within a block of one another and interact regularly in focused activities such as playing games and talking.

Instigating takes place only among those girls who regularly interact and judge themselves in terms of one another. This speech event reflects girls' rather than boys' social concerns. Boys make overt comparisons of one another through commands, threats, insults, and stories of others' cowardliness (M. Goodwin 1982), as well as in terms of skill in play activities and games. They therefore evaluate one another using fairly explicit standards.

Girls, by contrast, have few games that result in ranking; they spend most of their time jumping rope, playing house or school, or talking (M. Goodwin 1980a:170-172). Among themselves, aggravated speech acts are called into play only when serious affronts have been committed, generally when a girl learns that she was talked about behind her back. Operating with reference to what appears by comparison with the boys' group to be a form of egalitarianism, girls critique others who "think they cute" or "better" than others. They employ criteria that may exist as much in the mind of the observer as in the actions of the observed. Such critiques among status equals create what has been discussed by social psychologists (Simmel 1902:45-46; Caplow 1968; Vinacke and Arkoff 1957), as well as the girls themselves (Goodwin 1980b:683), as coalitions of "two against one"; this form of social organization and exclusiveness is reportedly more characteristic of girls' groups than of boys' (Eder and Hallinan 1978).

Both the timing and the framing of complaints against others within girls' and boys' groups differ as well. Although boys confront others directly, girls instead complain about other girls in their absence. This situation thus has parallels with norms of social order among the Makah (Colson 1953:233-234) and in the village of Vacluse (Frankenberg 1957), in which to maintain the appearance of harmony and friendship and never give grounds to say that one has insulted another, differences of opinion are expressed in talk behind someone's back. In the Maple Street group, when a girl learns she has been talked about behind her back, she may initiate formal proceedings against another in a public dispute. Such a course of action, however, occurs primarily in instances where the girl doing the confronting can be expected to win because of factors such as friendship alignments, verbal skill, or seniority. Among boys, aggravated accusations of the form "You did X!" are used in verbal contests; frequently, retorts are admissions such as "I know" or "So what!" By way of contrast, among girls the form of action opening a he-said-she-said confrontation is framed in indirect speech: "Y said you said I said X" (M. Goodwin 1980b). This formating of the accusation provides for deniable return actions; it therefore differs form the baldly stated actions of boys by protecting the face of both parties to the dispute.

structure in telling and listening to instigating stories

In this section of the paper I analyze how the activity of bringing about a future confrontation has direct bearing on the way the speaker structures her instigating story and the recipient responds to it. (A complete transcript of the stories under discussion appears in the Appendix,[6] a careful reading of which, at this point, will enable readers to understand the specific points to be made here.) The activity of telling a story that leads to a confrontation is compared with other forms of storytelling that occur in the group. Analysis then turns to how recipients' responses to instigating stories are differentiated, depending on the identity relationship of listener to figures in the story. Much of Goffman's (1974) work on "the frame analysis of talk" will be relevant here. Following this discussion I provide a closer look at the speaker's telling to examine ways in which the speaker makes use of forms of indirection to coimplicate the hearer in a form of future activity.

the telling Frequently, the stories told by girls concern others who are judged to have behaved in an inappropriate fashion. When girls talk about other girls they frequently do so in a guarded fashion, being mindful of the possibility that the present listener could report to the talked-about party what was said in her absence.

For example, in beginning a story about a nonpresent party Terry makes the following admonition to Nettie:

example 2   Ter: Don't tell nobody about what I said, Nettie. Bout- don't even tell Pam cuz I **know** Pam might go back and tell.

In stories about others' inappropriate activities, as well as in the instigating stories in the Appendix, certain features are common: (1) *the principal character in the story is a party who is not present;* (2) *the nonpresent party performs actions directed toward some other party;* and (3) *these actions can be seen as offenses.* Although much of girls' talk concerns negative evaluation of female agemates' activities, such talk need not necessarily lead to a confrontation if the activities of the talked-about party were not in the past directed toward the present recipient of the teller's talk. Thus, the feature of instigating stories that distinguishes them from other types of gossip stories is that: (4) *the recipient of the offenses is the present hearer, target of the cited offenses.* The placement of the present recipient within the story as a principal figure provides for her involvement in it and, consequently, for the story's rather enduring lifespan by comparison with other recountings.

Some evidence is available that the four features listed above are oriented toward the listener (offense recipient) by the teller in the construction of her stories (see Appendix), that lead to a confrontation. When one hearer leaves (following the completion of example A1), the speaker changes her stories. While the absent party remains constant, the recipient of her actions is changed so that the target of the offense remains the present hearer. Through such changes the speaker maintains the relevance of her story for its immediate recipient.

In Pam's instigating stories the nonpresent party whose offensive actions are described is Terry. As is the case for other societies, gossip is used among the girls of the Maple Street group "to control aspiring individuals," as Gluckman (1963:308) puts it. In the present case the girls are annoyed with Terry for previewing for them everything that will happen to them in junior high; though she is the same age as the other girls, she has skipped a year in school. The first group of stories (example A1), told in the presence of Maria and Florence, involves Terry's having excluded Maria's name from a hall bathroom pass. When Maria leaves and is no longer a recipient to the stories being told, Pam begins a series of stories (example A2) in which Florence is the target of a different set of offenses by Terry. Some demonstration is therefore provided that in building her stories the speaker is oriented toward constructing them such that the target of the absent party's offense is a listener in the present.

Stories may also be locally organized with respect to the figure selected as the offender. The fact that Terry is reputedly the agent of offensive talk in the story to Maria may well be why she is selected as a similar agent in the stories to Florence several minutes later. When the confrontation is played out it is discovered that it was actually Maria, rather than Terry, who said something about Florence in the past (M. Goodwin 1980b:678). Pam misconstrues the person rightfully occupying the position of offending party to create conflict between Florence and Terry. The structure of the immediate reporting situation is thus relevant to the organization of the description of the past and the figures in it being reported through these stories.

recipients' responses   In listening to a story a recipient is expected to provide some demonstration of his/her understanding of the events recounted (Sacks 1970, lecture 5:5). Places for listener responses are provided not only following a story (Sacks 1974:347–348), but also throughout its telling (Sacks 1974:344–345; Jefferson 1978).

According to Goffman (1974:503), listeners to replayings "are to be stirred not to take action but to exhibit signs that they have been stirred." The recipients of the present reports, however, are invited to be moved to action. These recountings are embedded within a larger realm of action, one that provides for a dynamic involvement of coparticipants and is not restricted to the present encounter. This prospect of future involvement provides for recipients' participation in the present in more active roles than generally occur in response to stories. The report of offenses in the he-said-she-said event is constructed to inform someone that she has (from the teller's perspective) been offended and thereby to invite her to take action against the offender.

A story might be told to several listeners, not all of whom are characters in it. Various forms of recipient response are available depending upon the occasion-specific identity relationship of the listener to the storyteller and the parties talked about. In explaining the types of identity relationships which are operative in responding to stories, some consideration of Goffman's (1974:516) critique of traditional sociological analysis that "breaks up the individual into multiple roles but does not suggest that further decimation is required" is helpful. While telling a story, a speaker not only portrays events, he animates figures within them (Goffman 1974:516–544). Thus, a single person, the present speaker, in replaying past experience, maintains both the identity of teller to listeners in the present and animator of "cited figures" (Goffman 1974:528) within it. Generally these figures are taken to be *principals* or originators of utterances, parties held responsible for having willfully taken up the position to which the meaning of the utterance attests (Goffman 1974:517).[7] In example A1 (see Appendix), for instance, Pam cites things said about Maria by Terry in Maria's absence (examples A1.14, A1.16, A1.22–A1.24). In the stories Pam tells Florence in example A2 (see Appendix), Pam recounts what Terry said about Florence (examples A2.1, A2.16).

Listeners as well as speakers occupy multiple identities, both vis-à-vis the teller in the present and the cited figures in the reported story. A listener who is a cited figure reported to have been offended may respond by directing counters to the charge of the cited figure who reportedly offended her, despite the fact that the cited figure may not be present in the ongoing interaction. One form of counter is a challenge to the truth of statements concerning her. For example, when Pam reports what Terry said that Maria said (example A1.16), Maria responds with a denial (example A1.17): "°No I didn't." Pam's report that Terry characterized Maria's actions in the past as "acting stupid" (example A1.14) is likewise countered by Maria: "But **w**as I actin stupid with them?" (example A1.15). Challenges also occur in example A2 when Pam reports what Terry said about Florence, that she had nothing to do with writing about her: "If I **wro**:te somp'm then I wrote it.=Then I got somp'm to do with it.=W'then I **wrote** it" (example A2.11) and "WELL IF I WROTE SOME 'N I HAD SOMP'M T'**DO** with it" (example A2.17). A second form of counter to a reported statement that is pejorative about the current recipient may be a return pejorative statement about the cited figure, as occurs in Maria's utterance "So: **she** wouldn' be **ac**tin **li**k**e that** wi' that **oth**er girl" (example A1.25, responding to examples A1.22–A1.24). Parties denied the opportunity to counter offensive statements about them in the past when the offenses were committed may deal with them in their retelling. In this way the offended party may also discover the present speaker's alignment toward the cited speaker's statements by observing her next utterances to the counter. Parties who were both present when the action described occurred and are figures in the story may not only respond to the story but also may participate in its telling, as Maria does (examples A1.25–A1.27, A1.37–A1.39). Such a collaborative telling is dependent on knowledge of the event and generally utilizes past tense.

A different form of recipient response is possible for a party who is not a figure in the story: providing comments on the offender's character, referring to ongoing attributes of the offender in the present progressive tense. For example, in response to Pam's story about

Terry's actions toward Maria, Florence, who is not a figure in the story, states: "SHE TELLIN Y'ALL WHERE TA S**I**T AT?" (example A1.28); "Terry **al**ways say somp'm" (example A1.19); "Terry-always-mad-at somebody" (example A1.9). These comments or "evaluations"[8] blatantly display what the point of the story is for listeners, an instance of Terry's inappropriate behavior.

Evaluation of this form may also be made by the party in the present who is offended in the story. However, the offended party can choose to make a far stronger evaluation of the reported action by stating that she will confront her offender; she may interpret the reported action as an offense and state that in response she will seek redress. For example, following Pam's stories to Florence about Terry, Florence states: "Well you **t**ell her to come say it in front of my fa:ce. (0.6) and **I**'ll **p**ut **her** somewhere" (example A2.2); "I better not see Terry to**day**. I'm a say 'Terry **I** heard **y**ou was talkin bout me' " (example A2.36); "W'll I'm tellin ya **I** better not catch Terry to**day.** Cuz if I catch her I'm gonna give **her** a wor:d from my **mou**th" (example A2.49). In response to the stories that Pam tells Maria about Terry, Maria states: "I'm a I'm a **t**ell her about herself to**day**" (example A1.33).

In listening to instigating stories recipients have available a range of possible responses. Through their descriptions instigators report events which can be seen as offensive and provide recipients the opportunity to assume the identity of offended party. The mere reporting of offenses is not itself sufficient to bring about a future confrontation; rather, a recipient must publicly analyze the event in question as an offense against her. In comparing the responses to stories in the Appendix, Florence takes a much stronger stance vis-à-vis Terry's reported actions than does Maria. Even though the events at issue would seem to be positive ones from Florence's perspective—not being found guilty for having written pejorative things about Terry (example A2.2)—the fact that Terry *said* something about Florence in her absence makes possible a response from her. The identity of the offended party is thus a position that is collaboratively brought into existence through both the teller's description of a third party's past activities and the recipient's orientation toward the absent party's past actions as offenses. The alignments offended parties maintain with the offending party may in part account for different types of responses. Maria is a close friend of Terry's, while Florence rarely plays with her or anyone in the older girls' group on Pam's street. Thus Florence, in contrast to Maria, has little to lose by confronting Terry.

Offended parties' responses of plans to confront the offending party are made in the presence of witnesses; they thus provide public displays of someone's intentions to seek redress for the offenses committed against her. Failure to follow through with a statement such as "I'm a **t**ell her about herself to**day**" can be remarked on as demonstrating inconsistencies in a person's talk and actions, thus reflecting negatively on her character. In the case of the he-said-she-said dispute being examined, later in the day of the instigating stories, when Maria could have confronted Terry but didn't, the following was said about her:

example 3   Pam: Yeah and Maria all the time talking bout she was gonna tell whatshername off. And **she** ain't do it.

People who refuse to confront someone once they have reported their intentions to do so are said to "swag," "mole," or "back down" from a future confrontation and may be publicly ridiculed in statements such as "You molin out." The fact that a statement about future intentions can be treated as a relevantly absent event at a future time provides some demonstration of how responses to instigating stories are geared into larger social projects.

teller's procedures for coimplicating offended party: features of indirection   Although I have considered the relationship of figures in instigating stories to participants in the present interaction and the actions generated in response to them, I have not yet discussed many details of the internal organization of the stories themselves. It has been noted that the description of the past is organized so as to display the status of that event as an offense. The actual presentation of past events is carefully managed, utilizing features of indirection.

Consider first the initiation of the story in examples A1.6–A1.11. This story beginning has the form of a reminiscence. Pam asks Maria to remember with her a particular event: "**How- how-** h- uhm, uh h- h- how about me and Ma**ri**a, ·h and all them um, and **Te**rry" (example A1.6). The proposed story concerns pejorative attributes of Terry. The telling of pejorative stories, especially in the context of the "he-said-she-said," poses particular problems for participants; that is, such stories constitute instances of talking behind someone's back, the action at issue in a "he-said-she-said." A party who tells about another is vulnerable to having that fact reported to the person being talked about by her recipient; the activity of righteously informing someone of an offense against her can itself be taken and cast as an offense. In the "he-said-she-said" under consideration, story recipient tells talked-about party (Terry) that teller (Pam) was saying something about her; subsequently, talked-about party confronts teller.

Are there ways by which a party telling such a story can protect herself against such risk? One way might be to implicate her recipient in a similar telling so that both are equally guilty and equally vulnerable. This still poses problems; specifically, it would be most advantageous for each party if the other would first implicate herself. This can lead to a delicate negotiation at the beginning of the story. In example A1.6 Pam brings up the story, providing references to the event, requesting the opinion of others, yet refusing to state her own position. In response Maria provides a particular description of her relationship vis-à-vis Terry, asking Pam "**Is**n't Terry **mad** at **me** or s:omp'm" (example A1.7). If Pam in fact provides a story at this point demonstrating how Terry is mad at Maria, Pam will have talked pejoratively about Terry before Maria has coimplicated herself in a similar position. Pam subsequently passes up the opportunity to tell a story, saying "I **'on'** know" (example A1.8). Then Maria provides an answer to her own question: "Cuz- cuz cuz I wouldn't, cu:z she ain't put my **n**ame on that **pa**per" (example A1.10). And only after Maria implicates herself does Pam begin to join in the telling (example A1.11).

I previously discussed how the teller presents the absent party's actions toward the hearer as offensive. This form of description is relevant to the project of constructing a future confrontation because it has the possibility of eliciting from the hearer promises to confront her offender. The figures of participants present at the encounter are also portrayed in a manner relevant to the present interaction. The target of the offense in the story, the hearer in the present conversation, is portrayed as someone whose actions were appropriate and exemplary, unlike those of the offender: "And Maria w'just sittin up there actin- actin:, ac- ac- actin sensible" (example A1.29). The present speaker is pictured as someone who defended the position of her present hearer against the offender (examples A1.29, A1.36).

In addition to carefully organizing the story beginning and demonstrating her alignment to the listener, the storyteller also suggests to the listener how she might respond to the events being described. For example, when Maria makes an evaluative comment, "OO: r'mind me a- you old b:ald-headed Terry" (example A1.39), at the close of the story about Terry's actions toward Maria, Pam states, "**I** should say it in fronta her **f**ace. (0.8) Bal: head" (example A1.39). Pam presents a model of how she herself would confront the offending party and thereby invites recipient to see the action in question as she herself does: as an action deserving in return an "aggravated" (Labov and Fanshel 1977:84–86) response, such as an insult.

Such suggestions, forms of indirection, also take the shape of embedded stories within the instigating stories. These embedded stories make use of variations on the same structural features used to inform the listener of an offense against her. Thus, one of the principal characters in these stories is the same absent party who appears in the informing stories; the other principal character is the present *speaker* rather than the present hearer. These stories also deal with offenses; the absent party is the recipient of these offenses, however, rather than their perpetrator. Briefly, the speaker makes her suggestions by telling her present recipient the kinds of actions that she herself takes against the offender, these actions being appropriate next moves to the offenses described in the informing stories (examples A2.21, A2.42–A2.46). In these stories Pam tells how she confronted Terry with aggravated insults. Specifically, she describes how she told Terry to her face that she had talked about her behind her back (example A2.21). In addition, Pam describes having performed insulting actions directly to Terry's face, issuing a direct command to her (example A2.44–A2.46). The aggravated nature of the command is highlighted by placing it in contrast to a more mitigated form (example A2.46).

Thus, through a variety of activities—passing the opportunity to align herself with a definitive position before hearer does at story beginning, presenting herself as having defended the offended party in the past, and portraying how she boldly confronted the offending party—speaker carefully works to coimplicate her present recipient in a next course of action. Features of indirection are evident in the reporting in several ways. In accordance with Kochman's (1970:157) definition of indirection, the teller presents a believeable picture of past events, involving what was said about the recipient, which arouses feelings of anger and hostility. In keeping with Mitchell-Kernan's (1972:166) analysis of indirection, the goal orientation of speaker in presenting her story is obscured. Although the report is reputedly a narrative account of past events involving teller and offending party, and speaker's alignment of righteous indignation toward these acts, it may also function to suggest future courses of action for present recipient.

future stories, retellings, and idealized models

Analysis so far has focused on the description of events in the past. However, Pam's stories about past events in which Florence was offended also permit Florence to describe future scenes contingent on possibly occurring events. To provide strong demonstrations of her understanding of Pam's stories, Florence makes herself a character who confronts Terry just as Pam had in the past. In these scenes Florence is the accuser and Terry is the defendant. These enacted sequences have certain regular features: (1) an evalaution of the offending party's actions, (2) an accusation, and (3) a response to the accusation.

In evaluating Pam's stories (example A2), Florence provides first a statement of how the offender should have acted and a warning for her: "So, she got anything t'say she come say it in front of my face. (1.0) I better not **see Ter**ry today" (example A2.8); "I better not see Terry to**day**" (example A2.32); "W'll I'm tellin ya **I** better not catch **T**erry to**day**" (example A2.49).

The next element in Florence's rehearsals is a statement of how she will confront Terry with a formal complaint: "I'm-a-say 'Terry **what you say** about me' " (example A2.8); "I'm a say 'Terry **I** heard **y**ou was talking bout me' " (example A2.32); "Cuz if I catch her I'm gonna give **her** a wor:d from my **mou**th" (example A2.49).

Following the offended's enactment of her own future action as an accuser, she projects how the defending party will respond with denials, actions that are expected following opening accusations: "She gonna say 'I ain't **say** nuttin' " (example A2.8); "Then she gonna say 'I ain't- **What I** say about you'" (example A2.34). At the close of the future stories in examples A2.36 and A2.49, Florence enacts additional parts of the drama, which are contingent on Terry's action to Florence: "An if she get **bad** at m:**e**: I'm a, punch her in the eye" (example A2.38); "An if she **j**ump in my **f**ace I'm a punch her in her **fa**:ce" (example A2.49).

These enactments of possible worlds (Lakoff 1968), in which Florence is confronting Terry, not only provide strong displays of her commitment to carry out a confrontation with Terry; but they also enable her to rehearse future lines in that encounter. In some sense such enactments might be viewed as idealized versions (Werner and Fenton 1973:538–539) of the sequence of activity in the actual confronting. That is, a minimal he-said-she-said sequence would, given this model, contain an accusation, a defense, and a warning or evaluation of offender's actions. Typically, anthropologists, and ethnoscientists in particular, employ elicited informants' accounts to substantiate their statements about the "ideational order." However, as these stories show, participants in their own talk provide images of encounters specifying minimal sequences of appropriate utterance types.

Indeed, encounters with others not part of the he-said-she-said event following the instigating stories display a similar orientation toward highlighting certain features of storytelling to the exclusion of others. Consider, for example, the following set of stories Pam tells Sharon after her reporting to Florence:

example 4   ((After Sharon answers Pam's knock on the door))
(1) Pam: Hey you- you n- you know- you know I- I- I had told **F**lorence, what um, what **T**erry said about her? And I- and she said "I **b**etter **n**ot **s**ee um, um **T**erry, b'cause" she said she said "Well I'm comin around Maple and I **j**ust **b**etter not **s**ee her b'cause I'm- b'cause I'm gonna tell her behind her- in front of her **f**ace and **n**ot be**h**ind her- I mean in front of // her face.
(2) Sha: She call her baldheaded and all that?
(3) Pam: Yep. And she said- she said- // she said "I'm gonna-"
((returning home from school Priscilla addresses her sister))
(4) Pri: Sharon what was all them teachers that was, holdin signs.

Pam's story in this example directly concerns the responses of a nonpresent party, Florence, to stories told her by the present speaker (Pam) about offenses to the nonpresent parties committed by someone else (Terry). It can be shown that these are the skeletal features of the stories by considering several of their features. An initial characteristic is the positioning of the part of the story regarding Florence's responses relative to other possible parts of the retellings, Pam's talk with Florence and her talk with Maria. The report of Florence's responses (example 4.1) occurs immediately following a brief summary of the statements by Pam that elicited them (talk with Maria, which had preceded talk to Florence, is omitted). Although it has been noted that clauses in "narratives" are characteristically ordered in temporal sequence (Labov 1972:359–360), here the ordering is altered. Florence's responses, rather than Maria's, project a future confrontation, and are therefore more relevant to Sharon.

The speaker marks the importance of the principal character's action not only by its placement, but also through its elaboration. Pam summarizes her own participation in the past recounting in a single statement: "I had told **F**lorence what um, what Terry said about her?" (example 4.1). Informing Florence of these events had in fact involved the major portion of the informing process (examples A2.1–A2.18). However, this is reported succinctly and in indirect speech. By contrast, Pam reports in direct speech what Florence said in response to her informings (example 4.1).

In response to Pam's replaying of her informing to Florence, both teller and recipient participate in constructing an imaginary event:

example 5

(1)	Sha:	Can't wait t'see this **a::kshu:n.** Mm**fh.** Mm**fh.**
(2)	Pam:	But if **Flor**ence say // she
(3)	Sha:	I laugh- I laugh I laugh if Terry say- Pam s- I laugh if Florence say, "**I wrote** it so what you gonna **do** about it."
(4)	Pam:	**She** say, she- and- and- and she and she probably gonna back out.
(5)	Sha:	I know.
(6)	Pam:	**Boouh boouh** // boouh
(7)	Sha:	And they she gonna say "You didn't **have** to **write** that about me Florence." She might call her Florence **fat** somp'm. = Florence say "**Least** I don't have no long: bumpy legs and bumpy neck. **Spot** legs, ·h Least I don't gotta fluff my hair up to make me look like // I hadda bush."
(8)	Pam:	Y'know **she**'s- she least she **fat**ter than her.
(9)	Sha:	Yeah an "**Least** I got bones. = At least I got **shape**." That's what she could say. (0.6) Florence **is** cuter than her though.
(10)	Pam:	Yah:p. And Florence got **shape t**oo.

In this sequence the party (Sharon) who was a nonparticipant in the informing stories but is present to the replaying of such stories projects herself as a spectator to an upcoming confrontation (example 5.3). The enactment of the possible event, however, is made up of forms of utterances that contrast with those actually enacted in a confrontation. Sharon notes that it would be an event that would evoke an unusual response, laughter, were Florence to actually admit the offense (example 5.3). In dramatizing what Terry would say to Florence, Sharon uses personal insults (examples 5.7, 5.9), actions that among girls may occur in the absence of the talked-about individual, but generally do not occur in her presence.

The informing about a past meeting with an offended party thus provides for forms of enactments about possible future events for those not occupying the identity of accuser or defendant in the confrontation, in much the same way that informing about offenses to an offended party provides for enactments by that party. In addition, the reporting is a way of recruiting future spectators to the event, in that it provides for their involvement in a future event.

The way in which Pam presents her description of past events to Sharon differs from her informings to Maria and Florence. Although in examples 1 and 2 Pam took precautions to elicit responses from Maria and Florence with regard to their alignment toward the offending party, building in opportunities for them to do so before indicating her own orientation toward Terry, with Sharon (examples 4–5) she launches into her story in an unguarded fashion. Because Sharon and Pam are best friends who complain to one another about both Terry and Florence, Pam can expect Sharon to side with her on most issues. In fact, as this "he-said-she-said" is played out when Terry confronts Pam for having talked about her, both Sharon (M. Goodwin 1980b:676–678) and Pam provide denials. The friendship alignments between girls are thus relevant to the structuring of gossip stories.

conclusion

Although the majority of anthropological research on gossip deals with its functions, content, and normative behavior, in this study I have focused on talk itself—on the activity of accomplishing gossip. In the "he-said-she-said" the identity of "offended party" is not one that recipient assumes automatically, but rather one that is collaboratively brought into existence through teller's reporting and recipient's cooperation in seeing the reported event as an offense. Thus, though a set of formal criteria for setting up a gossip confrontation is of central importance to the participants (and one way in which the analysis in this paper, especially that developed in the "telling" section, builds from the tradition of cognitive anthropology), it is the *interaction* between teller and recipient, rather than the properties of a formal structure, that make possible the unfolding of "social drama." By the same token, while researchers making use of speech act theory or formal cultural analysis may locate important structural features or organizations, these should not be considered in themselves adequate end products for anthropology. What is needed is a specification of the process of interaction through which such formal possibilities are made real and operative social events.

The stories examined in this paper concern past, future, and imaginary events and therefore differ from the forms of stories most frequently dealt with by students of stories. Although Goffman (1974:505) has noted the possibility of "preplays," most researchers have a narrower vision of what constitutes a narrative; it is generally defined as "a method of recapitulating past experience by matching a verbal sequence of clauses to the sequence of clauses which (it is inferred) actually occurred" (Labov 1972:359–360). Given this orientation toward the structuring of stories, it is not surprising that researchers of narrative make use of role-played data or elicited texts, assuming that narratives can be analyzed in isolation from the course of events in which they are embedded. And, similarly, professional anthropologists often assume that the accounts they receive from informants are context-free renderings of experience.

If we are to follow Malinowski (1959:312–313), however, and consider narrative "a mode of social action rather than a mere reflection of thought," then we need to investigate the details of how competent members of a society use language to deal with each other. This requires, first, methods of data collection that maintain the sequential structure of natural events (unencumbered by an anthropologist's elicitations) and make visible the process that these events are both embedded within and constitute; and second, a mode of analysis that, rather than treating talk as either a means for obtaining information about other phenomena or a special type of verbal performance, focuses on how competent members use talk to socially organize and indeed accomplish the ordinary scenes of their everyday lives.

In the stories examined here, the primary organization of the descriptions in them, as well as responses to them, is to be found not in the properties of the past events being described but rather in the structure of the present interaction, which includes an anticipated future. Indeed, that anticipation is possible because of the embeddedness of this entire process, including the constructing and understanding of the stories, within a larger cultural event the properties of which can be recognized in detail, the "he-said-she-said."

notes

Acknowledgments. The fieldwork constituting the basis for this study was made possible by a National Institute of Mental Health research grant (17216-01), administered through the Center for Urban Ethnography, University of Pennsylvania. I am indebted to Erving Goffman, Charles Goodwin, Gail Jefferson, and William Labov for comments on an earlier version of this paper.

[1] All too frequently, research investigating the internal structure of stories is based on stories that are "collected" by the researcher. The interviewer generally solicits the story from an informant by making an initial request for a story. For example, Watson (1973:260) reports, "A child who wished to tell a story responded to the eliciting frame, 'Tell us a story' " (see also Polanyi 1979:213–214). While

[2] For ethnographic analysis of how the telling of stories by urban black boys might function within larger social tasks, see Berentzen (in press) and M. Goodwin (1982).

[3] Among the children themselves the term "stories" is used primarily in the expression "telling stories"; this expression refers to false accounts in response to accusations, as in "And she gonna tell you another story anyway."

[4] See Sacks (1978:262) for a consideration of the motive power of preformulated talk.

[5] Although Haviland (1977) provides texts of gossip, they are elicited talk.

[6] Data are transcribed according to the system developed by Jefferson and described in Sacks, Schegloff, and Jefferson (1974:731-733). A simplified version of this transcription system appears in M. Goodwin (1980b:695).

[7] In fact, talk that is cited may well have originated in response to a question posed by the current teller. Consider the following in which the ethnographer's answer to a question is transformed into talk initiated by her:

((Boy skates by as Pam and ethnographer are sitting on steps.))
Pam: That boy have ugly sneaks, don't he.
Eth: Yeah,
Pam: HEY BOY THAT GIRL SAY YOU HAVE UGLY SNEAKS!

[8] On the multiple meanings that "evaluation" may have in research on stories, see Bauman (1977: 37-45); Labov (1972:366-393); Polanyi (1979:230-236); Pratt (1977:45-51; 63-68); Robinson (1981: 75-76); Watson (1973:255).

references cited

Abrahams, Roger D.
   1964   Deep Down in the Jungle: Negro Narrative Folklore from the Streets of Philadelphia. Hatboro: Pennsylvania Folklore Associates.
   1968   Introductory Remarks to a Rhetorical Theory of Folklore. Journal of American Folklore 81:143-158.
   1970   A Performance-Centered Approach to Gossip. Man (NS)5:290-301.
   1972   Folklore and Literature as Performance. Journal of the Folklore Institute 9:75-91.
Atkinson, J. Maxwell, and Paul Drew
   1979   Order in Court: The Organization of Verbal Interaction in Judicial Settings. London: Macmillan.
Austin, J. L.
   1962   How to Do Things with Words. London: Oxford University Press.
Babcock, Barbara A.
   1977   The Story in the Story: Metanarration in Folk Narrative. In Verbal Art as Performance. Richard Bauman, ed. pp. 61-79. Rowley, MA: Newbury House.
Bauman, Richard
   1972   The La Have Island General Store: Sociability and Verbal Art in a Nova Scotia Community. Journal of American Folklore 85:330-343.
   1977   The Nature of Performance. In Verbal Art as Performance. Richard Bauman, ed. pp. 3-58. Bloomington: Indiana University Press.
Ben-Amos, Dan
   1981   Review of The Social Use of Metaphor: Essays on the Anthropology of Rhetoric. J. D. Sapir and J. C. Crocker, eds. Language in Society 10:111-114.
Berentzen, Sigurd
   in press   The Contextualization of Behavior and Transformational Processes: A Study of Gang Formation in a Black Ghetto. In Transaction and Signification (preliminary title). R. Gronhaugh, ed. Oslo-Bergen: Scandinavian University Books.
Bilmes, Jack
   1975   Misinformation in Verbal Accounts: Some Fundamental Considerations. Man (NS)10:60-71.
Brady, Margaret K.
   1980   Narrative Competence: A Navajo Example of Peer Group Evaluation. Journal of American Folklore 93:158-181.
Bruner, Edward M.
   1980   Ethnography as Narrative. Paper presented at the 79th Annual Meeting of the American Anthropological Association. Washington, D.C.

Campbell, J. K.
   1964 Honour, Family and Patronage: A Study of Institutions and Moral Values in a Greek Mountain Community. Oxford: Clarendon Press.
Caplow, Theodore
   1968 Two Against One: Coalitions in Triads. Englewood Cliffs, NJ: Prentice-Hall.
Colson, Elizabeth
   1953 The Makah Indians. Manchester: Manchester University Press.
Cox, Bruce A.
   1970 What Is Hopi Gossip About? Information Management and Hopi Factions. Man (NS) 5:88-98.
Dorson, Richard M.
   1967 American Negro Folktales. Greenwich, CT: Fawcett Publications.
Eder, Donna, and Maureen T. Hallinan
   1978 Sex Differences in Children's Friendships. American Sociological Review 43:237-250.
Epstein, A. L.
   1969 Gossip, Norms and Social Network. *In* Social Networks in Urban Situations. J. Clyde Mitchell, ed. pp. 117-127. Manchester: Manchester University Press.
Fishman, Mark
   1980 Manufacturing the News. Austin: University of Texas Press.
Frankenberg, Ronald
   1957 Village on the Border. London: Cohen and West.
Frake, Charles O.
   1977 Plying Frames Can Be Dangerous: Some Reflections on Methodology in Cognitive Anthropology. Quarterly Newsletter of the Institute for Comparative Human Development 1:1-7.
   1980 Author's Postscript. *In* Language and Cultural Description: Essays by Charles O. Frake. Selected and Introduced by Anwar S. Dil. pp. 333-336. Stanford: Stanford University Press.
Garfinkel, Harold, Michael Lynch, and Eric Livingston
   1981 The Work of Discovering Science Construed with Materials from the Optically Discovered Pulsar. Philosophy of the Social Sciences 11:131-158.
Georges, Robert A.
   1969 Toward an Understanding of Storytelling Events. Journal of American Folklore 82:313-328.
Gluckman, Max
   1963 Gossip and Scandal. Current Anthropology 4:307-315.
   1968 Psychological, Sociological and Anthropological Explanations of Witchcraft and Gossip: A Clarification. Man (NS) 3:20-34.
Goffman, Erving
   1963 Behavior in Public Places: Notes on the Social Organization of Gatherings. New York: Free Press.
   1964 The Neglected Situation. *In* The Ethnography of Communication. John J. Gumperz and Dell Hymes, eds. American Anthropologist 66(6) Part 2:133-136.
   1967 Interaction Ritual: Essays in Face to Face Behavior. Garden City, NY: Doubleday.
   1971 Relations in Public: Microstudies of the Public Order. New York: Harper & Row.
   1974 Frame Analysis: An Essay on the Organization of Experience. New York: Harper & Row.
Goodenough, Ward H.
   1964 Cultural Anthropology and Linguistics. *In* Language in Culture and Society: A Reader in Linguistics and Anthropology. Dell Hymes, ed. pp. 36-39. New York: Harper & Row.
   1971 Culture, Language and Society. Reading, MA: Addison Wesley Modular Publications.
Goodwin, Charles
   1981 Conversational Organization: Interaction between Speakers and Hearers. New York: Academic Press.
Goodwin, Marjorie Harness
   1980a Directive/Response Speech Sequences in Girls' and Boys' Task Activities. *In* Women and Language in Literature and Society. Sally McConnell-Ginet, Ruth Borker, and Nelly Furman, eds. pp. 157-173. New York: Praeger.
   1980b He-Said-She-Said: Formal Cultural Procedures for the Construction of a Gossip Dispute Activity. American Ethnologist 7:674-695.
   1982 Processes of Dispute Management among Urban Black Children. American Ethnologist 9:76-96.
Grice, H. P.
   1969 Utterer's Meaning and Intentions. Philosophical Review 68:147-177.
Hannerz, Ulf
   1967 Gossip, Networks and Culture in a Black American Ghetto. Ethnos 32:35-60.
Harris, Clement
   1974 Hennage: A Social System in Miniature. New York: Holt, Rinehart and Winston.
Haviland, John Beard
   1977 Gossip, Reputation and Knowledge in Zinacantan. Chicago: University of Chicago Press.

Herskovits, M.
   1937   Life in a Haitiian Valley. New York: Knopf.
   1947   Trinidad Village. New York: Knopf.
Hymes, Dell H.
   1962   The Ethnography of Speaking. In Anthropology and Human Behavior. Thomas Gladwin and William C. Sturtevant, eds. pp. 13-53. Washington, DC: Anthropological Society of Washington.
   1972   The Contribution of Folklore to Sociolinguistic Research. In Towards New Perspectives in Folklore. Américo Paredes and Richard Bauman, eds. pp. 42-50. Austin: University of Texas Press.
   1975   Breakthrough into Performance. In Folklore: Performance and Communication. Dan Ben-Amos and Kenneth Goldstein, eds. pp. 13-74. The Hague: Mouton.
Jefferson, Gail
   1974   Error Correction as an Interactional Resource. Language in Society 2:181-199.
   1978   Sequential Aspects of Storytelling in Conversation. In Studies in the Organization of Conversational Interaction. Jim Schenkein, ed. pp. 219-248. New York: Academic Press.
Kernan, Keith T.
   1977   Semantic and Expressive Elaboration in Children's Narratives. In Child Discourse. Susan Ervin-Tripp and Claudia Mitchell-Kernan, eds. pp. 91-102. New York: Academic Press.
Kirshenblatt-Gimblett, Barbara
   1974   A Parable in Context: A Social Interactional Analysis of Story-Telling Performance. In Folklore: Performance and Communication. Dan Ben-Amos and Kenneth S. Goldstein, eds. pp. 105-130. The Hague: Mouton.
Kochman, Thomas
   1970   Toward an Ethnography of Black American Speech Behavior. In Afro-American Anthropology: Contemporary Perspectives. Norman E. Whitten, Jr., and John F. Szwed, eds. pp. 145-162. New York: Free Press.
Labov, William
   1972   The Transformation of Experience in Narrative Syntax. In Langauge in the Inner City: Studies in the Black English Vernacular. William Labov, ed. pp. 354-396. Philadelphia: University of Pennsylvania Press.
Labov, William, and David Fanshel
   1977   Therapeutic Discourse: Psychotherapy as Conversation. New York: Academic Press.
Labov, William, and Joshua Waletzky
   1968   Narrative Analysis. In A Study of the Non-Standard English of Negro and Puerto Rican Speakers in New York City. Report on Cooperative Research Project 3288. William Labov, Paul Cohen, Clarence Robins, and John Lewis. pp. 286-338. New York: Columbia University.
Lakoff, George
   1968   Counterparts, or the Problem of Reference in Transformational Grammar. Bloomington: Indiana University Linguistics Club Mimeo.
Latour, Bruno, and Steve Woolgar
   1979   Laboratory Life: The Social Construction of Scientific Facts. Los Angeles: Sage.
Lynch, Michael
   in press   Art and Artifacts in Laboratory Science. London: Routledge and Kegan Paul.
McCarl, Robert S.
   1976   Smokejumper Initiation: Ritualized Communication in a Modern Occupation. Journal of American Folklore 89:49-67.
   1980   Occupational Folklife: An Examination of the Expressive Aspects of Work Culture with Particular Reference to Fire Fighters. Ph.D. dissertation. Department of Folklore, Memorial University of Newfoundland.
McDermott, R. P.
   1976   Kids Make Sense: An Ethnographic Account of the Interactional Management of Success and Failure in One First Grade Classroom. Ph.D. dissertation. Department of Anthropology, Stanford University.
Malinowski, Bronislaw
   1959   The Problem of Meaning in Primitive Languages. In The Meaning of Meaning. C. K. Ogden and I. A. Richards, eds. pp. 296-336. New York: Harcourt, Brace and World.
Maynard, Douglas W.
   in press   Person-Description in Plea Bargaining. Semiotica.
Mehan, Hugh
   1979   Learning Lessons. Cambridge: Harvard University Press.
Mitchell-Kernan, Claudia
   1971   Language Behavior in a Black Urban Community. Monographs of the Language Behavior Laboratory, No. 2. University of California, Berkeley.
   1972   Signifying and Marking: Two Afro-American Speech Acts. In Directions in Sociolinguistics: The Ethnography of Communication. John J. Gumperz and Dell Hymes, eds. pp. 161-179. New York: Holt, Rinehart and Winston.

Nusbaum, Philip
   1976 Some Methods of Accomplishing Talk among Operatives in a Bagel Bakery in Queens, New York. Ms. Files of the author.

Ochs, Elinor, and Bambi B. Schieffelin, eds.
   1979 Developmental Pragmatics. New York: Academic Press.

Paine, Robert
   1967 What Is Gossip About: An Alternative Hypothesis. Man (NS) 2:278-285.

Polanyi, Livia
   1977 Not So False Starts. Working Papers in Sociolinguistics 41. Austin: Southwest Educational Development Laboratory.
   1979 So What's the Point? Semiotica 25:207-241.

Pomerantz, Anita
   1978 Compliment Responses: Notes on the Co-operation of Multiple Constraints. In Studies in the Organization of Conversational Interaction. Jim Schenkein, ed. pp. 79-112. New York: Academic Press.

Pratt, Mary Louise
   1977 Toward a Speech Act Theory of Literary Discourse. Bloomington: Indiana University Press.

Robinson, John A.
   1981 Personal Narratives Reconsidered. Journal of American Folklore 94:58-85.

Sacks, Harvey
   1963 Sociological Description. Berkeley Journal of Sociology 8:1-16.
   1970 Unpublished Lecture Notes. Mimeograph. University of California, Irvine.
   1972 On the Analyzability of Stories by Children. In Directions in Sociolinguistics: The Ethnography of Communication. John J. Gumperz and Dell Hymes, eds. pp. 325-345. New York: Holt, Rinehart and Winston.
   1974 An Analysis of the Course of a Joke's Telling in Conversation. In Explorations in the Ethnography of Speaking. Richard Bauman and Joel Sherzer, eds. pp. 337-353. Cambridge: Cambridge University Press.
   1978 Some Technical Considerations of a Dirty Joke. In Studies in the Organization of Conversational Interaction. Jim Schenkein, ed. pp. 249-269. New York: Academic Press.

Sacks, Harvey, Emanuel Schegloff, and Gail Jefferson
   1974 A Simplest Systematics for the Organization of Turn-Taking for Conversation. Language 50:696-735.

Schegloff, Emanuel A.
   1968 Sequencing in Conversational Openings. American Anthropologist 70:1075-1095.
   1980 Preliminaries to Preliminaries: "Can I Ask You a Question?" Sociological Inquiry 50:104-152.

Schegloff, Emanuel A., Gail Jefferson, and Harvey Sacks
   1977 The Preference for Self-Correction in the Organization of Repair in Conversation. Language 53:361-382.

Schegloff, Emanuel A., and Harvey Sacks
   1973 Opening Up Closings. Semiotica 8:289-327.

Schiffren, Deborah
   1980 Meta-Talk: Organizational and Evaluative Brackets in Discourse. Sociological Inquiry 50: 199-236.

Searle, John R.
   1970 Speech Acts: An Essay in the Philosophy of Language. Cambridge: Cambridge University Press.

Sherzer, Joel
   1980 Tellings and Retellings: An Aspect of Cuna Indian Narrative. Paper presented at the Fourth Annual Meeting of the Semiotic Society of America. Bloomington, Indiana.

Simmel, Georg
   1902 The Number of Members as Determining the Sociological Form of the Group. American Journal of Sociology 8:1-46, 158-196.

Stahl, Sandra S. K.
   1977 The Personal Narrative as Folklore. Journal of the Folklore Institute 14:9-30.

Szwed, John
   1966 Gossip, Drinking, and Social Control: Consensus and Communication in a Newfoundland Parish. Ethnology 5:434-441.

Turner, Victor
   1974 Dramas, Fields and Metaphors: Symbolic Action in Human Society. Ithaca: Cornell University Press.
   1980 The Anthropology of Experience. Paper delivered at the 79th Annual Meeting of the American Anthropological Association. Washington, DC.

Vinacke, W. Edgar, and Abe Arkoff
   1957 An Experimental Study of Coalitions in the Triad. American Sociological Review 22:406-414.

Vološinov, V. N.
   1971   Reported Speech. *In* Readings in Russian Poetics: Formalist and Structuralist Views. Ladislav Matejka and Krystyna Pomorska, transls. pp. 149–175. Cambridge: MIT Press.

Watson, Karen Ann
   1973   A Rhetorical and Sociolinguistic Model for the Analysis of Narrative. American Anthropologist 75:243–264.

Werner, Oswald, and Joann Fenton
   1973   Method and Theory in Ethnoscience or Ethnoepistemology. *In* A Handbook of Method in Cultural Anthropology. Raoul Naroll and Ronald Cohen, eds. pp. 537–578. Garden City, NY: Natural History Press for the American Museum of Natural History.

Wolfson, Nessa
   1978   A Feature of Performed Narrative: The Conversational Historical Present. Language in Society 7:215–237.

appendix

example 1   ((Pam (12), Florence (13), and Maria (12) are sitting on Maria's steps discussing substitute teachers during a teacher's strike.))

(1) Flo: Teach us some little **six**th grade work. (0.4) **Th**at's how these volun**teers** doin now. A little um, ·h **Add**in n all that.
(2) Pam: **Y**ahp. **Y**ahp. // **Y**ahp. An when we was in the-
(3) Flo: Twenny and twenny is // fordy an all that.
(4) Pam: How bout when we was in-
(5) Flo: Oo I **hate** that junk.
(6) Pam: **How- how-** h- um, uh h- h- how about me and Ma**ri**a, ·h and all them um, and **Terr**y, ·h // and all thum-
(7) Mar: Isn't Terry **mad** at **me** or s**:om**p'm,
        (0.4)
(8) Pam: I **'on'** kn//ow,
(9) Flo: Terry-**always**-mad-at somebody. °I // 'on' care.
(10) Mar: Cuz- cuz cuz I wouldn't, cu:z she ain't put my **n**ame on that **pap**er.
(11) Pam: I know, cuz // OH yeah. **Oh** yeah.
(12) Flo: An next she,
        (0.2)
(13) Flo: ⌈talk-bout-**peo**ple.
(14) Pam: ⌊**She** said, **She** said, that um, (0.6) that- (0.8) if that **girl** wasn't there = **You** know that girl that always makes those funny jokes, ·h Sh'aid if that **girl** wasn't there **you** wouldn' be **ac**ting, (0.4) a:ll **stu**pid like that. // °Sh-
(15) Mar: But **was** I actin stupid w//ith them?
(16) Pam: Nope, no, = And she- and she said that **you** sai:d, tha:t, "**Ah**: go tuh-" (0.5) somp'm like // tha:t.
(17) Mar: °No I didn't.
(18) Pam: She's- an uh- somp'm like **that**. She's-
(19) Flo: Te//rry **al**ways say somp'm. = When you **jump** in her **face** she gonna
(20) Pam: She-
(21) Flo: deny it.
(22) Pam: Yah:p Y//ahp. = An she said, ·h An- and she said, h that **you**
(23) Mar: °Right on.
(24) Pam: wouldn't be **ac**tin like **that** aroun- around **peo**ple.
(25) Mar: So: **she** wouldn' be **ac**tin l**i**ke **that** wi' that **oth**er girl. = **She** the one picked **me** to s**i**t wi'them. = ·h She said // "Maria you sit with
(26) Pam: Y:ahp.
(27) Mar: her, ·h and I'll sit with her, ·h an Pam an- an Pam an- an an // Sharon sit together.
(28) Flo: SHE TELLIN Y'ALL WHERE TA S**I**T AT?
        (2.0)
(29) Pam: An so **we** sat together, An s- and s- and so Maria was ju:st s:ittin right there. = An the girl, an- an- the girl: next to her? ·h and the girl kept

on getting back up. ·h Ask the teacher can she go t'the bathroom. An Maria say she don' **wa**nna go t'the bathroom w'her. An m- And Maria w'just sittin up there actin- actin:, ac- ac- actin sensible. An she up- and she up there talking bout, and she- I said, I s'd I s'd I s'd "This is how I'm- I'm gonna put Maria **na**:me down here." Cu- m- m- Cuz she had made a pa:ss you know. ·h She had made a **pa**:ss. (0.2)

(30)	Pam:	⌈For alla us to go down to the bathroom.
(31)	Flo:	⌊Y'all go down t'the bathroom?
(32)	Pam:	For ALLA- yeah. Yeah. For u:m, (0.4) for- for alla us- t'go to the bathroom.=I s'd- I s'd "**Ho**w: **co**:me you ain't put Maria name down there." ·h So she said, she said "That other girl called 'er so, she no:t **wi**:th **u**:s. so," That's what she said too. (0.2) So **I** said, s- so I snatched the paper wi'her. I said wh- when we // were playin wi' that paper?
(33)	Mar:	I'm a I'm a **te**ll her about herself toda//y. Well,
(34)	Pam:	Huh? huh remember when we're snatchin that // paper,
(35)	Flo:	An she gonna tell you another story any**way**.// (Are you gonna talk to her today?)
(36)	Pam:	But she ain't even put your **na**me down there. I just put it **down** there. Me and Sharon put it down.= An I said, and she said "Gimme-that-paper.=I don't wanna have her **na**me **d**own here." I s- I s- I s- I said "She woulda allowed **you** name." (if you star:ted.) (1.0)
(37)	Mar:	I said "Terry °how come you ain't put my name."
(38)	Flo:	Here go P//am, "uh uh uh well-"
(39)	Mar:	"You put that **o**ther girl (name down) didn't you, I thought **you** was gonna have- owl: a hall pass with that **o**ther girl." That's °what Terry said. I said (What's-her-problem.) OO: r'mind me a- you old b:ald-headed Terry.
(40)	Pam:	I should say it in fronta her **fa**ce. (0.8) Bal: head.
(41)	Flo:	Hey member when what we did th(h)e o(h)ther ti(h)me,

example 2		((The following occurs 45 seconds later (following example 1) after Maria has gone inside.))
(1)	Pam:	She shouldn't be **wri**tin things, about me. (0.5) An so- An so- so she said "**Flo**rence, Florence need ta **go** somewhere." (1.0)
(2)	Flo:	Well you **te**ll her to **co**me say it in front of my fa:ce. (0.6) And **I**'ll **pu**t **her** somewhere. (3.8) An Florence ain't got nuttin t'do with **what**.
(3)	Pam:	**Write**- um doin um, // that- that thing.
(4)	Flo:	What do y'**a**ll got ta do with it.
(5)	Pam:	Because because um, **I** don't know what we got to do with it. Bu//t she said-
(6)	Flo:	W'll **she** don't know what **she** **ta**lkin bout.
(7)	Pam:	But- but she- but we **di**:d have somp'm to do because we was **ma**:d at **her**. Because we didn't **li**ke her no more. (0.6) And **that's** why, (0.6) **So**mebody the one // that use-
(8)	Flo:	So, she got anything t'say she come say it in front of my face. (1.0) I better not **se**e Terry today. (2.5) I **ain'** gonna say- I'm-a-say "Terry **what you say** about m//e." She gonna say "I ain't **say** nuttin."
(9)	Pam:	((whiny)) (nyang)
(10)	Pam:	(behind her face) she meant- sh'ent You know you- you know what. She- she chan//gin it.
(11)	Flo:	If I **wro**:te somp'm then I **wro**te it.=Then I got somp'm to do with it. =W'then I **wro**te it. (0.5)
(12)	Pam:	And **she** said, an- an- she u:m ah whah. (I'm sorry oh.) I'm a walk you home. **She** said that um,
(13)	Flo:	She get on my **ne**rves.
(14)	Pam:	She said that um,=
(15)	Flo:	=**No**wn I got somp'm ta write about her **now**::. (0.5)
(16)	Pam:	Oh yeah.=She sai:d tha:t, (0.4) that um, you wouldn't have nuttin ta do with it, and every**thing**, An **plus**, (0.5) // um,
(17)	Flo:	WELL IF I WROTE SOME 'N I HAD SOMP'M T'**DO** with it.

"instigating"   817

(18)	Pam:	An she said, **I** wanna see what I was gettin ready ta say, (2.0) °An um,
(19)	Flo:	She gonna de**ny** every **word.**=Now **watch.** I c'n put more up there for her the:n. (2.0) // An in magic marker °so there.
(20)	Pam:	**What,**
		(0.6)
(21)	Pam:	Oh yeah, oh yeah.=**She** was, **she-** w's **she** was in Michele: house you know, and she said that um, that- I heard her say um, (0.4) um um uh uh "Mar**la** said y'all been talking behind my back."=I said I'm a- I'm a say "H:oney, I'm gla:d. that **you** know I'm talkin be**hind your back.** Because I- because **I meant** for you to know **any**way." An she said, I- said "I don't have to talk behind your back.=I can talk in front of your **face too.**" // And she said-
(22)	Flo:	That's all I wrote. I didn't write that. I wrote **that.**
		(1.2)
(23)	Pam:	Over here. **I** wrote **dis-** I cleared it **off.** Because **A**isha **wrote** and I- ·h // and **I** made it **bi**gger.
(24)	Flo:	Mmm,
		(2.0)
(25)	Pam:	So she said, // That first-
(26)	Flo:	And the other I did with my finger on the cars // and all that.
(27)	Pam:	An- so- I said, an- an so we were playin **sch**ool you know at Michele's house? And **boy we** tore her **all-** we said, I got uh y'know // I was doin some signs?
(28)	Flo:	I better **not** go around an catch Terry.
(29)	Pam:	An Mi**chele** called her **bald**headed right-in-fronta-her face. She said "You **bald**headed **thing.**" Because she was messin with Michele.=I said, and so she said, you know we were playin around with her? And she said "You **bald**headed thing."=She said, "MICHELE YOU DON'T LIKE IT?" I said I said // that's why-
(30)	Flo:	Yeah she gonna base in some little kid's // face.
(31)	Pam:	Yeah. And she said, // I said AND I SAID=I said I said "What-are-ya doin to her."
(32)	Flo:	I better not see Terry to**day.** I'm a say "Terry **I** heard **you** was talkin bout me."
(33)	Pam:	I'm a s//ay-
(34)	Flo:	Then she gonna say "I ain't- **What I** say about you." I say "Ain't none yer **bus**iness what you said.=You come say it in front a my face since what- you been tell everybody **e**lse." (0.4) ((falsetto)) OO::, And I can put more and I'm a put some- some °bad words in to**day.**
		(0.5)
(35)	Pam:	**She** said, and **she** was saying, // she said-
(36)	Flo:	**Now**:n I got somp'm to write // a**bout.** I better not catch you t'day.=I'm a (0.6) I'm a **tell her butt o**:ff.
(37)	Pam:	I said,
		(0.4)
(38)	Flo:	An if she // get **bad** at m:**e**: I'm a, punch her in the eye.
(39)	Pam:	I said, **I** s- I said, I said, Hey Florence I said, "Why don't you" um, I s- I- I- I- an "**Why** don' you stop messin with her." And she said she said "She called me baldheaded."=I said,
(40)	Flo:	That's right. // That's her name so call her name back.
(41)	Pam:	An so-
(42)	Pam:	**Guess** what. **Guess** what. Uh- we w- an we was up finger wavin?=An I said, I said, I said I said ((does motion)) like that.=I did. h An // just like that.=·h an I said an I an I was doin all those
(43)	Flo:	OO::,
(44)	Pam:	**si**g:ns in her face and everything? (0.5) ·h And she said that um, (1.0) And then she- an you- and she s- °She- roll her eye like that. ·h And she was leanin against- I- I said, I s'd I s'd I s'd I said, "**Hey** girl don't lean against that thing cuz it's **weak enough.**" ·h And she said and she said ·h she- she did like that.=She say, "Tch!" ((rolling eyes)) // like that. I s'd- I said "You c'd **roll** your eyes all you **want** to.
(45)	Flo:	Yeah if somebody do that to her- And if // you know what?
(46)	Pam:	Cuz I'm **tell**in you. (0.5) **Tell**in- I'm not **ask**in you." (0.4) An I ain't say no **plea**:se **ei**ther.
(47)	Flo:	mm hm.

(48) Pam: ((chews fingers))
(49) Flo: **Don**'t do that. (1.5) W'll I'm tellin ya **I** better not catch **Terry** to**day.** Cuz if I catch her I'm gonna give **her** a wor:d from my **mouth**. (0.6) An if she **j**ump in my **f**ace I'm a punch her in her **fa**:ce. (1.5) And she can talk behind my ba:ck she better say somp'm in front of my face. (1.5) ((Boy walks down the street)) OO: there go the **Tack.** ·h ·hh ·hh Eh That's your na(h)me. (1.5) ((starts down the street)) ·h See y'all.
(50) Pam: **See** you.

Submitted 13 March 1981
Revised version received 22 January 1982
Accepted 1 March 1982
Final revisions received 20 March 1982

afterword

JANET W. D. DOUGHERTY
University of Illinois, Urbana

JAMES W. FERNANDEZ
Princeton University

the convergence of cultures

The exploration that has gone on in these two special issues of the *American Ethnologist* (vol. 8, no. 3 and vol. 9, no. 4) as to the possible convergence of symbolic and cognitive approaches in anthropology recalls in part an old dialogue in the social sciences, framed as they are between the humanities and the natural sciences. In his *Geisteswissenschaft,* Max Weber, for example, sought to combine a profoundly subjective and intuitive approach to social action, characteristic of the humanities—the method of *Verstehen*—with the attempt to derive those typological and causal explanations of the course of social action characteristic of the natural sciences (see Feigl and Brodbeck 1953:20). In the late 1950s and early 1960s the humanities/sciences debate swirled around the *Two Cultures* thesis put forth by C. P. Snow (1959). Virtually ignoring the locus of convergence in the social sciences, Snow brings the two cultures of the sciences and the humanities into confrontation. Lloyd Fallers (1961), in an eloquent argument against Snow's technocratic naïveté as to the application of science to human affairs, reminds him of the existence of the Third Culture of the social sciences where, for upwards of 300 years, "powerful intellects—Hobbes, Hume, Smith, Toqueville, Marx—have been grappling with the problem of the proper application of scientific modes of thought to the systematic understanding of society and culture" (Fallers 1961:309).

This Third Culture, Fallers points out, has long been engaged in debate over just how far, and in what sense, science is applicable to human affairs. Despite extremists of both sides, Fallers (1961:309) goes on to say, there is "a solid central development towards successful synthesis of humanistic and scientific modes of understanding.... Arguments about science versus humanism are beside the point. Both are required for the understanding of the particular data which is the province of the Third Culture." It is the task of these two special issues, we argue, to go beyond the often used dichotomies in a convergent effort to recover the underlying unity of the human condition.

From this convergence perspective, argued previously by Colby, Fernandez, and Kronenfeld in *AE* 8(3), the two approaches to knowledge become influenced by one another because they are focused on the same complex phenomena for which neither can provide a full account. In fact, no total synthesis—no new whole persuasively integrating previously separated parts—emerges in any of the papers that compose these two special issues on symbolism and cognition. There is, nonetheless, plentiful indication of mutual influence, recombinations of research strategies, and emergent and new foci of interest that justifies the use of the term "convergence." We now address ourselves to these emergent foci of inquiry and to these new convergent senses of problem.

Copyright © 1982 by the American Ethnological Society
0094-0496/82/040820-13$1.80/1

the logic of the sciences and the humanities

The Weberian dilemma of subjective and objective approaches conjoined in the study of society and culture periodically reasserts itself, usually as a dichotomy to be overcome. Miller, Galanter, and Pribram (1960), in reacting to the overobjective and nonintrospective behaviorist approach of the 1950s, call for a "subjective behaviorism" in the study of the role of plans in the structure of behavior. More recently, Bourdieu (1977:87-95), in his *Outline of a Theory of Practice,* speaks of the dialectic in human life (and in the life of the anthropologist and sociologist, as well) between objectification and subjective embodiment. He seeks in his concept of the "habitus" to get to the center of human experience — to those "durable principles of regulated improvisation" that produce the regularities and creative irregularities of human life. At the heart of the "habitus" lies a principle of "mediation" of subjective and objective forces conjoined, but not reduced to, identity (Bourdieu 1977:79).

Anthropology cannot escape the human condition of creating and mediating oppositions. Each of the contributors to these two special issues has a unique perspective on the proper delimitation of the subjective, the objective, and the style of mediation. Drummond, for example, emphasizes the constitutive, culture-creating power of humans to subjectively generate the objective conditions of their own being, while Laderman, on the other end of the spectrum, relates the human capacity for subjectively generating meanings and imposing them on existence to the objective conditions of that existence, the ecological and etiological facts of Malay life. The dilemma is often cast in form/content terms. The forms or structures of ritual or kin relations are taken to have an objective reality, whereas the content is seen as much more diversely subjective, thereby giving each horn of the dilemma its due. Any adequate inquiry will be fully attentive to the interplay of form and content, and thus both scientific and humanistic in approach, as required (see Tambiah 1981).

These contrasts are evident in the convergence of cognitive and symbolic approaches to anthropology. Cognitive anthropologists, who founded this subdiscipline on rigorous methodology, verification, and explanation in a reaction to subjective interpretation, are reincorporating intuition into their approach. Symbolic anthropologists, always willing to employ the intuitive, have become more aware of the "situatedness" of their inquiry. With the common goal of understanding human behavior, this mutual influence across the traditions facilitates collaborative efforts that presage a more powerful social science.

Nonetheless, it is hard to escape the view that there is something paradoxical at the heart of our endeavors in the Third Culture. It is instructive, in this regard, to consider the effort made by F. S. C. Northrop (1947) in his, at the time, widely consulted collection of essays on *The Logic of the Sciences and the Humanities.* This book faces the problem of different systems of value — different cultural systems — in the world, along with the related problem of different methods of knowing. Northrop was both a world order advocate and a unified science advocate, and there is something fundamentally anthropological in his sense of problem. He was, it seems, deeply influenced by the culture concept. Northrop addresses the question of the possibility of verification and attendant human agreement in a world of normative diversity and controversy by emphasizing the primacy of the problem to be solved. His relativism is not absolute, however. Problem solving is sequential, proceeding by stages, each with its appropriate method and logic. Initiating research into human affairs is humanistic. A humanistic discovery procedure enables us to securely ground our inquiry in a local sense of problem and to avoid imposing norms and postulates alien to the problematic experience we seek to address. Problems of value — the essential human problems—must be approached, Northrop argues, by an intuitive logic and by methods of normative theory. Only in subsequent stages of theory can a deductive logic and Western scientific standards of verification—factual theory—be applied to reach some agreement about the diversity.

Northrop sought to bring about the convergence of world cultures in The Meeting of East and West (1946), and the convergence of academic cultures in The Logic of the Sciences and the Humanities (1947), the two convergences implicating one another. He also sought to overcome what he recognized to be the inevitable relativism of problem, method, and logic in the first, humanistic, or Eastern, stage of inquiry, by direct apprehension, or intuition. Subsequently, one postulates what has been induced (East meets West) and then applies, finally, a Western scientific logic of verification. This sequence of inquiry is compatible with the centrality in anthropology of the method of participant observation. Here, we first emphasize subjective participation and then reflective observation.

There are many problems raised by Northrop's sequential and programmatic solution to the dilemma of inductive-deductive, objective-subjective, intuitive-analytic, humanistic-scientific, East-West approaches. Nonetheless, when we compare his work with the contributions to our two special issues, we see emerging once again the primacy of problem over method, diverse logics of situations, transformations between levels of analysis, and, above all, emphasis on a fully situated and directly apprehended inquiry in which we are provided plentifully with local lexicon and text (see particularly Herzfeld; Roberts; Stoller; Quinn; and Goodwin).

Other authors transcend Northrop's concerns to inquire how categories and rules are created, applied, and manipulated according to situation, according to the participants' projects and tasks at hand, and according to the preoccupations and intentions of the larger cultural context in which participants find themselves (see particularly Dougherty and Keller; Goodwin; Roberts; and Edwards). We see here the humanist's interest in symbolic anthropology in the immediate apprehension of the situation of action converging with cognitive interests in the structures of knowing.

Northrop finds a paradox to be at the center of his endeavor to relate the logic and methods of the sciences to the logic and methods of the humanities. This "paradox of moral authority" arises from the fact that the sciences are concerned with factual judgments of what "is" and the humanities with value or normative judgments of what "ought to be." Although Northrop claims to have resolved the impasse of this paradox by sequencing inquiry through different logics and methods, the paradox of the "ought" and the "is" being confused in inquiry often leads to what he calls the "culturalistic fallacy." This fallacy consists of applying to normative social theory a scientific procedure (of verification) that is appropriate only for factual social theory (Northrop 1947:279). Although today one might debate the distinction between the normative and the factual, or the freedom of the scientific from the normative, Northrop does point to one of the main challenges the authors in these two special issues face: the culture-bound, contextualized nature of most of the "squirming facts," as Sapir calls them, known to anthropologists, which makes them unreliable subject matter for universalistic theories of verification.

Much of what anthropological inquiry knows of culture are normative statements of what "ought to be," both on the part of informants and on the part of anthropologists themselves in choosing to write from field experiences. So much of the material of anthropology is of the imaginative "as if," or judgmental "ought to be," or interpretive "one way to look at it" kind that we miss a great deal of it—probably its essential dynamic nature—if we treat it as fact that "is" subject to verification. We miss the essential value-oriented quality of human action in culture and anthropological action in interpreting and writing up culture—qualities that so many of these articles seek to make clear. In recent years this particular problem has been argued out in the debate over etic/emic approaches in anthropology and in the debate over descriptive and prescriptive grammars. It seems to us, however, that it is fruitful to remember Northrop's prior phrasing in which the normative, in the broadest sense, is recognized for the powerful role it plays in the paradox of social science. The preoccupation with the study of values in the 1950s—the enormous research effort directed toward this inquiry—while now discredited because of a faulty and artifactual research method and a pronounced, misplaced concreteness in conceptualization, nevertheless pointed us to the centrality of the normative in human affairs.

Whether these two special issues resolve "the paradox of social science," as Northrop felt he had done, should remain subject to debate. What these series of articles surely accomplish is to provide a deeper awareness of certain issues that lie at the interface between the symbolic and the cognitive approaches; an awareness that makes us less naive, less victimized by dichotomies, and more profound and comprehensive in our understanding. We are more deeply aware, for example, of the constitutive power in human behavior—the power to manipulate and reconstitute symbolic categories. We are more cognizant of the larger contexts, both individual and social, in which symbols and symbolic categories appear and which influence their relevance and evocativeness. Problems of ambiguity and consensus in symbolic and cognitive understanding have been redefined, and the difference between the didactic, categorical logic of the traditional cognitive approach and the argumentative, propositional logic of symbolic expression have been articulated. The tension between explanation and interpretation in social science is clarified, and an understanding of the possible relations between the two is within reach.

the constitution of social understanding

Without denying either the diversity of research collected in these two special issues, or the continuing resonance of the traditional "clash of paradigms" (Colby et al.; Ohnuki-Tierney; Whitten and Ohnuki-Tierney), a review of the contributions allows us to suggest a productive convergence from the perspective of what may be called a *constitutive view of social understanding*. From this view, culture is simultaneously to be regarded as representational and emergent, prepatterned and aimed at coming to terms with something sensed to be distinctly other. On the basis of experienced events and interactions, an individual is both taught and learns to represent perceived patterns and structures of behavior. These representations, or knowledge structures, are various, as Quinn points out—such things as prototypes of performance or interaction, images of desired or undesired conditions or situations, metaphors, key events remembered, fictional exemplars, pet theories, aphorisms, and proverbs. Definitions and rules (Goodenough 1981:57) and scripts and favored strategies (Schank and Abelson 1977; Dougherty and Keller) also play their role. Such representations operate as forestructures, providing goals and expectations for encountered events. These events, whatever their "real" nature and quality, are effectively constituted by the application of the structures of this previous learning.

Culture is also emergent, arising in events as they are ongoing. It is just this ongoing, symbolic action component that has been of most interest to symbolic anthropologists. Many of our contributors direct themselves to this emergent, reconstituted experience which is public as well as private.

A constitutive view of culture combines a perspective on cognition and knowledge structures with a perspective on the symbol and emergence. In this view, socially established symbolic systems are both a "condition and a consequence" (Giddens 1976:157; see also Drummond) of the interactions of individuals. Symbolic relations are a condition of interaction insofar as they forestructure events, and forestructuring itself takes various forms, of which Heidegger (1962:191) suggests three: (1) "Something we have in advance . . . a totality of involvements which is already understood." These would include the socially established structures of meaning as represented in the individual mind; what a person knows, in toto, the "stock of knowledge" (Wagner 1970:319). (2) "Something we see in advance," an initial stance derived from the totality of involvements. This includes the predisposition to understand an event in a particular way (Goodwin). (3) "Something we grasp in advance," an antecedent coding scheme by which behavior is rendered sensible (Boddy; Appadurai).

These symbolic structures of mind are a consequence of (inter)action insofar as they emerge in the construction of significance in particular situations: in the serving of a meal (Appadurai), in conversations pursuant to a taxi ride (Stoller), in celebrating cricket (Manning), in the telling of a myth (Drummond), or in the production of a project in iron (Dougherty and Keller). In these situations the effectiveness of symbols lies at once in their exterior, public, forestructured quality and in their interior, interpretive particularities that can emerge from the private to become a part of the public situation (Munn 1969). It is the power of symbols to link the exterior and the interior, as has been frequently demonstrated by symbolic anthropologists reworking Lévi-Strauss's (1963) classic paper "The Effectiveness of Symbols." This intermediation of microcosm and macrocosm is often accompanied by an element of uncertainty, ambiguity, emergence, and creativity, where the right word may be contingency. A cooperative, cognitive-symbolic anthropology should be constantly directing itself to these "contingent ongoing accomplishments of organized artful practices of everyday life" (Garfinkel 1967:11) in which the symbolic process operates.

This view of culture as ceaselessly constructed in the interactions of participants implies a constitutive view of the individual as well. "The self is both a product and an agent of semiotic communications and therefore social and public" (Singer 1980:489). The individual as a learner of culture is a learner of socially established significances that may be reshaped in representation. Emergence is as evident at the level of individual cognition as in the public arena.

This holistic view of culture as being and becoming is nothing new, although the paradoxically included middle element in it is antagonistic to the normal logic of Aristotelian inquiry. C. P. Snow (1965:62), in a "second look" at his essay on two cultures, points out that he originally chose to speak of culture because the term referred both to the development of the individual mind and to a society, the members of which are "linked by common habits, common assumptions, a common way of life" (1965:64). Spengler wrote in 1918 that "a culture as such is organismic and creative: it becomes" (quoted in Kroeber and Kluckhohn 1963:48). The Kroeber and Kluckhohn compendium is plentifully supplied with such double views. H. Schmidt wrote in 1922 that "culture is the mode of being of mankind . . . as well as the result of this mode of being, namely the stock of culture possessed or the cultural attainments" (quoted in Kroeber and Kluckhohn 1963:50). Indeed the emphasis on the constitutive in human affairs, the power to redefine situations already defined by that power, is Kantian in inspiration and broadly worked out in Cassirer's (1953:57) theory of symbolic forms and in Langer's (1962) divulgation of that theory.

The constitutive view of man that a convergent symbolic and cognitive anthropology contemplates is of an animal "suspended in webs of significance he himself has spun" (Geertz 1973:5). Significant and testable questions must be framed in terms of both the webs (structures and symbolic relations) and the spinning of these webs (interactions of individuals in the (re)production of culture). There has been diversity in the contributions to these two special issues as a result of contributors' emphases on the webs or the spinning, but all analyses anticipate an integration of the processes by which culture is (re)produced in action with the symbolic systems in terms of which culture is constituted.

The emphasis on process, on interaction and emergence, dissolves another of the older inhibiting dichotomies—that struck between stability and change. A constituted cultural order continually comes into being and never exists as a fait accompli. Instead, a culture is constituted and reconstituted with each social act. Whether the constitutive process in any given instance reproduces the system or innovates upon it will depend upon the contingencies of the situation. There is a tension between socially established meanings and emergent significances which is a natural concomitant of constitutive systems: the latter as constitutive of the former are continually subject to the particulars of situated social action. This tension creates an inescapable ambiguity in the experience of men and women in culture.

Reproduction of culture (Laderman), or change in systems of meaning (Herzfeld; Sallnow), and change in symbols of significance (Edwards; Sallnow), will be more or less pronounced as a result of the degree to which the constitutive acts are integrated and the degree to which represented structures tenaciously persist (Quinn; Sallnow; Herzfeld). The strength of integrity and persistence are continually subject to the tension between meaning and significance and an everpresent ambiguity.

consensus, variation, and relevance

What are the consequences of a constitutive view of culture for an understanding of consensus and individual variation? Not a novel problem for anthropologists, the issue of interpretive variability and individual or interactional creativity within a consensual sociocultural order is addressed by a number of the contributors to these two special issues. There are two initial aspects to the problem of consensus: consensus among whom and consensus with regard to what. Assuming, for the moment, that the "whom" is nonproblematic, a social group having been identified, we find consensus largely with regard to structural features of social action. At least three kinds of consensus can be recognized: (1) Common sense assumptions (Shutz 1971c; Garfinkel 1967) and formal procedures prerequisite to the construction of culturally recognizable events (Goodwin; also Goodenough 1981) are consensual. (2) Group members also agree on a set of "key symbols" for social discourse (Stromberg) and on the fundamental relations among them (Quinn; Laderman). (3) In any given situation the emergence of significant relations among particular symbols is public and therefore consensual (Goodwin; Stoller; Manning; Drummond).

Variability becomes evident in interpretation. Individuals will vary in the substantive interpretation of phenomena as a result of each person's unique experience and, consequently, uniquely constructed background knowledge (see Sperber 1975a), and as a result of an individual's selective use of consensual knowledge (Shutz 1971a, 1971b, 1971c; Sankoff 1980). Individual members of a social group do not share the totality of experienced social acts or interpretive frames of meaning. Each person's cognitive representations of events and symbolic relations is unique (to a greater or lesser degree). Such qualitative diversity at the basis of emerging consensus implies interpretive variability (Stromberg).

The selective application of represented knowledge (broadly consensual or not) also contributes to variability, and with the issue of selectivity, the question of relevance becomes primary. Individuals vary in their classification of a situation as appropriate for a particular interactional sequence. Whether a situation is right for the initiation of a gossip dispute (Goodwin) or for haggling over a taxi fare (Stoller) will be individually assessed. Individuals vary in their interpretation of experience as exemplifying an established "typification" (Shutz 1971a, 1971c; Wagner 1970). Whether a given utterance counts as "talking behind another's back" (Goodwin) or whether a given event counts as making a "commitment"

(Quinn) is an individual judgment. Individuals vary, as well, in the subset of potentially appropriate consensual procedures which are applied to a particular "typified" context and in the choice of significances to be conveyed (Appadurai).

Variability may also be related to the multiplicity of broad hermeneutic realms or levels with regard to which interpretation proceeds. Stoller reveals multiple possibilities for the interpretation of Songhay social interaction, including, at one level, the re-creation of the social order in symbolic expression, and at a deeper level, a more profound expression of Songhay being that integrates conceptions of time, age, wisdom, social mobility, and human dignity. Roberts argues in a similar vein for the recognition of levels of interpretive significance ranging from "psychological to sociological to philosophical to theological, all of which make sense unto themselves and each of which adds to the sense of all the others." This multiplicity promotes variability. Individuals may have differential knowledge of the various interpretive levels and/or may differentially apply segments of these interpretive schemes in specific situations.

Viewed from the anthropologists' (or other outsiders') perspective, these sources of variability guarantee a multiplicity of possible interpretations of experience within a consensual order. The essential vagueness of all social statements is the "operational principle" (Polanyi 1958) in the constitution of culture. Agreed upon symbols and their fundamental interrelations are continually employed in social action, enabling group members who, as a result of unique background experiences, necessarily hold different beliefs, to find the same statements and symbols meaningful (Stromberg). Contradictory as it sounds, social cohesion relies on this ambiguity.

To briefly return to the "for whom" of consensus, if a particular symbolic or structural element is held constant, inquiry can then be focused on its distribution. This is one of the primary tasks of Galt and, to a lesser extent, of Herzfeld (first issue). Galt focuses on the "evil eye" as a symbolic element of circum-Mediterranean distribution that is richly (but not identically) elaborated in numerous locales. The evil eye as an evocative image is widely distributed, and identification as a key symbol is consensual over this wide area. However, the evil eye does not convey a consistent meaning everywhere it is found. The image is evocative but also synthetic, as Galt, following Needham, points out. It is made up of a core of component features available for use but never entirely used in any given cultural situation. Only those components of the image relevant to a given cultural situation are employed.

The notion of the synthetic image is useful because it helps to mediate between widespread distribution of a general belief in the evil eye and, at the same time, considerable local variability in the shape of these beliefs. But it also raises again the question of relevance. If people pick out from more complex stimuli only some elements to feature in their situation, one must ask why these particular elements are relevant to them. The answer must be that certain elements are chosen to be featured because they speak to, resonate with, and are evocative of certain problematic experiences in that culture. The more humanistic notion of "aptness" in metaphor has been approached in this way. We are bound to relate the particular use we make of a symbol, the elements that enter into our discussion of it, to the available cultural context, the problems of which give relevance to these elements. It must certainly be true that there are many complex stimuli and images in the world available to many cultures, and some available to all. A fundamental question must then be why certain cultures select certain elements to feature in their imagery, to communicate about among themselves, and to construct themselves with. Ruth Benedict (1957[1934]) approached this problem in *Patterns of Culture* with a grand metaphor, "The Great Arc of Human Possibility." But a convergent cognitive-symbolic anthropology can be more precise. It can aim to specify the relation between the interpretation given to a symbol or a complex image and the available cultural context that makes that interpretation relevant.

That, indeed, is the Sperber approach in formulating a pragmatic theory of comprehension in culture—a theory of how culture carriers understand each other (Sperber and Wilson 1982). Sperber makes the principle of relevance, defined as an accessible relation between a cultural context and an utterance or proposition, central to such a theory of culture. One would assume that utterances in this theory include direct and indirect statements and displays of symbols and images whose relevance must be interpreted by culture carriers in relation to context. This theory has the virtue of pointing our inquiry directly at the very practical level where meaning emerges—at the level where culture carriers seek to make sense, to interpret, and to conceptualize the flow of information directly or indirectly impinging on them in their cultural environment. It is a theory that does not deny the presence of ambiguity in human experience but seeks rather to directly confront it in order to understand how culture is employed to disambiguate utterances and how mutual comprehension is achieved, one of the major goals of cultural anthropology (Quinn).

ambiguity and evocativeness

Two terms which have recurred in our discussion here, and which have increasing relevance for the anthropology we envision, are *ambiguity* and *evocativeness*. The polyvalence of symbols themselves—their susceptibility to a variety of interpretations by those who interact with them—has forced symbolic anthropologists to be aware of the ambiguities present in human experience. The "ambiguity of the constitutive," for the actor, lies in the tension between his obligation to "forestructure," on the one hand, and to the creative possibilities for restructuring, on the other. Ambiguity is created by incompatibility—as far as implication for belief and action is concerned—between the various knowledge structures. The knowledge coded in the prototypes of performance, for example, will be rather different than that coded in fictional exemplars or aphorisms and proverbs. Ambiguity is also created for any actor by his awareness of variability of interpretation in those with whom he interacts regarding the common items of interaction. These are but a few of the many examples of ambiguity in culture and in the situation of the actor.

A social science anchored in the natural sciences, where the task is to untangle puzzles and defeat ambiguities, is likely to be neglectful of the centrality of ambiguity in the human experience. But a human science sensible to the convergence of cognitive and symbolic approaches, and thus attuned to the wisdom of the humanities—where ambiguity is a central (and irreducible) concept—will keep the ambiguities of the human situation in full and direct view. Ambiguity is not simply something to be denied or explained away; it is not simply an error of method. It is a fact of human experience that both inhibits and motivates much behavior, and at the very least we should understand its role in cognition. Here, perhaps, the phenomenon of evocation offers us our best lead-in.

A complete ethnography should invoke the voices of its subjects. One characteristic of anthropology, well illustrated in these two special issues (that distinguishes us from many other social sciences), is to give voice to our informants, to not only register verbatim their responses to inquiry but also to record those texts that arise independent of the situation of inquiry. One is tempted to say that ours is an evocative science not only in the sense of giving voice to our informants but in trying to evoke by means of their voices, and by other devices, the "thickness" of human experience in culture. The complexity of this experience is not well assessed by the reduction characteristic of a certain kind of social science argument. A symbolic anthropology for which the "multivocality" of the symbol is central is, from the first, obligatorily attuned to that complexity and concerned to evoke it. It must contribute that awareness to any convergence.

Whatever may be said on this issue—it has to do with the particular "calling" of anthropology—the evocativeness of symbols themselves, and evocativeness in general, in our experience in culture is a necessary and fruitful topic on which a symbolic-cognitive anthropology can collaborate. The psychological experience of evocativeness of stimuli, so crucial in religion, ritual, and other expressive institutions, is also of direct concern to cognitive science. There is something puzzling in symbolic evocation and something edifying (Fernandez 1980) that a cognitive science is challenged to work out. What stimuli are evocative to begin with and why they are evocative (Brown and Witowski) remain salient questions. Are there certain stimuli that are naturally, if not universally, evocative, such as the stimuli that have appeared in these pages: catfish, lepers, hyenas, staring eyes, comets, pudenda, serpent's eggs? Or is all evocation subject to cultural contexts and, in fact, as Sperber (1980) argues, a creative form of conceptualization that takes place when the reasoned-out and well-understood schemata of everyday life are frustrated and prove inadequate? The role of authority in the use of the evocative and the way by which it figures in the charismatic continue the list of crucial questions, and they in turn raise more: In understanding the evocative will we not understand charisma more adequately than in any previous discussions? What is the role of cultural associations, of similarity and continuity relations, in symbolic evocation? Is the cultural associationism practiced by most symbolic anthropologists—in which, for example, the associations the milk tree has for the Ndembu (Turner 1967) are detailed—adequate to an understanding of the evocativeness of symbols? In symbolic evocation, surely, we see a central kind of human experience that implicates both symbolic and cognitive approaches. Ohnuki-Tierney, in her discussion of the perception-conception-symbolization phasing of human cognition, also approaches this problem. Evocation is surely central to the shifting of phases from one form of cognition to another. Sperber (1974, 1975b) argues that in symbolic evocation, and in the shift in processing of experience that it requires, we have the main impulse toward creative human problem solving.

the logic of symbolic relations

The view of culture as a constitutive system undergoing constant testing for relevance and characterized by ambiguity and evocativeness suggests a particular perspective on the "logic" of symbolic relations. Logic, here broadly conceived (Northrop 1947:viii), refers to sensible ways of making interconnections—sensible often being culturally (and sometimes individually) specific. In principle, meaningful interrelations of symbolic elements are unlimited, precisely because they develop in activities subject to the contingencies of historical process and individual creativity. It is the overriding notion of a project "towards-which" (Heidegger 1962:99; Sartre 1963) action is directed that provides an orientation for behavior that guides, *but does not determine,* the selection and structuring of appropriate, relevant, background knowledge (Dougherty and Keller). The elements of the world are conceived in a "ready-to-hand" fashion (Heidegger 1962:98) relevant to the "logic of the situation." The project provides an orientation that delimits zones of relevance within the world-as-taken-for-granted (Shutz 1971b, 1971d). Against this order of precedence, particular elements are "foregrounded" and interconnected in the construction of significance. The ordering that emerges may be a standard reproduction of a cultural segment or a (partially) novel interrelation of elements, which themselves may be conceived in standard categorical fashion or interpreted in a novel way in terms of the project. The particularistic sense that emerges is the propositional product of the immediate situation and the hierarchy of involvements in which it is embedded (Heidegger 1962; Goodwin).

While making sense, or finding relevance, in particular situations is an emergent process, it is constrained by various factors: functional or aesthetic constraints of a task (Dougherty and Keller), consensual symbols (Whorf 1956), recipes for action (Goodenough 1981), limits in individual knowledge (Shutz 1971b), and associated limitations in individuals' forestructuring of events. These constraints operate not to determine the outcome of the emergent process but to direct its path.

Interpretive freedom within these constraints is considerable. It is this freedom that allows Edwards to ask: What can catch the symbolic imagination? Or: What makes a symbol evocative? Edwards's answer, addressed to the issue of cross-cultural borrowing of symbolic forms, is that "given the range of [symbolic] forms that historically contingent factors produce," only some can be "coherently integrated" in terms of an established set of symbolic distinctions. This view is compatible with Galt's discussion of the synthetic image—a stimulus of complex properties only some of which can be relevantly employed in any given cultural situation. In situationally specific terms, the constraints of a project in conjunction with an individual's knowledge will select particular symbolic forms seen to fit the context. This is what one should mean by the "logic of the situation." In universalist terms, some forms may be natural symbols by virtue of their markedness, liminality, and ubiquity (Brown and Witowski; Roberts; Sapir; and cf. Galt). Such natural symbols will be widely recognized, although the semiosis that develops around them will still be culturally specific—that is to say, their relevance has to be determined for specific cultural situations.

Whatever the cultural system of symbols and socially established meanings, the essence of the system lies in creative manipulation in social action providing continuity and productivity in human experience (Herzfeld; Drummond). Human beings are not simply actors following a written script, or entities in a field of forces. They are self-conscious beings who must conceptualize and comprehend their environment in the face of the ambiguous, the anomalous, and the evocative. They must discover relevance and constantly disambiguate what they perceive, hear, or are told. In this process humans are constantly becoming. Humans are also, as so many of our contributors make clear, beings who are constantly arguing for what they conceive to be relevant and meaningful. We see this, simply to take the two articles that embrace this second volume, in the pleas made to excuse behavior (Herzfeld) and in the tattling people do to each other to maintain or change what they conceive as being meaningful human relations (Goodwin). We are also constantly employing the evocative, seeking to evoke in ourselves and others by means of an "argument of images" (Fernandez 1982), appropriate and meaningful feeling states and attitudes. In all this, humans are beings who are becoming. Only a convergent symbolic-cognitive anthropology can adequately come to terms with that truth about the human condition.

modes of interpretation and explanation

In this Afterword, as in many of the articles in these two special issues, it has been shown that knowledge vehicles of any kind—whether symbols, signs, metaphors, key terms, taxonomies, thematic preoccupations, genres of narrative, or storytelling; whether undertaken to excuse oneself, to explain comets, or to instigate rivalries in one's play group—are all "situated cultural objects," to employ Goodwin's phrase. They cannot be defined in any useful way independent of their situation, their context. Pharaonic circumcision can only be understood if we realize how deeply embedded it is in Sudanic village culture. The role of Western wedding cakes in Japanese weddings can only be understood in relation to Japanese notions of fertility. The creative allegorical use of comets in Central Africa can only be understood in relation to the problematic experience of Central African cultures vis-à-vis the expanding Western Imperium. In the practical, project- and task-oriented organization of everyday behavior, new constellations of conceptual units are constantly being produced. Creative reconceptualizations are present in the most prosaic human behavior in response to the particular tasks being faced. The concern of the traditional ethnoscience with knowledge structures—taxonomies and paradigms—necessarily has to be diversified as we study knowledge in action by focusing on contextualized processes of conceptualization and representation.

To have noted the situatedness, the embeddedness, of knowledge is perfectly anthropological. After all, we are a field discipline and we see knowledge not in the abstract but in use in shifting cultural contexts. The primary anthropological contribution to the social sciences may well be our disciplinary awareness of the variability of cultural contexts, which makes us most able, therefore, through the comparative method, to explore the effects of culture upon human nature.

Beyond the description of embeddedness and situational creativity, however, lie the problems of interpretation, understanding, and explanation—the problems of the contribution of anthropology to the ongoing inquiry of the human sciences into the nature of humankind. Here, symbolic anthropologists would be quick to point out that anthropological knowledge is situated as well, is subject to its own tasks and projects and to its own contextual constraints, which lead us to make some things relevant rather than others. Of course, as we have remarked, there are honest differences among contributors to these special AE issues as to the degree of objectivity possible in our study of human behavior. Taking this particular special issue alone, there are marked differences between Stoller, with his emphasis on hermeneutic reading of deeply lived local experiences and his use of aptly illustrative texts, and Quinn, with her emphasis on quantitative accumulation of interview texts so as to be able to factor out the three dimensions of meaning in a recurrent key term. The latter author takes a key term and seeks to find it broadly contextualized, to read it extensively. Her aim is to contribute to the precision of cognitive science by systematic analysis. Stoller's aim, by contrast, is to contribute to anthropological knowledge by increasing our ability to read local texts and make them more profoundly intelligible.

While emphasizing these differences in approach and style, it is unhelpful to simply return to an old dichotomy and label these approaches scientific and humanistic. It is just here that we see the convergence we have been discussing. Quinn emphasizes the system and verification in her analysis, and Stoller the intelligibility, coherence, and comprehensibility of the interpretation. Yet, Quinn's method does not escape interpretation; she recognizes that her three different senses of the word "commitment" are, in the end, an interpretation, intuitive in part, the appropriateness of which must become convincing to the reader. Stoller, by contrast, recognizes that no one text or experience can carry the burden of his interpretation; like Quinn, he must accumulate texts in order to deepen and validate his developing sense of the underlying coherence of the Songhay world view. The human sciences as science do not escape the need for the accumulation of corroborative data. However, there is always the need in humanistic inquiry to privilege an intuition, to let it stand for itself. The convergence we see occurring obliges the human scientist toward the corroborative detailing of intuition. But there is always the tendency in science, because of its preoccupation with method and abstract reasoning, to lose sight of its situatedness, its context-responsiveness, its value-oriented character. The convergence we see occurring here obliges the human scientist to an awareness that his propositions derive their relevance from the context in which they are put forth.

acknowledgments We would like to thank the authors for their thoughtful contributions to these two special issues. Dougherty also thanks Norman Denzin, Charles Keller, William Schroeder, Neil Weathers, and Norman E. Whitten, Jr., for their influences—direct and indirect—on the development of her thoughts. Provocations and interpretations are, of course, ours. Complete reference information for articles appearing in the two special issues on symbolism and cognition are omitted; reference is made by author only.

references cited

Benedict, Ruth
   1957[1934]   Patterns of Culture. New York: Mentor Books.
Bourdieu, Pierre
   1977   Outline of a Theory of Practice. New York: Cambridge University Press.
Cassirer, Ernst
   1953-57   Philosophy of Symbolic Forms. 3 vols. Ralph Manheim, transl. New Haven: Yale University Press.
Fallers, Lloyd
   1961   C. P. Snow and the Third Culture. Bulletin of the Atomic Scientists 17(8):306-310.
Feigl, Herbert, and May Brodbeck
   1953   Readings in the Philosophy of Science. New York: Appleton-Century Crofts.
Fernandez, James W.
   1980   Edification by Puzzlement. In Exploration in African Systems of Thought. Ivan Karp and Charles S. Bird, eds. pp. 44-59. Bloomington: Indiana University Press.
   1982   The Dark at the Bottom of the Stairs: The Inchoate in Symbolic Inquiry and Some Strategies for Coping with It. In On Symbols in Anthropology: Essays in Honor of Harry Hoijer 1980. Jacques Maquet, ed. pp. 13-43. Malibu, CA: Undena Press.
Garfinkel, Harold
   1967   Studies in Ethnomethodology. Englewood Cliffs, NJ: Prentice-Hall.
Geertz, Clifford
   1973   Thick Description: Toward an Interpretive Theory of Culture. In The Interpretation of Cultures. C. Geertz, ed. pp. 3-30. New York: Basic Books.
Giddens, Anthony
   1976   New Rules of Sociological Method. New York: Basic Books.
Goodenough, Ward H.
   1981   Culture, Language and Society. Menlo Park, CA: Benjamin Cummings Publishing.
Heidegger, Martin
   1962   Being and Time. John Macquarrie and Edward Robinson, transls. New York: Harper & Row.
Kroeber, A. L., and Clyde Kluckhohn
   1963   Culture: A Critical Review of Concepts and Definitions. New York: Vintage Books.
Langer, Suzanne
   1962   Philosophy in a New Key: A Study in the Symbolism of Reason, Rite and Art. New York: New American Library.
Lévi-Strauss, Claude
   1963   The Effectiveness of Symbols. In Structural Anthropology. pp. 186-205. New York: Basic Books.
Miller, G. A., E. Galanter, and K. H. Pribram
   1960   Plans and the Structure of Behavior. New York: Holt, Rinehart and Winston.
Munn, Nancy
   1969   The Effectiveness of Symbols in Murngin Rite and Myth. In Forms of Symbolic Action. Proceedings of the American Ethnological Society. Robert F. Spencer, ed. pp. 178-207. Seattle: University of Washington Press.
Northrop, F. S. C.
   1946   The Meeting of East and West: An Inquiry Concerning World Understanding. New York: Macmillan.
   1947   The Logic of the Sciences and the Humanities. New York: Macmillan.
Polyani, Michael
   1958   Personal Knowledge: Towards a Post-Critical Philosophy. New York: Harper & Row.
Sankoff, Gillian
   1980   Cognitive Variability and New Guinea Social Organization: The Buang Dgwa. In The Social Life of Languages. G. Sankoff, ed. pp. 153-168. Philadelphia: University of Pennsylvania Press.
Sartre, Jean Paul
   1963   Search for a Method. Hazel E. Barnes, transl. New York: Knopf.

Schank, R., and R. Abelson
　1977　Scripts, Plans, Goals and Understanding. Hillsdale, NJ: Erlbaum.
Singer, Milton
　1980　Signs of the Self: An Exploration in Semiotic Anthropology. American Anthropologist 82: 485–507.
Shutz, Alfred
　1971a　Equality and the Meaning Structure of the Social World. *In* Collected Papers II: Studies in Social Theory. pp. 226–274. The Hague: Martinus Nijhoff.
　1971b　The Well-Informed Citizen. *In* Collected Papers II: Studies in Social Theory. pp. 120–134. The Hague: Martinus Nijhoff.
　1971c　Common Sense and Scientific Interpretation of Human Action. *In* Collected Papers I: The Problem of Social Reality. pp. 3–27. The Hague: Martinus Nijhoff.
　1971d　Choosing among Projects of Action. *In* Collected Papers I: The Problem of Social Reality. pp. 67–96. The Hague: Martinus Nijhoff.
Snow, C. P.
　1959　The Two Cultures and the Scientific Revolution. Cambridge: Cambridge University Press.
　1965　The Two Cultures and A Second Look. Cambridge: Cambridge University Press.
Sperber, Dan
　1974　Le Symbolisme en General. Paris: Hermann.
　1975a　Rethinking Symbolism. Alice K. Morton, transl. London: Cambridge University Press.
　1975b　Porquoi les Animaux Parfaits, les Hybrides et les Monstres Sont-ils Bons à Penser Symboliquement? L'Homme 15(2):5–34.
　1980　Is Symbolic Thought Pre-Rational? *In* Symbol as Sense. M. L. Foster and S. H. Brandes, eds. pp. 25–44. New York: Academic Press.
Sperber, Dan, and D. Wilson
　1982　Mutual Knowledge and Relevance in Theories of Comprehension. *In* Mutual Knowledge. Neil Smith, ed. pp. 61–131. New York: Academic Press.
Tambiah, Stanley J.
　1981　A Performative Approach to Ritual. Radcliffe-Brown Lecture, 1979. London: The British Academy.
Turner, Victor
　1967　Symbols in Ndembu Ritual. *In* The Forest of Symbols. pp. 19–47. Ithaca: Cornell University Press.
Wagner, Helmut R.
　1970　Alfred Shutz on Phenomenology and Social Relations. Chicago: University of Chicago Press.
Whorf, Benjamin Lee
　1956　Language, Thought and Reality: Selected Writings of Benjamin Lee Whorf. John B. Carroll, ed. Cambridge: MIT Press.

Old Light on Separate Ways

The Narragansett Diary of Joseph Fish, 1765–1776

William S. Simmons *and*
Cheryl L. Simmons, *editors*

Anthropologists and historians have written extensively about New England Indians and Indian-White relations but have only recently begun to interpret the subsequent complex centuries of adjustment by the Indians to Euro-American society. Fish's diary of his efforts to set up a permanent school and mission on a Rhode Island reservation provides a "window into native life in the eighteenth century... This is a superb book and one that deserves a wide and appreciative audience."
—James P. Ronda, *Rhode Island History* $16.00

UNIVERSITY PRESS OF NEW ENGLAND HANOVER AND LONDON

"Articulate and provocative"
—*Library Journal*

THE PRIMAL MIND
Vision and Reality in Indian America

By **Jamake Highwater,** author of *The Sun, He Dies* and *Anpao.* In this thought-provoking, pioneering book, the noted American Indian author/critic explores history, ritual, art, and architecture to draw a vivid comparison between "primitive" Native American values and those of "civilized" Western society, then suggests ways in which these two widely divergent cultures might be reconciled. "Highwater shows himself to be in possession of real genius."—F.S.C. Northrup. "His intellectual curiosity and scholar's passion are aptly revealed in this fine work."—*Social Education.*

Ⓜ MERIDIAN F602 $6.95

At all bookstores or send $6.95 plus $1.50 postage & handling to NAL, PO Box 999, Bergenfield, NJ 07621.

NEW AMERICAN LIBRARY
1633 Broadway, New York, NY 10019

The Gift of a Virgin
Women, Marriage, and Ritual in a Bengali Society
Lina M. Fruzzetti
The author focuses on the separate domain of women, particularly their marriage rituals, as a means of understanding Indian society as a whole. She describes the actual rituals in detail, stressing that they are a reality for the women, not merely an idiom for expressing reality. "*Makes a complex system of caste and kinship intelligible without being a dull kinship study . . . . a considerable contribution to the scholarly development of Indian Studies in general.*"
—James J. Fox 170 pages, illus. $22.50

Palauan Social Structure
DeVerne Reed Smith
This study of a Micronesian island in the Pacific uses fascinating ethnographic data gathered by the author while living as a "daughter" of a Palauan family to introduce, in addition to the principles of descent and alliance, that of cross-siblingship. 345 pages $35.00

Rutgers University Press
Box A, 30 College Avenue, New Brunswick NJ 08903

Journal of LATIN AMERICAN LORE

The **Journal of Latin American Lore** examines the creation, preservation, and transmission of lore from prehistory to modern times. Studies in lore focus on the symbolic value and the connotative meaning of cultural manifestations. Lore is found in the records of ancient civilizations, among surviving tribal societies, indigenous groups, peasant communities, and in both the elite and popular sectors of modern urban society.

JLAL publishes in English, Spanish, and Portuguese and encourages interdisciplinary contributions to the study of Latin American lore. For the student of archaeology, ethnology, anthropology, history, politics, linguistics, natural science, literature, film, and theater, **JLAL** is the forum for applying innovative approaches to understanding the distinctive qualities of Latin American peoples and their ways of life.

Published biannually	Individuals $12/year
Institutions $20/year	Single issues $10/copy

UCLA Latin American Center
University of California
Los Angeles, CA 90024

CHICAGO

OEDIPUS IN THE TROBRIANDS
Melford E. Spiro

In this work Spiro analyzes all the available data on the Trobriands—including Malinowski's—and concludes that there is abundant evidence to support the hypothesis that an unusually strong Oedipus complex exists in the islands. Moreover, he contends that there are strong theoretical and empirical grounds for believing that the Oedipus complex is universal.

A Chicago Original Paperback $12.95 224 pages (est.)
Also available in cloth $26.00 December

THE WOMEN OF SUYE MURA
Robert J. Smith and Ella Lury Wiswell

This work provides a detailed portrait of the daily lives and world-views of the women of a Japanese agricultural village in the 1930s. Through Ella Wiswell's journal, sensitively edited by Robert Smith, we may understand these women's hopes and fears, see what amuses and angers them, and hear their comments on everything from adultery and illness to religion, magic, and the origins of the imperial house.

Cloth $20.00 Paper $7.50 336 pages 16 pages b&w photos
Available

ETHNIC IDENTITY
Cultural Continuities and Change
Edited by **George De Vos** and **Lola Romanucci-Ross**
With a new Preface

"This volume represents the work of fourteen anthropologists who participated in an international conference on ethnicity. The volume is unusual because (with just two exceptions) each author writes about ethnicity in his own society. All of the essays maintain a high level of scholarship and all offer something worthwhile to specialists in ethnic studies."—Robert V. Kemper, *International Migration Review*

Paper $10.00 402 pages Available

THE CHICAGO MANUAL OF STYLE
Thirteenth Edition, Revised and Expanded
Prepared by the **Editorial Staff of the University of Chicago Press**
Cloth $25.00 752 pages Illus. Available

THE UNIVERSITY OF CHICAGO PRESS
5801 South Ellis Avenue Chicago, IL 60637

Men, Women, and Money in Seychelles
by Marion Benedict and Burton Benedict
Two distinct approaches combine to add particular insight to this study of the society of Seychelles. Marion Benedict's Part One, an evocation in the form of a novella of an individual Seychelles woman's daily experiences, complements and illuminates Burton Benedict's Part Two, a traditional ethnography of the island society. $24.50, illustrated

The Politics of Divination
by Eugene L. Mendonsa
Divination in Sisala-land in northern Ghana is a religious ritual, but as this intriguing study shows, it is also a means of social control. Mendonsa shows that the elders effectively use the divinatory process as an exercise of personal and social power, to control their subordinates and to reinforce their own authority. His conclusions demonstrate that Sisala divination is a method of symbolic management and control of social reality. $28.50, illustrated

Person and Myth
Maurice Leenhardt in the Melanesian World
by James Clifford
This evocative study of Leenhardt draws extensively from unpublished letters and journals, and from the author's research in New Caledonia and Paris. What emerges from this biography of the themes and currents running through an unconventional man's life is a clear statement of the importance of Leenhardt's ethnographic work to modern approaches in the social sciences, and an analysis of the influence his quarter-century in New Caledonia exerted on this work. $28.50, illustrated

Three new paperbacks—

Rituals of Manhood
Male Initiation in Papua New Guinea
Edited by Gilbert H. Herdt
The authors of these original essays offer new descriptive data based on extensive participant observation fieldwork. Theirs is the first comparative ethnography of tribal initiation in New Guinea, or the Pacific, covering tribes in four ethnographically distinct regions of Melanesia. $10.95, illustrated

Saints, Scholars, and Schizophrenics
Mental Illness in Rural Ireland
by Nancy Scheper-Hughes
"A sensitively written account of life in western village Ireland."—*Medical Anthropology Newsletter* "A landmark in the field."—*Social Science Quarterly* "A sensitive study of lives frequently isolated and tragic. Compelling reading both for anthropologists and laypersons."—*Library Journal* $9.95

Musics of Many Cultures
Edited, with an Introduction and Preface, by Elizabeth May
"The most comprehensive and authoritative work available."—*John Barkham Reviews* "An invaluable resource."—*Choice* $19.95, illustrated, 3 records included

At bookstores or order directly from

University of California Press
Berkeley 94720

NOW AVAILABLE

1978 Proceedings of The American Ethnological Society

ETHNOGRAPHY BY ARCHAEOLOGISTS

William C. Sturtevant, Symposium Organizer
Elisabeth Tooker, Editor

The relationship between archaeology and ethnography are explored in this collection of papers originally presented at the Annual Meeting of the American Ethnological Society held in Quebec City, March 1978.

Questions addressed by the authors range from the use of ethnographic data in archaeological interpretations through the ethnographic study of archaeology itself and of the presentation of archaeological results.

Contents:
 Foreword
 Ethnoarchaeology: Some Cautionary Considerations, *Bruce G. Trigger*
 Ethnoarchaeology: An Ethnographer's Viewpoint, *Harold C. Conklin*
 Spatial Organization of Peasant Agricultural Subsistence Territories:
   Distance Factors and Crop Location, *Jane K. Sallade* and *David P. Braun*
 Ethnography and Archaeology of an American Farming Community:
   Silcott, Washington, *William Hampton Adams*
 Machines and Gardens: Structures in and Symbols of America's Past,
   Russell G. Handsman

Price: $4 to AES members $10 to all others

Published by the American Ethnological Society, 1982
 ISBN 0-942976-00-2
 ISSN 0731-4108
 LCCN 82-6802

GUIDE TO DEPARTMENTS OF ANTHROPOLOGY 1982-83

LISTS
414 US and foreign anthropology departments in academic, museum, and research institutions

DETAILS
- Degrees offered in anthropology
- Degree requirements
- Number of students in residence and degrees granted
- Academic year system
- Special programs
- Special resources and facilities
- Faculty/staff names, degrees, and subfields
- Graduate student support available

address all orders to

**AAA Publications Department
1703 New Hampshire Av NW
Washington, DC 20009**

please enclose payment with orders

$15.00
$10.00 (AAA individual members)

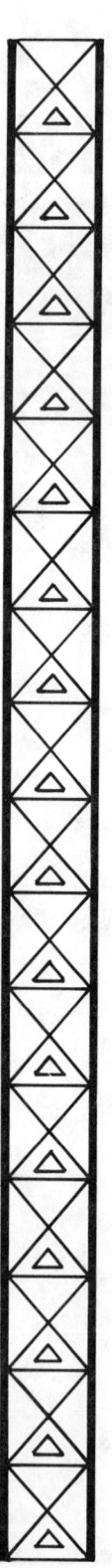

Cultural Transformations and Ethnicity in Modern Ecuador

Edited by NORMAN E. WHITTEN, JR.

"A landmark study of cultural change in a culturally plural country now undergoing centralized, planned integration through uniform nationalist development strategies. Whitten does a masterful job in his introduction in synthesizing the general literature on Ecuador and the papers of his 27 coauthors, thus providing a framework for understanding the contributions, which focus on various pieces of the total puzzle: clashes of ideologies, strategies, and stereotypes. The quality of the papers is very high; moreover, the volume is readable and well illustrated and indexed. Should be required reading." — *Choice*. 828 pages. $33.95

Order without Government

The Society of the Pemon Indians of Venezuela

DAVID JOHN THOMAS

The Carib-speaking Pemon Indians of southeastern Venezuela live by slash-and-burn cultivation, hunting, and fishing. The essence of their social structure, and the focus of Thomas's study, centers upon the Pemons' egalitarian principles of equality, personal autonomy, and the dispersion of power. "Will have great importance for anthropologists because it is packed with good, solid ethnographic data, which allow the testing of other theoretical models beyond the British structuralist approach favored by Thomas." — *Choice*. 328 pages. $15.00

Phone toll free 800/638-3030 (Maryland residents phone 301/ 824-7300) for credit card purchases.

UNIVERSITY OF ILLINOIS PRESS
54 E. Gregory, Champaign, IL 61820